PIONEER SPIRIT

Gareth Mitford - Barberton

First published in 1998 by Gareth Barberton.
Printed in Great Britain by Unity Print Limited, Corby, Northants, NN18 9EU

Note for Librarians: A cataloguing record for this book is available from Library and Archives Canada at www.collectionscanada.ca/amicus/index-e.html
ISBN 1-4120-8546-2

Printed in Victoria, BC, Canada. Printed on paper with minimum 30% recycled fibre.
Trafford's print shop runs on "green energy" from solar, wind and other environmentally-friendly power sources.

TRAFFORD PUBLISHING™

Offices in Canada, USA, Ireland and UK

Book sales for North America and international:
Trafford Publishing, 6E–2333 Government St.,
Victoria, BC V8T 4P4 CANADA
phone 250 383 6864 (toll-free 1 888 232 4444)
fax 250 383 6804; email to orders@trafford.com
Book sales in Europe:
Trafford Publishing (UK) Limited, 9 Park End Street, 2nd Floor
Oxford, UK OX1 1HH UNITED KINGDOM
phone 44 (0)1865 722 113 (local rate 0845 230 9601)
facsimile 44 (0)1865 722 868; info.uk@trafford.com
Order online at:
trafford.com/06-0302

10 9 8 7 6 5 4 3

DEDICATION

This book is dedicated to my first wife Pat
who encouraged me to begin the task
but did not live to see its completion;

to my second wife Judy who helped
with the completion of the first print
and with the revision of the second;

to my daughter Helen who designed
the Barberton Daisy cover;

and my sons Philip (and Brian who died young)
and their progeny who will transmit the
Barberton DNA down the generations.

INDEX

Introduction

Some members of the Barber and Bowker families, rooted in England for centuries, decided to emigrate to the Cape of Good Hope during the nineteenth century. A few of these moved on again to British East Africa (as it was then called) early in the twentieth century and later in that century some returned to the land of their forefathers. This account tells of their fortunes during the heyday and then the decline of the British Empire in Africa and ends with the writer's account of his return with his family to England.

These two families became united by marriage and maintained contact with each other and with friends and relations 'back home' by letter - all colonials refer to England as home, no matter how long they have been away. These would be passed around other relations and then returned to base. Many of these letters have survived to this day, dating from 1820 to 2000 and have proved to be a most valuable source of information.

In addition to this source are some diaries, notebooks, essays, poems, and accounts of events, some newspaper cuttings and three books written by my uncle, Ivan Barberton and his brother (my father) Raymond Barberton. At this point it is necessary to explain that the name Barber was changed in 1917 to Barberton to mark the discovery of gold by the Barber brothers (one of them my grandfather) at what became known as Barber's camp in the Transvaal province of South Africa, which was later named Barberton when it was designated a township. The first of these books was *The Barbers of the Peak* by Ivan and Raymond Barberton. The others, by Ivan Barberton were *The Bowkers of Tharfield* and *Comdt. Holden Bowker* and I have drawn from all these sources.

My father spent his life pursuing his interest in researching the family history and left me all his papers and his own life story which he called *Astride the Equator.* Another of my father's brothers, Alban Barberton, left me his scrapbooks and his mother's diaries (she was Mary Layard Barberton, née Bowker) and two tape recordings to which I refer later.

My own life has been spent in two continents, Africa and Europe, much of it separated from my parents and it was not till my parents died that I found that almost every letter I had written to them had been saved. I did not keep a diary, but these letters fill that gap. I left Kenya for secondary schooling and for Medical School in England and later returned to East Africa, joining the Colonial Medical Service in Uganda where I was obliged to write a monthly report to the Director of Medical Services. I kept a flimsy carbon copy of each of these, which, together with my letters have proved to be a useful archive. When Uganda (a protectorate, never a colony) achieved self government I returned to England to work as a Consultant in the National Health Service. By then it was known by many of my relations that I had an interest in old family papers and I have been fortunate in receiving further items to add to the family archives. This archive now comprises two volumes of old photographs and forty-five volumes of various documents, ranging from quill pen (some written horizontally, then vertically criss-cross the page on both sides), manuscript, typescript, telegrams, drawings, faxes and culminating with e-mail. It is from all these sources that I have been able to prepare this light-hearted account of an English colonial family from 1820 to the 1990s. British colonial history has developed a bad press in present, so-called politically correct, times but I look back with pride on the achievements of my forbears in South and East Africa - they (and I) did our best according to the *mores* prevalent at the time in the countries where we lived and worked.

Chapter 1

1820 The Cape of Good Hope

My great-great-grandfather, Miles Bowker, emigrated from the village of South Moulton near Salisbury to the colony of the Cape of Good Hope in South Africa in 1820, accompanied by his wife, eight sons, one daughter and 'eight stalwart indentured servants'. A second daughter was born on the voyage and a ninth son a couple of years later.

My great-grandfather on the other side of the family, Frederick William Barber, a twenty six year old bachelor at the time, emigrated to the Cape of Good Hope in 1839. Six years later he was to marry Mary Elizabeth Bowker, the older of Miles Bowker's two daughters. These two families, the Bowkers and the Barbers (later Barbertons) became eminent and influential pioneers in the early development of South Africa and Kenya.

The large Bowker and the smaller Barber families became very closely associated as friends, farmers, soldiers, gold and diamond prospectors and by more than one marriage and I have recorded in the appendix a six generation family tree of those who are mentioned in this account.

The earliest manuscript account in my possession of the emigration to the Cape of Good Hope was written by my great-grandfather, Thomas Holden Bowker, son of Miles.

He was twelve years old in 1820 at the time of the journey but the account was not written till "upwards of 40 years later" to use his phrase. He intended to continue the account "until time overtakes me or I overtake time" but the record is incomplete. It was written with a quill pen, for the writing gradually becomes thicker and less distinct until it suddenly becomes thin and clear again, when the quill was re-cut to a fresh point. The ink is fading and of variable colour - my father told me how they used to make their own vegetable ink from certain plants. I have quoted selectively from his account with his actual spelling: at the end he adds the names of the eight indentured men who accompanied him.

> "Miles Bowker of Deckhams Hall, not far from Newcastle, had two sons, my father, Miles Bowker, and Benjamin and three daughters. Uncle Ben died at sea after Grandfather gave up business which he carried on largely being a ship owner and exporting his own manufactures to the ports of the Baltic. Ben had become an officer in the navy and went on some cruise in the Leucadia Man of War from which he appears never to have returned.
>
> My great-grandfather went by the name amongst his friends of 'Manchester Tommy', where a considerable amount of family property was in abeyance to the Crown, having got into the family possession in consequence of certain Jacobinical predilections connected with the romantic sallies of the highlanders during the '45 when that, and much other property besides, was either left or mortgaged for the keeping of their heads upon their shoulders of my worthy ancestors, who eventually made their exit from the Tower, which few who entered there

> on the same account ever did, for few were rich enough to pay for keeping their heads on - as the history of the times written in letters of blood fully attest.
>
> I was the 4th son of Miles Bowker, who was the eldest son of Miles Bowker of Deckhams Hall, near Newcastle and Anna Maria Mitford, the youngest daughter of Capt. Mitford of Mitford Castle, Northumberland. Miles Bowker of Deckhams Hall claimed to be the lineal descendent of the Bourcher family, the seals of which were brought to this colony by the late Miles Bowker of Tharfield, being almost the sole remnants of the ancient family property which had been lost in the cause of the Pretender when the romantic loyalty of the Highlanders found an echo even in the western wilds of Lancashire."

Having lost a lot of the family property to the crown Miles Bowker gave up any idea of trying to recover this through Chancery and decided to emigrate with his whole family and settled for the Cape of Good Hope and:

> "He set about in earnest to recruit a party of settlers under the conditions and regulations by which it was proposed to fill up the vacant lands on the eastern extremity of the Cape Colony. The main features of the plan proposed by the govt. in this settlement was that every 100 acres of land should be occupied by at least one armed settler either as a freeholder or a servant on the rights of his master. Leaving his eldest son, John Mitford Bowker, to wind up the affairs of the large farm which he had rented for some years of Lord Pembroke, called Manor Farm, situated in South Newton he, with his second son Miles Bowker and eight stalwart indentured servants, one of them a family

man, made up a party of ten by which, in virtue of the regulations, he was able to become, upon reaching the location, a farmer of 1000 acres just the size of the Manor Farm mentioned above. The arrangements having been made for departure there was a huge black travelling carriage lent from the Earl of Pembroke's establishment to carry the family to Portsmouth and three or four large Scotch carts as big as wagons filled with every description of household furniture and instruments of husbandry, drawn by the teams of horses of the farm.

The well loaded carts and ponderous black travelling van moved down the main road toward Salisbury, leaving the fine old Manor House with its alternate squares of brick and flint upon its gentle rising ground, with its parterre or lawn in front, with its clumps of laurels and laburnums and the long garden wall and great white gates which opened upon the road which I and my brothers had so often climbed, contrary to parental injunctions, to see the mail Coaches pass, or to cheer the gaily decked carriages crammed inside and out with independent voters being taken by their respective candidates to the hustings in the times of county elections. The broad river Wiley ran parallel with the road for some distance and was a favourite spot of the coachmen, who often turned off the road and took a drive on the gravelly bottom of the river to cool (as we boys used think) their horses' feet. We soon passed the mill which was the last place in the long village of South Newton and the mill dam where my elder brothers used to set for Jack or put in night lines for eels and my father's long water meads that ran along the opposite side of the river, in whose ditches I had spent many a half holiday in wiring small Jack with a noose made of grass or picked out the crawfish from behind the boards of the numerous little flood gates and sluices - the 2 miles between South Newton and Wilton, over which I and my brothers had so often trudged to and fro' school where we were taught reading, writing, arithmetic and the catechism, which we repeated once a week or at least such answers as might come to our share as we stood in the row. Our schoolmaster was a very worthy man and was besides the mayor of the Town. His name that was Mr Phelps was a tall man of noble part and gentle manner and was held in high estimation by myself for the magnificent headings he used to put into our ciphering book. He also possessed an organ, to me then a great object of mystery, my being not only ignorant of the term of music but perfectly oblivious as to what it could be inside which produced the sounds. He also rose high in my estimation one day when he threw a whole handful of money out of the window, for the school was on an upper storey, to some foreign musicians who were singing in what was to me an unknown tongue but which I, from his liberality, at once judged that he must have understood and fully appreciated. Some of the boys said it was very fine but I must own I would have much rather heard Old Absolom Horn, a vagrant Ballad singer, that used to stop at the kitchen of the Old Manor House, to the great delight of all the servants, girls, carters and we boys who seemed never to tire of hearing his strange collection of ballads, which he sung of with a considerable amount of combined nasal and vocal ability - or the Musical Sailors, one of whom sang such songs as 'Dame Durden on the Washing Day' to the accompaniment of his blind comrade's German flute.

Wilton with its playgrounds, where as schoolboys we had spent many a merry hour at all sorts of games and the Wiltshire method of playing marbles or boss in the ring with iron tors, a kind of outdoor billiards in which great skill was occasionally displayed by the elder boys to the great loss of the juveniles in money or marbles as they often had to be repurchased when an unfortunate was cleaned out. Pence being in high esteem appeared to have been coined for no other purpose than tossing with old Tommy Ponting the pie-man, whose well known song of 'Toss or Buy' was sure to attract the fortunate winners of the coppers, a lucky throw with which sometimes secured to the fortunate gambler a penny pie for a halfpenny or otherwise the loss of the coin. The luck seemed genuinely to fall to Tommy whom we thought had some trick in guessing at 'heads or tails'. There were exceptions to this rule for one of the boys became so expert that Old Tommy was obliged to outlaw him and would only deal with him in the regular way.

There were many other objects of interest about Wilton which appeared to have been a place of more importance in former days for there were many old churches that appeared to be built into the streets and turned now to serve the purpose of more ordinary houses. In the outskirts of the Town on one of the fields there was a huge mound or barrow which I always associated with the spot, whether right or not, as corresponding with the record that a great battle was fought at Wilton between the Saxons and the Britons in which the former were defeated and their two leaders, Badanalph and Colgrim, slain who I devoutly believed were buried beneath the mound. There was another object of great interest to me

- the famous carpet manufactory with the long lines of gaily coloured thread which I used to delight to see, wove up into many a gay pattern.

Three miles more of the high road led on towards Salisbury, where I remember looking out over the Salisbury Plain to catch a glimpse of the mounds of Old Sarum which were, to me, an object of historical interest and to which some of my elder brothers had been when they witnessed an election or nomination for Old Sarum. Tho' reduced to little other than some circular mounds of earth with a single cottage near, it still possessed the very questionable right of sending representatives to parliament - the whole business of election being managed by two or three agents and such a very opposite manner to what the great bustling noisy crowded excitable county elections that I had seen at the Hustings, which were erected on two occasions on that same Salisbury Plain where the Frame weavers, in the pay of the ministerial candidates' committee men, seized and kept the Hustings armed with plough skilts, head stakes until they were ridden over and dispersed by the farmers and country gentlemen in the interest of the popular candidate, Mr Bennet, who had charged them with the cry 'Bennet Forever'. The red and blue colours of the equestrians waved in triumph over the sky blue of Mr Astley's dependants who had come down in a formidable body for the purpose of defending their party from the insults of their antagonists - they cut a sorry figure as they returned crestfallen by twos or threes.

But we are going through Salisbury with its tall needle-like spire where, some short time before, some of my elder brothers had been confirmed by the Bishop of Old Sarum and where I had once before been when my father and mother took us to see Wombwells splendid menagerie where I, for the first time, saw many of those noble animals with whose kindred I was one day to become so well acquainted. There were the first young lions that had ever been bred in England, great big soft dumpy puppies. There was the first gnu (our wildebeaste) that had ever been taken to England - a wonderful animal but far inferior in size and grotesque appearance to many I have since seen. There was, too, the Cape hyena - a restless, shy and ugly creature said to be untameable, tho' I have since held a young one as tame as a dog.

We took the coach through the New Forest where the houses are few and far between. On the way we had a distant view of Southampton and the sea, which I saw for the second time in my life, having once before seen the waves in the channel through a telescope from the top of the tower that stands in the centre of the woods near Draxe Grosvenor's Seat at Charborough Park. We were to embark at Portsmouth where we reached on the Gosport side where our large party took lodgings in an inn and we began to see new sights. At the same place was lodged a crew of Lascars who all wore red nightcaps and seemed to have a particular antipathy to the cold weather which had now set in, it being within a few days of Christmas. Here all the carts were unloaded of their multifarious contents and some now beginning to look the worse for bad packing and wet weather. I remember the smash which had overtaken some of a large number of gilded picture frames in which had long hung a number of portraits of old ancestors whose names I never knew but who had been taken from their frames which were destined never again to hold them and were rolled up together in one immense scroll and for ought I know have never been unrolled since. The straw with which many of the things were carefully packed, having got wet with the rain, looked ill-adapted for the preservation of veneered or inlaid furniture and cut a sorry figure when compared with the splendid sets of new and improved implements of husbandry which were being taken out to cultivate the new lands at the Cape of Good Hope. All these things in the course of a day or two were placed on board the 'Weymouth' with several of the carts and two artillery wagons which my father purchased for the purpose of carrying the furniture, farming implements, family and servants, one of whom was a married man with a family. The carters and drivers after being liberally treated at the Inn were sent back to South Newton as also my eldest brother John Mitford who remained to settle and wind up the affairs of the Manor Farm as the lease had yet some time to run.

The arrangements for the reception of these Settlers on board the 'Weymouth' not being completed - for they were finishing the poop cabins which the principal families were to occupy - to my Mother's great disappointment we were all put on board an immense old French three-decker called the 'Brave' where we were quartered until the 'Weymouth' should be ready to receive us. The tall old vessel which stood very high on top of the water and was a huge hulk, was made use of for the time as a tender to the 'Weymouth'. On board were many of the Weymouth's crew besides other parties of settlers. It was Xmas day in the morning when we went on board and, to us who had never seen or heard anything of how Xmas is kept on board ship, were very much surprised at all we heard and saw that memorable day. When we first found ourselves afloat we were all stowed in the cabin safe and secluded enough but not out of reach of the noise and bustle and riot that was going on board. It was a night long remembered by my mother who used to describe it as 'that dreadful Xmas night on board the Brave'.

From the lofty deck there was the next morning a grand and novel sight - we were just in the centre between Gosport, Portsea and Portsmouth and riding at anchor close to us were to me the noblest ships in our British navy. There was the 'Duke of York' and many others - but the ship which far eclipsed all the rest was the 'Queen Charlotte' which, tho' only a three-decker like the 'Brave', seemed to be 4 times as big and capable of fighting four or five ships such as the one I stood on. But this difference perhaps was enhanced by the fact that the old 'Brave' had long since been bereft of everything that pertained to a ship of war while the 'Queen Charlotte' was bristling with formidable rows of cannon and appeared to be fully rigged and ready to go to sea. Well do I remember how we used to assemble on the deck to see the morning or evening gun fired from the bows of the 'Queen Charlotte' and to watch that marvelous ring of smoke which flew across the harbour, which was said to be caused by the sailors greasing the muzzle of the cannon previous to its being fired. Not far off was another object of almost equal interest but less imposing appearance, this was Lord Nelson's old ship the 'Victory' on whose deck he fell while winning his country's battles and on which he issued that celebrated order which became from that hour the war cry of his countrymen by land or sea and which has cheered and carried them through many a trying scene of danger and difficulty in every quarter of the globe - 'England expects that every man will do his duty'. This great and glorious old ship once so formidable had lost her warlike appearance, being what was called "laid-up" in ordinary, the masts all taken down and roofed in. She lay at her moorings more like a second Noah's Ark and as harmless as an old Greenwich pensioner.

Close to us on the open or Spithead side lay another huge hulk something like the 'Brave' in appearance but much larger which was used for a prison or convict hulk where we saw the men wearing 'Derbeys' or square blocks of wood chained to their heels. The convicts were employed in the dockyards where strings of them appeared to be working two and two like teams of horses drawing huge blocks of timber. Their united power seemed to be far more than any team of horses that I had ever seen. They seemed to be under excellent discipline and were to me objects of great interest as they passed us morning and evening to and from their work in large boats or barges as thick as they could well be stowed. There were many other objects of interest, not the least of which was the fortifications or rather batteries of large guns whose dark mouths seemed to be but little above the waters edge and looking as if they were ready to sink any number of French Men of War that might be rash enough to venture within the harbour.

But to return to the men - they had their quarters in some place that was half dark on one of the lower decks where I often went to see them, for one of the men whose name was Charley had a great propensity for telling queer old stories and dry jokes and seemed to have become already a leading man amongst them. He was an old soldier my father had picked up at Salisbury to fill up the place of a great smock-frocked fellow of a carter called Lines whose heart had failed him when he saw that we really were going to the Cape of Good Hope so, to save himself from the dangers of shipwreck and the terrors of being murdered by the 'Caf-frees', had run away at the last moment - there was another too who must have been either a coward or a prophet who bore him company - the two men who supplied their places had to answer for the runaways when the names were daily called out as it was impossible at the time to make an alteration in the lists, the men long retained their false names after they had become unnecessary. The men as we called them soon reconciled themselves to sailors' fare, particularly the grog. They appeared quite comfortable and even jolly and had begun to make friends among the sailors who were soon attracted by the dry jokes and yarns of Charley. There was Grace, the purser's steward, as he was called, a fat jolly looking man not much like a sailor but clever at serving out the Biscuit and other supplies.

After remaining a few days on board the 'Brave' the time came for our going on board the 'Weymouth'. The 'Weymouth' like our old friend the 'Brave' had seen better days and had been a frigate but had, in consequence of not being a good sailor, been taken out of the fleet and turned into a transport or troop ship. She was however commanded by a regular set of officers and crew but in a reduced number. She still had some few guns on board and looked like a ship of war. We had but a little way to go in the boat to where the 'Weymouth' lay at anchor just a little beyond the old 'Victory', which lay quietly on the waters and seemed to have nobody about her, while the 'Weymouth' appeared all crowd and bustle, there being many parties of settlers already on board and others going on board like ourselves. The 'Weymouth' seemed as large as the old French Man of War we had left but was not so high out of the water. But we were soon all on board when we met a crowd of gentlemen one of whom, a tall good-looking man with a white beard, had addressed my father by his name and asked him if he was any relation of Ben Bowker of the 'Leucadia' and, upon my father telling him that Ben Bowker was his own and only brother, he appeared delighted to have found a friend of his old comrade bound for the same new country as himself. Captain Campbell of the Marine Service and my father became friends shortly, told each other their histories, nor did they ever get to the end of their conversation and their friendship terminated only in the end of their natural lives

I am now only beginning the voyage of the goodly ship that was to carry us to the Cape of Good Hope but the task I am undertaking is the description of what might be called the voyage of life, for it is now upwards of 40 years since we went on board the 'Weymouth' where we spent 17 weeks before landing in Algoa Bay. In writing this history I shall follow the course of the vessel to our destination and then, taking up the family progress up to the time that I became my own master, go on until time overtakes me or I overtake time. The race, whether I win or lose, will be a record of some interest when the generation of the settlers of 1820 shall have been gathered to its fathers and the young generation of their children, free from the disappointments and disasters which beset and hindered the Pilgrim Fathers of Albany, shall have time and leisure to read the stories of the works and wars of the hardy pioneers 'who not to be wearied, not to be outdone' toiled on and on until they tamed not only the stubborn soil of South Africa but its more stubborn sons of the soil, the wild natives who would neither improve themselves nor allow others to reap the advantages that a healthy climate and fertile soil held out as a reward of prudence and industry. I do remember well the high hopes felt and expressed by many of the settlers, of the great things they expected to find worth having or doing when they should reach the Cape of Good Hope - to us a land of Hope indeed - a land of Hope it was then and a land of Hope it is now to me. After the chequered fortunes that have befallen me during my Pilgrimage of 40 years duration, I still trust and hope that I may yet under the blessings of that Providence which has led me through 'perils a many and fights a few' enjoy a season of rest under the shade of my Vine and Fig Tree, in common with the thousands who have been enabled to take advantage of the cessation of frontier troubles, which few care to think how it was arrived at or at whose cost but who rather take it as a matter of course like, the rain that falls from heaven that falls upon the just and the unjust, the labourer and the laggard alike, while the maker as well as the writer of history spend their lives for the benefit of the generations who come after them.

On looking about the ship you might peruse the most incongruous assortment or rather confusion of articles. The settlers of all classes high or low had most of them become travellers for the first time in their lives and were only beginning to gather by degrees as their ill-packed and assorted goods went to smash, that experience which was wanted to teach them how to pack up things properly or what to have left behind - lucky appeared the ordinary class of immigrant who, having only a single chest, could sit upon it at his ease while those who had larger possessions saw them go down into the hold or piled up creaking and breaking to make room for more. But in a short while all these things were sent down below, except some of the larger articles. My father's long carts were stowed upon the Booms before the main mast, the wheels were sent below, so were the two artillery wagons. They had been constructed especially for the purpose of transport either of baggage or of themselves for they could be easily unbolted and taken to pieces, their wheels being so constructed that the high wheels could change places with the low ones and thus enable the vehicle to keep upright in a position so slanting as might have upset it altogether. Then there was my father's Agricultural Implements, a complete set. The plough excited the notice of the frame weavers who wanted to know whether Mr. Bowker was going to plough up the seas. So little did some of the Townspeople know about country life that Mr. Bowker's establishment of agricultural implements came a matter of amusement to them. They appeared to be not even acquainted with the rudiments of agriculture and probably unable to appreciate the fact that they were leaving their old country to become landowners and agriculturalists in the new one. One of them, a carpenter who had been brought up in some large Town before tradesmen's holidays were invented, told us, when he was doing some carpentry work for my father shortly after our arrival in Albany that he had never been digging or knew the use of a spade till he came to this country.

The arrangement and stowage of the goods was soon completed - all the luggage, with the exception of a few wheels, being sent below while the settlers were confined with the numerous families, amounting to nearly 700 in number, to the small berths in double tiers arranged on each side of the orlop and main decks and the berths being occupied mainly by the women and children, while the men slept in hammocks in a long row in front of the berths. On the upper deck there was a range of cabins called the poop cabins which were allocated to the most respectable families. On one side was my father's cabin with his eight sons and one daughter - on the opposite side was a gentleman whose family consisted of one son and nine daughters. A long dining table reaching the whole length of the poop cabin served for all purposes, each party occupying their own side. In consequence of the arrangements not being completed, myself and brothers were sent down to sleep in one of the long ranges of hammocks on the main deck where we slept but one night - but it was a most remarkable one. The novelty of the arrangements, which the people were entirely unaccustomed to, led to a thousand mistakes which kept up a state of excitement that lasted till the next morning. An arrangement was made the next night for us to sleep in cots slung above the long table beforementioned. The arrangements for the voyage being nearly completed, the vessel was moved out to Spithead opposite the Isle of Wight and cast anchor close to the buoy which marked the spot where Admiral Kempenfelt, with all hands on board, went down in the 'Royal George' which lay almost beneath us, the tops of the masts were said to have only disappeared a year or two previously. There we remained several days taking in livestock, sailors and stragglers. The eventful time for our starting soon arrived - the anchor was hoisted, the sails set and away we went with a fair wind for the Needles. There was great speculation among the landsmen as to how we were to get through the Needles which were much further off than I expected - we had not reached them when the day closed and gradually the swell of the sea and the motion of the vessel sent us all below to bed with sea-sickness. I stood it out for a long time as it was a light evening but the wished for sight of the Needles never appeared. The seas became rougher and I was obliged to take to my bed like all the others - I have not yet forgotten the dreadful sufferings endured during the first 3 or 4 days, when I next saw the sea we were rolling in the Bay of Biscay with a heavy swell and a fair wind.

On the deck were many of the sailors and also some of the settlers come up to see the sun again for it was shining on us. Our man John Austen told me he had never been ill at all but had been eating and drinking all the time. He said it was (illegible) day and that everybody on board a ship on such days eat plum pudding. Soon after he brought us some which he said he had made himself, this was very likely for when I came to taste it I found all the stalks in it - returning appetite and the novelty of eating 'Sailor's Duff' as it was called made it agreeable. The change too in the weather was also agreeable to everybody, for we had left the frost and snow behind us at Portsmouth and were fast running into a warmer latitude. We seemed to have forgotten for a time our native land, our thoughts became occupied with what we should see next and everyone looked towards the time when we should pay a visit to some of the Canary Islands which we were fast approaching. Captain Turner one day informed my father that Tenerife was somewhere on our starboard quarter. My father took me up to the poop deck with him to watch for the first sight of the peak which we did without saying anything to anybody. Soon after my father went down below for something leaving me to watch. He had hardly been gone two minutes when I saw the peak glistening above the clouds in the broad sunshine. I slipped down to the Captain's cabin with the news and told my father who came up with the Captain to see it. The news spread through the ship in one minute and there was a general turnout of the people to see the famous peak. Gradually we came in sight of more land, either the clouds had dispersed or our near approach had rendered it visible. We were now leaving the peak behind us and running along within sight of a high mountainous country, it had at the distance a barren appearance. We saw a few houses here and there but the Captain said he would go on to the Chief Island called Palma, where he expected to find some of the many vessels that were going to the Cape with settlers. On the following day we cast anchor in the Bay of Palma where we remained for twelve days taking in water, tho' I had an idea that we took in but little more than kept up our supply. We found, however, none of our companions in the Bay. None of them had touched there tho' some of them called at the different Islands, got supplies of fruit and such things as were to be had and sped on their voyage.

Our ship, from its considerable size and the remarkable nature of its living cargo of English people of all ages sexes and sizes, proved a great attraction to the inhabitants of the Island and they came in numbers every day, some to see the ship and others came with quantities such as oranges, apples, bananas, limes and Canary wines to sell, others came to trade and purchase various articles which the settlers had to dispose of. The Captain allowed parties of these people to go on shore and see the place and purchase for themselves. Every day parties went on shore. Then the Captain gave a grand entertainment on the occasion of the Spanish Governor coming on board. With him came nearly all the elite of the Island, both Ladies and Gentlemen, much to the astonishment of Mrs. Turner and the Captain's cook who little expected to have to provide for so large a party. From this apparent dilemma they were soon relieved for the sea-sickness attacked both Ladies and Gentlemen and by the time they had gone over the vessel, and even before, many of them were glad to go ashore again. Others who remained were not in a condition to touch many of the good things that were provided so, after all, there was enough and to spare. Captain Turner was well supplied with wines and a very large party managed to keep off the sea-sickness while they drank with no little enthusiasm the health of the King of England and their King and Queen, Ferdinand and Isabella.

After this visit there was a large party of Gentlemen and some Ladies went on shore. My father's friend, Captain Campbell, who was a bachelor, was fortunate enough to make a love match with Mrs. Turner's niece, who little expected that her protégée was going to the Cape to become one of the settlers. Here for the first time I saw pumpkins and mealies. My father brought some away for sowing at the Cape when we should reach our new country in which he saw, in anticipation, all the tropical fruits produced at the Canaries growing in his own garden and which he afterwards realised on a large scale. The pumpkins grew to upwards of 70 lbs weight and the Indian corn maintains itself to this day - it was in fine large yellow grains with a deep indentation on the outside of the grain like what the Americans call Horsetooth Corn.

The town of Palma lies at the foot of a high hill, there appeared to be no level country at all. Among the many who came to see us, not the least remarkable were the Priests with their enormous Black Hats rolled up at the edges at each side but sticking out in an immense way before and behind, this without their long shabby surplice-like robe of dingy black was quite enough to make them look like so many Guys rather than anything resembling the neat gentlemanly Country parsons that I remembered having seen in England. The great contrast here exhibited, together with their ill looks and my historical reminiscences of popery, raised in me anything but a reverence for these horrid queer men.

Our ship was anchored a long way out from the landing place but I remember a novel contrivance for beaching the Boat. We could see from the ship a strong team of oxen on the beach whose employment was to pull the Boat through the surf by means of a tackle that was prepared for the purpose outside the surf. This enabled the Boat to make a rapid passage through the surf and prevented them from being turned out of their course and swamped, which is constantly happening, in spite of skill and boldness, in heavy surfs where there are no such contrivances.

The names of the eight indentured men were:
JOHN HAYTER: A young man from Wakeford - from Dredger's the celebrated nurseryman and maker of a medicine of then world-wide reputation, called 'Dredger Healall' and was at that time the only remedy in which I had any faith as it was a certain cure for all cuts, sores and bruises - the concoction of this famous embrocation was a profound secret, tho' Hayter said he had often helped to make it all he knew was that he had often worked for hours churning it until it was of the consistency of thick cream.

GEORGE FLOOKS: Also a labourer, came from some place near Wilton where he was said to have some respectable connections.

WILLIAM INGRAM: A labourer from near Salisbury.

JOHN AUSTEN: Was an old soldier supposed to be a deserter, had been abroad and wished to remove to a warmer climate.

HENRY ADAMS: Was a bricklayer and mason, was said to be a clever workman, he was to build my father's house at the Cape.

WILLIAM BOWLES: Alias 'Lines' - was a young man who professed to be a carpenter but knew little of the trade.

CHARLES BEZANT: Was an old soldier, had been in the Peninsula and in many of the battles there. He knew a few words of Spanish and as many of French which, together with his old stories and dry jokes, made him a man to be looked up to amongst his fellows. He had a ready answer for everything and he soon became the delight of the ship's company and was never at a loss for a glass of grog or a pair of canvas shoes or trousers in payment for the jokes he retailed.

JOHN STAMFORD: Also an old soldier, had a wife and family. He had seen no foreign service like the other man - he had five children - Jack the eldest and Tilley the next, a pretty little girl, and three smaller ones. The overseers at South Newton complained to my father that he was taking away too many of their young men and they offered him 10£, which he accepted, to bring away John Stamford instead of one of the younger men who was less likely to be chargeable to the Parish. Mrs. Stamford tho' she had not seen 'foreign parts' had traveled about England a good deal with her husband and was supposed to know a good deal more than the common people."

Here Thomas Holden Bowker's account ends and there is no record that it was ever completed. He was fearless and before he was a grown man had killed two leopards (they called them tigers, which do not exist on the African continent) one with a club and the other with an assegai. His brother Bertram recorded these episodes in his journal:

". . .one Sunday Holden, Robert and me were out with the cattle near the sea and one of us said "Let's go and hunt for a bees' nest." It so happened that three of our dogs were with us. We had not got far into the bush when the dogs Tuck, Turrie and Folly went furiously past me in the bush, down to where Holden was. After a while I heard them barking as if they had something at bay. After a while they ceased to bark and Holden called us to come. When we got to the place he had killed a large tiger. As we had neither guns nor assegais we asked "How did you kill him?" "I cut that stick". The stick was about as thick as a pick handle and a little longer. "While he was sitting against that bush keeping the dogs off with his claws I went quietly behind him and just as he had his eyes on the dogs I caught him behind the head and down he went. The dogs pinned him and I gave him 2 or 3 more and that settled his hash for him." Holden was not a man then. He was about 16 years old.

When (I was) a boy my father sent to say that the tiger had killed another sheep in the kraal and he wanted us to come and hunt him. William, Holden and myself started with the dogs. We had five miles to walk and could not find the tiger in the bush by the kraal but, with the scent and assistance of our well trained dogs, we followed his track across a plain, 2 miles into another and larger bush where we soon found him. He would not mount a tree, as they generally do when hard pressed by dogs, but ran into a large pond of water, dogs in with him. Dogs mauling the tiger and the tiger the dogs. William and Holden jumped into the water up to their waists. William was about to shoot the tiger when Holden, with his old presence of mind, said "Don't shoot, you will spoil the skin." I was standing on the bank, looking on when Holden, with his hunting spear, watched his chance and thrust it into the tiger's mouth and down his throat into his chest and killed him without spoiling the skin."

It was Holden who taught his young brother Bertram how to read and write. The two of them would be sent out all day to herd the cattle as they grazed and Bertram wrote later in his journal:

> "I never thought about learning to read or write. Holden often told me about it but I always said "I know nothing about books." He had learned a little in England and read every book that he could get. He was a regular book-worm. I said "If you will help me I will try to learn." Holden was very good to get me at it so he used to make me learn in the fields when herding the cattle and at nights but candles were always the difficulty for night work. We used to have a little tin with fat in and a piece of rag for wick. I used to learn all figure tables in the field. Holden always made them for me but I never got further than the multiplication tables."

Thomas Holden Bowker became a man of influence and he served as a Member of the Legislative Assembly and in various of the so called Kaffir wars. In one of these, in 1835 the family homestead was sacked but not before the family silver had been buried for safety, never to be recovered despite many searches. During another of the Kaffir wars he heard a baby crying and on investigation found a Kaffir baby boy who had been hidden in an ant bear's hole with a flat stone placed across the entrance. The child was half dead from exposure and Holden surmised that he had been secreted there by his fleeing mother. He took the boy back to his farm where he was brought up by a Kaffir woman on the farm and became known as Resurrection Jack, growing up and becoming a family retainer for many years. Thomas Holden Bowker was the designer and founder of Queenstown and was promised, but never received, a grant of land for his services. He composed light hearted verse and was prey to the insecurities that we all feel from time to time: he resolved on 15th November 1858 to:

> 'Do all my work quicker than I have done. Keep up my journal again. Work up all my memorandums'.

Frederick William Barber, my great-grandfather on the other side of the family was the son of Thomas Barber, a notable portrait painter in Nottingham. Thomas Barber had given his son enough money to start as a sheep farmer in the Cape of Good Hope. He married Mary Elizabeth Bowker, daughter of Miles and sister to Thomas Holden Bowker. She was a most talented artist and naturalist who corresponded with Charles Darwin and other naturalists of the day. They raised two sons and a daughter. One son Henry (Hal) Barber, later Barberton, was my grandfather. Frederick William Barber was, like everyone at the time, involved in the Kaffir wars. He supplemented his farming income by digging for diamonds near Bloemfontein in 1870 but did not make his fortune. He wrote from his farm on Jan 16th 1871 to his brother Alfred in England, giving an account of diamond digging:

> "As our Transvaal diamond fields seem to be exciting some attention in England you will perhaps like to hear something more about them than you may have seen in the English papers; there seems to be a notion at home that a man has only to be on the ground and he will soon make a fortune. This is quite a mistake for although every man who works hard and sticks to it is pretty sure to find diamonds sooner or later, yet the large diamonds are few and far between, although the proportion of them to the smaller ones is far greater here than in the Brazils.

As I have been for four months on the fields, and as our party was looked upon one of the successful ones, you will perhaps like to hear an account of our doings.

Our party left in a bullock wagon drawn by sixteen oxen with stores enough for six months consumption in the shape of maize meal, coffee, sugar, rice etc and with a supply of shovels, pickaxes and three tents. We were thirty-three days in reaching the Vaal River a distance of about four hundred and fifty miles. We traveled a good deal at night so as to allow the oxen time to graze in the day-time when they could be watched to prevent their straying away.

The diggings on the Vaal are confined at present to the close proximity to the river and the water is convenient for washing the gravel in which the diamonds are found. When we were there all the habitations were of canvas, either stretched on wooden frames or in the shape of marquees and tents of all sorts and sizes pitched close to the wagons, some close to the river banks, others on the higher ground but still not far from the river. Each white man can mark out for himself four hundred square feet of ground to work on wherever he likes, providing of course that the ground is previously unoccupied. It is expected that each digger pays to the committee two shillings and sixpence on entrance, besides taking out a licence to dig which is one shilling per month. At the time that he pays the two and six entrance fee he is expected to sign the 'Diggers Duties' which embody a sort of mutual protection association for defence and mutual assistance in the event of any quarrel with natives. You are also ensured in the possession of your 'claim' which, had you not signed the rules and paid the two and six pence, might be taken possession of by any other man who had signed. After marking out your ground you go to work with pickaxe, shovel and crowbar. After throwing out a quantity of gravel or soil as the case may be it is taken to the river in carts and thoroughly washed till the pebbles are clean. They are then thrown out on to a table and carefully looked over. With a bit of iron hoop or knife the stones are scattered over a part of the table. You see at a glance whether there be a diamond amongst them, if not they are at once swept off on to the ground. You would wonder to see how rapidly this is done after a little practice. At first I 'sorted' as it is called very slowly, being afraid lest one of the bright pretty crystals might be a diamond, but after finding one and comparing it with a crystal, you learn to detect at once the difference.

The large gems found here are in much larger proportion than the small ones found in the Brazils where one of eighteen carats will not be found amongst 10,000 but here they are much more commonly found. Amongst our twenty six stones there were of the following sizes: one of eight and a half carats, one of eight and a quarter, one of seven and three eighths, one of six, one of four and three quarters, one of three and three eighths and so on down to five eighths of a carat and one little fellow of one eighth of a carat, all but two of the first water and free of defects. It is a great mistake to suppose that they may be had for the picking up, a man may be so lucky as to find a valuable stone as soon as he begins but in ninety nine cases out of a hundred it requires months of hard work to pay expenses. I know of a man who had worked for six months and washed and sorted five hundred cartloads of gravel without finding more than one small diamond, the value of which was required to repair his cart which broke down with the very load which contained the stone. Then, to anyone accustomed to the comforts of home, tent life is not very pleasant and the want of milk, butter, vegetables etcetera is felt. There are men of every class and character on the fields, military officers, lawyers, doctors, farmers, carriers, bank clerks, merchants, shop keepers, mechanics of all sorts, newspaper editors - in fact all classes are represented. You see a fellow working away with pick and shovel sweating like a horse 'bearded like the bard' in woollen shirt and moleskin trousers, his face covered with dust as also his clothes, with high or low blucher boots, a leather belt round his waist and a fur felt 'smasher' on his head: go and speak to him and you will see at once that he is a gentleman, polite and courteous who at sunset will plunge into the Vaal, make soap and towel do their work, don clean toggery for the rest of the evening.

We have got an advance on our diamonds of only sixty-five pounds each (nine of us) which I take to be about one third of their value. They are sent home for sale. A lucky season at the diggings and I should try hard to see my native land once more before I go hence and be no more."

In 1876 Frederick William Barber had moved to the richer diamond mines of Kimberley and he wrote again to his brother Alfred in England:

"Kimberley Diamond Fields South Africa Good Friday 1876. You see from the heading of this sheet that we are still at the diamond fields where we shall have been four years by the end of next month. So far, we are but little better off than when we came up, in the hope of making a fortune in a few months, as so many have done but we have not been digging all the time neither have we all been here all the time. I left off digging twenty months ago to take over this soda water business which has not turned out quite so well as we expected. But this has been occasioned by two causes - one, that owing to competition we were obliged to lower our price by ten per cent and also to make another fall of ten per cent a few months ago and a falling off of twenty per cent in the profits of a business tells seriously on one's income. The second cause is that two more men have also commenced in the same line and of course all the business they have has been derived from what they got from all the other makers. When we first began, the profits were between seventy and seventy five per cent if the bottles were all returned.

About twelve months ago my eldest son Frederick and Hugh made a journey, in company with two other friends, to the Victoria Falls on the Zambezi River which you will see marked down on any recent map of South Africa. His sole object in going was sport: he is a splendid shot, rider and sportsman and had always a strong hankering to be amongst the large game. He was away a little more than nine months and had a very pleasant trip, killing nearly all the large game with the exception of lion and rhinoceros, neither of which he ever saw, although lions were very often prowling around their camp at night and frightening the horses. But he shot with his own gun four elephants, fifteen giraffes and any amount of the other large game. After leaving Zeerust, a trading station just outside the Trans Vaal border, the road is almost dead flat but covered with `bush' i.e. different sorts of thorn trees, which are so thick that although you can ride through the bush yet you can't see many yards about you and it is necessary, when you leave the wagon, to have a compass with you, so as to know how to return to it, more especially in misty or rainy weather. Suppose you are going north, you notice when you leave the wagon whether you go on the right side of the road or on the left. So long as you keep on the same side, you know that to return to the road you must ride west, when you reach the road you see at once by the tracks on it whether you are in advance or north of it or behind it. If there are no fresh wheel tracks then you know you are north or in advance of the wagon and accordingly you ride south to reach the wagon. Here and there are large barren places free from bush where the soil is very salt and where, in rainy weather, there is a large salt pan as we call it. At other places you travel for a day or two through deep sand which knocks up your oxen, necessitating a few days rest afterwards to recruit them. The holes of water are so far apart that it sometimes takes a whole day to go from one to another. Once they were four days without water for the oxen and had only a very scanty supply for themselves and lost an ox in consequence. When about sixty miles from the Falls you have to leave the wagon and walk to them, unless you have a donkey to ride. This is on account of the Tsetse fly whose bite is death to oxen and horses. This fly frequents certain well defined tracts which are known and through which you cannot take your wagon unless the tract is narrow enough to allow of your travelling through it in one night. Fred and his party were away from the wagon for a fortnight shooting, camping out at night and they had a number of natives to carry their food, bedding, guns, ammunition etcetera. They heard the roar of the falls in the night when twenty miles off. They are the finest falls in the world, not excepting Niagra, being two thousand two hundred yards wide and about three hundred feet deep, whereas the Niagra Falls are only eight hundred yards in width with a fall of a hundred and sixty-five feet. The whole of this immense body of water passes through a gorge only about forty yards wide and many miles in length.

The mine here is one immense hole of about two hundred feet deep and of about six acres in extent. The diamondiferous soil is drawn out in buckets and casks, running up and down wire ropes, either by means of windlasses worked by natives or by horse or steam power. Some claim owners draw out forty and more scotch cart loads a day, which some of them sell at ten shillings and twelve shillings per load. As a rule all the large-ish diamonds are found in the claim itself, which the owner keeps but, after the ground has been thrown into the box which supplies the carts, the seller of the ground has no more right to it but the person who is being supplied. You may imagine what many such claim owners make. A friend of ours who has been selling to Fred found an 83 carat stone lately which, at the present low prices, is worth five hundred pounds and, a day or two afterwards, another not so big but very valuable.

Kimberley Diamond Fields, 12th November 1876.
When we came up more than four and a half years ago we intended to stay for only six months. I suspect we shall have to stay until we have made some money but money is not so easily made now as it used to be. Diamonds are considerably lower in value than they used to be and the

expense of obtaining them is very much greater. Some of the machinery pulls out the ground so fast that the owners give it out in shares to be washed and this is how Fred is working. He has a machine for washing and has hired a well and depositing ground.

The temptation to appropriate diamonds is so great that the claim owners have to be very particular as to whom they have to wash for them as it is almost impossible to find out if there is any dishonesty being carried on. My boys are so well known as being hard working fellows and thoroughly to be trusted and as keeping a keen eye on the natives when at work, that they have no difficulty in getting ground to work and Fred is a capital hand at selling his finds - his partners, the owner of the claim, preferring that he should sell his finds himself. It was a great mistake of Fred's in my opinion going on his hunting trip to the Victoria Falls on the Zambezi, the portions of claims that he had to sell when he started have since been sold for five thousand pounds. When he sold them they were not worth much more than as many hundred pounds. But that is the way here: the price of diamonds and the price of claims fluctuate so much that either is quite a speculation and a man may make or lose a fortune in a few weeks. This town, with very few exceptions, is composed of buildings either of galvanised iron, wood, or of canvas stretched over a framework of deal. There are a very few buildings of unburned brick plastered over to protect them from the rain. There are no good building stones in the neighbourhood and the expense of wood hinders people from burning the bricks. Drink is the great moral curse of this place and indeed of all the diggings. There are about two hundred canteens, places where drink can be had and it is a sad thing that so many of the natives are acquiring a love for drink. Just now I have only three men but they all drink. They get their wages on Saturday night about sunset. An hour afterwards they are generally all drunk and keep so all Sunday and very often again on Monday. Ten shillings a week with food, fuel, water and a place to live in is the usual rate of wage or one pound per week if they find themselves in everything; but they can live for about one shilling or one and sixpence per day so that they soon save enough to take them back to their own country with a gun, ammunition, a blanket or two, some beads, brass wire, perhaps an American axe, a knife and some clothing and, if they have made good use of their opportunities, most likely a diamond or a few, as their chances have been. There is no doubt that many of our largest diamonds are stolen by the natives and sold either here or up the country to illicit buyers and traders. I was told by a man, on whose word I can place every reliance, that he had himself seen far away in the interior, a handful of diamonds purchased from natives by a trader. There is a class of men here, both jews and gentiles, who carry on this game to a great extent. They are trying to stamp it out by what they call severe measures such as one year's hard labour and a flogging but the punishment is not half severe enough. The flogging with the cat ought to be in the Market Square at Market Time instead of in the prison. If they had made illicit buying and inducing natives to sell a hanging business with confiscation of all the man's known personal property it would have stamped it out long ago. There is a Jew now undergoing punishment for illicit buying and inciting natives to steal. He was sentenced to one year's imprisonment with hard labour on the roads and to have thirty-six lashes with the cat. He received twenty-eight lashes yesterday and then the medical inspector thought he had had enough, as much as he could bear. This fellow two years ago was in destitute circumstances. Not long before he was `run in' he is known to have sent home two drafts on a bank at home, each for four thousand pounds; most of this money it can be proved has been made unlawfully by inciting natives to steal. Many a man here has made a fortune in a year or two by such practices to the ruin of many an honest digger, who has invested his all in the necessary plant, left his wife and children at home and worked on here year after year running all risks from the burning sun, accidents in the claims and chance of fever or dysentery or lung disease, all of which are common here. The natives are such adroit thieves that it is almost impossible to prevent their stealing. Even if you are in the claim within a few feet of them and watching them with `all your eyes' they will still steal before your face. Sometimes if the diamond flies clean out with the blow of the pickaxe he will quietly put his foot on it and pick it up between his great toe and the next one keeping it there till he has a chance to secure it. Or under pretence of lighting his pipe he will take out a box of matches let a few drop on the ground as near the diamond as he can and when he picks up the matches pick up at the same time the diamond and put it with the matches into the box again.

The natives are well paid, well fed, well housed and there is a hospital for them when sick, attended to by the district surgeon. They come here of their own choice, stay or go just when they like but the law provides that every servant, white or native, must enter into a contract for a specified time with a master, either for one month or for as long as he chooses. This is to prevent loafers hanging around the town without any visible means of subsistence. This contract the master keeps and the native receives a pass which is on a piece of pasteboard stating his name, tribe, name of master, length of engagement, a number of claim in which he is to work and this pass he must always carry with him. If found without it by the police he is liable to be put into jail for a night as a vagabond. The natives often come from a long way in the interior, from the country about the Zambezi and beyond it and are many weeks on the journey. As they can't carry enough food for the whole distance they often have to enter into service with some Boer on the road until they have earned a little money or gained strength to proceed. They nearly all arrive here in a very emaciated state, quite unfit to do any work for some time after their arrival; many die on the road from exhaustion or sickness or inclement weather which, in their weak state, soon kills them, especially as they have nothing but their miserable scanty skin for clothing. Besides their pay they have the chance of stealing and selling diamonds and then going back to their own country well off. They came here miserable half starved naked wretches and go back fat sleek and, for them, rich. If a native dies here, master unknown, he is buried by a convict party at government expense but if in service, a fee of seven and sixpence is required for the expense of digging the grave. It is not an uncommon thing for natives to be found in out of the way places or in the streets dead from drink and exposure especially after inclement weather."

Chapter 2

The Barbers of South Africa & British East Africa

Henry Mitford Barber (later Barberton) 1850 - 1920, usually known as Hal, was the second son of Frederick William Barber. He married his cousin Mary Layard Bowker, daughter of Thomas Holden Bowker in 1894 and they raised four sons and had an adventurous life together. He was a hardy pioneer who dug for diamonds in Kimberley, mined for gold in Barberton and Johannesburg and farmed ostriches. He was a fine shot and went on many hunting trips, survived being gored by a buffalo and mauled by a leopard and had many other very close shaves at the hands of big game. He later emigrated with his family to Kenya, known at that time as British East Africa where he and his sons farmed successfully.

In 1877 Hal Barber (aged twenty seven) and his older brother, Frederick Hugh, took time off from diamond digging to go on a hunting trip to Matabeleland. Hal intended to try ostrich farming and took £300 in gold with him for the purpose of buying ostrich chicks on their return journey. This enterprise was abandoned when he nearly died as a result of being gored by a buffalo on 16th June 1877. His brother described the event as the most trying and terrible day of his life. Hal's own account of the event was written later:

"We came across an Elephant Cow's spoor which we decided on following and, having tracked it for some distance down a very bushy and grassy valley, we came to a stony piece of country which was difficult to track the Elephant's foot prints on so we separated, my brother keeping to the right of the stones and I myself the left, with the idea of finding the spoor where it left the stones. I had not gone more than a couple of hundred yards when I heard a rush in the bush but as it was a very windy day and a great noise going on in the trees it was difficult to see exactly in which direction the rush or noise was in, when I suddenly saw a large Buffalo Bull approaching me at full canter only a few yards away when I made a rush for protection for the nearest tree but, before I reached it, the brute was on top of me and lifted me up with his left horn and twisted me round not unlike a windmill, having struck me through the left thigh, the horn coming out at the back making a fearful gash fully 7 inches long at the entrance and 3 at the exit; he carried me 7 or 8 yards like a weather-cock on his horn, grunting all the time then tossed me off several yards away in the bushes, bleeding and mauled and half killed. My brother then came up and finding the Buffalo had cleared he ran a few yards on his spoor but as he had made sure his retreat my brother came back to me and, finding I was losing blood freely, he tore up his underclothing and bound up my wounds. Making a litter they carried me to our camp about 3 miles away where I remained for about 3 months under the trees and it was only by my brother's most constant care and nursing that I am here to tell the tale as the wounds were most severe & the main artery of the thigh in one place could be seen stretched across the wound like an aqueduct across a ditch, the flesh being all torn from it. I

> was at the expiration of three months carried out to the wagons at the Lunquasi [river] where I hobbled about on crutches, which I did not throw away until quite a year afterwards on arriving at the Diamond Fields".

Fred related how he heard a terrible cry which he recognised to be his brother's voice, how he came upon him with his dreadful wound right through the fork of the thigh below the abdomen and out at the back almost severing the leg from his body and the stock of his heavy rifle was broken at the hand grip. He told how he called for the Kaffirs, one of whom had a calabash of water which he used to revive Hal, whereafter he tied up the wound as best he could with his shirt. He sent two other Kaffirs back to their camp to bring their bottle of brandy and offered them a blanket each if they would return speedily. Fred made a litter of branches tied together with tree bark, dosed Hal liberally with brandy and had him carried back to their camp where he washed the wounds with warm water, extracting several pieces of corduroy trousers and then sewed the wounds up with needle and cotton. Against all the odds Hal survived, Fred nursing him there for three months, poulticing and bathing his wounds with water and a concoction of herbs brought by the local natives. At the end of this time Hal was well enough to be carried back the seventy miles to their wagons and he was left in the care of some Dutch women while Fred continued on his hunting trip, during which he shot nine elephants. After another couple of months Hal was fit enough to travel to Cape Town where he was eventually able to regain the use of his leg, albeit with a limp for the rest of his life.

In 1884 Fred and Hal Barber struck gold in the De Kaap valley. They noticed a streak of quartz running up a hillside, took some specimens which they crushed and panned with a good show of gold. So they pegged out their claim and moved their camp to the foot of the hillside. The news spread like wildfire and they were soon joined by hundreds of other prospectors; bars, shops, restaurants, canteens and a post office soon appeared and became known as Barber's Camp, which was soon large enough to be designated a town which was named Barberton. At the naming ceremony, in the absence of champagne, a bottle of gin was broken over a boulder. Hal later changed his name from Barber to Barberton in order that the connection should not be forgotten. The gold was soon extracted from the Barber reefs so the brothers returned to the Cape to farm ostriches. But gold fever was in their veins and in 1886 they went to Witwatersrand (the Rand) where gold had been discovered. They mined at Ferreira's Camp, which later became Johannesburg. Three years later they left their thriving business in the hands of a friend while they visited England and returned to find that it had collapsed and it took them about five years to pay off their debts and get back on their feet. When Hal married Mary Layard Bowker he ended his partnership with Fred and left the Rand. He spent the rest of his life farming, firstly in South Africa and later in Kenya.

Mary Layard Bowker was held in great affection by her father Thomas Holden Bowker whose nick-name for her was 'Wild Cats' from which we may infer something of her remarkable character. She received her early education from her talented mother Julia Eliza Bowker and at the age of sixteen was sent to complete her schooling at the Hugenot Seminary at Wellington. Her diaries of 1879 and 1880 have survived; within the cover of the first is inscribed in her hand:

"Leaves from the life of 'Wild Cats' during her residence at the Hugenot Seminary, Wellington, from 1879 to 18.... 'Certainly a woman's thought runs before her actions"

It was a three day journey from her home to Wellington (not far from Cape Town), first by horse and cart, then by train to Port Elizabeth and finally by sea to Cape Town. She recorded the journey in her diary:

"Thursday November 21st 1878
Left Oakwell at six o'clock this morning, in a private cart, with two spanking horses, en route for Cape Town. It was a very bad morning, nothing but mist and rain, the horses kept sliding about. Dear me, I did realise then that I was leaving home for an indefinite time. I looked out of the back of the cart as we were driving off and saw the trees and house wrapped round by whirling masses of mist and rain, and that was all. The last time I saw my people they were standing on the steps. I couldn't say anything at that minute but, just as I went down the step, I said "write to a fellow, eh?" A most becoming speech for a young lady leaving home for school!

We past *(sic)* over the hills and far away. We had a long way to go before we could get to the first station. We out-spanned once by the side of a little bush. The rain had gone away but it was too wet to get out, so Aunty and I sat in the cart. I had charge of the canary which Mama had given as a present to Douglas. The railway seemed to be getting on nicely as far as I could see and we passed under a splendid arch - the first I had ever seen. At last, after passing through the most lovely valleys, we descended a steep red road to Alicedale, a pretty little village in a snug little corner and the first station. We arrived at something to twelve and were obliged to wait till one before the train came in. Uncle H took me to see it and I can't say what my first impressions were. I only thought what wonderful things men were able to invent. We got into a small compartment, all to ourselves, so comfortable with nice cushions to lean against. The noise dashing along the cut roads in the hillside was awful. The echoes thrown from the caves and blasted rock were past description. We couldn't hear each other though we yelled.

After a while we got into the open country, and the mountains in the distance were grand, range upon range, all shapes and sizes. The hills were worth seeing, all covered with little trees, with the exception of the tops which were covered with soft green grass. Uncle and Aunt had a nap but I was too excited to do anything but gaze out of the window. At last, after six hours, we reached Port Elizabeth. The first glimpse I caught of the sea was at a place called Salt River. It felt like meeting an old friend and the odour of brine from the ocean was so comforting. At the station there was such a crowd and, in great fear lest we shouldn't find room in the hotels, Uncle hailed a cab and away we drove to the Phoenix. Before asking, we whisked out our luggage on to the stoep, when a man came out with the pleasant fact that there wasn't one room left. The Diamond field coach had just come in full of passengers. We went off to another hotel, that was full too. At this point the driver suggested our trying the George Hotel, where we got two rooms. I had a little room at one end of a long passage, Uncle and Aunty were put at the other end and next a little sitting room, where Aunty and I wrote our first letters to Mama. At supper

I saw gaslight for the first time. I rolled up my hair in a Quackie knob, Uncle H asked Aunty if it was right, Aunty said no, and offered to do it properly the next morning, which she did.

My window looked out into the Bay. Before going to bed I blew the candle out and watched the ship lights moving about on the waters and listened to the waves crashing against the shore. Somehow I felt so happy, which was strange considering. I lit the candle again and getting into bed drew the mosquito curtain close round. After a while, hearing strange noises in the room, I lit the candle and peered about; ugh! the floor was covered with horrid cockroaches which disgusted me not a little. At last I fell asleep to dream about the dear folks I had left behind.

Friday November 22nd 1878

This was the day to start for the Cape by sea. I rose betimes and dressed quickly as I wanted to see as much of the town as possible but there was such a gale blowing that going out wasn't thought of. After breakfast Uncle came in to tell us to prepare to go on board at once as such a gale was coming on the sailors were afraid to wait. So we got into a cab, and drove to the wharf. I was in terror lest I should be treated to the sight of nude Kaffirs but the coast was clear. The wind howled along with such fury that I kept my standing with difficulty. What the little canary thought of I never found out. After a deal of fighting they got the boat near enough. I was the first to go down the steps. Two sailors grabbed hold of me and I held on to them till I was seated. Then Aunty and Uncle. It was a long time before the four sailors could push off, the waves beat against us with such fury and great white breakers crashed under the wharf and roared like angry bulls. It was half an hour at least before we reached the Nyanza. The sailors pulled hard, Uncle looked grave, Aunty held hold of me like a vice, looking as white as a sheet. She told us afterwards that she prayed the whole time. I was too green to be frightened, so thought it jolly fun. When we reached the ship the sailors crashed down the gangway and gave us a rope to which we had to hang till we could jump on to the steps. I was the last to go, I verily believe my heart didn't beat till I was safe in the steamer. We all sank into the nearest seat. The Captain came and spoke to us, and said he was glad to see us safe on board after the danger we had come through. There were crowds of passengers, some bound for England. After dinner the rest of the passengers came by the steam tug. It was such fun watching them being hauled up in the basket and shot out on to the deck.

About four in the afternoon the ship started. Everyone began to look queer and began to disappear from public to groan in their cabins. Aunty and Uncle H went first. I didn't feel a bit sick only the same sensations as swinging gives one came over me. I rolled up in a Kaross and went into fits of laughter. The gentleman who took Aunty down came and asked me if I would like to go to the other side as the waves were dashing by me. So I went and he gave me a comfortable chair where I remained till it was quite dark, when Mr Dunn took me down to my cabin. I wasn't pleased to find my cabin mate, a young girl, looking green and acting queerly. However I mustered courage and broke the ice by asking her how she felt. We waxed chummy after that and talked freely. Before retiring I sat on the sofa looking out of the porthole till it was too dark to see any more. Then I disrobed in the most comical manner, taking my clothes off by jerks, between the lurches which kept dashing me from one corner to the other. I wound up the day by eating some stale bread and butter that Mama had packed up for our lunch the day before. It was very stale but to me it was manna because it had been prepared by Mama. Said my prayers and lay down and fell asleep on the great waters.

Saturday November 23rd 1878
I was waked by the noise of scrubbing on the deck. As ladies are not allowed on the deck 'till eight we had to wait. When we went up they hadn't finished scrubbing and it was such fun to watch the sailors tearing about with naked feet splashing water everywhere. We had a very pleasant day. I made chums with Captain Ballard, such a jolly looking fellow. He explained ever so many things to me. Hearing the log was very interesting but as there was some mathematical somethings in connection with it I gave it up. There was a rather pretty girl on board but she was too ill to do anything but lie on the deck all rolled up. Late in the afternoon she fainted away, was taken down and didn't appear again. We touched at Mossel Bay and Uncle went ashore. The ship rolled dreadfully. An under officer, with whom I was having a nice little chat, told me that it was always so in that bay. Ships rolled almost over sometimes. There was a queer old doctor Paul on board. Such a chatty old fellow he talked so much that I couldn't get a word in sideways even! Aunty and Uncle were bad all day so I looked after myself. Aunty retired early but Uncle and I sat up till very late watching the lights on the coast. I saw a lighthouse which the Captain said was on Cape Agulhas.

Sunday November 24th 1878
Rose betimes and went on deck. A sailor boy brought us each a large cup of coffee. We walked about getting warm and talking about Cape Town which we were to reach some time that morning. Soon we came in sight of land, there were some high peaks all along the coast called the "Twelve Apostles", then Table Mountain came in sight and there was such a rush on board to see. Uncle explained to me as we neared the town, pointing out the different places. The docks with stacks of masts and crowds of small boats, the Lions hill with the flag staff and flag up announcing our arrival. Then we got into dock. There was a great crowd on the land - all excitement. I dashed away to say goodbye to the Captain and made him promise to take me home in his ship".

After completing her schooling at the Hugenot Seminary, Mary Layard Bowker was later to return there as a teacher. In 1889 she received The Public Schools Certificate issued by the Cape of Good Hope Department of Public Education, passing with honours in English, Handwriting, Arithmetic, Geography, Outlines of History and Animal Physiology for the Fifth and Sixth (Highest Elementary) Standards; in 1890 she obtained the Elementary Teachers Certificate of Competency in English Language, Arithmetic, Geography and History, School Management and Lessons on Objects, Handwriting and Drawing. Many years later my father presented a copy of her 'Wild Cats' journal to the school. It included a lot of schoolgirl chatter and some entertaining comments about the school:

Sat Jan 25 1879
Alice and I drank eau-de-cologne to make our eyes sparkle

and were both nearly sick.

Friday 8th March 1879
Mr Collins the drawing master kept me so long that I was tardy for dinner. Mr Collins is hideous! red beard, red hair, red nose, loud voice reeking with tobacco and sits so close to one while showing us how to draw and bellows into one's ear, as if the drum thereof was built of cast iron! When I came to bed I saw something black running on to the bed so took hold of it and looked and, oh, it was a bug. Only think, a bug!! I shall surely die if I stay here much longer.

May 21st 1879
Oh yes, on Tuesday Miss Palmer gave me the hottest lecture I have ever had. She said that I was wronging everyone and myself too, that I must make a wide departure as it could not be allowed any longer or I should be expelled. She said a dozen horrid things and cheeked me dreadfully, so I cheeked her and we fell out fearfully. I was so angry. She frightened me a little when she said expelled but I laughed it off and pretended that I did not care.

May 28th 1879
Have had a dozen lectures from the teachers, was sent to my room for a long time from before seven in the evening till after breakfast the next morning. I screamed because Henrietta Bulmer tickled me and Miss Palmer got so angry and I was cheeky, so that's how it came to pass. She came to lecture me and acted most foolishly, shut the window, turned down the lamp, shifted about uneasily, me standing darning, scowling like seven demons, so she went away and left me there for further punishment. That

evening I was sent from table for laughing and made to sit for two hours in the dark parlour".

Mary Layard Bowker left scrapbooks containing many interesting jottings and the following account is illustrative of prevailing attitudes to wild-life at the time:

"Wild Dogs. Aug 24 1891 Tharfield
An old Hottentot while walking over from Fletchers to Elliotts was followed by two large wild dogs, he had a small dog with him which probably induced the wild dogs to follow him. It was dark and, in mortal terror of being run to earth and devoured, the ancient Tot took out of his ragged coat pocket a dinner knife, this his sole weapon and resolved to fight to the last. The dogs, huge grizzly animals broad in the chest and dreadful of fang were close upon him. With native instinct he fell upon the ground and screamed and roared with his mouth close to the earth. This stratagem had the desired effect of frightening the dogs who fell back a little and gave the old man time to recover his legs and use them in flight - fright added wings to his clumsy veldschoen and he soon reached his home across the valley with a tale bristling with gesticulation and exaggeration. A few days after, Mr Elliott caught a bitch in a trap set for tiger. They then visited an old hole from which they had once dug out a porcupine and there they found traces of the wild dogs who only live in holes when they have young ones. They dug the hole out and found five wild dog pups, the dog was away at the time. They destroyed 4 of the pups and kept one to tame. This little creature refused to eat anything that was offered until one of the boys shot birds with a catapult and then it eat *(sic)*. At night it used to

> howl and the old dog answer it. One night, a night or two after they had captured the pup, the foot prints of the dog were found near the house and a large piece of bush buck meat had been brought and left there evidently for the young one. Mr Elliott took the meat to the little animal and it devoured it eagerly when it would take nothing else, it recognised the smell of the poor father whose canine instincts taught him to bring and leave the food near where he knew the puppy was imprisoned. The dog was finally captured, the pup was placed in the hole as a decoy to the father who was caught in a trap in the entrance. The pup also met its fate when it had accomplished that of its father for in attempting to reach the trap where the old dog was caught it jumped over a bank of earth and was hung by its chain."

Hal Barber, whom she later married, had in 1890 become engaged to someone else. Her sister Katie wrote to her on 20 February that year with the news:

> "Ma wrote to you last post and told you the news - fancy Hal engaged after all. Wish he had rolled up to you, he might have paid the mortgage off for us. I wonder what they all think of it, Mrs A. must think it is fine - such a rich son in law. I guess Fred will hunt up a cook next".

In 1894 Mary Layard Bowker wrote to her mother (her father had died nine years earlier) with the news that she wanted to marry Hal Barber; she was now thirty one years of age and Hal was forty four. Her mother was obviously delighted, judging by the tone of Mary's next letter:

> "Your jolly letters came this afternoon; we were very glad

to get them and know that you are pleased. I am sorry to feel that it means leaving my dear old home but I guess I shall always be coming back . You can imagine that I am dreadfully happy. As to Old Hal, he is slightly mad, looks years younger, goes about whistling and saying he can't imagine why it did not come off two years' ago. You've no notion how pleased people are. Aunt Mary has got quite young and skittish over it and says the `same old rot' to us. I send you Alice's effusion to laugh over, as we did. I am going to telegraph to her tomorrow on the chance of beating your letter and give her leave to tell first or she'll bust. I am sure Uncle Henry will be pleased. You must not be sorry and think that I am `clean gone' like the wicked. I shall often run home and drag Old Hal. Hal has given me a jolly revolver and lots of shooting lessons, he says I am an awfully good shot. I hit a condensed milk tin eight times running, ten yards off - will soon be able to knock down a bullock".

Hal's proposal was obviously well received by Mary's mother Julia, to whom he wrote:

"It is with great pleasure that I now take up my pen to answer your most welcome letter and I really do not know how to thank you enough for the great gift you have bestowed on me. The only way I can now think of showing it is by promising to be kind to your daughter and this I shall indeavour *(sic)* to do all through life. Aunt Julia you little know how delighted I am about it as I really believe we are most suited for each other as our tastes are so much the same. You are perhaps aware that Fred and I were quite ruined in 1890 during the terrible downfall of the share market etc but I am now pleased to tell you that

> we have managed to 'pull ourselves together' fairly well and are now in pretty good circumstances again so I am not asking Mary to share a life of poverty with me. We are building a comfortable house in a very nice part of the town and in two months time or even less I hope to have it finished when I shall go down to Tharfield and ask you to hand over that gal".

In letters between Hal and Mary at this time the name 'Phyllis' is mentioned several times and it transpires that it was she who had been Hal's first fiancée. The first mention of Phyllis is in a letter dated 9 February 1894 from Mary:

> "I was quite nervous as we alighted at Craigieburn and the probability of meeting Phyllis and the feeling increased as I neared the town and when I looked round the hall after we had taken our seats hers was the first face that caught my eye. Hal, it nearly kills me to think of her so young and fair and so ill fated. If she had written to either of us after our engagement I would know how to act but, as it is, I am afraid to make any advances and yet I want to meet and speak with her. I was down town all the morning shopping with Mrs and Miss Hemming, such nice gentle ladies. As ill luck would have it I chanced near Phyllis twice but not near enough to speak to tho' of course she saw me and I saw her. She did not appear to recognize me tho' she passed within a few yards. What am I to do. I wish we were half way to the Zambesi, this atmosphere is too depressing".

Mary next mentions Phyllis in a letter to Hal dated 18 February 1894, which has an irregular hole through the centre, made by termites. It is a delightful lover's letter in which she asks Hal to either burn her letters or keep them safely locked away.

> "There were several for me. I kept yours till the last and read it in my room. I wonder how many times I have read it since! If you receive all my seven letters in succession you will find all your questions answered and, I hope, your doubts at rest. Satisfied! of course I am. I feel positively walled in with satisfaction. Only you are so far away and it is years since you kissed me, Hal, 26 days really, only a short time. I wonder how many complete 24 hour lengths will get measured off before you come, if you know how much I would like to have you here. If I suppose you are really busy about the house, if you are not coming till March and we are to be married at once, Mama and all of them will have seen nothing of you. If I'm to meet you in town you must telegraph in time for me to meet you and if you time your train to tally with the Kowie down train we can leave the same day as I don't wish to spend more than absolutely necessary in Grahamstown. I hate it and last day there quite finished me. I met Phyllis in a shop and I went up to her and shook hands and we just looked one another in the face. It nearly killed me, so how must she have felt, poor child. I began this letter in the afternoon after returning from the mealie lands, half a mile away, carrying heap of mealies on the stalk tied together with monkey rope, revolver dangling ready for action. I laughed to myself over an imaginary encounter with some J'burg swells I know. You could never have got the letter I left in S. . . to be posted or you would not bemoan the long intervals between my postings when you ought to have had a letter from me every three days on average. Our letters always seem to have crossed

somehow, you have only answered two of mine directly since I left, all the other five seem to have dropped into oblivion. Its nearly the time when we used to say goodnight. It is curious how the tide of thoughts sets to you with these hours. Please burn my letters or lock them up or something. I am quite nervous about them getting into a storm and blowing over the town. I inquired in town about the King W'town post cart. It leaves Weldons in High Street at 6 am Monday, Wednesday and Friday, fare £2, baggage 30 lbs, overweight 6d per lb. However, we can talk over where and how we are going when you come. Haven't I written too often to you? Please say so and I'll stop at once! I am obliged to read your four letters over and over, guess I know them pretty much word for word. You must have my photo by now, posted last Wednesday. Want to know where I keep yours? Shan't tell you - so there! Goodnight dear Hal - Mary.

P.S. Please seal your letters, I am positive that they read them in the Kowie office. I remember you all day dear Hal".

The last mention of Phyllis is in Hal's letter dated 21 February 1894, in which the matter of Phyllis seems to have been laid to rest: she is not mentioned again. He wrote:

"You need not worry about my writing to Phyllis as I have now stopped for ever. There certainly was a misunderstanding between us as she wrote to me before I went to the bush velt saying that her face was so bad that she had to go to town and that the doctor said she would most likely have to undergo a plastic operation and, in that case, she would have to give up all thoughts of ever getting married.

> I concluded from that that it was equal to breaking off the engagement as I have no hopes of her face ever getting well, so gradually left off writing to her and had not written to her for about six months or more when a very short note came asking why I did not write any more? I then wrote and told her that I was most likely going to the Matabeli country & that our engagement had better come to an end & for several other reasons that I gave. (This was long before I had any idea of proposing to you.) To this she answered in a very sad letter saying that she also thought it best to end the engagement not for the reason I gave but on act. of her face. Mary you must not worry yourself about her poor girl for it can't do any good".

What had happened to poor Phyllis' face? This is not recorded in any of the letters that I have but one possibility is that it had become severely scarred, perhaps by smallpox which was endemic throughout the African continent at that time, or by burns. Whatever the reason it is clear that Phyllis had suffered some calamitous facial scarring after her engagement to Hal in 1890 and that this was at that time regarded as a barrier to marriage. To complete this little saga I must relate that Mary, too, had been previously engaged: my father told me that he came across an old photograph of his mother wearing an engagement ring some time before she was engaged to Hal Barber. This had never been spoken of and no details are recorded but the previous engagements offer an explanation for the fact that Hal and Mary were older than most at the time of their engagement and marriage.

Hal and Mary were married at Bathurst on 28th March 1894. They and most of the guests travelled to the church on horseback. Mary's mother Julia Eliza Bowker lived far away and could not attend the wedding and Mary wrote to her that very day:

> "Dearest Mother, Katie's letter just turned up and I am answering with the wedding ring on my finger. I am awfully pleased and happy and Hal says that I must tell you that he seems happy (to look at) and is. It is all awfully funny, I don't know who I am in the least so will not sign myself particular but everything in general. Emma was awfully nice to me & quite took the edge off the loneliness. She is sitting in here now while I am writing, talking about everything. Holden will tell you everything and I'll contrive to write from everywhere. We found Bathurst for once but when we turned our backs on the church it faded like a whisp *(sic)* of mist and became part of the great 'white'. Love to Robin and Katie, dear Mother and 'Don't cry for me', as I am most lucky, being undeserving I'll be haring home dragging Hal with me. Ever your loving child, Mary L Bowker Barber".

She and Hal raised four sons: Ivan the sculptor; Raymond (my father) who was a farmer, genealogist and writer; Renshaw, farmer and engineer; and Alban, violinist, farmer and engineer. There was a mystery about a fifth son: when my father was sorting through old letters and papers quite late in his life he came across an envelope on which was written in his father Hal's handwriting: 'Finger nail. Hal and Mary Barber's 4th son nail . . . aged 20 days not named yet. 18.11.1904. The Castle.' If he died on that date he would have been born on 29 October 1904. Alban, who we all knew as the fourth, son was born on 9 Dec 1904 at the house called The Castle at Port Alfred, so was the unnamed son (born eleven weeks earlier) Alban's twin? My father Raymond recalled his uncle Holden mentioning the matter in an unguarded moment but none of the four surviving brothers knew about it at the time. In my career as a Consultant Obstetrician I heard of twins born days, even weeks apart so it must be a possibility that Alban was the surviving twin.

Hal walked with a limp for the rest of his life as a result of his affray with the buffalo. Later he added to his troubles by being mauled by a leopard and then by falling from a pear tree. He was not fit enough to work for some time and it was fortunate that, at this stage of his life, he was wealthy enough to be able to live on the investments derived from his mining and speculation on the stock market. He must have become restless with the inactivity for, in January 1906, he travelled from Port Alfred on the coast into the Transvaal where he spent five months looking for a suitable farm. On 14th May 1906 he bought the farm which he called 'Terramena' near Potchefstroom and wrote enthusiastically to Mary:

> "My dear Mary: I did not write on Friday or Saturday for I had such a lot to do seeing the people about the option on the farm and going out to see it. I have now quite decided on buying the farm I went to look at and, last evening, the Attorney came down and brought all the diagrams for me to see and I told him that I would take the farm, so tomorrow I have to sign the deed of sale. So not till then will I count this farm as my own. I have got one of the cheapest bargains on the Mooi River, comprising 1500 acres in all, out of which there are quite 100 acres on the river under water and a splendid rich soil when water is abundant. Lucerne grows like 'blazes' as Edgar says. I'm paying £3800 for it and with transfer

dues it will cost about £4000. I am quite delighted at the thought of moving up in about September when is the time for us to come up, as it is too cold and risky to come up now. Beside the two houses on the farm are common flat roofed red brick houses such as most 'taak haar' Boers build, so I shall have to build pretty soon but I may first patch up the one house soon for us to get a foothold in until we can get a better house built, so this is what I expect to do. The farm has fine large lands and a few nice poplar and other trees on it and one grand large wild tree, just where I intend building, but you will have to come up and help choose the site and 'mind the dairy while I will guide the plough'. Edgar thinks I will be able easily to make £2000 a year out of this farm once it is under Lucerne, so I must tackle it at once and shall put men in to plough as soon as I have actually got it. I will wire you tomorrow as soon as I have signed the deed of sale so it will be with you before this letter reaches you. I hope you are all well my own dear ones at home and dear little Pog. I just dream of you all night and day my dear and its not nice living away from you all but I am sure I have done well by coming up and would not take £500 profit on the ground I have bought if it were offered me. The Evans' farm is abt. ¼ of an hour distance off. Mine is ½ an hour from town so the boys will be able to bike and drive in to school with them in just no time. I am sure if all goes well we will like coming up here. Lots of love. Yours Hal".

It was a full six months before Hal had upgraded the house sufficiently to bring Mary and the four sons up. Throughout this time Hal and Mary wrote almost daily, only his letters have survived and give details about how the house was coming on:

"Terramena 7th Sept. [1906]
My dear Mary: I am fifty six today as it is my birthday. Born 7th September 1850, more than half a century ago by six years. I am quite an old man now and have had a long and happy life with but a few cares and a great lot of happiness; lots of nice friends and a loving wife and four of the nicest children man has ever been blessed with. I am fairly well off and prospects good, so what more do I want? What I now want most of all is to get my family round me again, so all I have to do on this my birthday is to enclose you a small cheque of £50 to get what you require and to pay your fares up with. The single First fares will come to about £20 if you bring a nurse with you; a single fare is about £6 but you must arrange for the children at half price. Pog [Alban] is still in arms, comes for nothing or one quarter, so you must fight a hard battle with the ticket issuer and get them through cheap. You must come First Class or you won't get on to the train de lux at Alicedale or De Aar, which you will find a great comfort as you will have all your meals on board in a nice large pretty dining car. You will get 11 o.c. tea, in fact tea at any time you care to order as they always have tea and coffee ready to make at a moment's notice. So do things comfortably when you do start. Stay a day or two over at The Grand if you want Davis to do your teeth, for I know nothing about these dentists. Break the journey at Hales Owen if you wish to and be ready for De Aar and wire to De Aar Hotel to meet you there. Catching train at about 11 next day, this will give you all a nice night's rest. You will still have another night in the train and reach Potchefstroom at 6 o.c. next morning, where Miles will meet you but you must wire when you are leaving Grahamstown, so that we can know when to meet you. We get our letters daily at 10 from the

> PO so your wire must reach the PO before that on the day before your arrival. My, it will be a happy day for me when you all are here. In your one letter you say get a Pearl stove and now a Fortress No. 9, so which am I to do? I think a Fortress is the best and we can always get spare in. Miles back all right, says Mitford is on the track of a diamond mine but the owner will have to make terms to give us a share in if it is a mine; can't tell yet. Lots of love to you all. H.M. Barber".

Five years later Hal was afflicted by wanderlust again and went to visit British East Africa [BEA] as it was then known, later named Kenya. He wrote to Mary in glowing terms of the country and in 1912 sold his farm in South Africa and bought a farm which he named Ivanhoe at Kyambu, close to Nairobi. Mary loved the country and wrote a description of their early days which she called 'Pioneering in East Africa':

> "For pure melancholy give me a windy day in Central Africa, for we are now in the gales. These must have their appointed times and come round on their old paths as regularly as the rains and seem to delight in whistling over these vast regions of ripe yellow grass. I always picture the wind as hurrying with eyes strained to the horizon, girdled to the loins and sandal-shoed grey with the dust of deserts passed. One sees great fires too in these months - the Masai are burning the old to make place for the new and rolling columns of smoke and racing flames, mounting and falling as they devour the short and the long, burn terrifying holes in the blackness of night. I stand and wonder how the frightened animals fly, and how the small and weak shriek and die. How cruel is fire - we light a match in the dry

hedge as we walk and go home to sleep, millions groan and die. But fire is a wonderful stimulator of vegetable life in hot Africa, and a few days after it has swept the face of the country the grass peeps out of the blackness and many shrubs put out fresh leaves from the top of their scortched *(sic)* stumps, dead trees smoke for days and finally fall in a mass of ashes, the oribi and rietbuck come skipping back to crop the fresh verdure. This morning, when I was looking around at dawn with the glasses, I counted 19 ruddy little antelopes on the slope across the valley, all gaily at breakfast. They are so graceful and, when surprised, they dance off springing at intervals and showing their white bodies as they skim over the grass and run and jump again and when at a safe distance turn nose on to gaze. Then one can hardly see them at all as their colour merges with their surroundings. The other day our dog chased a kid from the grass close to us, we all ran and screamed to save the tiny creature when, to our astonishment, the mother dashed amongst us, rushed up to the hound who immediately followed her and she fled off and so led him away while the kid escaped, a wonderful piece of strategy acted under our very eyes. All the antelopes in these wilds astonish one; they are all beautiful and so at home, feeding in great herds, many species together and all seemingly at peace together. Here we see oribi, jackals, topi, rietbuck, congoni and zebra, hundreds of these all cropping the short grass on the marsh and a pair of big bustards, great birds with rufous neck and powder blue breasts. They walk gracefully, occasionally dashing their beaks at some choice beetle. They are always splendidly fat and one we had lasted 3 days, finer than roast turkey and finally came back in soup from the bones. They really ought to be domesticated for the benefit of humanity, but as they only lay 2 eggs each season the problem would not be half solved. Odd eland are also here and one occasionally comes across a family of giraffe, wonderful creatures. You see and don't see them when suddenly all their spots hit your eyes at once as they lunge forward and appear to be going to fall but really break into a sweeping gallop and, when they go over a rise, you still see their mighty necks long after their bodies have disappeared. They are supposed to be voiceless as their voice is not heard - what a pipe that length of neck might boast! Last night we were sitting round our fire when the gruff voice of a leopard broke the stillness; we all rushed to a small mound hard by and stood listening. The animal was making for the stream in the valley below; he was evidently calling his mate as they always live in pairs - such a rough rolling voice, I was glad to be safe and near guns and good shots. These leopards have lovely pelts. We have found several oribi killed and eaten in the grass not 600 yards from our camp, so we are planning open war to save our game. One can not walk in these wilds without guns as you never know what will turn up. The lions are very quiet, I have not heard them lately. Heard in the stillness of the night all other sounds sink to whispers when this mighty voice shakes the solitude. I am so glad I have lived to feel the wonder and terror of the lion calling to his mates in his own wilderness. When the roar rolls on the ear one's whole face seems seared with the concussion. After leaving the train at Londiani we tracked up to the great hill of cedars to the plateau over which our road led. The road has been cut through the solid forest for nearly 40 miles. It is up and up, colder and colder, till one reaches the highest point, 9000 feet, and over the berg as it is called there, down on to the plateau, a long grassy elevation called by the natives the 'uasin gishu', and streams of cattle. There

> are many legends of old time wars and tribal fights for this rich strip of open veld. The first night in the cedars was a weird experience. We made a mighty fire at the edge of the road, the light gleaming on the huge boles of the dark cedars served to deepen the ebon shadows that stretched away into their depths. I was afraid to look anywhere in case I saw something and when a colobus monkey began shouting close by I sprang up in terror. A hurried meal round the windblown fire and into the wagon and under the blankets, all ears and shivering with cold, I lay as in a castle enchanted in an unknown land".

They were hardly established on the new farm when the 1914 - 1918 war broke out. One might imagine that in those remote parts they would not be affected by the war in Europe but they were: their two older sons Ivan and Raymond both served in the campaign in German East Africa (later Tanganyika, now Tanzania) and Portuguese East Africa (now Mozambique). Mary kept a diary from which I quote but a few entries:

> "First day on Farm January 21st 1914 A few miles and we were on our home farm & finally we drew up under the big fig tree on the Momeas road, loaded off the wagons & slept there. Early the next morning Hal went away & left us & we were actually alone with our things & servants, one tent, the cart & wagon. We walked about a lot the next day trying to find a suitable place for a house but could not decide. That night, about ten, I was lying awake when a lion roared close by & the lioness answered at once With one bound I tried to shut the hut door but it was hooked open & a big box was in the way so Mary [her niece] and I lit the lamp and stood it at the door and

sat and waited while Hal and the others in the wagon got out guns & put the 4 lamps round the span on the yokes; however, we heard nothing more and after a long time we went to sleep till morning.

August 6th 1914 War! England declares war with Germany - how awful. How it must have startled the world & the news shook our peace in these East African solitudes. We were all agog for news & sending to Kyambu often twice a day to learn the happenings in the outside world - not much has come through yet but men are gathering in Nairobi to help defend this colony if necessary. Mr Bromage came here & went into town the next day to join "Bowkers Horse". Hal, Ivan & he drove in & saw Russell in town, he is getting up a corps of men, everyone vastly excited. Wessells also getting up a band of men, mostly Dutchmen. We hear all phases of news, sea fights & land battles & sieges in Belgium - plucky little country! Cecil Harris & his small brother `Bobs' were here for a couple of days. They have very little petrol & Harris took half a bottle we had & filled it up with paraffin to take him back. We send as often as we can to Kyambu for news. We are not losing so far but war is too terrible to think about all the young & the brave dying to satisfy the greedy ambition of the German Emperor. We hear that all mules & horses are to be commandeered for civil use so we do not drive to town in case of losing ours. We hear that the Germans are posted every 7 miles down the boundary. Also that they were marching on Kisumu in Nyanza but it was false. The Governor proclaims the awful fact that England has declared war with Austria, how truly fearsome it has become, where will we hide our heads during these awful days, it is a terrible thing war in these days of Dreadnaughts & aeroplanes. We hear that an air ship has been seen over Nairobi at night but the men were so convivial that they are likely to see things.

Sep.1st 1914 Tuesday We hear that the Germans have attacked Belgian Congo, the Belgians are acting on the defensive. Two Germans were caught by our men near Voi. They were asleep near the railway line & seem to have had a terrible time crossing the long stretch of waterless country full of scrub & aloes that divides Voi from their border. They had 10 porters & cases of dynamite & were probably bound for our bridges to blow them up. Instead of shooting them our men took them prisoners & they are now in Nairobi.

Nov 22 1915 Ivan & Ray off!! I drove to town & saw Ivan & Ray go off in khaki to help with the transport, dear boys, I could not stop them doing their `bit' as the saying is, but I am always afraid & hoping madly for the best. We have heard from them, they are happy & busy. Ivan's first letter was much censored.

New years eve! [1915] We came back in the dusk & saw a jackal very near in the road, Miles fired at him twice, he went like the wind, so did the dogs but lost the trail. We got home & a few minutes later in burst Ivan & Ray come on bykes [sic] from Nairobi having walked from the Athi station where they are resting the transport oxen for a week or two. We were so glad to see them, tired & dusty & it was so good to see how glad they were to be at home. My very dear sons - so happy to see them in bed & still safe & in the night I waked & blessed them unaware as they slept in a room close by, my most dear sons! How happy they have made my life & do not regret one hour spent for them. I am glad I lived my life with them all their young years. We spent quite a happy new years day together - they must away at 8 o'clock on the 2nd day of the new year. I watched them go & thought long, long thoughts.

May 22nd 1915 We have had a few wonderful sights of Kilimanjaro a pink wonder at sunset. The men from the border say no words can picture its beauty seen close by, poetry is dumb & art hurls her brush in the dust. Deadly things happen down there. After a fight, a wounded man lying by his dead chum was left all night at his request on the chance of our men returning in the morning - which they did & fetched him away but his hair was white, as in the grim & awful night the lions came and eat his poor dead friend close to him & growled at him. At Longido two wounded men 50 yards apart were entertained all night by a party of furious lions who eat a mule lying dead between them. Also, worst of all, the Germans or askaris or both or together actually cut buttons off our poor wounded & gouged out their poor pleading eyes that asked for mercy & put the buttons into the sockets - & God is in heaven! Then heaven must be too remote to help us in any way & we've got to set our teeth & fight these fiends to the finish.

June 22 1915 Ray, always Ray! dropped on us this afternoon & we have spent a lovely evening together singing & talking books. Half the night is gone as he waited for the moon which is evidently hung up somewhere in the eastern steeps as she didn't appear. So after coffee Ivan, Ray & `Mother Mary', we three that have been together these many years separated once more, I ran to bed. Ray rode into the night with a lamp hanging on his bicycle. It is after 12, cold & dark. I went out & saw a speck of light far off in the forest & blessed my dear sweet son & remembered all his loving ways to me when he was yet a small boy. I am so glad in my children. Goodnight.

November 22nd 1917 Two years ago today since dear Ray went away in Khaki to help his King & Country & now he is far in East Africa at a place called New Dabaga quite unfindable on the map, but high & healthy he writes. We seldom get letters & have to wait & wait till we can scarcely breathe with anxiety. He has had fever 4 times but is better in the high country, he is at a food depot loading & forwarding wagons to feed the forces that are pursuing the Germans. Mitford is also down there with a carrier corps following the Belgian forces & walking through grass 12 feet high & my Ivan has been six months at Dar es Salaam at office work & then minding prisoners of war & is now sick in The Hospital at Morogoro, also in the highlands & still the war rages, but this particular piece of fury is really abating but, in Europe, the tornado of shot & shell continues & things are now so complicated that its like the house in Josh Billings `so divided against itself that it don't know which way to fall!' What with Russia falling out & cutting her own throat & Italy getting driven back & treason in high places our hair is just waving with fright & wondering what will be the end of it all. When history dips his pen in the inkpot of fixed politics & writes `Finis' who'll be top & where will the sinner & ungodly be with poor old righteous man trembling in his shoes! We just live on & plant & work & sow & gather coffee & write letters & watch the days pass & wait & wait & our hair is greying & time racing to our end & still all our children are far away & still the war rages & men die by the 100 thousand.

Nov 14 1918 I am trying to make a small garden for green things & there I was battling with a primeval bit of Africa when Hal came calling down waving a piece of paper. I thought it must be good news & this is the immortal scrap - I paste it in.

> "14/11/18 Dear Mr Barberton, Mail hasn't arrived yet but should do so today. Good news. GERMANY Surrendered on 12th inst. No particulars. Hope you are all keeping well. Kind regards to all.
> Yours sinc D A Johnston"

Peace! All day I thought as I listened to the wind racing over this vast solitude. The guns are silent in Europe! I was not happy thinking of the empty chairs and the Unreturning Brave. But down in my mind I knew that my darling sons were alive & I was very thankful. Johnston sent runners all over the country with the news. Now who shall roll us away the stone from the door of the sepulchre? All the wise heads in the world are trying to tidy up - but it will take a long time & many strong brooms. The Kaiser is in Holland & little Willie `along of his father', they must sleep on thorny pillows & get little satisfaction in contemplating the ash heaps of their mutual achievements".

In 1915 Hal had visited the Trans Nzoia District further north where his eyes had lit upon some of the finest land in the world on the foothills of Mount Elgon, with fertile valleys. He bought four farms totalling twenty thousand acres which they did not occupy until 1919, when he sold his farm Ivanhoe at Kyambu to a wealthy South African. At the time the currency in BEA was changed from rupees to pounds, shillings and cents and Hal benefitted from a favourable exchange rate to the tune of an additional two or three thousand pounds. Mary left Ivanhoe with sadness where she had germinated and nurtured thousands and thousands of coffee and fruit trees. Her third son, Renshaw, later recalled how she would work alone in her coffee nursery and on her vegetable garden by the river some distance from the house, till darkness had fallen, with only her .38 nickel plated revolver for protection against the wild animals which were plentiful at that time. She wrote of her sadness in her diary after they had moved to the new farms:

> "December 1918
> A long, lonely, dry month with two great events standing out. Ray went to Eldoret about the sale of Ivanhoe, he was gone one morning & back the next night. Then we got deeds of sale which we signed & returned. A Mr Randall from the Cape bought it for £17,500. I was not happy thinking of all the many happy years there spent with our children & Mary & all my many plant children grown from seed & watched for years, all gone with the stroke of the pen; but we are here & will make a new home quickly & perhaps go travelling a little".

Hal survived the post war epidemic of Spanish flu in 1918 and then died in 1920 from Blackwater fever. Mary lay unconscious with cerebral malaria at the same time, only recovering after his funeral had taken place.

Chapter 3

1912 -The Barbertons of Kenya

Among the items which I received after my uncle Alban Barberton died was a tape recording made in 1971 of a conversation between an Afrikaaner named Piet Roets and Mitford Bowker, Alban's cousin. Piet Roets had come to British East Africa from South Africa as a boy in 1908 and his recording gives a vivid account of life at the time, which will have been very similar to the experiences of my grandparents. Piet Roets was articulate and my edited record of his account preserves most of his own language. He spoke fluent but archaic English in a rich Afrikaans accent and the following quotations are from my transcript of his story which became known as the Van Rensberg Trek:

> "My first experience before we came to this country, which was called British East Africa at that time, was with my father who was a farmer in the Transvaal in South Africa. He used to farm maize and we had cattle and sheep. When the winter starts we used to trek with the sheep and the cattle down to the bushveld; we would stay there for months. Then when the rain starts again in the highveld we would start ploughing and getting our crops in.

A few years after the Boer War there were some advertisements in the English papers that people were wanted in East Africa for farming. My wife's grandfather, Mr Jan van Rensberg and another man came up by boat in 1906 to Mombasa and they came up to Nairobi and met the Governor of those days. He told them that he wanted to get some farmers up from South Africa to farm in the Uasin Gishu district. He said that if Mr van Rensberg would get him thirty families he would open the Uasin Gishu plateau for them to choose where they wanted to settle. He came back to South Africa and he had meetings in several towns and in 1908 he brought forty-seven families which wanted to come with him to settle in British East Africa. We did not bring any cattle but we brought horses and wagons and our ox gear and some horse carts and nearly everyone brought one or two dogs and their families. The total of men, women and children were four hundred and two. We came up to Mombasa by the Windhoek which was a German boat. We came by train as far as Nakuru and there we camped.

An expedition was sent from there, eleven men on horseback, Mr van Rensberg was their leader. They came up through the plateau, looked around. They went back to Nakuru and reported to the people there that they think it is quite a good place, a nice plain with rivers enough, water enough and they think it a good place to settle. There was any amount of game - zebra, kongoni, topi, oribi and reedbuck. There were lots of lion; sometimes we used to see sixteen together. There were jackal and wild dogs.

While the expedition was away the people had bought some oxen and some cattle from the trading Somalis and from the natives and we started training the oxen, then we started trekking up from there by wagons. We cut through heavy forest; the first forest was five miles and the second forest three miles, the next one was two miles, then there was a little one and then we came to what we call the Tribost. From there we went on to what we called the Brusspruit and we outspanned there for one day. From there we came straight through to the Plateau and all the rivers we came to we had to make drifts. There was no chance of making bridges because there was no timber. We had to take enough firewood on to the wagons to last about a week. We outspanned at mid-day for our lunch, then we went on travelling in three columns - seven wagons and then ten wagons and another ten wagons. We stopped at Sergoit for a few days; some went downstream, some crossed the river and some went upstream - every man more or less where he wants to pick his farm - so we went and put our camps on our places. Later the government sent up a surveyor, a Mr Scobie, who surveyed the farms and we got the farms on condition that we do three years development. After three years if you have done the development satisfactorily, you are a tenant and later on you can get your title deeds.

After we had pitched tents and camps on the farms we very soon got busy building houses. Some built mud houses, some just with grass but most of the people started building permanent houses with stone and mud. Then the people said we have to get some land ready for planting, although it was late in the year. We did not know the seasons - we thought it was the same as where we came from - so it was late in November when we started breaking up a few acres of land and put in some maize and oats which we had brought with us. We had a little rain; it did come up but it didn't mature. Some people took water furrows from the rivers for irrigation and started gardens and that was very successful.

Any food, sugar, coffee, tea, groceries and things like that, we had to go back to Nakuru for. That was our nearest shops and that was our nearest post office. There was no road to Londiani - as we came up there were only footpaths. We had to cut the roads for the wagons. The flour we got in those days was called Indian Superfine Flour and we bought that at thirty-seven rupees per bag. The posho we got in those days was very very poor because it was that mixed blue and white and red maize which we got from the natives. What saved our lives mostly was the game, the meat. We used to buy wimbi (millet) and crush it with little mills - we bought it from the Nandi. We bought some maize and some beans.

Shortly after we arrived on the farm we didn't have shoes and boots with us so some people started tanning their own leather. My mother was very expert at that, so it wasn't long before we made our own veldschoens by tanning eland hides for the soles and kongoni for the leather. We used to tan oribi hide, which is very thin, to sew with instead of cotton. We didn't have any nails so we used little pegs made out of bamboo to put into the boot. We couldn't make them out of wire because we had no wire.

The ploughs which we used in those early days used to turn the soil over about nine inches deep. Later on we had a Jambo plough and an Elephant plough, all single furrows which cut about twelve inches. Our first harrows we made by cutting some poles and we drilled one and a half inch holes in it and made some pegs out of olive, drive the pegs in and those were our harrows which we used to harrow the maize in.

After the second year we had enough to eat which we had grown on our farms. After about eighteen months the farmers thought we have done more or less enough now, we must approach the government to see what more we should do in the way of improvements. A committee was appointed and was sent down to Nairobi to the Governor and he sent a valuer up to value all the work and improvements on the farms. There was not a single man whose farm was taken - everybody passed. Then we were considered as tenants and everybody could work for his title deeds.

We didn't have much produce to sell because we had to take it down to Londiani by wagons. Later on, when the road was better, we sold wheat at four and a half rupees a bag and maize at three rupees a bag. The prices weren't very much but we were making a living. We often ran short of food - sugar and things like that - for several weeks at a time. We had to send the wagons down to Nakuru and it would take them three weeks, sometimes four weeks, to return according to the weather so sometimes we had to do without coffee or tea. If we ran out of coffee some took some potatoes, boiled the potato to a certain extent then cut him in small slices and dry him out in the sun and then they roasted that and that was coffee. Some did it out of maize; you boil the maize a little and put it out and dry it, then you roasted it and that was coffee too.

We had to be very careful with our lamp oil and when we did run out we used to use what we call a fat candle - our mothers used to make them. Some used a mould like a marrow bone, some used bamboo which is hollow inside. They used to take a piece of rag, narrower than my little finger. Then they twist it until it is nice and round and then they double it and then they put it in the bamboo straight down, with a little stick on top across and they boil the hot fat in there and leave it to get cold: ordinary fat from the game, kongoni fat and eland fat - it must be hard fat. Then when it is cold you pull it out of the mould and there you've got your candle.

Later on when we got our title deeds we carried on - we came with the intention here to stay and to farm. A few went back to South Africa a few years later but the majority stayed here. I am here now living on my father-in-law's farm, a portion of it. My wife came with my father-in-law and later on I bought this piece of land from him, so I am settled here. In the early days when they were still in a tent with a small grass hut on the side for a kitchen, she always used to get up and do the fire early in the morning to cook the kettle for coffee. One morning she got up and lit the fire and it was foggy and she looked out and she saw something, for the kitchen was a little way from the tent. She went to the grass hut where her father and mother were sleeping and cried "Father, Father" she says "here is a big pig". Her father jumped out and he didn't know what it was and he saw it running there, it was a rhino about twenty-five yards from the tent. He went back to the bedroom and he got his rifle and he shot it about a hundred yards away and he killed it. Some of the rhinos have a lot of fat in them. We had no hippos in the swamps here; the nearest hippos were in the Nzoia river. Hippos always had a lot of fat.

We were very successful starting with sheep and cattle in the first days. Then in 1912 the first epidemic of rinderpest broke out and we had very heavy losses because there were no veterinary services. After that East Coast fever broke out and after the East Coast fever we had very little cattle left. We were very unlucky with cattle until about 1937-38 when we started building dips and then cattle farming improved again. In 1913 and 1914 there was a disease among the sheep. Some people lost hundreds and some mornings when you get into the boma there are about a hundred, all dead. They didn't know what killed them, until a lot later on when they sent some by wagon to Kabete to the veterinary station.

From Londiani we used to do transport to Eldoret right up to Elgon, in the early days. When the sawmills started here we had to import very heavy machinery - great boilers and the saws - and we had to load the wagons very heavily, for some of those boilers were over five tons. If you put a boiler weighing five tons on one wagon on these muddy roads you will, on some days, have great difficulty in getting through the forest with the mud tracks. On some days the teams of oxen drawing the wagons were up to their bellies in mud and they had to pull the wagon through that too. It was very difficult and very hard on the cattle. We once had the experience where one boiler rolled over with the wagon. There were no cranes there, so we decided to unhitch the oxen and we loosened the ropes and let the boiler lie by the side of the wagon, then we pulled the wagon away from the boiler with the oxen.

On the other side we dug a long trench and pulled the empty wagon into it right beside the boiler. The wheels were below road level in the ditch, and we took the wagon jacks - we had several wagons, each one with a jack - and we jacked the boiler up until we could roll it on the wagon again. We took three teams of oxen and pulled it out of the ditch, so we carry on again. It took us a whole day to do it.

Sometimes it took us twenty-seven days from Londiani to Elgeo sawmills in the very wet weather. Sometimes a wagon wheel broke; perhaps some of the spokes broke so you cut some timber, took some of the ox reims and you tied it together again and the work went on. There were no blacksmiths on the road. Sometimes the disselboom broke so you just cut a tree, or the branch off a tree which was thick enough and you put that in and you carried on again. Once I had a very nice experience in the Uasin Gishu district: I was travelling along early in the morning and I heard some shots in front of me - two shots. I thought to myself it was probably somebody shooting lion or something, for there was any amount of game in those days. About ten minutes later I came across a Scotch cart in front of me with a few Europeans and Africans. I stopped and said "What is the matter?" There were five people who had come up from Londiani on the Scotch cart and they were going to look for their farm. There were some trees very close to the road and the Scotch cart wheel caught one of the trees and the oxen swung the other way and they broke the disselboom of the Scotch cart and they did not know what to do. They were English speaking people from Nairobi. When I got to them they said "Can you help me?" They said

"Our driver cut one of those trees but we have no augers, so we marked the holes with a pencil and tried to fire a shot through the wood with a 9 mm. rifle". They fired two shots and the whole thing was split and finished. I outspanned my oxen and went to my wagon and got my auger and my axe and I chopped that pole nicely so that it would fit in between the two iron arms and I drilled the two holes and within half an hour the thing was fixed. One of them said to me "What is that?" and I said "That is an auger" and he said "I think we've got something like that in the box on the cart". He opened the box and there was every tool you could think of but they didn't realise how to use them.

Another time I was on the road to Londiani with five wagons loaded with maize. When I outspanned there were four or five wagons in front of me just starting to inspan. There was a young chap called Jamieson who had four wagons and some African drivers. He asked me where I was going and I said to Londiani. He said so was he but some of his drivers were sick and he was finding it very difficult. I told him that I was outspanning here now but that I would be inspanning again at half past six and that I would meet him at the next river. So we had our dinner there and inspanned and left and about eleven o'clock in the evening I found him again, outspanned. He was sitting by the fireside making his food as his cook was also sick. He said "Don't leave me behind, let us go from here together". I said "All right, but I want to start very early in the morning. We will move off at four and will start inspanning at three". He said "That's very nice; will you call me?" and I said "Yes, I'll call you". So we went to bed and, at three o'clock in the morning, I awoke and I shouted "Inspan! Inspan!", so all the workmen started inspanning and I gave him my driver for one of his wagons and another wagon of his was to follow my wagon and another behind that and I would take the lead. Before dawn we came to a bridge and I took my wagons through. Then came one of his wagons and the driver wasn't quick enough and he overturned the wagon from the bridge into the river which was about four feet deep. He said "What are we going to do now?" I took my team of oxen from my wagon and put it on to his wagon in the river and I pulled it upright so it stands on its wheels again. We got all the drivers together and loaded the wagon up and pulled it out and we were outspanned just as the sun was rising. He said that's the very best trip he has ever had for a very long time. He said "We capsize a wagon, we reload it and we pull it out and the sun is just rising now."

Once I was leading the oxen for my father - my father and my brother were sitting on the wagon, my father was driving and it was just after sunrise. I was looking to my right and I heard something and there came two old lions, one chasing the other. I stopped the oxen and shouted to my father "Lion." He had a rifle on the wagon and came to me and said "Where are they?" and I said "Sitting over there" and there was a lion sitting watching me. So my father shot him and he ran about fifty yards when he dropped. We went into the thorn trees there and collected some firewood and picked up the lion and put him on the wagon and took him home.

My father was a very good shot and hunter for lion - he killed over two hundred - but the two hundredth one knocked him over. It didn't hurt him, he had a little scratch on his leg, that was all. A lion jumped up at him and he fired a shot but it wasn't a very good shot and he ran off. He was walking along leading his mule when, suddenly, out jumped the lion just the other side of an ant-heap and landed nearly on top of him. He pulled the trigger but the bullet didn't hit him but, when he got up, the lion was just about three yards off him and he turned the rifle round and killed him. Of course the mule ran away and it is away to this day, probably still running. We used to get elephant here; they came across from Mount Elgon to the Elgeo forest in the very wet weather and as soon as the weather breaks, they go away again. Several times we have had more than a hundred passing through the farm in a day. Sometimes they would stay two or three days in amongst the thorn trees and then they would walk off again. Once at Sergoit, they came through a farm right by the farmer's house, about a hundred and fifty of them. They got scared by something and started running away and left behind two elephant calves. He caught them and sent them to Nairobi. Later on when we had more crops, they used to do a lot of damage passing through the maize fields.

The most damage done to the animals on the farm was done by leopards. Mr Joubert, up at Burnt Forest had a boma with a thatched roof and a leopard got in through the thatched roof and killed ninety of his sheep. He heard them stampeding inside and he took one of these Dietz lamps and he walked over and opened the door and out jumped the leopard and knocked the lamp out of his hand and ran off. Near Kipkarren, near the Nandi border, there was a man called Boswick and he had about five hundred head of merino sheep and he got a couple of good rams as well. He had a stone-walled boma; my father built it for him, built with mud and stones but with big ventilation holes through because you must have some air inside. He put the rams into the boma and for the first three or four nights it was all right. One morning he woke up and went to open the boma and found both rams dead and also fifty of the ewes. A leopard had got in through the ventilation hole and killed the sheep and got out again. A man at Suam had about seven hundred sheep in a boma made of thorns about a mile from the house and there were two herdsmen there and they used to sleep there. One morning, the herdsman came early and called him and said "The leopard has eaten some sheep." He went there and found ninety-seven killed, the ninety-eighth he took away with him. He followed his track and about half a mile away, he put it in a big fig tree right up at the top. He went and set a trap gun for it and about half past seven the following evening he was dead, shot with the trap gun. They used to take sheep by the neck and suck the blood until the heart doesn't pump any more, then they would leave it and get another one and when he has had enough, he takes one away with him.

We had very big herds of zebra here and they used to do a lot of damage to the crops. We used to have night guards and put up some white flags which disturbed them a bit. Later on we got them shot out. Eland too used to be in very big herds, sometimes two hundred, but even more were the kongoni.

The place Zuiker Vlei got its name from the Jan van Rensberg trek in 1908. We camped at a place and, the

> next morning, we came to this very muddy vlei, like a swamp, with a little stream of water running through it; it wasn't very deep. There were no roads or bridges. The people went up and down the stream looking for a narrow place to cross but they couldn't, so everybody pushed as best they could to get through. At ten o'clock there were about twenty wagons all stuck, so they put two teams and three teams of oxen and pulled them out one by one. That evening, when it got dark, there was one wagon which was too heavy and we couldn't get it out and it had to stay in the water during the night. We slept in the wagon and the water was so deep that it was just touching the bottom of the wagon. During the night, a bag of sugar got wet and melted and that's what gave it the name, Sugar Vlei. The wagon belonged to Mr Steenkamp. In the morning we got three of the best teams of all and we pulled it out. From there, we went to a place called Diploff and we camped there. From there we came to a nasty vlei over near Kipkabus and we outspanned for three days and cut plenty of brushwood and built a bridge."

When Mary and Hal Barber emigrated to British East Africa their two older sons, Ivan and Raymond, stayed behind to complete their schooling at St Andrew's College in Grahamstown. The two younger sons, Renshaw aged eleven and Alban aged eight, accompanied Mary and Hal to Kenya on a ship called Prinzessin, one of the Deutsch Ost Afrika liners which plied between Europe and South Africa at the time, round the west coast of Africa or through the Suez canal and the Mediterranean. Alban found the actual date of their arrival, 12 December 1912, on a permit from the customs for a gun which his father had brought into the country. They disembarked from the Prinzessin into a rowing boat which took them to the shore and Alban was picked off the boat by a large Swahili boatman who carried him ashore. Alban recorded his memories of these events on tape fifty nine years later and it is from this tape that I have been able to construct this part of the family narrative, augmented by my father's manuscript 'Astride the Equator.' The roads were of sand and there were light trolley lines around the town and they were pushed on a trolley from the port to Mombasa town where they stayed in the Manor hotel. From Mombasa they went by train to Nairobi on the Uganda Railway.

Hal Barber bought a farm at Kyambu near Nairobi and planted a hundred and fifty acres of coffee, much of it grown from seedlings cultivated by his wife Mary. Alban recalled the abundance of rats at the time, which would scuttle with alarm across the corrugated iron roof of the house when the clock struck the hour. These rats, or rather the fleas on them, were the harbingers of plague, outbreaks of which would occur from time to time causing serious illness and many deaths in the African population. Hal prudently packed his family onto a wagon for a safari to Mount Kenya while the epidemic raged. Ray, the second son, recorded the events thus:

> "Not long after settling at Ivanhoe there was an outbreak of bubonic plague and Nairobi and the surrounding districts were put into quarantine. This did not worry my parents much. Nairobi was eight miles away and there was no need to go there for the moment. Then one evening a rat appeared from behind a cupboard, crept as far as the centre of the room, put its head between its paws and died. My father quickly wrapped the body in a newspaper and sent it to the local Medical Department. Next morning

they sent a message confirming that the rat had died of bubonic plague. This was an alarming situation. Everyone went to be inoculated and Dad bought a quantity of insecticide, which was even put inside our socks. All food and water was made inaccessible to the rats, except for a barley stack near the stables. The rat population was encouraged to come to this stack and plenty of food and water was put there to entice them. Immediate evacuation of the house was decided upon and a safari to Mount Kenya was arranged. Hernando Saa was left in charge and ran the farm for a month. On my father's instructions he locked all the water tanks around the house and removed all food that rats could live on. At the stack of barley he put down dishes of water. When Saa had decided that the local rodent population was gathered safely into the barley sheaves, he set a fire to burn round the base of the stack so ensuring that no rats remained. The trip to Mount Kenya was enjoyed by all who went. Mother and the young people climbed to the crater's rim while Hal occupied his time shooting his last buffalo."

Renshaw, the third son, was ten years old when the family moved to Ivanhoe and recalled that they took their dog Otto with them from South Africa:

"He was a golden setter. I remember that when we got into the train at Klington siding Otto was put in the guard's van. He was wearing a collar and a chain was attached to it. As the train moved on Otto stuck his head out of the van window about two carriages behind us; Alban and I called to him just to let him know we were also on board and Otto jumped out of the van window and was suspended in mid air for a while, then his head slipped

> through and he fell clear; luckily the guard was quick and he stopped the train and Otto was picked up. At Kyambu I used to go hunting reedbuck in the big circular swamp. Otto used to go with me and when a reedbuck was put up Otto would get onto the shorter grass and chase the reedbuck round in a circle and, in this way, I just waited till the animal came round to me and I would bowl him over with that old single barrelled gas pipe gun that Chesnaye used to lend me. On another occasion Otto put a serval cat up a tree and I shot him down. I thought that I had shot a young leopard, I was most disappointed when Dad said it was only a cat."

Alban learned to read and write while at Ivanhoe. This was achieved by importing a governess for him from England. Her name was Winifred Cass and she later married a farmer named Cecil Harries. In 1914, when Alban was ten years old, the Government auctioned farming land in the Trans Nzoia district on the foothills of Mount Elgon, three or more days journey to the north, first by train to Londiani then onwards by ox-wagon. Hal Barber bought four farms unseen in a block for £200 each, one for himself and three others in his sons' names, it being conditional that the farms be developed without delay. Alban recalled the surveyor telling them that they would find one farm beacon near a white lime patch on a rock caused by the urine from coneys which used to run out onto the rock, which was visible from miles away with binoculars. Ray Barber gives more detail:

> "The first sale of farms in the Trans Nzoia took place in Nairobi in 1913. The sale was fairly well attended considering the scanty European population at that time.

Most of the farms were sold for two rupees per acre and my father bought Farm No. 20 on the slopes of Mount Elgon. My brother Ivan bought the farm next to it No. 22. He was asked his age and when he replied that he was seventeen the farm was put up for sale again but not sold. Subsequently Miss Mary Bowker (our cousin) bought it and sold it to my father. Very soon after this sale, my father and Ivan railed a mule cart and two mules to Londiani. Taking a Kikuyu servant, Kagume by name, they went up-country to see the farms. They drove in the cart up through the Burnt Forest to Eldoret (on Farm 64). They slept the first night near the little Lake Narasha and got to 'Sixty-Four' in the dark of the second night, crossing a stony ford and stopping outside a small building with a thatched roof which called itself the Eldoret Hotel.

At this time Eldoret consisted of about six houses, the Plateau having been settled rather earlier than the Trans Nzoia. In Eldoret my father and Ivan hired a wagon and together with four others, ventured forth for the delectable country. Two walked ahead to look out for ant-bear holes and to cut down odd trees in order that the mule cart which was next in the procession could proceed. The wagon brought up the rear. There was no road or track so they headed for Mount Elgon crossing the Sergoit River where the little town of Turbo now stands.

They reached the Nzoia river the next day somewhere near the spot where the present Nzoia Bridge crosses it. Here they camped and searched up-stream and down for some miles trying to find a fordable spot. There was a small river running into the Nzoia west of the camp. Somewhere in this vicinity Ivan, wearing only his pith helmet and carrying a gun, waded across the river and found a hard, flat bottom. So they decided to cross at this spot. There was a high bank on the south side of the River, so the native servants were put to the task of digging it down. Having successfully negotiated the mule cart across, the wagon soon followed. It ran down the steep bank, nearly over-running the back oxen. On the Nzoia side it became firmly stuck in the mud and the draught pole broke. Everything had to be off-loaded and carried up the bank. They tied up the broken pole with a chain and the empty wagon was pulled laboriously to the top of the opposite bank where they camped while they cut and fitted a new pole. Crocodile tracks were seen in the mud and Ivan remembered how he had waded three feet deep through the river the previous day! The next day they travelled through corkscrew trees and reached what is now known as Lion's Fountain, where my brother Alban farmed until 1975 when he sold this land retaining only his house in which he and his wife Mary lived.

Peering through field glasses Ivan saw a metal beacon on a lava spur some miles away. "If you can see what number is on that beacon" my father said "we shall be able to find our position on the map." It was already late but Ivan rushed off taking Kagume with him as gun-bearer. Following a valley, he climbed past a huge rock with nearly vertical sides (now called the Castle Rock) through trees and long grass until he found the metal beacon. On it was the number 20 and a small furrow indicated the direction of the boundary. Ivan got back to camp after dark. My father was very pleased as the farm he had bought and for which they were now looking was number 20.

Next day they went down taking both the wagon and the mule cart and made camp under a Mukuyuni fig tree on Farm 20, just beyond the age-old Karamoja Track, used by the Arab slavers for centuries before any Europeans came. My father and A K Macdonald were the first landowners to locate their farms in the Trans Nzoia. Dad and Ivan stayed for several day while another of the party went to find his farm. When they had accomplished this, the whole party returned to Eldoret, my father and Ivan driving back to Londiani and then on to Nairobi by train.

About January 1914 my father returned to the Trans Nzoia farm to start development. This time he was accompanied by Mother, my brothers Ivan, Renshaw and Alban and Miss Mary Bowker. They also had with them a faithful native of South Africa named Jacob Maidi, two Indian carpenters and stone masons and several Kikuyu servants. They intended to start building a house at once.

My father followed much the same route as before when travelling from Londiani and, eventually, the heavily loaded wagon with its building materials, personal possessions and so on reached the Mukuyuni tree on the farm now called Caverndale. The very first house, built of stone, was ready in a few months, all but a few details. It was never lived in. About this time my mother became very seriously ill. She was taken back to Nairobi where, after many months she made an unexpected recovery. Mother was nearly spared the effort of making a recovery - an African carrying a loaded shotgun succeeded in firing a charge of buckshot so close to her that her skirt swished round her knees. While my brother Ivan and I were on active service my father struggled on with the Kyambu

> farm and it was not until the end of 1918 that we all returned to the Trans Nzoia. Here we found that coffee planted by contractors was two miles distant from the new house so we set to and built another house, pulling down the old one".

In 1917 his parents, Hal and Mary, took Alban back to South Africa to school at St Andrew's College where his brothers had been and where he remained till 1921. Ray Barber left school in 1914 when he was seventeen years old, too young to join the army yet and fearful that the war would end before he could do so at eighteen. So he went north to join his parents and Ivan on the farm, Ivanhoe, till he was able to join up in 1915. He wrote of the events at that time:

> "I left school at the end of the 1914 Christmas term, when I was aged 17½, too young to join the army. Many of my friends were on active service. Some had fallen in action in the early months of the 'Kaiser's War' and many more were to appear on the Roll of Honour before the tally was complete. I wanted to see my parents and brothers in our new home in British East Africa which, from all accounts, sounded a most exciting country. I travelled for five weeks after leaving school seeing friends and relations in various parts of South Africa and then booked passage to Lorenço Marques in January 1915.
>
> I went to the station to catch the night train and, looking for my reserved carriage, I was delighted to find my cousin, Archie Hope-Bailie, was to share it with me. He was returning to British East Africa to rejoin his regiment after home leave. At Lorenço Marques, having passed

through Portuguese Customs without hindrance, we embarked upon the small British-India ship SS Pundua, crewed by Lascars and carrying a dense crowd of Asians with deck passages, who also were bound for Mombasa. We arrived at Moçambique and its great castle-like fort built on a small island close to the mainland. Archie and I went ashore to see this remarkable place - remarkable because the stone used in its walls all came from Portugal as ballast in the sailing ships which traded up and down the East coast in the sixteenth and seventeenth centuries. Near the main entrance there was a prison and, behind the iron bars, we saw men and women both white and black locked up for their sins. They were plaiting baskets which they sold to visitors to earn the money to pay their way to freedom. Here Archie laughed in his irresponsible way, "I was in there once" he said. "We had a party and it got a little rough. Oh, my head when I woke up in the morning. A warder handed me a piece of paper with my fine written on it - 25,000 reis. Heavens, I thought, I shall be here for life, then a fellow passenger came along and I was free for about ten shillings."

At Zanzibar, just outside the town, we could see the masts of HMS Pegasus, sunk by the German cruiser Emden a few months before. Zanzibar was a most unusual city; only in the main street could a vehicle pass through and pedestrians had to step into a shop or up on to house steps to let this happen.

My great excitement was our landing at the island of Mombasa - my feet actually walking on the soil of this British Colony. Mombasa Old Town was a harbour only suitable for dhows and smaller vessels. The port for all modern ships was Kilindini, about a mile up the deep water channel forming the Southern approach to the Island. Here the Pundua anchored and we were rowed ashore in boats. Having been cleared through the Customs, Archie and I hired a rickshaw to take ourselves and our belongings to the railway station. A wood-burning engine dragged a mixed train of food wagons and passenger carriages into that delectable country I had waited for four years to see. Brimful of excitement and with eyes bugged out so as not to miss anything, I sat opposite Archie as the train puffed very slowly and laboriously up the rising ground through the palms and huge spreading mango trees, climbing all the time to the higher altitudes. Too soon it was dark, too dark to see anything. The whole sky was beautified by fireflies from the engine. Our carriage was roomy with four bunks, two above and two below and a wash basin. There was no communication between carriages. You had to wait until the train arrived at a station. Refreshments were not then available on the train and meals were served at certain stations along the line, where we stopped for sufficient time to eat the excellent meals, all done by Goanese men. There was a plethora of chillies, onions and peppery curries at these Dak bungalows as they were called, but they were spotlessly clean.

Farther on one looked to the left to see Africa's highest mountain and it looked like a huge Christmas pudding, snow-clad for the last 4000 feet. Its height was 19,321 feet and its name was Kilimanjaro, which means the cold mountain. It was a long way from the Railway line but still impressive. In the foreground were giraffe, elephant, kongoni and the brindled gnu. This was still, in

1915, a land of vast animal populations and these were nomadic, always searching for water and pastures new. As these became climatically deficient the game moved elsewhere in constant search. Most numerous were the zebra, great herds of which made the plains look as if they were a moving black and white board. Near Nairobi the line crosses the Kapiti and Athi Plains which were tick-infested but still rich in game, and where lion could be seen. Just outside Nairobi we came to Athi River and Stony Athi, so called because the river bed was strewn with large boulders. Those who tried to get through these with ox wagons found the task almost impossible. At last we arrived at Nairobi where we were met by my parents and brothers accompanied by pretty Mary Bowker, my mother's niece. The whole family was there on the platform. What a wonderful moment that was. My mother, whom I had missed so much all the three years of our separation

Nairobi in 1915 was a shanty-town. Wood and iron houses, streets of earth, everything about it made it totally unlike anything I had seen before. But to hell with Nairobi. We were coffee planters, countrymen and this was our very own adopted homeland. Excitement rose as we left the town and drove northwards through the Ruaraka Forest on a narrow track. Tall Mahogo trees and thick undergrowth restricted the vehicle - a spider drawn by two mules - and deep ruts were unavoidable in places. The Ruaraka stream was crossed by a narrow wooden bridge and then we soon got into more open, undulating farmland. In a mile or two we arrived home to 'Ivanhoe', the stone-built cottage with its detached wood and iron kitchen, rondavels and outhouses. Close behind the kitchen Dad's first planted coffee trees were already nearly six feet high and producing a crop. Beautiful green (or red when ripe) cherries the size of a small marble were already showing how quickly a profitable income could be derived from this undertaking.

From February until the November of that year I started my life as a coffee farmer. Then Ivan and I went on active service - but that is another chapter. By this time 'Ivanhoe' was a hive of activity. Apart from the coffee, the thousand acres was as yet untouched. It occupied two ridges cleft down the middle by Sarara stream which oozed through a papyrus soak about a hundred yards wide and crossed only by wading through water like tomato soup.

Around the house and down the slope to the marsh and later, beyond on the second ridge, we planted coffee. Sarara stream was dammed nearest its highest point and a water furrow brought a strong flow of clear water to a 'factory' where the coffee berries were pulped, fermented, washed and then put on to drying trays - soon to number some hundreds - on top of the ridge near the homestead. Ivan and I were kept very busy. We personally manipulated the coffee chains, marking out the new acreages for planting coffee trees which had to be spaced eight feet by eight feet. Pegs were put to mark where each hole had to be dug to receive a seedling. Saa, the headman, with his gang of Kikuyu workers, dug the holes about two feet in diameter and eighteen inches deep. These were filled in with surface soil leaving a small hole in the centre where the seedlings were planted on wet days by an experienced man. If rain fell again within a day or so of planting, there would be no need for hand watering. Gangs of Kikuyu women picked the ripe coffee, using four gallon paraffin tins as receptacles. A full tin was paid for at the rate of twenty-five cents. These women were extremely fast and earned a good deal of money this way. Wages were low in those days but they augmented their incomes in various ways.

Pangas, used for digging and cutting saplings and a multitude of odd jobs, disappeared in their hundreds. In one year the farm lost over two hundred. Many men came for work just to be able to steel a panga and then deserted on the same day. Most 'Kukes' were named either Njoroge or Kamau and it was always the absent Njoroge or Kamau who had so shamefully robbed the Bwana. "The scoundrel" they would say, "he must have come from Meru." Saa did not think so: "All same, Kikuyu, all bad." Saa's English was refreshing and his interpretation of modern inventions were equally so. He was quite sure that when a telegram was sent the message was dragged in some magic way along the wire to its destination. Though he never actually saw anyone doing this he was convinced that it could be done no other way. He was married to a local woman, also of Portuguese ancestry. She was a heavy drinker and poor Saa was as putty in her hands when the booze was on the table. It went to his head too!

Work on the farm was progressing well and it was encouraging to see the Estate, as we now called it, becoming productive. Hill, Wood, Sprenger and Macmillan were all Standard Bank clerks who had bought farms. All had to leave because of the war, to join the Army. At Ivanhoe we were merry and had tennis at weekends. Girls were a little scarce, but with Mary Bowker at Ivanhoe and Cathleen

Cronwright at Bell's just next door, both of our age group, we had fun and enjoyment for a brief time before most of us went to report for active service. Macmillan had a beautiful voice and, with Sprenger and Hill, our musical evenings were the better for help. Then these three went off to the 'front' and Macmillan was killed in his first action at Longido West. Both Hill and Wood were wounded and we did not see them again.

In November 1915 Ivan and I enlisted and served in the East African Transport Corps as we knew a certain amount of Swahili. I was away for nearly three years and saw most of German East Africa and a good chunk of Portuguese East Africa at the expense of His Majesty King George V. We all suffered much from malaria and were in and out of various field hospitals; we grew tough, brown and hardened but all had recurring malaria in our systems when we were finally discharged. I was released from the Army on 5th September 1918; my father's birthday was on the 7th and the war in East Africa was nearly over. It was strange getting back to a different Ivanhoe, now a productive concern bringing in dozens of tons of coffee every season. In fact my Father had two whole crops of coffee in his stores in 1918 with no available shipping to carry it away. He was over-worked, and my return was opportune."

Ray spent the whole of his war service, almost three years, moving supplies on pack donkeys to the British troops in German East Africa (later Tanganyika, later still Tanzania) and in Portuguese East Africa (Moçambique). Seldom in danger from enemy fire, he was fortunate to survive the diseases which afflicted them, most particularly the virulent form of malaria which was prevalent. He wrote this account of the Kilwa Campaign in German East Africa in 1916 – 1917.

"In September 1916 the first British Troops landed at Kilwa to oppose a strong German force that had moved in from higher and healthier country. The Kings African Rifles (KAR) were some of the first arrivals and soon a considerable force was built up, which included the 3rd infantry Brigade, the 1st Division and the 2nd Infantry Brigade. Then there were the Loyals, the 40th Pathans, some Baluchis and still more re-organised battalions of the King's African Rifles. Collectively, these troops amounted to a considerable army and it was our job to carry food and supplies for most of the long distances behind the lines, a task made more difficult by exceptionally wet weather, insect pests and disease.

It was a bright clear morning when our transport ship steamed into the pretty estuary at Kilwa Kisiwani, carrying our personnel, numerous animals and equipment. Mules for loading, pack and draught donkeys, pack saddles, carts etc. were soon off-loaded into the jungly mango forest. "Kal-yu-kal-kal" shouted the soaring fish eagles, flying between us and gathering clouds in the West. What a beautiful country it looked, but we were to learn otherwise.

The East African Transport Corps came into being about 1915 and carried supplies during Gen. Smuts' rapid attack on the German forces until the campaign shifted from the higher terrain into the swampy coastal belt. Here, heavy wagon transport was impossible and pack donkeys were used instead, with light Asiatic transport carts as substitutes for the wagons. Our personnel were Europeans from British East Africa, South Africans, both European and Bantu; our drivers were both Bantu and Somali from East Africa.

Kilwa Kavinji was the only town we saw after leaving the ship and there we were organised into convoys of pack animals and animal transport carts and we moved inland, often working backwards and forwards between two points for a monotonous period. But we were soon up against a major obstacle: belts of tsetse fly were prevalent throughout this hinterland and our splendid animals were soon bitten and doomed. Our mules were the first to die, but the donkeys were tougher and survived for several months as beasts of burden.

At the height of the rains I was with a convoy that arrived at the Mchemera River, usually a fordable stream but now a flowing torrent about forty yards wide, swiftly flowing, completely holding up the forward delivery of supplies. A swimmer had to be found to carry a cord to the opposite bank, a most dangerous and hazardous task as the dark waters were filled with hidden obstacles or floating snags. Some gallant Africans came forward and, one by one, swam from various places farther up-stream in the hope of reaching the opposite bank. The first man to dive in disappeared immediately in that boiling torrent. The second swimmer went still further up-stream but he, poor fellow, became entangled in the cord attached to him and was swept past our feet, just visible from where we stood. Still undaunted, a third man plunged in and succeeded. The cord he carried made it possible to drag a rope and finally a heavy cable to the further bank. In the meantime the Engineers had improvised a pontoon, using as floats about 100 empty 4 gallon cans all bound together to form the platform. A gang of workmen on either bank dragged the pontoon backwards and forwards. Foodstuffs were protected by tarpaulins in transit but much was damaged and went forward in a fermenting condition. We spent very long hours and weary days on this work. One pontoon broke loose and several people on board were drowned; one of our officers 2/Lt. Cooper luckily got ashore a long way down the river. One day about ten KAR soldiers and their Sergeant, each man carrying his ammunition, slung rifle and haversack, were being dragged across. In the middle of the river where the current was strongest the pontoon submerged: the men were up to their waists in water. The Sergeant coolly gave his orders, the men locked their elbows together and hung on to what ropes there were for dear life. Yells of dismay from either bank speeded their safe delivery to the farther shore. Our Sgt. Major Stein was decorated for his good work here but the swimmers who gave their lives and the one who succeeded in first established contact with the shore beyond - what was their reward? We were never told.

Most of us were quite new to the hazards of this swampy, unhealthy country. We took few precautions, drank muddy or contaminated water from streams or water-holes, put up with the mosquitoes and soon, one after another, we went down with malaria, dysentery or something else. My first attack of malaria came on while we were on convoy, in the heat of the day. Quite suddenly I found that I could no longer sit on my mule. I tethered him, put on my greatcoat and lay down in the grass by the side of the track. Somebody covered me with my blanket, the column moved on and I was all alone. Towards evening I woke up feeling better and rode forward, finding the convey camped for the night. Extra quinine and 'sweating it out' was how we dealt with malaria, avoiding field hospitals if possible, recovering as best we could

As second line transport we were seldom near enough to the enemy to get involved in action. Just occasionally we were ambushed, as happened to me later in the campaign. The enemy doubled back and surrounded one of our conveys in dense bush country late at night, inflicting heavy casualties. Near Mchemera we only experienced snipers. Sgt. Major Stein had crossed the river with me and we were near an Animal Transport Section in an open glade when shots from a nearby thicket clapped in our ears like a whiplash. Stein lamented: "Oh, Barbie, they are trying to kill us and I'm a married man!"

The KAR and many other troops fought in and around Kibata Mission about this time. The rains were at their worst. We were seldom dry by day or by night; it was very hot so this seemed of little consequence. But for our poor animals, blighted by the tsetse infection, it was horrible indeed. Pack donkeys, unable any longer to carry their heavy loads fell one after the other and had to be destroyed. Their packs and saddles would then be put on to another already loaded animal, often to bring these down in a short distance. In hollows where the muddy water lay deep in the paths, animals fell and were drowned in liquid mud or we fired into the writhing mass to end their misery. Nor at night were they at peace: lions carried some away. We carried a very inadequate supply of tents;

most of us improvised by pitching a small tarpaulin as a covering. When you had crawled into this low and very uncomfortable contraption, your mosquito net was difficult to adjust or you did without it.

Newspaper correspondents used to speak of Smuts' starving army but this was an exaggeration. In the Kilwa area all we could hope for and often did not get when due, was bully beef, biscuits, tea, sugar and soap. Sometimes we were able to purchase a few vegetables from the local inhabitants, or we shamelessly robbed them if they had fled the scene. Arrowroot was often available and so were sweet potatoes, a great luxury then. Fresh meat was rare but very occasionally we were able to shoot an antelope, most of the game having moved away.

Hospitals were to be found only in the larger camps; in the field we had first aid posts or clearing stations. As we approached the Muhero River in the Rufiji Delta some of us went to hospital with malaria; we were taken there by cart - a long hot journey. It was no fun lying in a tent in that heat. Light diet consisted chiefly of condensed milk and, of course, there was plenty of liquid quinine to speed one's recovery. While I was in hospital a South African soldier walked from his sick-bed into the bush and disappeared. Searchers failed to find him but with so many sick on their hands the incident was soon forgotten. Some years after the war I travelled in a ship going north with this man's parents on board. They were Afrikaners and in conversation they told me that they were disembarking at Kilwa to search for their son. They had never given up hope that he would some day be found.

One day our carts were taking some sick from one hospital to another. Among them was an emaciated miserable little man, Plikey by name, from South Africa. He lay alone on one of my wagons for half a day as we convoyed on. Later when we halted for the night I found he had died with his arms fully outstretched. Thus I buried him in a posture a saint would have chosen. Two drivers dug his shallow grave with a narrow trench for each arm and thus we left him in the wilderness. At Muhoro I buried one of our men in a grave that filled with water as we dug it. I was censured later for burying him in his greatcoat.

Wine, women and song - A soldier's life is supposedly more tolerable if he gets enough of each of these. Wine - there usually wasn't any and often the rum ration was in short supply; by mistake it was occasionally delivered over-proof. These were memorable occasions. Song - occasionally we had found some bright fellow who could cheer the heart with his singing, especially after the over-proof rum ration had drowned our sorrows. Women - there always seemed to be women, even in these swamps and jungles. One night I reached one of our camps late at night in the pouring rain. Tired and hungry, I was looking for food and somewhere to sleep when two of our NCOs offered a shake-down in their small bell tent. "We've got some girls, there won't be much room" they remarked casually. Neither of the two girls could have been more than fifteen years old. Before sunrise they had prudently scurried into the bush to their homes.

By the time we reached the Rufiji, only about three months after landing at Kilwa Kisiwani, our unfortunate animals were of little use. One by one our pack donkeys had been falling down under their loads and these we would have to destroy on the march. Then we reached Muhoro village on the river and orders came that all remaining donkeys were to be destroyed. Taking them by hundreds into the open glades away from the paths we shot them one by one through their skulls. It was a quick end to a useless existence. Looking back I often think of those green remote places littered with the bleaching bones of those simple creatures; of the occasions when mares produced foals on the march only to have them destroyed as soon as born - and memories worse than these.

Our pack saddles and equipment had now to be loaded on to a small ship tied up at Ndundu some miles away on the river. I was sent to do this, our drivers doing the porterage. A severe attack of malaria laid me low while on this duty and the ship's doctor pushed me into a bunk to sweat it out. I sent a pencilled message to my OC by the hand of one of the drivers telling him I was delayed but this note was never delivered. Back in camp I was posted as 'missing'. I remember little of what happened after that until I became aware that I was lying in the Kaiserhof Hospital in Dar-se-Salaam wearing a youthful beard (I was nineteen) and rather surprised at the turn of events. After about a month I was well enough to rejoin my unit at a base camp near the sea beach and here, in time, re-appeared several of my companions from the Kilwa area. They had a very bad time marching on foot from Muhoro all the way back to Kilwa Kavinji; most of them had been ill, some had died on that hard return journey through the mud. But still the war went on and we went with it; a long weary journey lay ahead. The gallant German Commander General von Lettow Vorbeck and the

> remnant of his forces evaded capture throughout the War, finally surrendering at Abercorn in 1918".

Ray spent 1918 in Portuguese East Africa and finished that campaign (as he had the Kilwa campaign) in hospital, seriously ill with recurring malaria. He wrote this account of events:

> "When General von Lettow Vorbook invaded Portuguese territory I was one of the lucky ones ordered to that sphere of operations. We were sent to Dar-es-Salaam, the main port in Tanganyika Territory. Here we were hustled aboard a very evil-smelling old troopship with pack saddles, donkeys and native drivers and were soon steaming out of the harbour. It was, however, not until the SS. Clan McPhee turned her nose south that we guessed our destination. Packed like sardines, with frequent shifts of attending to the donkeys between decks or in the stifling hold, we were glad when the short voyage ended and we steamed into the wonderful harbour of land-locked Pemba Bay where the little village of Port Amelia crowns a hill near the narrow entrance. We landed without incident on New Year's Day 1918. As everyone wanted to celebrate the advent of the new year and the new campaign, we had soon managed to purchase a goodly stock of wine and were a very drunken crowd that night and for several nights following. Then we moved to a new camp outside the town, thirteen miles away, pitched our tents on the sand no more than fifty yards from the waves and settled down. The cool breezes blew over the Indian ocean through our camp. We revelled in the inactivity, bathed, ate, drank and were sorry for several days.

Our enjoyment was short-lived however and we were next ordered to proceed to Mtugi, a camp beyond Pemba Bay. We marched round the Bay under KAR escort, arriving after sunset. Mtugi will remain in my memory for ever as a stinking swamp where man and beast died like flies and hungry hyenas devoured both with equal relish. I shared a tent on the route to the cemetery so saw more burial fatigues than we had bargained for and heard the howls of the hyenas exhuming corpses throughout most nights. I went forward with a convoy to a Portuguese post called Ankuabe camping at Namarala which had regular convoys run into it and sometimes as far as back to Mtugi. This was a dreary and monotonous business through tsetse fly infested country and we disliked being bitten. Boredom was relieved when, on one occasion, I was sent back to Port Amelia to buy a few necessities before we moved inland.

At Bendari landing stage on the Bay I boarded a small dhow which was beached in the mud. At midnight the tide lifted us and we sailed through the tranquil waters to the port. By 9 a.m. I was once more aboard with my purchases. After much tacking we were about half way across the Bay and some four miles from land when a heavy squall came sweeping down upon us. The dhow, heavily laden with a cargo of sugar, pitched and rolled in the most alarming manner and the three natives of its crew were completely unnerved, so much so that they decided to go about and run for port. This meant shifting the straining mainsail to the opposite tack. In the process the sail took complete command and was swept from their hands. Panic reigned as the heavy canvas, with about twenty feet of rope, blew into the air like a flag. Now completely out of control, our craft wallowed broadside in the trough of the waves. She was shipping water rapidly and her yelling crew were attempting again and again to lasso the flying mainsail. I had made up my mind that we should all be drowned when they managed to recover the sail. We raced back to port and, as we arrived, the storm subsided so we had the weary process of tacking back to Bendari again. We reached our destination at midnight.

Two marches beyond Ankuabe lay Medo Boma where our forces drove the Germans from their strong position. The attackers had exhausted most of their ammunition and were as low as five rounds per man. I had some small share in their replenishment, volunteering to take an ammunition convoy through to Medo and I was able to deliver these valuable loads safely before sunrise. We had marched through the night in almost completely silent movement, seeing many dead and wounded on the track.

There were man-eating lions in the area and, on our first night encamped at Medo, one of our men was dragged from the camp. His blood-curdling yells awoke everyone and the men threw fiery sticks into the air and yelled and shouted at the tops of their voices. The lion bolted in terror, leaving his prey. One night near this spot a lion walked into camp between a group of us sleeping on the ground. He then stood with both feet making heavy imprints in the soft ground at the foot of an Officer's camp bed. I have often heard that lions would not touch meat that is repulsive to them but they relished our donkeys. On one occasion when we were having breakfast, we heard a great stampede of the donkeys and terrified scuffles as a lion pounced upon one of them not forty yards from us. The lion is a noble animal who makes a decision in a split second without any dilly-dallying, unlike other creatures seen during our stay in the area. There was a large green chameleon who climbed a telephone pole and ventured forth upon the wire. When first seen he was about mid-way between two of the poles walking with slow deliberation towards Port Amelia a hundred miles away. Late that afternoon on our return journey he was still up there, dithering in the opposite direction.

Beyond Medo our progress was quicker and we followed the KAR through bamboo and elephant grass. We could hear gunfire all day and the thumps of a Stokes mortar. At 'Battle Camp' we came upon quite large trees which had been severed by machine gun fire and had fallen. Here the enemy had suffered heavy losses from shells. Later we marched into Karanji. The shells from our guns were bursting on the enemy positions as darkness fell. The day after we reached Karanji we heard rifle fire to the rear of the camp and at about 11 am the first motor convoy arrived. They had been ambushed a few miles from our camp and had casualties. They had stopped to return the enemy fire, dispersing them. Our animals had to give way to these motorised units and often our donkeys became entangled in dense bush, their loads dragged off and the pack saddles swinging under their bellies. We were coming down a corrugated road beyond Karanji when we had to leave the road to allow some lorries to pass. One of them exploded a mine on the path, thus saving us from walking on to it.

The women of this area were unusual. In the past, to escape Portuguese concubinage, they had found a hideous custom expedient and its usage had survived the necessity for it. They perforated the upper lip and inserted wooden discs of ever-increasing circumference until they had discs of up to seven inches in diameter lying on their chests. This had afforded them some immunity also from the slave traders and was in time adopted as a tribal custom. These women were willing to barter goods with the army and for such commodities as American cloth (known as americani) they would exchange arrowroot, sweet potatoes and grain.

The Germans had a hospital at Nanungu and this was captured by the KAR. Our unit was sent there with a load of sweet potatoes. The Carrier Corps followed behind us with more valuable supplies. About eight miles short of our destination we walked straight into an ambush. Rapid machine gun and rifle fire was opened in the centre of the convoy and there was a general stampede. I had not thought it possible for a somnambulant donkey to be metamorphosed into a Derby racehorse, yet this transformation took place. Our Kavirondo drivers too made haste to escape, yelling and falling over one another in their panic. I jumped off my mule - which immediately scampered away - and started firing from the cover of a tree. At once the enemy fire was directed on to me and I was glad when four KAR soldiers came up and fired volleys at the enemy, who then blew 'Cease Fire' on a bugle and moved off.

It was about this time that the War shifted to the Moçambique area. The Germans had crossed the Lurio River and were moving southwards. There were stretches along this route where water was very scarce and, one day, we halted at a stream where the stagnant water was a bright green colour. When boiled this was palatable.

Soon after this I developed a severe attack of malaria. It was not possible to rest owing to protracted marching every day. The Lurio River was wide and fast-flowing. The engineers had made a pontoon bridge across which our donkeys were taken twenty at a time. Several fell from the bridge and were swept away by the currents but to our surprise all got ashore in the end. We had to fire several rounds to scare away interested crocodiles. After we had made camp at the Lurio I applied to be put into hospital to try to shake off my malaria. I had hoped to be evacuated to the Moçambique area but, to my disgust, I was-put aboard some lorries returning to Port Amelia. Tents had been erected for patients, of whom there were a great number, many dying and many sick awaiting evacuation. It was surprising how many strong men who had survived the entire campaign to date died of disease during the last two months of the war. I was sent to Dar-es-Salaam in a hospital ship and spent a few weeks in a fever ward. Then I was discharged, just in time to celebrate my twenty-first birthday. My brother Ivan was at the time stationed with a POW Camp nearby and he came over and we had a grand celebration".

Ray was released from the army on 5 September 1918 about five weeks before the end of the war and returned to his parents farm Ivanhoe. His father had completed the arrangements for the sale of Ivanhoe at Kyambu so that he could concentrate on developing his up-country farms, Caverndale in the Trans Nzoia district and Merrowdown at Soy. A wealthy elderly man called Randall bought Ivanhoe for £18,000. Soon afterwards the Government stabilised the East African rupee at two shillings and in the new 'florins' Randall found he had to pay a total of £23,000 for the estate! Ray recorded the return to the up-country farms by ox wagon:

> "Towards the end of 1918, a wagon was loaded with necessities and then put on the train. It was to be accompanied by several trustworthy Kikuyu servants and sixteen trek oxen and harrows. Dad, Mother and I left for Londiani Station. This was the last stopping place on the line and further journeys had to be made by ox wagon or mule cart on a route opened up by the Plateau farmers a few years before. Our journey from Londiani to Mount Elgon is very bright in my memory because it was the first long journey I had done in a wagon with my parents into almost uninhabited country. It took about three days to get through the forests and hills, keeping to wheel tracks made by the carts and wagons of the earlier settlers to the Plateau. Weaving our way along, we climbed many steep hills. In some places we had to make our way between tall trees and in others along paths which were almost obscured by heavy bush. The higher we climbed the more wonderful were the various views across those vast tracts of country that had never known any form of civilisation and had never been inhabited by any but primitive nomads and the wild animals of thicket and grassland. Of the latter we saw, one early dawn, a male and female bushbuck step out of the dense undergrowth on to the open hillside. Mother could never be caught napping when on safari. She would get up almost in the dark hoping to see the night folk who hide by day, she was rewarded now by these lovely creatures. Mother's

early rising had its material comforts also: while the rest of us were still yawning and stretching there she would be, bringing a brimful beaker of hot coffee to the sluggard menfolk. What a cheerful and valued companion she was on these long expeditions. She had seen many remote parts of the continent of Africa since marrying my adventurous father and she was eager to see and to help to tame the Elgon farms at the end of this journey - no easy task.

Over the summit of the high ridge we eventually came to semi-open country called, at that time, the Burnt Forest. Here, years before, a great forest fire had destroyed a large cedar belt. Thousands of charred tree skeletons and huge blackened stumps could be seen for as far as the eye could discern. Almost equally surprising was a sudden end to the mountain and forest areas through which we had struggled. Ahead lay a vast, totally treeless plain: nothing grew on it except long, waving yellow grass. Here were great herds of game: kongoni, topi, zebra by the thousand. Less numerous were the smaller animals such as Thompson's gazelle, oribi and Grant's gazelle, to mention the more familiar creatures of the region.

A first view of the plateau would be dull indeed were it not that, from this high ridge, one sees in the far distance the azure silhouette of massive Mount Elgon - the 'delectable mountain' of our dreams, where most of us were to make our home for many years. We crossed the plateau, paid a brief visit to its administrative centre - then known as Sixty-Four - consisting of six wood and iron buildings, which later became known as Eldoret. We then headed north through the long grass west of Eldoret."

Ray's system was ravaged by malaria as a consequence of his war service so he went to South Africa for a prolonged course of treatment to eradicate the malarial parasite from his liver and blood. After eighteen months he returned well and strong and wrote this account of his return to BEA:

> "After an absence of about eighteen months in South Africa, my return to East Africa in May 1920 was opportune. My father had decided to develop Merrowdown Farm, a place he had bought in the Uasin Gishu district about halfway between Kitale and Eldoret. I found Dad, Mother, Ivan and Renshaw all hard at work. They had built the usual wattle and daub house under thatch with a detached kitchen. Dad had a gang of Bugishu workers digging out ancient cedar stumps and we were soon ploughing the fields for flax growing. This commodity had been scarce since the war and its price was high at that time. Dad, always a hard worker, used to say: "Go for the main chance - that is the important thing in all farming operations. Flax is now our main chance for a better return." We were all enthusiastic and happy but this was short-lived, for trouble and sorrow came soon. I had been home only a fortnight when first Dad and then Mother went down with malaria. First Dad started shivering and we put him to bed to 'sweat it out'. He did not ask for a doctor. 'You boys must do what you can for me' he said. It was all he expected, and we were not alarmed. Malaria, we had lots of it and survived. Then Mother too remained shivering in bed and we spent most of our days looking after them both. When Dad and Mother became unconscious we were thoroughly frightened and the doctor and nurse were called. Dad died on 20th May 1920 whilst Mother was in coma with cerebral malaria. She recovered only to

> find her dearly beloved Hal gone forever. We had made a rough coffin out of heavy-sawn timber and had buried him in Eldoret eighteen miles away, taking him there on an ox cart".

Renshaw, the third of Hal and Mary Barber's sons, was nineteen years old at this time and helped build the first house on Merrowdown farm in 1920. He described one event that took place:

> "I went into the forest to get some straight poles and we found a bees' nest in a tree by the river. The two Nandi boys cut a suitable tree and we found that it was a new nest (with little honey) and just then a honey bird, attracted by us, came and started chattering so I told the boys that I would follow the bird. I went fifty yards and was about to vault over a fallen tree when a lion which was under it gave a terrific roar and threw me and my 8mm German Mauser in the air. The gun fell in the river and only the butt of the stock was in sight. I gave a great leap into the water and grabbed my gun, I whipped the bullet out and sucked the mud from the gun muzzle and by then the Nandi boys came rushing up to see if I was being eaten alive. They wanted me to follow the lion but I decided that I had had enough as I began to shake, so we all went back to the camp at the wagons"

The newly completed house on Merrowdown was occupied by Ivan, the eldest brother and his new bride Cecile Hoole whom he had married in South Africa. Raymond continued his account:

> After living for some years in his new house, doing

perhaps more sculpture than serious farming, Ivan became restless. The soil seemed very poor, the flax was a failure and maize produced about two bags to the acre which did not seem good enough. He decided to sell the western part of the farm and this was bought by Alan E Turnbull. Ivan went to London to study art and I was left with his Power of Attorney. Alan Turnbull sent for me to Eldoret to receive one of the payments and I had to wait several days whilst he sobered up sufficiently to sign the cheque. When the next payment fell due I guaranteed it and the bank paid Ivan - but they took the money from my account, Turnbull's being 'in the red'. The last visit I made to Merrowdown many years later, the place was a prosperous cattle ranch. I saw many changes. Gone was that neat little wattle and daub shack that once stood nearby, where my parents had lived and where my worthy old father had died. Memories came crowding back: Dad had been of a kind and cheerful nature, generous with his money for those in real need. Many were the loans he had made knowing that he could expect no repayment and his friendly hospitality was at times completely misunderstood. People would be handed his last bottle of whisky, out in the blue where replenishment was not easy and they would guzzle the lot. Dad would have to go without his sundowner and would remark: "Well, I didn't think they would do that!" But he never did learn.

Some time in 1918 Dad, Mother and I had walked from Caverndale along the Karamoja Track to look at Farm 7, which Dad and I had bought from the Macdonald estate. I had saved 800 Rupees from my Army pay which we put towards the purchase price, which was about R2.50 per acre. The Karamoja - Mumias Track is one of the oldest known routes in this part of the country. If all the miserable slaves brought down this route could shout with one voice, they could be heard in Europe. Now all was serene, tribes no longer sold their neighbours to heartless Arab slavers and colonialism had made it possible to move about in safety (safety from man, that is) through this wilderness where the lion, the buffalo and all the lesser creatures were still so numerous and, for the most part, harmless if you left them alone. We were well pleased with No. 7. It was very rich-looking mountain soil, and the bigger trees were mostly mimosa with flat tops. It was a farm of hills and valleys with dense ribbon growth along small streams that passed through it. These water courses were apt to dry up in some hot seasons, I was to find later. By the laws of Crown Colony British East Africa, all European-owned land had to be developed, which meant that land had to be occupied and crops had to be planted.

We all started to fulfil these conditions about 1920 on our various properties. We had brought with us from Kyambu a very reliable headman, Hamisi by name and this middle-aged man I put in charge on Farm 7. The language difficulty was being overcome gradually. Up-country tribes were acquiring a smattering of un-grammatical Kiswahili. However, it was not easy to get farm hands to understand what was wanted or to make a man, who was untrained and had never worked at such tasks in his life, undertake them and do them well. It was mostly by manual demonstration that work could be started and constant supervision had to be maintained all the time. In this way could a shack be built, trees stumped out with their roots to a depth of at least three feet in order that ploughs could be used; wells had to be dug, also latrine pits and all the hundred and one tasks had to be overseen with care. Often work had to be undone and started all over again.

I marked out a 24ft x 12ft shack, which was to be built with olive poles and wattle daubs. The roof was to be thatched thickly with the beautiful long grass that was plentiful everywhere. Twenty yards or more away, Hamisi was instructed to get a latrine pit dug where the soil was deep enough. At the back of the shack and ten yards from it, a kitchen hut of 8ft x 8ft was also put up. All this was easy for Hamisi, he was used to making houses of this nature. He was a man of about 45 years, already distinguished by a greying beard, very handsome and well in command of his wild labour forces with whom he dealt sternly and not always with a light hand. The men we had to employ were an unruly lot; they had never known discipline and were reluctant to obey any manager, black or white. Money? Some of them had never owned a rupee in their lives. It was customary in those days to have 'tickets'. These were cards marked out with thirty-one squares, one for each day of the month. On to these you entered the days on which the particular man had worked. The workman was then paid for the days he had worked during that month.

Wages varied but were low in those early days. R3 per month was gladly accepted and often reluctantly paid by the Bwana. In addition to this princely remuneration, each worker was given two pounds of maize meal (posho) per day, some salt and, occasionally, there was meat when the farmer was able to shoot an animal such as antelope for his own larder. The best was taken for the farmer and

> the rest shared between the labourers. Of course all tools and implements had to be taken over to Number 7. It was only designated as a farm because corner beacons had been put in by early Government surveyors. These were generally miles apart and, when you were lucky enough to locate all four of your angle-iron corner pegs, you could explore your tract of country and decide whether it was worth all the toil and sweat of the effort to make something of it. Many had one look and then sold out - if they could find a buyer - and disappeared, leaving the development of the Trans Nzoia to the real pioneers. I lived at Caverndale until my shack on farm 7 was ready. About once a week I would walk up and spend the night there to see what progress had been made".

Following his father's death, Ray started work in earnest: he owned two farms, one named Ballymere and the other (Survey Number 7) named Standard Hill after the Nottingham house of his great-grandfather Thomas Barber, the portrait painter. He sold number 7 and swapped Ballymere for farm number 6 which he worked until he retired. This farm was called Dunbryonne, to which he brought his bride and on which he reared his family, myself and my sister Hazel. He wrote of these early events in his account 'Astride the Equator':

> "Farm No 6, which adjoined No 7 (called by us Standard Hill) became my property by exchange. In dividing up the farms, it was seen that the land we had called Ballymere was too far away to be conveniently worked by me. In consultation with my mother and brothers, I took No. 6 and we decided to sell Ballymere when an opportunity offered.

I became engaged to Peggy Nisbet towards the end of 1922. This added a tremendous impetus to my easy-going methods of farming and progress. We all spent a lot of time visiting neighbours and eating of their venison instead of our own. Perhaps in their larder would be hanging a young oribi or a tasty antelope, whereas in mine there was nothing better than a shoulder of kongoni. Wherever we lived, Mother fed us very well. She always grew vegetables, usually under irrigation. At Lion's Fountain we were a very happy family and it was a sad day for me when I packed a wagon load of gear, clothes and essentials, and left home for good to work my new farm at No. 6.

My two farms, Numbers 6 and 7, now formed an area of land nearly rectangular in shape and roughly three miles long by three miles wide, making a total of 6022 acres. What an interesting terrain it was, beautifully situated on the lower slopes of Mount Elgon. I sold farm No 7 on fairly easy terms and this gave me sufficient money to start developing No 6, to build an inexpensive house and to get married. Dunbryonne, as I named it, was one of the most interesting tracts of country in the whole of the Trans Nzoia. Saboti, or the Round Hill, formed its south-east corner with the farm beacon on the summit. It is a hard climb to get to the top, but you get there and your reward is a wonderful long view. The Karamoja Track skirted below the escarpment, or the higher part of the farm as you walked northwards. A sparse growth of thorn trees (mimosa) covered all those slopes; in places the soil was very shallow and water trickled down the solid lava under tufts of grass. But the valleys! Ah, that was where the rich soil had accumulated since before Adam was a little boy. I soon found that the arable land on the farm consisted of about eight fields. Rivers and ridges had to be crossed to got to each ploughable area. In looking for the arable land and generally exploring, I found big lava caves tucked away in dense forest-filled valleys. Wonderful places these caves were, dark and gloomy and haunted. A stream of water gushed from the mouth of one of them; another had five entrances, numerous murky tunnels and these were hundreds of yards long. Bats! They were in millions and nettles five feet high stung and kept you at bay at every entrance. More wonderful still were the fossils: elephant tusks were found in several places, together with other recognisable bones and shells.

I decided to build my permanent home on the last ridge but one, overlooking the fast-flowing Kaubeyon River. This was a splendid permanent stream rising almost at the summit of Mount Elgon. It was a bad house site from the point of view of a garden, for the soil was shallow where we needed deep, rich soil for lawns and flower beds.

My neighbours the Macdonalds had built their house at Saboti. Alexander Macdonald was not a farmer, he was a big game hunter and an adventurer: a man with a roving spirit that had taken him to Paraguay, Abyssinia and other out of the way places. He had allowed a few Kitosh families to built huts on the slopes below Saboti and these wild people did odd jobs or went hunting with him. Now I needed labourers, so I sent for these squatters. About a dozen men came along, dressed for the most part in skins slung over one shoulder. These kept the sun off the back and the rest did not matter. Foremost among them strutted Marauni, self-assertive, self-appointed headman, who coolly informed me that he was a 'neopara', always had been and would continue as such and this was his gang. Marauni had his heart's desire, headman don't work - they watch others do so. The others don't work either if they can get out of it. It was a long uphill task trying to get work out of men who had always made his women do the hard work while he strutted about telling them how to do it. They, the females of the species, were less deadly than the males and a great stand-by too. They were strong and capable at harvest time, the women and girls were invaluable at coffee and maize picking times.

So, on this last ridge but one, I first erected a grass rondavel to live in and cleared the immediate area of scrub and other obstructions. A makeshift smaller one served as a kitchen, where a makeshift cook-boy functioned to the best of his ability. We could make bread fairly well if the yeast worked and a hole was dug in an anthill to serve as an oven. We used to keep a stock-pot permanently in the kitchen for convenience, into which meat and vegetables were thrown .to make a stew. A cast iron pot with three legs was a most convenient utensil and you were a poor fish indeed if you hadn't one. A cook could hardly go wrong with a leg of oribi, potatoes and onions simmering in this pot for his master's dinner. Breakfast was also a simple matter: mealie-meal porridge, eggs, bread and butter or ghee and a mug of coffee or tea. When short of sugar, as often happened, we sweetened things with honey. The Wanderobo from the forests and caves would appear every now and then with a mass of honeycombs squeezed into a large mutungi and we paid a very small price for this sticky mess. Then we heated and strained it to get the clearer honey we liked. What could be nicer than a large soup plate of posho and milk with two tablespoonfuls of honey? All this and heaven too! Then the eggs and coffee and you were set up for a hard day's work or play, as the mood dictated.

'Batching' in wild Trans Nzoia was a carefree existence. When you had spent six days alone on your farm, you felt you had earned a weekend somewhere else. I generally spent my weekends at Lion's Fountain. Before I possessed a push-bicycle, this entailed walking for nine miles down the Karamoja Track and it seemed twice as far in wet weather, when all the smaller gullies were running brooks and the two rivers were thigh-deep and slippery with mud under the water. Elgon Masai grazed their large herds of cattle on these lower slopes of the mountain, which are now farms. Animals driven up or down the track kept it open. There were a dozen tracks you could follow between any of the farms and particularly between mine and Lion's Fountain. I often walked down by moonlight carrying my .303 rifle in case I met a lion, a leopard or a buffalo. Lesser animals did not matter. Surprisingly, one seldom encountered anything.

One of the first acts in almost uninhabited country is to hunt up your neighbours. I was lucky: two miles to the north lived two families, the Kemps and the Oliviers. I made contact with them almost at once. There was no road and no bridge over the rushing Kaubeyon River, which cleaved the north end of my farm but I found where the natives crossed this river by fallen trees, which made a natural bridge. The Kaubeyon is a lovely, permanent mountain torrent and this was the asset which made me sell the upper part of the farm and move down to my final land on this lovely river. John Kemp was a Cornishman from St Ives. He fought in the Boor War and then settled in South Africa, where he married Bessie Robinson of Queenstown. Later he bought his farm on the Kassowai River and moved to the lower slopes of Mount Elgon and that was where I found them when I walked over from my grass hut, crossing the fallen tree bridge and wandering along the snake-like foot-path until I came upon their cottage of four rooms. This was on a slope running down to their river which, like the Kaubeyon, was fast-flowing. John was jovial, rather indolent and very friendly, as was his wife Bessie with her round, cheerful face. All were welcome in their tiny home. Bachelors were given a bed on the floor, on the dining room table and even on the veranda, when we used to congregate there for company and for tennis - I think theirs was the first tennis court in the district.

In an easy country to live in like BEA in those days, many were carefree. We had maize, luscious and plentiful in the growing season. We had posho during the dry months and a buck could be shot at any time. As families increased, the situation deteriorated. My following verse puts this in highlight to enlist your sympathy. I wrote this masterpiece during the depression when maize was fetching only two shillings and fifty cents per bag but it fits anywhere in the early days. It did not refer to anyone in particular.

My young wife and I were most terribly poor
We struggled to frighten the wolf from the door
He would prowl round the house, and the sound of his feet
Had scared all the tradesmen right out of our street
Cried Molly: "Oh, Jimmy we ain't got no bread
Here's a lawyers demand for our payment instead"

The butcher won't butcher the beef for the stew
The grocer won't groce and the brewer won't brew
Each day our lean finances shrink, till our dread
Was a horrible bogey - we wished we were dead
And the wolf - how we plotted to scare him away -
Was the bane of our lives and the care of each day
Then Molly she ups with a brainwave and said
"Let's sell all we have, only keeping the bed"
"Saved! SAVED!" I cried wildly, "My sweetheart divine!"
But I'm glad the suggestion was Molly's, not mine
For alas, the few florins we got for our things
In less than a year, they had all taken wings
The wolf (he had wandered) came back from his walk
And close on his heels Molly spotted the Stork!
And this, mean, sneaking bird that had kept out of view
While we guarded each entrance came in down the flue!

The Oliviers, who lived next door to the Kemps, were Boers. This was before the name Afrikaaner was generally used to define Afrikaans speaking South Africans. They were friendly, simple people of little education though, like the Voortrekkers, they were completely at home in the wilderness. Old man Olivier was a tall, strong man and having no money, he contracted to plant coffee for John Kemp in exchange for that part of Kemp's farm on the east side of the Kassowai River. Here, on this little farm, Olivier and his wife and family settled. The rank tobacco that old man J J Olivier grew, cured and sold in cloth bags to all of us who smoked pipes, was a greenish, dreadful weed which he named "Olivier's Celebrated Golden Leaf Tobacco". It must have had some excellent qualities as most of those who smoked it outlived the age and the BEA we know.

Big thunderstorms often meant running madly in from the work on the farm to take shelter. I was coming up past Lion's Fountain when a raging storm overtook me and I was soaked to the skin. I changed direction and walked over to the Newdigate farm, glad to have escaped a huge flash behind me. I had no sooner reached Newdigate's when an African came running behind me to say the house had been burned down and two men killed. Hurrying back, expecting to find all my possessions burned, I met Abdullah, my cook and the hero of the occasion. He had not only managed to drag the two unfortunates from under the burning veranda but had rescued my clothes and all my bedding. Not a vestige of the house remained. Of the two men killed, one was a total stranger and was unmarked by the lightning; the other was Mavachi, a regular farm hand living on the farm and a married man. The flash had burned a strip of skin like a ribbon from his neck to his hip. Mavachi was duly buried. His wife then carried his spear wherever she went.

My rondavel had served its purpose whilst I built the brick and thatch house to accommodate Peggy and me when we were married. Bricks were made nearby and the stone for the foundations was quarried down the slope some four hundred yards away. Early in 1923 the house was finished, all but the dining/sitting room floor. I had run out of tongued and grooved flooring boards but more were on order from Sunde's mill. What a job it was to get to this mill - up into the forest some six miles through dreadful earth tracks behind Kemp's farm, a steep climb all the way. We even succeeded in breaking a steel wagon axle getting there on one occasion.

My next task was to build a kitchen, pantry, bathroom in wattle and daub. This was to be a small structure directly behind the main house and some 25 yards away. Kitchens are often burned down accidentally and this one was no exception, building them separately lessened the chance of the entire dwelling going up in flames. I remember the tremendous fun we had when it caught fire for the first time. The roof was thatched and the tin chimney which passed through this became so hot that the grass round it ignited. A gang of workers nearby, both men and women, dashed to the rescue and, finding water near at hand in a 40 gallon drum, hurled it wildly towards the flaming roof. Most of the water fell short of the flames and everyone was shouting so loudly that no orders could be heard above the din. I rushed out from breakfast put a ladder into position and organised a bucket gang. Soon the fire was out but about 24 square feet of the roof was useless and had to be re-thatched.

My house had four rooms - two bedrooms, a dining/sitting room and a store/pantry. It was L-shaped and the nook was covered to form a small veranda. The walls were only seven foot high and there was no ceiling. You looked up into the thatch, and you could climb over the walls anywhere to get into the next room. By this you can see how we played into the hands of thieves and, in time, we found that they had more hands than most people and climbing came naturally to them.

My fiancee, accompanied by her mother, Mrs Emily Caroline Fleming Nisbet, arrived in the 'Gloucester Castle' at Kilindini on 19th June 1923. I went to meet them and would have been far more terrified of this encounter had I known that half the ship's passengers were agog to see the wild man from the equatorial interior - he who had the remarkable good fortune to espouse such a gem! However, this encounter I survived and I have never ceased to count my many blessings.

Mother, Mrs Nisbet and Peggy came up in the wagonette to spend the weekend. It rained hard and water seeped in through the foundations and lodged under the floor - a bad beginning for a new house! I nailed gunnybags over the open windows and we made up beds for the ladies as best we could. Peggy and I decided on the 25th July 1923 for our wedding day. This meant getting all concerned in to Kitale for the ceremony so my brother Renshaw went there in a neighbour's car to fetch our family's new Model T Ford car. This was a pedal model, most popular at that time and suitable for the bad wagon tracks we called roads.

Mrs. Nisbet said afterwards that if she had known what conditions were like in East Africa she would never have agreed to her daughter's marriage. Peggy, however, was a girl of spirit and determination, for her the future held no fears. A hard, rough life lay ahead and it was many years before prosperity came our way. It had to be a civil wedding as there was no registered parish in the district then but we had arranged with the Reverend O H Knight, an itinerant Church of England padré, to marry us properly immediately after the civil ceremony, at which we said a few words before the District Commissioner Mr la Fontaine, and signed our names before witnesses.

Peg and I went home to No 6 and to our unfinished house

> and to face married life in the hard and uncomfortable way prevailing then. Jim Matthews had persuaded his cook to come and work for us. This man hardly knew a thing but he filled a gap in the kitchen for a while. Peg, equally inexperienced, tried to improve on the culinary shortcomings. At weekends we used to escape to Kemps, where Bessie would feed all comers, mostly lean and hungry bachelors from nearby farms. When the rainy season burst upon us soon after we had moved into our new home we found the site, chosen during the dry months, completely unsatisfactory. The rains averaged some forty inches a year. Below the foundations lay a lava bed which was about three feet below the surface. The surrounding soil had become saturated, and I had to dig a kind of moat close to the walls. Willy-nilly we had to live there for a few years before we could demolish this house and build on a better site nearby".

Alban Barberton's account of these early days contains many vignettes:

> "The first car that we had was a Model T Ford in 1921, which we bought in Kitale and which we all learned to drive by getting in and trying. We used to get our supplies in 1921 in Eldoret and Soy, which were quite well developed then. When we first came, in 1912, the bank in Eldoret consisted of a large grass hut with a safe in it. The coins then were florins and cents. There was the Nandi Trading Company, which was an iron building on the other side of the street and they sold blankets and salt, hand tools and nails and all sorts of things. It was a real outpost trading company. Everything came by ox wagon from Londiani. We were quite lucky here in

the early days because my father brought a light spring wagon, about half the size of an ordinary standard wagon and we used to send this through to Eldoret and later to Soy to the shop, with a driver and a note. We used to get coffee and sugar and wholemeal flour and that was about all one wanted. I remember the soldier settlers coming after the war: a lot of them were around me here and a lot of them left.

People came into the Trans Nzoia by ox wagon, like we did after the 1914 land sales. It was a condition that you had to put £400 into it within two years, so within two or three months people who had bought farms were there. Some people had quite a job finding their farms; you knew roughly where it was on the map but you had to find the beacons and the beacons were hidden in long grass. Some people mistakenly built their first houses on somebody else's property. There was no money made here for many years. We came in with capital: my father sold his Kyambu farm and we used that capital to develop these three farms. Eventually, there came a day when the capital was finished and we were not making any money at all, so we were really hard up in the early days. We lived on posho and on shooting game and that was about all but we had a happy life - life was an adventure. The coffee that we planted was the only thing that brought a little money in; practically every farm put in a little patch of coffee. Then, later on when the railway came, the Trans Nzoia became the maize growing country it is today. Much too much maize was grown in the country for local use so it was exported and you could shift a bag of maize from here to Mombasa for one shilling. In those days people got about six shillings a bag, so one shilling of that went on transport by rail and you had to pay somebody about a shilling to get it into Kitale, so you got four shillings a bag for your maize. We were young and life was great fun and, whatever you were doing, there was great enthusiasm for it. We were all a great family and people used to meet at weekends. We even had dances here, in the early days, with a gramophone with the old acoustic recordings. They used to put a tarpaulin down and dance on it.

The slump in 1929 and the years after came slowly here because, being an outpost of civilisation, we weren't affected by the sudden fall of stock markets. The price of maize went down and down until, in 1931, it went down to three shillings and fifty cents a bag. I don't think any food has been as cheap as that. Imagine 200 lb. of very good food for three shillings and fifty cents - it must be a world record. Some of the European farmers had no money at all during the slump. I know a settler here who sold a serval cat skin for six shillings and he walked nearly thirty miles to try and collect this debt. You can imagine how much money he had if he walked thirty miles to try and collect six shillings. We had no money here, at all. Fortunately we had caves containing bat guano. These caves were discovered by an explorer called Thompson, who was gored by a rhino, just up here. We dug bat guano out of these caves and sold it to the coffee farmers round here for what I thought was a tremendous price, which was sixty shillings a ton. Some of the coffee farmers had a little money and they used this guano to fertilise their coffee trees.

One of the things I remember is that we used to buy a

Japanese coloured shirt blue or yellow, white or cream, for two shillings. Another thing I remember is that you could buy a seven pound packet of nails for two shillings. Another extraordinary thing is that the Japanese brought a bicycle into this country, complete with chain guard, which sold for thirty shillings: imagine a whole bicycle, for thirty bob and what's more they lasted. About eight years ago an African brought me a bicycle for repair and said 'my son is using this bicycle and I bought it in 1935 for thirty bob'. So there it was, thirty or thirty five years afterwards and the bicycle was still going.

The Asian has made a success as a business man because he lives in his shop and is there all day long. In the early days, the Asian spread right across Kenya. Wherever there was a little village, in no time there would be a duka. They did a tremendous amount of good because, if you were stuck on the road, you could walk to the nearest village and you could find tins of biscuits and tea. And if you went to an Asian duka at least a hundred miles from Kisumu and asked for whisky (I never did this myself but I heard of it happening) the Asian would say 'Oh no, no, I haven't a licence' and then, as you went out of the shop he would say 'Ah, but I have a bottle of my own. I am sorry, I can't give it to you, but you can have it for (whatever the local price is) twenty-five shillings'. That was their business acumen, to have everything that anybody wants and if he hasn't got it, he runs to the shop next door. The Asian never misses a sale.

When I was a schoolboy I was made to learn the violin, which I hated like poison: then when I left school, I began to like it and started to learn it seriously and I became a player by ear; most things that I hear I can play simply by ear and it is a hobby of mine. If you play the violin, people are always giving you violins and I have five of them hanging on the wall. One came from Woolworths and cost about twelve shillings; one belonged to an old Frenchman, it was broken and I made the top table that is on it today; one is an Italian violin that I picked up in Ethiopia - I was carrying the hygiene section of troops and when we were at their barracks in Adis Ababa one of the sergeants said to me 'Oh, there is a violin down in our mess, would you like to have it', and he brought it along to me. It was on top of a cupboard and I tied it onto the roof of my truck and it came home with me, one of the booties of war. Another violin is one that I made myself during the war in Ceylon and Burma. I took a violin with me wherever I went in the army through Ceylon, Burma and Ethiopia. Spare parts for aeroplanes came packed in big cases made from Canadian maple and I used this to make the violin. In my workshop bench there was one piece of wood, 8 inches by 1 inch by about 2 feet, which was deal and from this Canadian maple and this piece of deal I made a violin. I worked on it very carefully, mostly at night, when I had some off duty. One time I lost it; I had a small attaché case and all the parts, as I completed them, went into this case. After about a fortnight they were found miles away and somebody happened to know that they were mine so I got them back; otherwise, it wouldn't have been here today".

Chapter 4

1925 - A Kenya childhood

I was born in Kitale on the slopes of Mount Elgon in Kenya, during an eclipse of the moon in 1925. Kenya was a British Colony at the time and I felt it to be a privilege to be a member of the British Empire. I had a sense of great pride about this for, when I studied the atlas so much of it was coloured pink and I was part of a multitude of people and countries with King George V at our head. Although my forbears had left England for the Cape of Good Hope in 1820, I felt and called myself English and referred to England as 'home'. Surprise, surprise for me, therefore, forty years later when, after changes in the British Nationality Act, I encountered difficulties in establishing my nationality and right of abode in England, the land which I loved and to which I had given unquestioned loyalty and allegiance in my mind since I could first remember. I owe it to the then Member of Parliament for Wellingborough, Peter Fry (now Sir Peter) and later (after further legislation altered the Nationality Act once again) to Roger Freeman, MP for Kettering (now Lord Freeman) for establishing without remaining doubt my right to citizenship of the UK and also that of my children.

My father was a keen and knowledgeable amateur astronomer and told me many times about the eclipse of the moon at the time of my birth which he thought to be a good omen. Maybe it was, for my life has been filled with good fortune and interest. My babyhood nickname was 'Clipsie' but fortunately this fell into disuse before I went to school. He recorded my birth in his diary: on 8th February 1925 late in the evening he wrote "Eclipse of the moon nearly total" and, on 9th February, "Our dear son Gareth deBohun Mitford-Barberton was born about 5 minutes past midnight. He weighed 7lb 15oz." In the back of his diary for 1924 there was a list of boys and girls names and I escaped being named Eustace, Mervyn, Ralph, Bryan, Desmond and Terence. Had I been a girl the selection was no better and had fortunately been revised by the time my sister was born.

My maternal grandmother, Emily Nisbet, wrote from South Africa with advice for her daughter:

> 'At four and a half months you will quicken, and don't give way to fainting. Think of everything that is beautiful, be in your garden, be quiet, happy and peaceful and do not listen to unpleasant talk, for all this has a direct influence on an unborn child'.

She could dance quietly - but not the Lancers; tennis was proscribed and she wasn't to lift her arms to hang anything at a height. To prepare her nipples she was to make a mixture with equal parts of castor oil and eau de cologne (or brandy) to be applied morning and evening. My paternal grandmother Mary Layard Barberton sent a pram, very second hand and with it a letter to my father:

> 'I send the pram up. The tiny cushions want a lot more

> drying so stand up on edge so they can get dry all round on your veranda, and pram wants all mending and straps ordering, and repainting, and generally everything. I washed it so it is as clean as can be, only looks derelict'.

Late in her life my mother told me how a Masai tribesman who worked on the farm had made a cash offer for me when I was a few months old.

I was brought up with a sense of pride in the family. My father was a farmer in Kenya and a genealogist who spent a lifetime researching our ancestors and family connections. He traced the family in the direct male line back to the 17th century to yeoman farmers from the High Peak of Derbyshire. Through collateral lines on his mother's side I was proud to know that the blood of Charlemagne flowed in my veins; also that of John of Gaunt, Duke of Lancaster and of many other figures in history with romantic names and titles: Joan the Fair Maid of Kent; Richard Strongbow Earl of Pembroke; Otto the Great, Emperor of Rome; Richard, Earl of Cambridge who was beheaded in 1415; the Mitfords of Mitford Castle; and my great-great-grandfather Thomas Barber had also brought distinction to the family as a portrait painter. Ever since I can remember there have been portraits by him hanging on the walls and six of them have come my way by inheritance. His paintings and drawings are lovingly cared for by his descendants and many others are held in the art gallery of Nottingham Castle. Thomas Barber was buried in Nottingham in 1843 and my uncle Ivan recorded the details on his gravestone on a visit in 1925. When I tried to find the grave in 1994 the stone had crumbled to dust but I was able to trace its position with the help of the Nottingham City Council and I erected a replacement stone to mark the spot. Even more recently my uncle Ivan had added yet more lustre to the family name with his great talent as a sculptor and his position as lecturer in Fine Art at Cape Town University. I have several of his bronzes which will become family heirlooms and many of his works adorn public buildings and areas in South Africa. This artistic talent has cascaded further down the generations.

I was born onto a Kenya highland farm when the European population was very sparse. Our nearest neighbours were two or three miles away and there were no local schools: from an early age children had to be sent away to the few boarding schools which served the needs of the farming community. I suppose now that I would be regarded as having a solitary childhood but I didn't know otherwise and I certainly did not feel deprived in any way.

In my early years I had a friend named Ken Bolton who lived on a nearby farm. We would meet often, particularly on the weekly visit to town. Friday was the farmers day when they would forgather in the Kitale hotel to compare crops, prices, stock and have a glass of Tusker beer and I recall the beery smell of the bar at the end of the veranda. Ken and I went to the only secondary school in the Colony, the Prince of Wales school in Nairobi. We were friends and rivals in everything. The back of his house had a half wall, perhaps three feet high, on which we would stand and see who could pee the furthest. Years later when I was reading medicine at Oxford I learned that he had been senselessly killed when someone ran into the back of his car.

One of my earliest memories was about the time my sister Hazel was born in 1928 when I was three years old. It was of a searing pain in my buttock which I later learned was due to an injection of quinine because I was seriously ill with malaria. Malaria was a common cause of death at that time and everybody knew somebody who had died of the condition. Drug prophylaxis against malaria had not been developed and people slept under mosquito nets to protect themselves from the bite of the anopheles mosquito which transmitted the disease. My next attack of malaria was when I was eight years old, when I was sent to a boys holiday camp at the coast near Mombasa while my parents and sister went on a visit to England by ship. My exclusion from the visit to England was to have been broken to me tactfully but my sister let the cat out of the bag prematurely and I felt left out of what was sure to have been a great adventure.

The holiday camp wasn't particular fun. I won a fight, with whom and for what reason I cannot recall. On Fridays we were lined up for a weekly purge of Epsom salts. The matron erected a folding wooden table in the shade under a fig tree on which she had a large enamel jug full of ready mixed Epsom salts, an enamel mug and a bucket of water in which she rinsed the mug between each boy's dose. It tasted foul but with the matron's eagle eye on us there was no getting out of it. When the time for departure came I was struck down by malaria and found myself lying in the bottom of a small boat, clearly delirious, with the sun burning into my eyes and when I reached hospital I once again felt the fire of pain in my buttock. A few days later, when I had recovered, they wanted to be rid of me and I was handed over to the care of my uncle Alban who happened to be in Mombasa. Alban and a friend of his named Warburton, both impecunious young bachelors, had been provided with free accommodation at the Manor Hotel in Mombasa in return for playing in the dance band every evening, Warburton on the piano and Alban on the violin. They had little idea of how to look after a young boy, gave me more money to spend than I had ever seen, didn't send me to bed when my mother would have done and took me to the cinema late at night. The film was 'The Woman from Mars' featuring an evil looking woman who had long black fingernails - it was a black and white film and I now realise that her nails must have been red. She featured in my nightmares for a while and flashed into my imagination for the first time when I gave myself an electric shock at the hotel where we were staying. I had never seen electric light before, studied the bulb bayonet fitting, removed it and touched the two brass prongs in the base.

At the end of the holiday I returned to Kitale by train with Alban and Warburton, the journey lasting two days and two nights. Each compartment served for sleeping as well, had a WC, a washbasin and fold away table. The squab of the seats hinged upwards and fixed horizontally to convert to the upper sleeping bunks. There were no corridors so, to visit the restaurant car, one was supposed to wait for the train to stop at a station and the same again at the end of the meal. But this would not do for two young bachelors - they clambered along the foot-board on the outside of the moving train holding onto the hand-rail, myself between them. This huge adventure was the first thing I told my mother when we were reunited, with resultant commotion.

My third attack of malaria was when I was about thirteen years old at the Prince of Wales School but it was not as bad as the others and I did not receive or need the dreaded injection on this occasion. Quinine tasted almost as bad as it felt by injection and as Nairobi was a much more malarial area than my home at Kitale we were now supposed to take a tablet a day as protection against the disease. The boys from each dormitory were lined up at dusk and given the daily tablet by the matron, Miss Lane, and I cultivated the art of seeming to toss it to the back of my throat while concealing it in my palm. I then walked to a flower bed, made a hole with my finger and dropped the tablet in and covered it. The consequence was inevitable and I departed to the 'san' for about 10 days where I had to take the dreaded quinine three times a day. I tried to spin out my recovery for I was secretly in love with Miss Lane but she caught me putting the thermometer into warm tea to try and make out that I still had a temperature.

I did not go to school till I was seven years of age but my mother had taught me to read by then. My first school was at Eldoret about 60 miles away, The *Loreto Convent for Roman Catholics & the Children of Gentlemen* as the painted sign on the roadside proclaimed. My mother took pains to make me understand that I was Church of England and that I was not to participate in the religious proceedings at the convent. I was a bit puzzled about being Church of England as, living on an isolated farm, church had not featured much in my life and I wasn't aware that we were church of anything. Mother Borgia was in charge and the nuns ran a strict regime. My first day I was given a reading primer and told to 'look at that' and was disbelieved when later I said that I had read it through. I was challenged to prove it and I did so aloud, without hesitation, including the small print which said 'Printed in London, New York and Toronto'. I couldn't understand why the nun thought I was being cheeky.

It was my first time away from home and they say that I was unhappy but, if I was, I didn't realise it. Certainly I was naughty but maybe it was only high spirits. I was told by a catholic girl that I would drop dead if I touched the sacred heart depicted on a particular religious card so I didn't chance it. There was no electric light so when I put ink in the holy water no one noticed when crossing themselves at dusk at the evening service. It became all too plain who was the culprit as I was the only one without ink stains. Also I was said to have disgraced myself and the school for chattering, laughing and larking about on a solemn and important occasion, with a band playing, flags flying and people in uniform and wearing medals marching about. They sang a hymn and then all fell silent for a while. I was sent for by Mother Borgia who told me off in no uncertain terms for having so little respect for the dead, my father having been a soldier as well. Only later did I learn the significance of the occasion which was the first Remembrance Day ceremony I had attended, this being only fourteen years after the end of the Great War. The last straw was when I was caught in the girls' dormitory at night tying a rope to the leg of the bed of my chief tormentor; my parents were asked to find another school for me. This was without rancour and I have happy memories of the place. A few years later, when I went back to Eldoret on a special outing to see a new coloured film called Snow White and the Seven Dwarfs, I encountered Mother Borgia who welcomed me warmly as an old member of the school.

The first letter I wrote has been preserved, dated 18th September 1931:

> "Dear Mammy and Daddy, Thanks very much for your nice letters. I am very happy at school there are four other boy boarders here. How is Valerie? (my sister, also called Hazel and Boo) When will I see her? I told Sister what to write and then I went over her writing. Love to all from Your fond child, Gareth. Please send me some stamps." And, added as a postscript by Mother Borgia: "Dear Mrs Barberton - Gareth is very well, thank God".

Mrs Ida le Poer Trench had been trained as a teacher before she married her husband Cornelius who had a farm perhaps fifteen miles from my father's. It was, therefore, fortunate that she started a school around the time that I left the convent and I continued my schooling there, receiving an excellent grounding which has stood me in good stead for the rest of my life. Mrs Trench taught her three children as well as myself (and later, Hazel) and four or five other farm children. There were no buses or any other form of public transport and the roads were awful so we all boarded. Being close to home parental visits were quite frequent and I was happy there for sure and didn't spend my time getting into trouble. Mrs Trench usually had one assistant though these tended to come and go. One in particular was a young Frenchwoman whom we called mademoiselle - I never knew her name - who taught me French without recourse to grammar lessons with the result that I learned the language naturally as my own and, in the fullness of time, I obtained a distinction (the only one I had) in my School Certificate examination. When it came to the time for me to move to secondary education at the Prince of Wales school in Nairobi I came fifth and Mrs Trench's son Jim came third out of seventy seven boys taking the entrance examination. That wasn't because we were clever, it was because we were well taught.

We also had plenty of extracurricular activities. Games of course and picnicking, fishing, gardening, even hunting, all activities befitting farm children in a country which was very underdeveloped at the time. Needing a new pair of tennis shoes I drew round my foot on a piece of paper and sent it to my mother who was in England at the time. Wishing to impress her I copied out a simple rhyme which appeared on a calendar and claimed to have written it myself. In her letter back she asked if I had really composed it myself and to my shame I insisted that it was all my own work. I was always asking for items to be sent to me which were at home - my fishing rod, dictionary, cricket bat, more stamps, ink and so forth. Once I needed my old belt because the new one had fallen down the 'long drop' toilet (not an infrequent occurrence) together with other treasures from my pockets such as marbles, birds eggs and my pocket knife. The 'long drop' toilet was in a mud and wattle thatched hut about fifty yards from the dwelling house, containing a hole about twenty feet deep with a wooden seat. There was a red flag on a stick which we would push into the thatch to indicate that somebody was within. Flies bred in profusion in the pit and we used to throw burning sheets of newspaper down to kill them off. Once a spider or suchlike ran across the underside of the seat and across my bottom which caused me great alarm.

We devised a game which we called 'French and English' on a bit of ground about the size of a tennis court with a centre line and another at each end. Opposing teams had about twenty maize cobs laid behind their lines and the object was to capture the opponents cobs without being captured one's self. If captured, the person was held prisoner behind the line with the maize cobs and no more cobs could be seized till the prisoner had been rescued. Maize was a major crop and cobs were in plentiful supply. At this time Mussolini had sent Italian troops to invade Abyssinia as it was then called and we renamed the game 'Abyssinians and Italians' and the boys made the girls play the part of the Italians.

Mr Trench, or Corney as we called him, had the occasional young man out from England as a farm pupil and these also came and went. One had a powerful rifle and I was sickened when I saw him shoot a monkey high up in a very tall tree. I had been accustomed to my father shooting game all my life, but only for meat for ourselves and the farm workers, there being no butcher's shop, but never for fun. I saw the monkey struck by the bullet, saw him fall and grasp a passing branch with one hand, hang on till his grip weakened and he crashed through the branches to the ground.

Around this time the value of farm produce fell through the floor and many farmers, already heavily mortgaged, went bankrupt. The price of a two hundred lbs. bag of maize fell to Shs. 3/50 (17p) which was less than the cost of the bag in which it had to be transported to be sold and that certainly would not pay the grocer or the school fees. My father took another job prospecting for gold for a consortium and employed a farm manager named Patsy Hendren Frost who was a friend and honorary uncle to me. My father received a monthly salary from the prospecting consortium which enabled him to avoid bankruptcy. He was one of the people who discovered the Lupa goldfield near Kakamega so his employer received good value for money. He worked a long way from home and we would only see him now and again when he managed a few days back at the farm. On one visit he brought me a gold nugget in a small glass bottle and I was the envy of the whole school. I was relieved of it with little delay. Gold prospecting was a very dusty job and I have a photograph of my father taking a bath in a wheelbarrow in the open air at that time.

Gold certainly got us through a very sticky period and I was proud that my grandfather and now my father had made a living for some time from mining gold. I learned when very young to recognise quartz stone, in which my grandfather had found gold and I kept my eyes open to the possibility that I might strike it lucky. There came a day when I saw something which I thought to be gold shining in a large lump of quartz and ran home with the news as fast as my legs could carry me, my heart bursting with excitement - but it was only mica. I became familiar at an early age with the price of gold and its daily fluctuations, which I used to follow on the wireless. The wireless ran off a wet battery and had a long aerial to the top of the house which was once struck by lightening, doing the wireless no good whatever. Thereafter we disconnected the aerial every night and whenever there was a thunderstorm. Nairobi broadcasting station was number 7LO - "This is 7LO Nairobi calling" said the news reader. We received the BBC on short wave from Daventry which was 2LO. Reception was best at dawn and I would hurry down from my bedroom in time for the 6 am news from England to listen to the price of gold. At the end of the news programme the national anthem was played and I would stand stiffly to attention, mindful of how I had disgraced myself at the Remembrance Day ceremony while at the Loreto Convent school.

My father built our house on the farm himself using bricks made from clay he found by the river. The roof timbers were from gum trees he grew on the farm, but he bought the floorboards from Sunde's saw mill higher up Mount Elgon. The roof was made of corrugated iron which made a characteristic noise when it rained and was particularly noisy when it hailed. There was a large L shaped veranda, the bedrooms were upstairs on the first floor and there was a central tower which rose to a third floor with battlements on the top. There was no electricity and lighting was by oil lamps. I used to carry a hurricane lamp upstairs to my bedroom, bending my elbow to stop it from knocking on every step and I longed to be tall enough to mount the stairs without hitching my arm up. Earth tremors were frequent because of our proximity to the Rift Valley but they seldom did much damage. After a larger tremor than usual a crack a couple of inches wide developed in one of the walls of the central tower of the house. My father filled it with cement and bound it together with heavy gauge fencing wire wrapped round a couple of the turrets. The house had a lightening conductor at the highest point which was often struck in the violent thunderstorms. The wood fire in the kitchen stove was always doused before we went to bed. Grass fires were a common event and the grass was kept short for a distance around the house – a year's crops had once been lost through fire.

This happened when a farmer friend came to visit and was taken to see the maize crop which had just been gathered into one large barn. He was admiring the quality of the dry maize cobs, took out a cigarette, lit it and threw the match to the ground and that was the end of that year's produce. The field where it happened was thereafter known by his name, "Lynn's Folly". The farm fields were given appropriate names: the Fig Tree field, the Forge field where there had been an ancient forge, the Peter Pan field where there was a hollow tree, the Dalla field (another of my nicknames) and so on. Disasters seldom come singly - the next year's crops were lost to locusts and avoiding bankruptcy was a continual struggle. The locust swarm could be seen as a dirty brown cloud moving slowly some miles off and how we prayed for them to settle on someone else's land. Driving the car through a locust swarm was a messy job and the windscreen (with a hand operated wiper) was soon so splattered with locust corpses as to be almost obscure and you could hear the crunching of their bodies beneath the tyres. At dusk they settled on the ground, the crops, the trees, and their very weight frequently broke off tree branches.

Everything possible was done to scare them away; fires were lit; empty kerosene tins, saucepans and plough shares were beaten to create a cacophony, mostly to no avail. The next day the scene was desolate; everything that had been green had been eaten, the crops were gone, many of the smaller tree branches hung broken, my mother's flower and vegetable gardens were destroyed. We and the farm workers wandered around disconsolately, hunger and poverty staring us in the face. And the locusts, having no further use for us had moved on.

Before I went to the Prince of Wales school I had never seen a cricket match but I had read about the game and used to play by myself on the veranda which was a reversed L shape, perfect for practising my bowling. My mother did bat once or twice for me but refused to do so after I hurt her with a bouncer; my sister was too small and my father was out working on the farm. I became familiar with county cricket results because the matches were published in full detail in the weekly edition of the East African Standard. Also I would hear the results on the wireless first thing in the morning when I was checking the price of gold. I supported Derbyshire (who else, in view of my ancestry) and kept up to date with the batting and bowling averages and with the county championship. In what awe and admiration did I hold Harold Larwood who seemed to have the measure of the Australians.

I grew out of the child's cricket bat I had been given and needed another one. I mentioned the matter with some diffidence for I knew money was tight. My father, never one to sit back for want of money or an idea, asked me why not make one. Later I found an entry in an old diary of his:

"Never buy what you can make or grow".

So he helped me select a small tree whose diameter was about the width of a bat and, under his instruction, I sawed through the trunk at about my eye level. Then I sawed down the trunk from top to bottom either side of the centre, two long cuts about an inch and a half apart, creating a plank between the cuts still attached to the trunk below. Then I cut horizontally from each side at the bottom of the vertical cuts and discarded the outer bits which fell away, still leaving the central plank attached. All this took several days, much sweat, some blisters and all manner of interruptions from my mother for meals, bath, bed, visitors and so forth. Then I made two more vertical cuts of appropriate length for the handle and two more horizontal cuts at the right point to make the shoulders of the blade. Then in triumph I cut it off at the bottom and went off to the farm workshop with my rudimentary bat, clamped it into the vice, spent another day shaping the blade and the handle with a spoke-shave and made it look authentic by binding the handle with insulating tape. I was too impatient to varnish it, got somebody to bowl to me (I had a real cricket ball by then), gave the ball an almighty swipe with a resultant shock wave which jarred my arms to my shoulder sockets and caused the blade to fracture from the handle.

Church did not figure largely in my life before I went to secondary school because there was nowhere nearby to attend. We occasionally attended the thatched Mount Elgon Church, some miles away, the vicar having several other churches to oversee. To begin with it was Pardré Knight who had christened me using one of mother's cut glass bowls on a visit to the farm. He was succeeded by someone whose sermons were never dull to a young boy but no one had warned me about his use of the rhetorical question. "Who is the Saviour of Mankind?" he boomed. Diffident at supplying the answer among so many grown ups I held my tongue and waited for one of them to respond but to my amazement none of them seemed to know the answer. "Who is the son of God, who is our Redeemer who died upon the cross for our salvation?" he continued and again none of the adults replied. My amazement at their ignorance could no longer be contained and I jumped to my feet and raised my hand as high as I could. Seeing me and entering into the spirit of the occasion he called out "There is a boy who knows the answer" and I cried out "Abraham, Sir". Another thing that surprised me was how little the grown-ups knew about hymn singing. I thought the letters at the beginning of the lines denoted who should be singing, *f* for females, *mf* for males and females, *p* for people and *cr* for crowd. When it said *f*, why were the men singing as well? *Cr* for crowd obviously included children and I did my part with gusto. I couldn't understand the subtle distinction between *p* and *cr* but what did that matter if the adults didn't even know the difference between *f* and *mf*. I never did work out the meaning of *dim*.

My sister Hazel and I were both taught to shoot with a .22 rifle from quite an early age and she became, and remained, a better shot than I. And of course we were taught how to handle a gun safely, to keep the barrel pointing to the ground at all times when carrying it and never to point it in the direction of anyone even if we knew it to be unloaded. There came a point at which I was a good enough shot and could be relied upon to handle the gun with safety so I was allowed, on my own discretion, to take the gun and a few rounds of ammunition to shoot mouse birds (so called because of their long tails) in the orchard, which were a major pest, stealing much of the fruit. I would have been about twelve years old and these birds had a hard time of it for a while but there were thousands of them and I did not make much difference to the bird population or to the fruit supply.

Mouse birds I regarded as vermin and they did not qualify for burial in my private animal cemetery. I had found a dead lizard to which I accorded a solemn burial under a hedge with quite a lump in my throat, marking the spot with a small cross fashioned from twigs bound with string. I added to the cemetery as I came upon a dead frog, a dead worm and so forth, marking each spot with a fresh cross. Then for several days I couldn't find anything dead with which to fuel my childish grief so I had to kill something to be able to continue my burials, so out came my catapult with which I slew some innocent sparrow.

Life was simple and there were few luxuries, partly because they were not available and partly because we were, in common with all Kenya farmers at the time, distinctly hard up. My father had a motor cycle when he was first married and bought his first car, the model T Ford, not long after I was born. It cost him £198 and was delivered to him on his farm. A few days later someone came out to give him and my mother a driving lesson, the only one they ever had. I have but one recollection of that car and that was of my grandmother, Mary Layard Barberton, being taken ill in it while we were on a safari holiday in a remote area of Kenya. She became so ill that when we stopped she got out and lay on the ground and my father stood in the hot tropical sun so that his shadow fell over her while my mother tended to her. Later they took her to a remote farmhouse where she died a few days later, another victim of blackwater fever. Her other sons were summoned from some distance away and she was buried there out in the bush. No doctors - there wasn't one near enough; no death certificates or formalities, just the age old custom of sons laying their mother to rest and marking the spot with a cairn of stones. Many years later the cairn was replaced by a large stone and bronze plaque.

When I say that all our shoes were hand made it seems to belie the fact of our poverty at the time, but this is not so because those were the only shoes available. There was an Indian shoemaker in Kitale and he and two others would sit cross-legged on the floor, cutting, shaping, stitching and nailing shoes for the whole neighbourhood. There was a stone for sharpening their knives which had become smooth and shiny from frequent and prolonged usage. The shoemaker had a big heavy book in which he would trace his customers feet. He then took two measurements, the widest part of the foot and around the instep and recorded these together with the customers name, the date, the colour and style required. He would flip back through the pages to find a previous record and there were always lots of 'oohs' and 'ahs' at how my feet had grown. The shoes were always ready the same day one week later, for that was the usual interval for farmers to return to town. Many years later my father and I turned out to have feet of identical shape and size. When he was well off and I was an impecunious young doctor he would get an extra pair of shoes made for himself and slip them somewhere for me to find. My shirts and shorts were made by my mother with her hand operated Singer sewing machine but the better off families used an Indian tailor. These would ply their trade sitting on the veranda of their shops using a treadle machine, always a Singer. The materials were chosen from the back of the shop where customers were also measured up. The dressing in the cloth had a characteristic sweetish smell which I associated with the excitement of having new clothes.

The Kitale hotel was the gathering point at midday after the weekly shopping had been done. Tea and biscuits were served for the women and children, the men apart at the bar for a beer and farming talk. On rare occasions my father said we could stay for lunch which was a great treat as I could have fish. We were two days train travel from the sea, so we could not get sea fish but the memory of fresh water tilapia from a nearby river still sets my tastebuds tingling.

We collected the mail on the weekly visit to town. There were three Barberton brothers and their wives so they all shared the same Post Office Box, number 32. Having a box meant that you could collect your mail at any time and did not have to depend on the post office being open - there was no delivery. It was incumbent on each to take mail for other members of the family if going their way and letters from relatives living abroad were passed around to keep everyone up to date. Two of the three brothers and two of the wives had the same initial so there was plenty of room for confusion with inadequately addressed mail being opened by the wrong person.

The wireless reception was awful so it was only used for the news, most particularly the price of maize, wheat, coffee and gold and the news from Europe about Franco, Mussolini and Hitler and the county cricket and test match reports. I overheard the grown ups talking in hushed voices about a scandal concerning a Mrs Simpson but they clammed up when they knew I was listening. The wireless was never used for music so we made our own. My mother played the piano and sang and I was taught and expected to sing as well. Never again do I want to hear:

'I never dreamt that I should see
a poem lovely as a tree'

which I trotted out on more occasions than I care to remember. My uncle Alban played the violin and later made one while serving in the Burma campaign of the second world war, following the example of his great uncle Bertram Egerton Bowker who had made one in about 1825. Alban's violin was passed on to me when he died but within the case I found a note in his hand saying that it was to go to David Hopcraft in Kenya to whom I sent it. We had a His Master's Voice wind-up gramophone and some records, '*O play to me Gipsy*', '*Isle of Capri*', '*Down Mexico Way*', and there must have been others, which were played endlessly. The grown ups would put a record on and dance at the slightest excuse and in my father's diary there is an entry of a record to be purchased '*Columbia. Who tied the Can on the Old Dog's Tail. Vocal, Fox Trot. 3135 (80341)*'. Dances and amateur cabarets were held at the Kitale Club with my mother a keen participant.

Reading books and writing letters, poems, essays and articles for publication all contributed to home enjoyment and a day without receiving or making a visit was an occasion for comment. Bridge was a frequent means of enjoyment and the cards (one pack only) were used for patience when no one else was around. I wanted, and was not allowed, to use the pack myself (too sticky already) so nothing daunted I decided to make one out of brown paper which took me ages. I cut them to the correct size, drew and painted the cards copying from the real pack, stacked them in preparation for the inaugural game of patience and then found they could not be shuffled.

My father had made a tennis court close by the house

which was extensively used by the family and visitors. It was made of earth, levelled, raked and rolled and played surprisingly well. There were no grass courts at all in Kenya and I was surprised to find that grass was used when I got to England. The court was marked out with white maize meal flour: a length of farm twine would be stretched between sticks as a guide a farm worker would carefully release a little of the maize meal from between his palms until the court was fully marked. Play had to begin soon thereafter as the birds and our cat Mickey would set about eating the meal. There was a small brick tennis house with a bench for any spectators and refreshments. I was watching with my uncle Renshaw when he had run out of cigarettes. In desperation he crushed some dried canna lily leaves and rolled them in a bit of newspaper to smoke, but the experiment was a failure as it burst into flames when lit.

Invitations to tennis to the Stradling family who farmed three miles away across the Kabeyon valley were sometimes made by heliograph, which method of communication my father had learned during the 1914-18 war. We had no telephone and it was time consuming to send a farm worker with a note so my father would flash a morse code message across the valley, using the sun and my mother's hand mirror. Of course someone the other side had to be looking in order to reply so it didn't always work. They had an agreement that heliograph messages would only be sent at certain times so they knew more or less when to keep an eye open to the possibility.

One of my prize possessions was a Meccano set which was added to year after year without seemingly getting any larger as pieces seemed to disappear without any explanation. Then I found the reason for this when I caught my sister poking one strut through a crack between the veranda floorboards. I hit her on the head with an enamel chamber pot, fortunately not hard enough to earn me retribution. Putting my eye to the crack I was able to see plenty of Meccano parts which I was able to retrieve when my father took up a couple of floorboards for me.

Farming in Kenya in the 1920s and 1930s was barely mechanised. Ploughs and wagons were drawn by teams of eight bullocks with a driver who wielded a long two handed whip. I used to think he lashed the poor beasts unmercifully but then I realised that it was mostly show, the driver priding himself on the loudness of the crack of the whip, if he could do this just above the head of an ox without actually touching it, so much the better. The cracking of the whip was accompanied by loud and frequent shouts of encouragement and exhortation, some of them directed at a young boy whose job it was to operate the wagon brakes and at another whose job it was to lead the teams along the most favourable route. The loads were heavy and the routes rough, often through heavy mud which brought forth groans of effort as the beasts strained their shoulders to their yokes. They worked a six day week and seemed to know when it was Sunday: that was the day that they were taken to the salt lick and they would set up a chorus of lowing in anticipation of the weekly treat. We kept a few cows for the household milk supply in the charge of a woman named Veronica. The milk had to be boiled before consumption as it was not pasteurised and thick cream rose to the surface and clotted there.

The bullocks and loads were secured by reims, also used for the whiplash. When an ox died or was killed for meat, its skin was pegged out tightly on the ground in the sun till dry and was then cut perhaps an inch wide round and round the perimeter of the skin, into a long continuous piece. This was then looped over a sturdy branch about eight feet high, reaching almost to the ground and a pole was put through the loops at the bottom. The skin, all rough and hard, was then softened by applying generous quantities of fat from the beast and a lad would be put to twisting the reims by walking round and round with the pole till it was twisted up tightly and had reached head level. He would then release it and it would spin round till near the ground; he would then twist it again in the opposite direction and so on for a couple of days, applying more fat as needed until the reims were soft. At night the loop would be tied up high to the branch out of reach of hyenas who would have eaten it given the chance. When soft enough, it would be taken down and cut into suitable lengths and would serve some useful purpose for a couple of years or more, for securing loads, for harness and for making a whiplash.

There was no mains water or drainage and it was many years till we had our own piped water supply and could install flush toilets. Rain water from the roof was collected into tanks but, during the dry season, water had to be brought from the river daily in a pair of forty gallon drums mounted horizontally on a small cart drawn by two bullocks, with a driver and a lad. The lad's job was to lead the oxen, to hurry to the rear to apply the brake if needed and then fill the tanks from a four gallon kerosene tin while the driver smoked his pipe sitting in the sun or shade. The hill down to the river was quite steep so the return journey was accompanied by much shouting, heaving, groaning and sweating. That supply had to last the day because the man, boy and oxen would then go off to undertake some other work on the farm, so woe betide anyone who wasted water. The bathroom had a wash basin, jug and a bucket for the used water, which was saved for the garden. Bath water was heated in four gallon kerosene tins on the kitchen stove and Hazel and I used to share the same bath water. River water was, of course, contaminated so had to be boiled and filtered before it could be drunk and it says much for my mother that we never suffered from contaminated water or food. Many years later, after the second world war, my father installed a 'ram' pump at the river which drove water through pipes to a large concrete tank on the hill above the house and this transformed life. The years of serious poverty for Kenya farmers were by then a memory and he installed the plumbing, water-borne sanitation and washing machine which we now take for granted. I had by then grown up, married and gone out into the world.

Several streams flowed through the farm and my father made a dam to conserve water when it was plentiful in the rainy season, for irrigation, for fun and to provide power for a mill to grind maize into posho, which was an important part of the diet of the farm labourers. The dam wall was made over a period of many months with stones and earth using manpower, picks, shovels, kerais (the local name for mortar pans) and wheelbarrows. There was a sluice gate through which water could be allowed to escape if needed and a new road was constructed to go over the dam wall. The dam took a season to fill. It was a great success and was soon colonised by water birds. I was taken on a trip to catch tilapia fish from someone else's dam with which to stock our new dam. Several of us each caught twenty to thirty tilapia, put them into drums of water in the back of the pick up-truck and hurried home to tip them, gasping by now, into our dam where they flourished - till carried away a few years later after the dam burst following several days of heavy rain. The dam was used for swimming, fishing, picnicking and boating, the boats being made on the farm. One Christmas one of the farm labourers who could not swim took a boat, fell into the water and drowned. The alarm was brought to the house half way through Christmas lunch and everyone hurried to the dam and dived and dived in search of the man, but to no avail. He rose to the surface a couple of days later bloated by death and great wailing accompanied his funeral obsequies.

The owner of the dam from which we had stocked ours with fish was my father's cousin Mitford Bowker. He was known to my sister and myself as uncle Mit and was a great favourite. He was for many years a bachelor and lavished on us the affection he would no doubt have bestowed on his own children but, sadly, when he did marry he and his wife remained childless. His farming speciality was pineapples and he grew the biggest, sweetest, juiciest and tastiest pineapples in the world - so we thought and so he said. He described himself as the Pineapple King and certainly his fruit travelled throughout the land. I bathed in reflected glory when I took one of his pineapples to school and claimed him as a relative. Ronny Macdonald and I once stayed with him on his farm for a week, free from parental discipline and discovered to our chagrin that he expected us to join in daily prayers. Swimming in his dam on one occasion he dived in and came up minus his upper plate of false teeth. We laughed our heads off but, in truth, it was no laughing matter for there was no dentist in Kitale and new teeth could only be obtained in Nairobi, a day's journey away. Despite much diving the teeth could not be retrieved and Mit ended up by opening the sluice to empty the dam and the teeth were then recovered. On another occasion one tooth broke off the plate and he skilfully repaired it with a tiny screw.

Electricity, by way of a generator only, came to the farm long after I had left home - as a child we used oil lamps and candles. My mother succeeded in banning candles after my grandmother, who was an inveterate reader even by candle-light, set fire to her mosquito net. She was also subject to dreadful nightmares. One recurring nightmare was of her sleeping in a long row of beds in a dormitory. A man with long white hair was at the far end of the row, crawling under each bed and popping his head up between, getting closer and closer. She would hide under the bedclothes until her terror got the better of her when she would leap out of bed, flee and waken the whole household with her shouts.

A young lad known as the kitchen toto was employed for the purpose of keeping the kitchen fire going through the day. That was before my father built a school room, employed a teacher and made schooling compulsory on his farm. This lad also collected firewood, stoked the fire when required for cooking, riddled the ashes, damped it down when nothing was on the stove, heated the bath water, doused the fire in the evening and rose before dawn to get it going again, putting on the kettle for the early morning tea and shaving water. Matches were sometimes in short supply. A load would arrive from Europe by sea and there would be plenty in the shops but then stocks would run low before the next shipment had arrived. My father and his brothers got over this problem by splitting the match stalk and the head carefully down the middle with a razor blade, thus converting each match into two. The shortage of matches affected the farm workers and their wives and I can see in my minds eye one elderly woman, bent with age, with gnarled hands, carrying away a red hot ember from our kitchen fire to her hut, tossing it from hand to hand so as not to burn herself.

Writing in March 1912 my grandmother made first mention of the kitchen *toto*. She, her husband Hal and her two younger sons, had just arrived in the virgin territory of Kenya and were camped in the bush. After a night made restless by excitement, the novelty, the cold and the calls of the wild, she fell asleep only to be wakened by her hen Minorca announcing that it was 4 o'clock in the morning. So she rose, saw the last star fade and the sky turn to gold as the sun rose and witnessed:

> 'the fascination of all Africa in the shape of an almost nude toto warming his stomach by the fire he has made, watching without a wink your white hands brew the scented cup ...'

It was the responsibility of our kitchen toto to test the eggs which were brought to the house for purchase at 3 cents each, there being a hundred cents to the shilling. He would bring a bowl and a bucket of water and place each egg in turn in the bucket. If it floated it was bad and was rejected, if it sank to the bottom it was transferred to the bowl. Then came the business of calculating how much was to be paid for the eggs to a person who had received no schooling and knew no multiplication. My mother had a collection of one cent coins and would set three of these aside for each egg purchased. When the process had been completed the one cent coins were counted out in tens, to be replaced with a ten cent coin and in this manner was the transaction concluded. With thirty three eggs to the shilling (with one cent left over) it was seldom that any silver coins needed to be used.

Living on isolated farms without any telephones, we placed great importance on keeping in touch with neighbours, friends and relations, near and far. This was not just for social reasons but also for security, to give and receive succour at times of illness, injury or death and to share any good fortune which was bestowed on one. The Post Office provided a remarkably good and fast service without the benefit of air mail and we regularly wrote to and received letters from England and South Africa.

Keeping in touch with local friends and relations was by hand delivered note by one of the farm workers who would wait for a reply to bring back. The note was somewhat grubby by the time it reached its destination having been held in a sweaty hand or stuffed into a pocket perhaps none too clean. So someone had the idea of splitting the end of a stick and slipping the note into the cleft, the messenger then carried the stick and thus the note remained clean. The note would often be accompanied by a gift of fruit or vegetables from the farm garden.

By far the best method of keeping in touch was by visiting and never a week went by without making or receiving calls; as often as not the visitors would end up staying overnight without any prior arrangement. The sound of a distant car engine approaching would quicken the pulse, my mother would check me for cleanliness, comb my hair with her fingers and smooth my eyebrows with saliva on her thumbs, a hand on either side of my face. It was an important part of the Colonial ethic to offer unhesitating and unstinting hospitality to friend, relation or stranger. People would be down on their luck and out of funds and could rely without question on receiving sustenance and accommodation for as long as was necessary - there was no other form of social security. St Paul's injunction to the Hebrews was observed:

> 'Be not forgetful to entertain strangers, for thereby some have entertained angels unawares'.

Many years later my wife Pat was round eyed with surprise and then with understanding when she heard her mother-in-law relate how my father's friend, Phil Cooke Collis, had once come for Christmas and stayed till Easter. Visits were filled with fun, laughter and song, not much alcohol - they couldn't afford it.

We lived quite close to the Uganda border so we often made camping trips there for holidays. The coast was three days travel away so holidays by the sea were a great rarity. Kenya farmers and their families were past masters at camping safaris, sometimes two families going together in a couple of cars. Tents, bedding, mosquito nets, primus stoves, paraffin lamps, food, drinking water, guns and ammunition, spare clothes, spare petrol and so forth would all be piled into the car. There would be no fixed itinerary, just a general decision to 'go and see Lake Albert' or to 'visit the Mountains of the Moon', the very names conjuring up excitement in my breast. We would suffer punctures and breakdowns, normal day to day occurrences and these would be repaired by the roadside. My uncle Renshaw, with us on one occasion when we blew a gasket, was a mechanical genius. He took the lid off my mother's fibre suitcase (to her chagrin) and cut a new gasket from it which served till we reached civilisation again. Years later he wrote in a letter an account of how, on another occasion, he had made a piston ring for his motor cycle out of fence wire while returning from a safari in Uganda.

> "The rings in my Norton all packed up and you had to give me a good push to start the bike. I hammered the

> wire square and, by cutting the piston ring groove as wide as possible with a flat file, I fitted the ring and it worked well for some time as I had to order a new piston and rings from England".

When we reached Lake Albert we hired a dug-out canoe hollowed from a tree trunk - unstable and prone to capsize - and went to explore a small island. The lake was infested with crocodiles who watched our progress with eyes and nostrils just above the water and the island was criss-crossed with lines which had been drawn in the sand by their tails dragging behind them. I had been told how crocodiles rushed from the water to grab their prey and then kept them under water for days till they were good and rotten before eating them, so I kept a very apprehensive look out.

One safari to Kampala wasn't much of a holiday for me as I went to the Namirembe Mission Hospital to have an operation to correct a squint, undertaken by Dr Stone. His reputation was legendary for he had saved or restored the sight of many, many Ugandans. After the squint operation I spent days and days (so it seemed) in darkness with my eyes bandaged. I was given a musical box operated by a cranking handle and also a yo-yo with emery paper around the diameter on which a flint rested. As the yo-yo spun, sparks were thrown off the flint and were dazzling in the dark. None of the dire consequences which were promised if I peeped round the bandages came to pass and I came to realise that adults often prevaricated and exaggerated from the best of intentions. While my eyes were bandaged I suffered my first bed bath. Hands, arms, face, back and chest I accepted as sensible and necessary but with mounting anxiety and apprehension - would they go any further? My worst fears were realised when my pyjama trousers were whipped off and some totally strange woman washed my very private parts.

On another safari I was sent to catch a bird by putting salt on its tail. The adults were packing up and found my childish interruptions irksome and, in desperation, someone poured a teaspoonful of salt into my palm and explained how to catch a bird with it. There were plentiful large white birds around which would fly lazily away as I approached and then land again some twenty or so yards away. I realised that I would have to move much more quickly if I was to succeed and before long I was bathed in sweat, the salt dissolving in my hand. I eventually gave up and returned sheepishly to the adults, preserving silence as I did not wish to admit my failure. When asked if I had caught one I replied yes, actually, but it had got away.

Travel abroad in my childhood was by ship. My first time was, as a baby, to relations in South Africa and we went there again when I was four years old. My first visit to England was at the age of fourteen when I went to secondary school. Air travel was in its infancy so we did not even consider it. Flights did take place from England to South Africa and the flying boats took several days to make the journey, stopping overnight where there was water suitable for landing and take off, the passengers sleeping in a local hotel. Our nearest landing place was at Port Bell on Lake Victoria and Uganda safaris took in a visit to see a flying boat land or take off. Sea trips were long in the planning, expensive and infrequent, so no one went away for only two or three weeks holiday: it was for two or three months, often to relatives, often involving house rental. My father couldn't be away from the farm for that length of time and either didn't come or came and joined us later. The Union Castle Line ran a regular and reliable service from London or Southampton to the Cape, either down the west coast of Africa or through the Suez canal, often out one way and back the other and all my travelling was done on Union Castle ships, but until the first world war saw the end of German colonisation of East Africa there was strong competition from the Deutch Ost Afrika Line.

My father had booked me into Hailebury school while I was young, as secondary education in Kenya did not adequately prepare one for the possibility of entry to university. As a boy I learned that the best university in the world was Oxford and, in order to prepare myself for entry, my education had to be finished off in England. Thus, when I went to the Prince of Wales School at Kabete, near Nairobi, I knew it would only be a year or two before I went on to England. I was the youngest boy in the school on entry to the Prince of Wales in January 1937 - 11 years and 11 months. To get there I went by train from Kitale, departing at about 4 pm and reaching our destination at about 3 pm the next day. There were about half a dozen of us from Kitale and other boys joined the train at various points thereafter. The departure by train was quite a social occasion and adult relations and friends would come and see us off, bringing a gift of some sort, chocolate, sweets, fruit or jam to sustain us for the journey and start the term off well. Sammy Weller, a bachelor who was honorary uncle to everyone, always came along and set me off with a jar of Pan Yan Pickle. New boys were readily recognised and the lump in their throats on leaving home suppressed their appetites to the extent that they were easy prey to those who were already established at school - we would buy their supplies for a paltry sum and even sold some back to them at a profit a few days later.

We were unsupervised on the journey but behaved pretty well under the circumstances. We were few in number and would have been easily identified with sure and certain retribution when we reached school. There were no corridors so we had to wait for the train to stop at a station to get out and wander around and explore. I had my introduction to the morse code on one of these journeys, finding a station clerk tapping a message out on his morse key down the line. The engine burned wood and a magnificent shower of sparks could be seen coming from the funnel at night when we rounded a bend. These sparks would sometimes ignite the dry grass by the railway. We crossed the Great Rift Valley and a second engine had to be coupled to help haul us up from it. At this stage of the journey the train could barely exceed walking pace and young African children would scamper alongside selling fruit to the passengers. The copper coinage had a hole through the centre and we would tie the correct money to a piece of string and hang it out of the window for the fruit-seller to grasp. On one such occasion my hat blew off and my negotiations for some bananas were abruptly cut off as my fruit-seller ran off after the hat. At that time direct sun on the head was thought to put one at risk of developing sunstroke and I was conditioned to wearing a hat between eight o'clock in the morning and four in the afternoon, even if I briefly put my head out of the train window. On another occasion I snatched the money from the fruit-sellers hand as he was about to grasp it, having already received my fruit. I could hardly complain when he struck my hand with a stick the next time I lowered the money with which he escaped.

The school was close to the railway line a few miles out of Nairobi and the headmaster arranged for the train to be stopped to off-load us, to save having to send the school lorry to pick us up at the railway station. A master would stand beside the track and shout for us to open the doors, pass down our luggage and then jump down the two or three feet to the ground. Then the train would start up again, leaving an untidy gaggle of boys - perhaps twenty or thirty by now - and their baggage. We would help each other to carry our bags uphill to the school about three hundred yards away. I was rapidly nicknamed Four-eyes because of my spectacles, Yellow-skin because of my complexion and Daisy because of the Barberton Daisy named after my grandmother.

The journey to school was always tinged with sadness at leaving home and apprehension at the start of a new term. The journey home at the end of term was anticipated with excitement, especially by the boys from Kitale. Kitale was at the end of a branch line and there was only one train a week which seldom coincided with the day appointed for the end of term. Boys from Kitale therefore enjoyed the benefit of leaving two or three days before the rest. We were normally derided as from the back of beyond but, come the end of term we were envied, the more so because we had the company of Kitale girls from the girls school on the same train. I was too young at the time to personally appreciate their favours but I used to carry notes from an older boy at the school to one of the girls and this childhood romance was, in due time to become a marriage. One girl of my age would embarrass me by ogling at me and I would do my best to keep out of her way. When morning came we knew that Mount Elgon, on the slopes of which my family lived would be in sight and how slow the last fifty miles to Kitale would seem. As we came into Kitale station boys and girls would jostle for favourable positions through the train windows to catch first sight of parents who had come to meet us.

The Prince of Wales School had a tough reputation and certainly the discipline was strict, possibly harsh, but nobody seemed to think that this should be otherwise. There were initiation ceremonies to be endured at the end of the first term which were always worse by exaggeration and in the imagination than in fact. Songs had to be sung before one's class and this never harmed anyone. A 'soap pill' had to be consumed made of any noxious substance which could be obtained - soap, shoe polish, toothpaste, paraffin, mustard and so forth and this was said to be so awful as to be greatly feared. But my concoction was mild and innocuous. And then there was a ducking in a bath of cold water on the last day of term and rumour had it that many narrowly escaped drowning. But again I found it a tame affair, none of my fears being realised.

One of the new boys in my group, Ebbie (for Ebenezer) Smith, was a couple of years older than I and tried, with some success, to make my life a misery whenever he could, teasing and tormenting me and others. He didn't have a Sunday tie and when mine disappeared and he turned up sporting one I drew the appropriate conclusions which were confirmed when he called me at the end of the day. "Barberton" he said, "come and brush my tie", this in his clipped Afrikaans accent. Being younger and smaller I did as I was told and was able to see the needle marks where he had removed the Cash's name tape which my mother had sewn on. I endured this additional affront but imagine my delight when this supposedly tough guy was found to have run away from school the day before the end of term to escape his initiation ceremony. And how the tables were turned the next term when I was able to deride him for his cowardice.

The headmaster was an ex-Naval Officer named Captain

Nicholson who was succeeded by Mr Astley a few terms later. Caning was normal and both were greatly feared. In truth, few people were caned - myself only once - and those who were seemed to accept that they deserved it. Two boys who ran away were given a public caning, held by two others over the gym 'horse' before the whole school and this certainly created a lasting impression. Smoking was a caning offence but I never knew anyone to be punished for this. Fighting was common and when it led to injury, the participants could expect a caning. Two particular boys who were implacable enemies pursued a vendetta against each other, one fight only being concluded when one of them sustained a broken arm. When he came back from hospital with his arm in plaster he issued an immediate challenge for another fight the day the plaster was removed and we all awaited the event with bated breath. Such was the sense of anticipation on the appointed day that one of the masters got wind of it, caught them at it before any damage had been done and carted them off to the headmaster.

The school boasted an Officers Training Corps with a school band for which all new boys had to volunteer. I volunteered to be a bugler, having had some practice on a bugle my father had looted from the Germans in the Great War or, failing that, a drummer. So they sent me to learn the flute and we had to practise some two hundred yards away, by the water pumping house, which was where I learned to smoke. Or so I thought, till Ebbie Smith realised I did not know about inhaling. So he showed me; I inhaled, my head felt as if it would burst, my lungs felt on fire, my eyes started out of their sockets, the earth spun and I became dizzy, almost falling. Desperate not to make a fool of myself in front of my chief *bête noir* I managed with difficulty to maintain my composure. "You didn't do it properly Barberton" he said "do it like this" taking a long drag and inhaling deeply. I complied and felt even worse and with a superhuman effort avoided the ignominy of collapsing. Puzzled and surprised he walked away shaking his head with disbelief, just far enough for me to disappear behind the pump house and vomit unobserved. But the seed of tobacco addiction was sowed and I smoked for the next thirty years till I gave up, with a much greater effort than that needed to start when seeking to impress Ebbie Smith. I never did make the band and had to be content with admiring it from a distance, especially the bandmaster Philip Abrams. He would turn and spin and throw his silver headed mace high into the air as he marched in front and I dreaded the possibility of his failing to catch it as it descended. And how the polished silver head gleamed in the sunshine. The OTC and its band played an important part in school life, the Union Jack was raised every morning and lowered every sunset. Empire Day was a school holiday and the OTC and band put on a special display for that day and on the King's birthday.

Being the youngest in the school for my first year I was always last in every queue and the first to be allocated any of the school tasks. One of these was 'trades', setting and clearing the tables before and after meals. Four boys at a time were on trades and, if you were on the first week of term (which I was), it was likely that you would end up doing it more times than those who were on later in the term. Being last in all the queues I learned that I could recognise every boy in the school by the shape of the back of his head, a talent I never subsequently found useful.

Most of us came from some distance away and had to board but about a third came from Nairobi and attended as day boys. We were divided into four houses, Rhodes (my own), Hawke, Grigg and Clive, all illustrious Imperial names and intense competition was encouraged between the houses, mainly sporting - scholastic ability didn't count for much in the 'Cock House' competition. Winning this was rewarded by a celebration meal. Different terms were devoted to rugby, cricket and hockey, all of which I embraced with enthusiasm but not a great deal of skill. It was while playing cricket that I first saw a person die. A boy my age named Jackie Powell was standing in the outfield and suddenly dropped dead. We didn't attend his funeral - I expect that was held at his home town - but the special service held in the school dining room (there was no chapel) was a poignant occasion.

Groups of us formed ourselves into gangs. The one to which I belonged comprised Ken Bolton, John Morgan, Ronny MacDonald and David ('Danny') Danziger. Ken Bolton died young in a motor accident. John Morgan also died young in North Africa as a pilot in the RAF during the 1939-45 war. Ronny MacDonald I lost touch with but Danny Danziger I next heard of about forty five years later when he was working in England. He was the accountant to a large business and dealt with my account for surgery rendered to one of their employees. His mother was very kind to me while at the Prince of Wales School. My own parents lived too far away to be able to take me out on leave Sundays and she included me on a number of outings. The best of friends fall out and we were no exception - I once called Danny "you dirty Jew". He replied "just you remember that Jesus Christ was a Jew" and I retired crushed, wiser and chastened.

Down the hill towards the railway was a barbed wire fence and beyond it lay the line itself with another fence the far side. Between the fences was kept clear of vegetation and this zone was strictly out of bounds. I would put my ear to the rail and listen to the faint sound of a train approaching long before it could be heard or seen. And I would put a five cent coin on the rail to be flattened as the train went over it. Either side of the fences was dense scrubby bush and the gangs made dens within this. The entrance was made between two bushes, disturbing them as little as possible so that it seemed invisible. But within we would clear an area perhaps ten feet in diameter, leaving a cover of branches and leaves. Here we would smoke, spin yarns, hatch plots and feast on anything we had been able to lay hands on. African children from the Kikuyu tribe lived in homesteads the far side of the railway line and when they found one of our dens they would destroy it by opening up the entrance and removing the roof cover, or by setting fire to it. So there grew up an enmity between them and us which resulted in many pitched battles.

The railway was the front line, the weapons were catapults and slings and we used the stones comprising the foundations for the railway sleepers as our ammunition. The catapults and slings were home made. We used empty jam and sauce bottles (given to us at the beginning of term) for target practise. With a sling, a larger stone could be thrown much further but it was a very inaccurate weapon. The winners (usually the Kikuyu) were determined by their superior numbers and the losers (usually ourselves) would flee through the barbed wire fences. Injuries were infrequent as one could see the stone coming and dodge but one boy had his scalp sliced open and I sustained a scar down my back, caused by fleeing from their superior numbers and being pulled up a bank between the strands of the barbed wire fence by a friend.

Every boy in the school carried a knife, many of us

two. Never were these used for aggressive purposes; they were used for such important purposes as skinning animals, cutting string, sharpening pencils, peeling bark from a stick, carving initials and for throwing at targets. I had a sheath knife on my belt and a Joseph Rogers pocket knife; I also carried a small sharpening stone. It was a matter of pride that the knife be sharp enough to shave the hairs from ones' arm or leg and any spare moments were spent honing the blade to perfection after every use. We used to carve our initials and the date on desks and trees and, for a while, there was a vogue for doing so on one's skin. We wore shorts so the favoured position was on the front of the thigh but high up where the masters wouldn't see it. Mine was but a faint scratch and did not rate high in the virility stakes. I also carried a mouth organ and played the popular songs of the day: *'Twas on the Isle of Capri where I found her', 'There's a lovely Lake in London' and 'South of the Border down Mexico Way'.*

My letters at this time contained the normal schoolboy reports of events, results of matches, promises to try harder, apologies for the brevity of the epistle and for its lateness, requests for stamps, money, books and items left at home and needed at school. Once I needed ink and to illustrate the matter filled my fountain pen with water, the resultant letter being pale but still legible sixty years later. I knew how short we were of money and was conscious of the need for economy. Postage was 5 cents and I asked my mother 'Your last letter had a 20 cent stamp on it, why did it'? I asked for my geometry set and birthday book but added the stricture that they should not be sent if they were 'too heavy and costs too much'. Many of my letters were brief to say the least and I once sought to excuse this in case the postage on a longer letter might cost too much.

There were mentions of other important matters which had impressed themselves on my young mind, the Spanish Civil war and the Coronation of George VI. 'Thank you so much for the Coronation Calendar' I wrote and later I said that the Coronation gift had come in very useful. What that gift was I cannot now remember. I had sent for a microscope advertised in England and was worried about the duty which might be payable and was concerned that it might have been lost at sea in a ship sunk by a mine in the Spanish civil war. I asked to be told of 'any interesting news about the Spanish War that comes over the wireless'. And 'In your last letter you said that ...... had fallen. I could not read the place; was it Madrid?'. And later 'Did Malaga belong to the Rebels or the Royalists'?

My mother wanted me to tear up her letters to me, to which I agreed 'although I like keeping them'. She was concerned that my bowels act regularly and sent me to school with a supply of phenolphthalein (which I was proud to be able to spell) for the purpose and a small bottle of mercurochrome for application to wounds. I had to ask for a reminder about the instructions for taking the laxative and later reported that I had taken 'half a one and it worked alright'. Her ideas of school were derived from *Tom Brown's Schooldays* so I was sent off with a tuck box and soon found that I was the only boy with one. When the boys from my dormitory saw that it contained fruit cake, cheese, biscuits, chocolate and so forth, they fell upon it like ravening wolves and everything was consumed in a trice. We were weighed and measured every term and I attributed my growth to taking a Vikelp tablet every day - from memory it was made of dried seaweed. One term I reported that I knew I had grown because I had previously been able to walk under a certain window which had just touched my hair and could no longer do so without banging my head.

I suppose that I would now be regarded as somewhat of a creep, but I wrote in all sincerity at the time 'Every night when I go to bed I think of you and Daddy and my little sister and think how much I love you all. I do not forget my prayers but kneel up in my bed every night after lights out and say them'. It takes but little perspicacity to realise that I hadn't the courage to do so before lights out when I would have been observed.

I had a stroke of good fortune when my uncle Renshaw became engaged to a lady who lived in Nairobi. Her name was Marjorie Eaton and she was nicknamed Moth. She took me under her wing and became a firm favourite for the rest of her life and, as it transpired, I was the only person from the family to attend their wedding in Nairobi, far from Kitale where we all lived. So Moth took me out on leave Sundays. She had a box Brownie Kodak camera and afforded me the luxury of lending it to me with a film; thus I became hooked on photography. I stalked a herd of giraffe and was disap.pointed when I could only just see two tiny giraffes in the distance in the photo. Moth told me how Renshaw had taken her on safari to see Mount Kivu in the Belgian Congo which was in eruption at the time. It was a very cold night and they stood on the hot edge of the crater looking down into the molten volcano when he proposed to her. Renshaw and Moth were childless, eventually they adopted an orphaned brother and sister, the children of Warburton who had played in the band with my uncle Alban at the Manor hotel in Mombasa years before.

I only spent two years at the Prince of Wales School before moving to England. My father had realised that he would not be able to meet the costs of the school intended for me. He had an up-to-date copy of Whittaker's Almanac, turned to the Schools section and looked at the right hand column which listed the fees payable. In this way Stamford School in Lincolnshire was selected. No doubt the decision was aided by the fact that Stamford was a fine country town with many historical associations; the school was ancient with a fine record and an eminent headmaster, the Reverend Canon John Duncan Day, who was to have a profound and beneficial influence on me. War broke out while my mother was in England preparing me for school and she was trapped there while my father was isolated in Kenya. So he joined the army for the second time in his life.

Wanting to see as much of me as possible before I went to England, my father withdrew me from the Prince of Wales School for my last term and I was schooled close to home by a Mrs Baldenhofer, an Irish lady married to a German farmer. There were two other pupils, Anne and Jill Matthews, whose widowed mother had married my uncle Alban. Mr Eugen Baldenhofer was believed to be a Nazi. Certainly he had a portrait photograph of Adolf Hitler on the dining room wall; certainly he had evening gatherings of German men at his house when they would converse (darkly in my view) long into the night; certainly he gave vent to outbursts of violent anger. All these I believed to confirm him as a Nazi and indeed he returned to Germany unexpectedly a month or two later. I had no doubt that he had been summoned to serve 'der Fuhrer'. Mrs Baldenhofer was said to have a bad heart and took tablets. She would swoon away sometimes during one of her husband's rages and I feared that she would die. When this happened he would stop in mid tirade, fearing he had gone too far this time but he never failed to revive her with some amber coloured fluid from a silver flask. I cannot remember many lessons at the Baldenhofers but for Anne and Jill I carry a lasting affection. Ann, widowed for years, lived in Kenya with her tame cheetah till she died and Jill, a successful and talented writer, has an animal sanctuary in Zimbabwe. Jill has reminded me that even then I wanted to be a doctor, how I killed a frog and then cut it open with my pocket knife and showed them that the heart was still beating. Gruesome.

The time of my departure for England to Stamford school was accompanied by gathering war clouds and there was a sense if uncertainty in the air. I was to be away from my family in any case for a number of years but I have no doubt that my father and mother were filled with anxiety about the mood of political insecurity that prevailed. We felt strangely close to the possibility of war although far away from Europe, for we had quite recently experienced the proximity of the Italian - Abyssinian war in our own back yard as it were, Kenya having a common border with Abyssinia. We had read of the air raids and gas attacks on the Abyssinian troops and people after the ineffective response of the League of Nations had been peremptorily brushed aside by Mussolini. But we kept cheerful concerning the great adventure on which I was about to embark and looked forward to meeting again when my father found himself able to visit England. He proposed to throw in a trip to Iceland with me when he came and I maintained this fiction in letters to him long after the possibility of doing so had passed.

So the preparations for our departure went ahead. Tickets were bought for the passenger liner Dunvegan Castle, returns for my mother and sister and a single for myself. My father was to stay behind to look after the farm. Clothing suitable for a northern clime was bought and I found my first pair of long flannel trousers very restrictive. My father, perhaps sensing a longer separation than we imagined, took every opportunity to impress his love on us and every minute possible was spent together, where normally he would have been out and about on the farm for hours at a time. Down the path to the orchard, the garage and the 'long-drop' toilet, was a large pomelo tree which had been grown from seed by my grandmother. My father would pass this tree two or three times each day and Hazel and I wired little mementoes, a bakelite Mickey Mouse and a pencil sharpener, to a branch at his eye level. We knew he would see them and be reminded of us. That was in 1939 and they were still there when I next visited Kenya in 1951, the wire rusted and eaten deep into the branch. My father took us to catch the train to Mombasa where we were to board the ship and we were seen off by a crowd of friends and relations, himself in the forefront. His brothers Renshaw and Alban and their wives were there, his cousins Mitford Bowker and Harold White, all of them my loving kinsmen for longer than I could remember. I feel the sense of desolation to this day and only as I have reached mature years have I realised how much greater must have been his sadness at the departure of his wife and children. The war separated us till I was eighteen years old but we kept in touch by letter despite all the vagaries of wartime mail across the continents and seas.

My sense of smell lives with me through many of the events of my life, sad and happy, great and small. The first rain striking the dust at the end of the dry season in the tropics, the heavy scent of frangipanni at dusk, the wholesome smell of a clean baby, agricultural smells of oxen groaning at the plough, the fig tree on my father's farm, coffee roasting in the kitchen, wet dog drying off in front of the fire, the fearful smell of death; the faintest trace of any of these awakens instant and evocative memories. As powerful as any is the smell of a ship and the Dunvegan Castle wakened a memory dormant since early childhood, a mixture of paint, oil, cooking, salt sea water and stale air imprisoned in the ship when it was built and never yet fully displaced. The ship was later to be torpedoed and sunk during the war while carrying troops and fortune has protected me from experiencing the foul stench of a dying ship as the trapped air is expelled as it slides below the sea.

The throb of the engines carried me further and further from home and closer and closer to the other place I had called home ever since I was very young, but it didn't feel a bit like it. Each early morning, the steward delivered to my cabin an ice cold apple which I had never tasted before; we passed through the Suez canal built by Ferdinand de Lesseps; in Suez we visited the great emporium owned by Simon Arzt and bought tourist trinkets and inhaled the luxurious smell of the leather goods; in the Mediterranean I was allowed to stay up late to see Mount Etna; in Marseilles I was seduced by the size and cheapness of a huge bar of chocolate which was later the main reason for my succumbing to *mal-de-mer*; the Rock of Gibraltar, that great bastion of Empire was dutifully visited, admired with awe and photographed. The Bay of Biscay did not live up to my fears, my childhood reading had impressed its ferocity on my mind but my apprehension was misplaced as we made a calm crossing. Approaching our destination all was activity; I was sent below decks to the 'Baggage Not Required on Voyage' to put away my tropical garb and get out my English clothes. The ship's loudspeaker endlessly repeated a popular song of the day

I'm a little prairie flower
Growing wilder every hour
Nobody cares to cultivate me
For I'm as wild as wild can be.

We docked at Tilbury and were met on board by Irene Johnson, a loving ex-Kenya friend who shepherded us through the formalities. Dockyard workers swarmed all over the ship collecting baggage, piling it into rope cradles which were swung over the side by derricks, whence it was taken to the huge Customs Hall where it was sorted alphabetically. I was filled with apprehension lest we were thought to be carrying contraband but we were soon on the train to Victoria. Irene had rented a flat in Kensington for all of us for a week or two till we found other accommodation and she showed us the sights and sounds of London.

We had left my home in Kitale on March 20th 1939 and arrived at Tilbury docks twenty four days later. My mother then had three weeks in which to find accommodation and to kit me out for entry to Stamford School as a boarder. We moved to accommodation on a farm in Devon near Totnes which, together with Paignton and Dartmouth, were our homes till my mother returned to East Africa after the war. We couldn't afford a car so my journeys to school were by train, the Great Western Railway line to Paddington, by taxi with my school trunk to Kings Cross and then by the London & North Eastern Railway to Peterborough and Stamford. On that first journey we failed to change at Manton and had to get out at Ashwell in Rutland, return to Kettering and, thence, to Stamford. This was my first visit to Kettering where I was later to spend twenty-five years of my working life. In Stamford we stayed at the George

Hotel and bought my kit at the school outfitters Parrish & Sons, unaware that I would do so twenty-three years later with my daughter and two sons, when I brought my family back to England, the boys going to the same school as myself and my daughter to the companion school for girls.

Parental finance was very tight and my mother wrote with anxiety to my father in Kenya asking for money to pay the first terms fees. She was already alarmed at the cost of accommodation in Devon which was £5 a week for the three of us. My school kit, including linen, clothes, black Sunday suit with waistcoat and pin stripe trousers, white Sunday shirt with starched collar and straw boater had cost £18. The farm in Kenya had been plundered by locusts again and my father wrote that half his wheat crop had been eaten by them - he considered himself fortunate as his neighbour had lost the whole of his crop. It was therefore with a sense of relief that my mother reported to him that I had been awarded a bursary - for £15 a year. War now seemed very likely, throwing into uncertainty the plan for my mother and sister to return to Kenya which was going to cost £174. £90 was put on one side for my first years fees.

My fees were £31.8s a term, less £5 because of my bursary. Later, to make ends meet Hazel was withdrawn from her boarding school so that I could continue at mine. My mother's letters were a catalogue of expenses and she reported with dismay how it had cost 22s.6d for a single train fare from Waterloo to Southampton. To supplement Hazel's schooling I was paid 1s. a week to coach her in mathematics.

A naval disaster took place at this time, the accidental loss of the submarine Thetis, only four men being saved from the whole crew and this seemed an ominous warning about the shape of events to come.

Chapter 5

1939 - Stamford, Oxford and St Mary's Medical School

I entered Stamford school in April 1939 full of apprehension and left it in July 1943 happy and confident and qualified for admission to St Edmund Hall, Oxford to study medicine. Stamford was steeped in history and tradition and the headmaster, the Reverend Canon John Duncan Day upheld the finest standards of English education. He was named as my guardian should it become necessary and became an influential figure to me for the five and a half years that I was separated by the war from my father. He was respected and feared and did not hesitate to use the cane, normal at that time. I had my share of punishment, none undeserved and never felt any sense of injustice. Some forty years later an article in the school magazine portrayed him as a cane happy authoritarian and I take this opportunity to rebut the dishonour done to him by a latter day contributor who never knew the man or came under his inspirational guidance. Canon Day lived in the headmaster's quarters attached to the school and his wife was intimately involved in helping to look after those of us who were boarders. 'The Gaffer' as we called him was often out and about and did not like to catch us unawares. He always heralded his approach with a discrete characteristic cough a few seconds before he came into view so as to give us time to refrain from whatever misdemeanours we might be perpetrating.

Chapel, according to the rites of the Church of England, played a prominent part in the life of the school and we attended every morning during the week and twice on Sundays. The services were short and to the point and I became familiar with the fine language of the Authorised Version of the Bible and of Cranmer's compilation of the Book of Common Prayer. I sang in the choir and did my stint of reading the lessons. Canon Day, great and authoritarian in my eyes, never failed to impress me with his humility when intoning the prayer of Humble Access during the Communion service. And he regularly used the prayer of St Chrysostom, fourth century Bishop of Constantinople, which became a precept to me of which I thought my absent father would approve:

> 'Teach us good Lord to serve the as thou deservest, to give and not to count the cost, to fight and not to heed the wound, to toil and not to seek for rest, to labour and not to ask for any reward save that of knowing that we do thy will'.

Oak pews had been installed in the Chapel not long before my arrival and one could help to defray the cost by paying £5 for one's name to be carved thereon, which my mother did on my behalf. Also around the Chapel walls were oak panels on which were carved the names of the boys who had been killed in the 1914-18 war, soon to be augmented by those of schoolboys of my generation.

My entry to school in April 1939 was soon to be followed by the outbreak of the war on September 3rd and memories of both are closely intermingled. My first term was quite a culture shock coming from Kenya. Living in the colonies and coming from pioneer origins I felt sure that I would be more than a match for English schoolboys and it was a surprise to me that they were fully as tough as myself and that they were indifferent to my wider experience of life. On the end wall of the school chapel was a gargoyle, the head of an old man and I suffered the indignity of all new boys in having to kiss this at a formal ceremony before the whole school. This was at the beginning of term, and worse was to follow at the end when new boys had to sing a song before the members of their house. The imagined terrors of these initiation ceremonies far exceeded those of the actual occasions and I can honestly say that I was happy at school. I had my moments of home-sickness, perhaps the more so because of the complete separation from my father. I would waken often at six o'clock in the morning, normal for a farm lad bred in the tropics and would shed a few tears in the privacy of my bed. A train left Stamford station at this time each day and the sound of a steam engine used to conjure up for me memories of my happy childhood with my parents and sister on the Kenya farm.

Gas masks in cardboard boxes with a tape to carry them over our shoulders were issued at the beginning of my second term. To begin with we carried them everywhere but after a while the rule obliging us to do so was relaxed. We were drilled regularly wearing them for ten minutes or so as an exercise. Breathing through them was surprisingly hard work and I greatly feared having to wear a mask for hours in the event of a gas air raid. One abiding memory remains: a teenage girl cycled past with gas mask slung over her shoulder. A gust of wind lifted her skirt and I was rewarded with a glimpse of her thigh, unusual at that time.

There were no air raid shelters to begin with but sandbags and covered trenches were soon provided at the school. Stamford, a medieval market town, was hardly a target with any degree of priority for the German air force and I remember few air raid alarms and only two or three occasions on which we were wakened from our beds to take shelter. When I became a prefect I was given fire watching duties during air raid warnings and while this gave me a sense of importance I never once saw a fire. A few bombs were dropped one night a long way away. The only time that I saw any action was without any prior warning: from an upstairs school window I saw a low flying German plane fly past at roof level, machine-gunning the High street. It dropped a bomb which failed to explode and we were all evacuated to Stamford High School for girls school for three days while a bomb disposal crew came and dismantled it. We took blankets and slept on the floor of the school hall. Our excitement at being amongst the girls, who were out of bounds normally, waned rapidly for we were strictly segregated. Lessons were abandoned for the three days and we were sent out to help a local farmer gather in his crop of peas at 8d a day. It was dirty and tiring work but I didn't mind a bit because the farmer's daughter had dancing eyes and favoured me with a shy smile.

Blackout regulations were introduced at the very outset of the war. All street lamps were extinguished and frames with black cloth were made to fit all windows. Before opening an outer door we would put out the light within and close the door quickly. Air Raid Precaution officers who wore an arm band reading ARP patrolled the streets on bicycles and shouted "PUT THAT LIGHT OUT" at any offending household. Car head-lamps were masked with a black disc with a horizontal slit about four inches wide and half an inch high to restrict the amount of illumination. Petrol was rationed to two hundred miles a month for essential users only so there were very few cars on the streets and many people put their cars up on bricks in their garages for the duration of the war. For the first time, I believe, white paint was used for road markings to make it easier for people to get about in the unaccustomed darkness.

School food is popularly thought to be some of the worst in the world, but given the ravenous appetites of growing boys and a plentiful supply of bread and potatoes we did remarkably well and certainly had enough to grow in stature and to fuel our energies. Food rationing began in January 1940 and one of my letters home reported that 'now that butter is rationed we get more than we did before'. The headmaster's wife kept an eagle eye on the quality of the food served to us. A sample plate of the meal we were to receive was brought to her for inspection and I was once witness to this event: "Take it away, it's horrible" said she but it was served up to us nevertheless. Each boy had a third of a pint of milk daily which had an inch of thick cream at the top of the bottle. Not everyone drank their milk and one or two bottles would become sour and I tricked some of my friends (and enemies) pretending to pour a bottle of milk over their heads. They were duly relieved when it turned out to be a spot of innocent fun because the milk had gone solid - that is until I did it to my friend Lewin over whose head the evil smelling mess flowed. He was hurt and I was ashamed and the quality of our friendship was never the same again as he had lost trust in me. Today, many years later, I repeat the apology which seemed hollow to him then. I would supplement my butter ration at school by making more from the layer of cream on top of the milk. I would suck out the milk below with a straw leaving the cream and would gather the cream from two or three bottles into one, replace the cardboard disc to seal it and go around shaking it for a couple of hours. The butter fat would coalesce to a rather soft creamy butter to which I added a little salt. Another way that we used to expand the volume of the butter ration was to add some margarine and flour, then stirring it to an even consistency.

Had war not broken out my mother would have returned to Kenya with Hazel but they stayed in England for the duration while my father put a manager on his farm and joined the East African Reconnaissance Squadron. All this had serious financial repercussions and my mother's letters reported on how she was managing on the meagre finance available. Till the war got going in earnest letters were sent by airmail which was cheap and efficient at 1½d and would reach my father in Kenya in a week. Later it rose to 1s.3d and later still airmail was suspended altogether and it took up to fourteen weeks for my father's letters to arrive, many failing to do so, presumed sunk at sea. In 1941 a technical advance took place, the introduction of 'airgraphs' for servicemen overseas. The letter was written, or preferably typed on one side of a form designed for the purpose which was then photographed and the negatives were then sent in bulk by air. At their destination the negatives were enlarged to prints five inches by four, the writing or typescript being rather small but quite legible.

Two of his communications (in case he was killed) were never sent. One was written in a notebook which I found many years later when I received his papers after he died. I found an entry in his pocket book, written in July 1940 just before the battle of Ajau in Abyssinia as it was then called:

> "Sweetheart Peggy, God bless and keep you and my darling Dalla and Boo. My dearest love to you all and my brothers. Raymond. 8th July 1940".

Later I came across a sealed letter dated 10th Feb 1941, written to my mother during the war. It was endorsed on the envelope:

> "To be posted in the event of my death. Register if possible'. Again he told of his love for us and added 'I tremble now thinking of the dreadful days that are upon us and I'd give a lot to be with you and take care of you all, perhaps into some happy old age together".

This last sentiment came to pass and they lived happily well into their eighties.

My mother had to earn some money and did so by helping to run a large house called Longcause near Totnes owned by a bachelor called Mr Martin, my sister and I being accommodated there as well. Mr Martin was somewhat crusty but was very stimulating to a teenage boy. He would take me on to the lawn at night and show me the constellations and we would find some of the planets with his small telescope. The house was old and had been occupied by Cromwell's men, and it was possible to decipher the names on the doors which had been over-painted - 'Armoury' and 'Buttery' I remember. It was said that part of the house had been burnt down or demolished and one winter morning I woke to observe the old foundations etched in frost on the lawn. I tore downstairs to alert Mr Martin and we hastily gathered canes from the greenhouse to mark them before the frost melted in the morning sun. Mr Martin would play chess with me of an evening and always won, but on one occasion I very nearly beat him. I laid a trap for him which he spotted at the last minute, escaped and went on to beat me. To this day my pulse races when I think how close I came to defeating him on that single occasion.

Later we moved to Paignton and lived in Manor Road with the Slann family who ran a holiday boarding house. Summer holidays were more or less suspended for the duration of the war so the Slanns took in several people like ourselves who were in need of long term accommodation. A few people still came for short summer holidays but the Slanns could not have survived on the greatly reduced income from that source alone. My mother joined the Womens' Voluntary Service in Paignton to help with war work. Four thousand evacuees arrived from London and she helped with their billeting. Once a week she bathed thirty six evacuees at the public baths. She also worked in the food office which issued ration books. I was by now sixteen years old and was old enough to carry out fire-watching duties at night. Hazel was thirteen and knitted warm socks and balaclavas for the troops. Boys with bicycles (I did not have one) often got interesting jobs dashing around with messages, so I resolved to save up for one. I got as far as 2s 4d when my father sent me the balance, about £5, from his meagre pay. I bought a bicycle with a three speed derailleur gear which was guaranteed for the unlikely period of fifty years, as I reported in one of my letters. It went with me to and from school by train each term, went to Oxford with me for my three years as an undergraduate, was stolen by a convict escaping from Oxford prison and was recovered because I had registered its serial number at the Police station. Finally I sold it for £2 to a freshman who came to Oxford in 1946 when I left to go to Medical School. It was by then in sorry condition and had not stood up to its guarantee, but had been my sturdy and invaluable steed over many hundreds of miles. I now confess that I stampeded a young insecure freshman into paying me more than it was worth.

I progressed up the school ladder becoming a house prefect, school prefect, head of house and then head boy of the school. In 1942 the previous head of school left and a sense of excitement prevailed among the school prefects wondering who would be his successor and have his name emblazoned in gold paint on the boards displayed in the school hall. The headmaster sent for me and warned me that he would announce my succession at the next day's assembly. I knew without being told that I had to keep silent about this until then and how the adrenaline flowed in my veins till the announcement was made. I was a keen but undistinguished sportsman and struggled to keep a place in the first cricket team. Scholastically I was thought to be above average but I have always disputed this. The reason that I got on well was because I was always curious and had been well taught; a succession of teachers had stimulated my interest so that it had been a pleasure to do my school work well. I became what was called a 'double five', that is five for work and five for conduct, being the highest grades awarded – (*Creep!*). I won the Crighton-Maitland prize for common sense, a sovereign, a pocket knife and a piece of string. War time restrictions meant that sovereigns were not available so I received £2 (in £1 notes) instead; there were no pocket knives to be had in the town and they forgot the piece of string.

All boys were encouraged to join the Officer Training Corps and we were issued with uniform, taught to drill and march and sent on exercises learning to map read and cross a bit of countryside with the help of a compass. We learned the Morse Code and how to transmit messages. I've forgotten most of it but recall how we were taught to remember F and L (for French Letter). For F one said 'did it *hurt* you' (dot dot dash dot), and for L 'of *course* it did' (dot dash dot dot). For good measure I also joined the Air Training Corps but made little progress. As the pace of war developed and invasion by Germany became a real fear, it was decided to evacuate the school from Lincolnshire where there were a lot of RAF aerodromes which would therefore be likely to be a prime target. So off we went to Cors-y-Gedol Hall, near Barmouth in North Wales with a skeleton staff of school teachers. My name and destination were written on a luggage label tied to my jacket lapel. My mother came to help with the domestic arrangements at the school. It was a golden idyll, a lovely summer, but didn't last for long. When the risk of invasion had receded we moved back to Stamford and normal school work. I cannot remember much teaching being done at Cors-y-Gedol but I did learn to fly fish for trout.

During the school holidays teenage boys were expected and were keen to do something to aid the war effort, so I joined the Home Guard in Paignton where we were now living. The Home Guard consisted of over-aged men and boys below call-up age and we took our duties very seriously; it was much more exciting than the school OTC as we were doing real work. I had a weekly stint guarding an ammunition dump over-night with three others, each of us being issued with a .303 rifle and a single bullet and each doing a two hour watch. My eyes would become strained peering into the darkness looking for Germans and in my imagination I would see moving shadows which made the hair on the back of my neck and on my arms stand on end. Paignton was not exactly a war target but it did suffer the occasional air raid, aircraft perhaps dropping bombs left over from a raid on Plymouth and once sixteen people were killed. Five parachute flares were dropped at the same time and hung in the sky - they were bright enough for me to read by easily. Plymouth was bombed night after night during one dreadful period and we would stand outside in the dark and see the flash of explosions, the glow of fires and hear the crump of exploding bombs across the south Devon night sky.

Some of the masters at school were over age for call up but the younger ones were not and disappeared to the war. The maths master was replaced by his wife who had been a teacher. She was a comely young woman who was always ready to explain a problem. She would come to one's desk and lean over to see what the problem was and it wasn't long before we noticed that we could get a good view of her cleavage when she did this. The school groundsman was called up and another boy and myself were press-ganged into marking out the rugby pitches till an over age replacement could be engaged. Some of the older school leavers went straight from school into the services or became 'Bevin Boys', doing their war service down the coal mines. It wasn't long before a boy who had joined the RAF was killed, soon to be followed by others and new names were carved into the oak panelling in the Chapel. The newspapers told of a shipload of children going to Canada to escape the rigours of the war, who were drowned when their ship was torpedoed and we became inured to the fact of sudden and unexpected death.

A month or two before my 18th birthday I registered with my age group for call up into one of the services and was exempted because I was to study medicine at Oxford. I had already passed the necessary three subjects in the Natural Science Preliminary examination, spending three days in Oxford doing so. These were heady days for a schoolboy and to mark my maturity I started smoking a pipe. I bought an ounce of Gold Flake tobacco and must have used several boxes of matches trying to keep the pipe alight, ending up with a very sore tongue.

I still had to pass in Latin at the required standard. Subject to this, I had been accepted by St Edmund Hall, failing which I would be called up into the army. Canon Day, the headmaster had been a classical scholar and took me in hand with an hour of coaching every evening and he almost despaired of my learning when to use the subjunctive. The right hand page of my exercise book was for my work and the left was reserved for his comments and, in exasperation, he drew a tombstone on the left hand page and wrote on it my initials GMB and below them RIP. Beneath the gravestone he inscribed 'Always / remember / that ut / is followed / by the / subjunctive' saying it, and stabbing the paper with his pen, in the rhythm of a hexameter.

This diagram and the rhythm of the hexameter did the trick. I passed at the required standard and the vital document certifying this modest achievement, on which the rest of my life hinged read thus:

UNIVERSITY OF OXFORD

I CERTIFY that it appears by the Register of Examinations that

Gareth de Bohun Mitford-Barberton

whose name was entered by the authorities of

St. Edmund Hall

satisfied the Masters of the Schools in Latin only at Responsions, in Hilary Term, 1943, having previously produced a Certificate exempting him from the remaining three subjects.

UNIVERSITY REGISTRY *S. Caldwell*

OXFORD *Assistant Registrar*

Nearly fifty years later I related this train of events to a consultant friend and colleague at the hospital lunch table. He had never studied Latin at school but resolved to impress his son, a classics scholar, with this choice bit of knowledge. I met him again at the lunch table a day or two later, deflated. His son had replied "but do you know the exceptions to the rule"?

At the end of the summer term in 1943 I left Stamford School and entered St Edmund Hall at Oxford. Entry to Oxford I found bewildering and exhilarating, with regulations to be complied with; tutors, dons, lecturers, laboratories, clubs and libraries to be identified; and social and sporting activities to be fitted into the work schedule which often took me well into the night after the evening meal. Admission to the College and to the University were by two different ceremonies. The College ceremony consisted of signing the register after reciting the Latin oath which had been used for centuries, but which sadly has not been used since 1970:

> "Ego in aulam sancti Edmundi admissus do fidem quod statuta et consuitudines aulae, quaternus me concernunt, observabo: ita me deus adiuvat, tactis his sacrosanctis evangeliis".

The Matriculation ceremony for admission to the University was conducted, again in Latin, in full academic dress, before the Vice Chancellor and as there were many of us we were admitted in batches. Full academic dress consisted of dark suit, white shirt, white bow tie, black shoes, gown (a commoner's gown in my case) and mortar board. The Vice Chancellor was also in academic dress but the effect was somewhat marred by his wearing bright blue socks.

My matriculation certificate of entry to the University was again in Latin and read as follows, the hand written entries being shown in italic:

OXONIAE, TERMINO *Mich.* A.D 1943
Die *XV* Mensis *Oct.*
Quo die comparuit coram me
Gareth de Bohun Mitford-Barberton
ex *Aulâ Sancti Edmundi*
et admonitus est de observandis Statutis hujus Universitatis, et in Matriculam Universitatis relatus est.
W. D. Ross
Vice-Cancellarius.

I had been warned beforehand that I would be inundated with invitations to join this club, that society and that I should hold my hand and be selective, which I was. I did join the St Edmund Hall Boat Club because from an early age I had been led to take an interest in the outcome of the Oxford - Cambridge boat race. I had never rowed (except a dinghy) before but they took me in hand, licked me into shape and turned me into a passable oarsman except for my only being ten and a half stone in weight. The Hall boat in which I rowed went head of the river in Torpid races, following which I became Secretary, and later Captain of the Boat Club. By good fortune I had a few outings in the University boat trials but was not up to the required standard. The feel of a boat propelled by eight oarsmen in perfect unison is poetry in motion and the memory is still vivid many years later, as is the total exhaustion at the end of a hard race.

Money was tight, very tight but I was fortunate to get

a Kenya Government Bursary for £50 a year. I calculated that I would need £225 a year to manage, including £25 a year for personal spending on clothes, cigarettes and beer. Fortunately St Edmund Hall was one of the least expensive colleges, there were many other undergraduates in the same position as myself - there was at that time no such thing as a University grant. I was told that I would need a dinner jacket at Oxford which presented a problem so I scoured the second hand advertisements in the local paper and saw one advertised. I went along on my bicycle to the address given with £4 in my pocket and the lady who opened the door to me burst into tears and said "He was just your build." She sold me a dinner jacket suit, waistcoat with mother of pearl buttons, starched shirt with gold studs, a starched collar and a black bow tie for £3. It had belonged to her husband who had died not long before and it served me well for years until I gave up smoking and gained weight. It languished in my wardrobe for a few years until I passed it on to a young friend who was going up to Oxford: I sold it to him for the same price as I had paid for it, imposing the condition that he continued the tradition on the same terms to the next generation, imposing the same condition yet again.

Whatever the thrill of getting to Oxford it was soon dispelled by hard work. I had absolutely no conception of just how much work was required of me and my first two or three terms were spent in scraping through the necessary exams, with my tutors and lecturers reminding me that I would rapidly be out and into the army if I did not come up to scratch. Indeed I had a very narrow shave. I had left Oxford, passed my medical for the army and was about to report to barracks in Northampton for training when I was recalled by telegram to continue my studies. On review of my work the authorities had decided that I would after all make the grade. I had gone round my mother's friends saying goodbye and had received various going away presents, some money, a chamois leather money belt to keep it in and a pocket New Testament in which the donor had written 'Be thou a good soldier of Christ'. I then had to go round again and explain that I was returning to Oxford and offering to return the presents. I was told to keep them with the exception of the money belt which was reclaimed by its donor.

Entry to Oxford was restricted during the war. Some undergraduates like myself were there because their training was thought to be more important than entering one of the armed services. Others who were destined for call up but who had earned entry, were admitted for a year before going off to join the war and were offered re-entry on conclusion of hostilities; towards the end of my time in Oxford many men in this category were starting to return to the university. They were more mature and less restrained by discipline than school entry undergraduates and they added greatly to the life of the university. Others who were unfit for military service obtained entry without restriction and three of my close friends at Oxford fell into this category.

Duncan Amos Watson (known always as Tubby) was blind and was a man of huge character and I was not surprised to learn that he had risen to be Chairman of the Royal National Institute for the Blind and had been knighted. We all smoked cigarettes and would offer our pack around those present, often sitting round the Hall well in the centre of the quadrangle with our feet resting on the protective wrought iron grill. When Tubby did so we would sometimes take three or four cigarettes each so that when he came to take his own from the packet there would only be one left. His response to this would be to leap on the nearest person and envelop them in a bear like grip which he maintained until the person could barely breathe and begged for mercy. In one respect he had the advantage over the rest of us and that was mounting the staircase to our rooms in College at night. Due to the blackout there was no lighting and we with sight would feel and fumble our way up the stairs while Tubby ran up just as he did in daylight. Tubby used to employ readers to read to him from the many legal tomes he had to study but one of us would sometimes be press-ganged to do this of an evening. He had a prodigious memory and would direct me to "a big book on the top shelf by so-and-so. On page number xxx you will find a paragraph starting thus ... begin there". He had a tandem bicycle and would find volunteers to ride and steer and take him hither and thither. He came to my wedding in 1946. The only surviving wedding present (a silver toast rack) still in existence sixty years later was from him.

Francis Morley had lost an arm in a childhood accident, he was half French and was a full blooded Francophile. If he felt it necessary to defend himself he would shake his good fist under the nose of his opponent then swing his empty jacket sleeve against his face, all in good fun of course. When in 1945 I became engaged Francis put on a mournful face and went to his room and returned wearing his black tie. He was a very passable tennis player and would weave his way one handed on his bicycle to the tennis courts through the traffic (not much of it at the time) clutching his racquet under the stump of his missing arm, a bag of balls hooked onto the handlebar, his bicycle basket full of books and papers. When serving he would hold the racquet and ball in his one hand, throw the ball into the air and then strike it with great effect.

Eric Williams, a live-wire slim Welshman from Liverpool had overcome serious illness and surgery and invested the whole College with laughter. Francis, Eric and I shared lodgings down the Iffley Road and later on Eric and I shared rooms in St Edmund Hall above the Principal's lodgings. The disadvantage of living over the Principal was offset by the fact that the rooms in question were the best in the College. We and others spent many late nights up there drinking tea, making toast and putting the world to rights. I etched my name on a window pane with a quartz crystal and the Head Porter (who had been a young 'scout' in my day) recognised me and reminded me of this when I visited the College some thirty years later. My father had gravitated to England during his war service and used to send me his free issue of cigarettes and when I was in training for some rowing race I would pass these on to Eric. He and I attended each others twenty first birthday parties, his in Liverpool and mine in Dartmouth. The war in Europe was over by the time of his twenty first birthday and he had obtained by some means some Champagne on which was printed in French and German *'Reserved for the Wehrmacht'.*

The Principal was A B Emden, known as the Abe, a man of great learning who wrote several books about the Hall. He was greatly respected and feared and if one's work was not up to the required standard he would leave one in no doubt as to his opinion about this. The Rev John N D Kelly was the Vice Principal, a man of erudition, charm and authority. His outstanding ability took him to the Vice Chancellorship of the University but his term of office was cruelly curtailed by illness. He once detected me climbing into Hall after hours and invited me to join him for sherry during which the anticipated admonition did not materialise. When he became an octogenarian he was entertained at a special ceremony at the Hall by many generations of graduates. The VP as we affectionately called him is commemorated as a gargoyle (bearing a squash racquet) at St Peter's in the East, which disused church he acquired from the Church Commissioners for conversion to the Hall library. Other Dons in my day were Ramsay, Fletcher, Brewis and Irvine and we used all their names to the tune of Frère Jaques on convivial occasions in the Junior Common Room:

A B Emden, A B Emden
Kelly too, Kelly too
Ramsay, Fletcher, Irvine
Ramsay, Fletcher, Irvine
And old Brew, and old Brew.

After my first year of study of the preliminary sciences I started on Anatomy and Physiology of the human body. The Anatomy Department dissecting room had about half a dozen metal tables, each bearing a human body preserved in formalin, each body in various stages of dissection by half a dozen students. The smell of formalin was deeply ingrained in the room. Working on the arm one afternoon I fell in love in an instant with a bell like peal of laughter from a young woman student working away at a table behind me. She was of surpassing beauty but I was too shy to approach her. Dissection of the body was carried out under the eye of a number of Anatomy Demonstrators under the direction of Professor Le Gros Clarke. The most feared of these was Alice Carlton, a lady known to, and feared by, generations of medical students. We dissected the body in sections, an arm, a leg, the head and neck, the brain and central nervous system, the thorax and the abdomen. I wrote to my father that I had 'started on the thorax now that the arms are off'. Each Friday we were grilled by one of the Demonstrators on the week's dissection to make sure we had learned every detail and as the day approached my anxiety level would increase in case it befell that Alice was to conduct my Anatomy 'viva voce' that week. She always had a blue rinse hair-do on Fridays and would arrive in none too good a humour; yet we were drawn to her like moths to a candle, for if you satisfied Alice it was a great accolade, you really knew your stuff. If you did not satisfy her probing questions you had to face her again on the Tuesday following, a fate to be avoided if at all possible. We also studied Physiology, analysing our own body fluids to learn their constituents. Urine presented no problem, but to test our stomach contents we had to swallow long rubber tubes and aspirate the contents. We took blood samples from each other for analysis, hurting each other in the process because of our inexperience. At that time it was thought safe to use the same needle time and again, boiling it between each use.

Oxford has always been a centre of excellence in all academic disciplines; in my day research on Penicillin and Ergometrine made these drugs available to the world and were of incalculable benefit to people I treated in the rest of my professional life. When I left Oxford for the hospital part of my training I went to St Mary's in Paddington where Penicillin had been discovered by Professor Alexander Fleming who was later knighted for this great achievement. A mobile exhibition in a converted bus used to travel round the country collecting funds for *'St Mary's Hospital, the hospital that gave you Penicillin'* which was emblazoned on the side. It was, however, Drs Florey and Chain, researchers at Oxford, who identified the chemical structure of Penicillin which led to its manufacture, firstly for war casualties and later for the whole world. Ergometrine has saved countless lives of women in childbirth by preventing haemorrhage after the birth of the baby. It was extracted from ergot, a poisonous fungus which grew on rye: indeed unscrupulous bakers had in the past caused the death of many people by using contaminated flour which caused gangrene by constricting the blood vessels. Midwives and doctors had for long made a weak non-poisonous extract of ergot for use in childbirth. Research in Oxford found that the constituents of Ergot were Ergotoxin (which caused gangrene), Ergotamine (later used for treating migraine) and Ergometrine which acted on the uterus only and was much more effective and less toxic than the crude extract of Ergot. Now almost every woman in the civilised world receives an injection of Ergometrine immediately following the birth of the baby to reduce the risk of haemorrhage.

Those of us who were fit and who were at Oxford because we were exempted from war service had to undergo some part time military training. This included a visit to a training camp near Aldershot where we spent a week being licked into dubious shape and were harangued by a Sergeant Major of fierce disposition. The V1 'doodle-bug' was being targeted on London and the home counties at this time and we were all familiar with the distinctive sound of its engine which cut out a minute before it hit the ground and exploded. If the engine did not cut out it went on its way and you knew you were safe. While I was at this camp we heard a doodle-bug engine cut out as it approached and we all hit the deck without delay, myself faster than the person who landed on top of me. The sharp edge of his tin hat hit me on the back of the head and knocked me out. When I came to I was much relieved to find that it had not been the doodle-bug which had done the damage. At the end of the camp we dispersed, myself back to Oxford and I agreed to take someone else's kit-bag with me as he was going home. When I got to Oxford station I found the last bus had gone and I had a long walk to my lodgings the far side of the town, the walk being redeemed by a couple of girls who gave me a wolf whistle. I reached my digs tired, sweaty, dirty and hungry, cast the two kit-bags into the corner of my room and threw myself on to my bed - and the ceiling fell in covering me and my room in plaster and dust. As I had not been expected my landlady had no food for me and the bath water was cold.

The war was now going in our favour and we knew that the invasion of Europe was imminent. The suspense of waiting for D-day (the invasion of Europe) was at last ended and we followed the news day by day as our forces regained the low countries and France and then crossed the Rhine. The Pathé News reels at the cinemas gave us graphic pictures of the progress of the war. Winston Churchill crossed the Rhine into Germany with unconcealed glee with his homburg, dark coat, cigar and walking stick and the news reels showed him being cheered by the soldiers. He wore a broad grin, gave the familiar V sign and waved his homburg high above his head on the end of his stick. And in May 1945 came V-E day, the end of the war in Europe, with the surrender of the German forces. Oxford, in common with the rest of the country went wild and the happy celebrations lasted three days. I ran out of money after two or three drinks so couldn't get drunk but that didn't stop us from disorderly behaviour. I stole a lump of sodium to drop down the covered well in the St Edmund Hall quadrangle and the resultant explosion created little stir because it was muffled by the depth of the well. I laid several reels of magnesium tape in the gutter of a crowded High Street using a pebble to join the end of one reel to the beginning of the next and ignited one end. There was a spectacular brilliant flash which travelled up the street at speed and the crowds fell apart on either side but fortunately no one was hurt by this foolhardy prank. I was briefly arrested and released without charge by a good natured policeman. Every church bell pealed wildly, bonfires were lit, there was singing and dancing in the streets, pubs and clubs, no one attended lectures, tutorials or prepared essays while the pent up emotions of the years of war were released in a glorious binge of unrestrained happiness and celebration, all stained with sadness at the great human cost. Beer was in short supply and the pubs ran dry but we did not need alcohol to fuel our joy. When we had had our fill of this we returned to work. The war in the far east had yet to be finished and it was with great foreboding that we imagined the cost of this in human suffering, not knowing how its duration was to be shortened by the atomic bomb.

The summer of 1945 in Oxford was a time of intense happiness. The European war was over, I had survived some close shaves with the examiners and my presence as a medical student now seemed secure. My father whom I had not seen since 1939 had managed to obtain a transfer to England after service in the army in Abyssinia, Italian Somaliland and Palestine, so the whole family was able to get together again. They all came to see me in Oxford during 'Eights Week'; I had booked rooms for them at the King's Arms for sixteen shillings and sixpence [eighty two and a half pence in decimal money] each a day, meals included, hoping that it was not too expensive for them. I was captain of boats and enjoyed rowing hugely but we did not cover ourselves in glory. Later in the year my father was demobilised and was sent back to Kenya so the family was fragmented again but we were well used to this. Food was still rationed and he started sending us food parcels, once with dire results - a bottle of honey became broken and ruined the other contents.

While Oxford now has nearly as many women undergraduates as men, it was predominantly a male preserve in my time. Sexual continence seemed to be observed by the majority of my circle of friends but one summer's day heavy rain, after a long dry spell, deposited a collection of old french letters at the bottom of a down pipe in the college quadrangle. We concluded that the undergraduate who occupied the room on the top floor had been disposing of them in the gutter above his bedroom window. My time in Oxford was before 'the pill', before termination of pregnancy was lawful or safe and before the discovery of antibiotics revolutionised the treatment of venereal diseases of which we had a great fear. I once saw adjacent posters which read:

VENEREAL DISEASE IS DANGEROUS	GET IT AT THE CO-OP

Pregnancy for a woman undergraduate was unthinkable because it would have been the end of her university education and marriage prospects. The public lavatories all carried notices about the dangers of venereal disease and told the address of the nearest VD clinic. So I was celibate, which was not all that difficult with relatively few women around, with good male companions, plenty of essays to write, text books to study, lectures and tutorials to attend and violent sport for sublimation. Maybe I was naive, but I never aware that I knew a single homosexual while at Oxford or for that matter at school before that.

There were four womens' colleges and I took pains to get to know some of their inmates, one of whom, Pat Thorpe was to play a central part in my life. She had earned her place at St Hilda's with an open scholarship to read modern history and it is likely that she would have achieved a first class degree but for my intervention in her life. She died from cancer one afternoon as the clock struck four after we had been married for forty three years, having three children and seven grandchildren. She had a fine brain, unshakeable principles and a fearless temperament and spent her life helping and stimulating others. She earned our daily bread when we married while I was still a medical student, she managed on my pitiful remuneration when I was an impoverished young doctor, she encouraged and stimulated me while I was working for higher qualifications, she did more than her share of bringing up the family because of the nature of my work. She had a ready wit, an articulate and sometimes sharp tongue, didn't suffer fools at all let alone gladly. She exasperated me, goaded me, loved and cared for me. I now recognise how I took her for granted and was insensitive to her needs. I now pay tribute to her beyond her grave; I am now enjoying the fruits of the life she helped me make. She told me when she knew she was dying that I should find someone else to share my life with but I could not at the time conceive of the possibility. But as usual she was right.

After three years my time at Oxford came to an end when I satisfied the examiners and became a Batchelor of Arts in Human Anatomy and Phsiology and I prepared for entry to one of the London medical schools. St Mary's Hospital Medical School had a great reputation for rugby and it was believed that good rugby playing medical students could be sure of entry. This wasn't my game so at my interview I made much of my rowing. I then rowed for the hospital on the tideway for the next couple of years until the pressure of work made it impossible for me to continue. I was one of twenty five medical students accepted at St Mary's in the summer of 1946 and the fees were fifty guineas a year. The teaching staff and honorary consultants there licked me into sufficient shape to satisfy the Oxford examiners three years later and I have been grateful to them ever since. I found lodgings in the Harrow Road, Wembley at a cost of £2 per week, breakfast and an evening meal and all weekend meals included. Pat, now my fiancée, had a one room flat in Richmond and we managed to meet once or twice a week. I thought I had worked hard at Oxford, but it was but an introduction to what was expected of me at my teaching hospital and this in turn was but a gentle precursor of the demands to be made on me as a doctor. At an early stage it was made plain that the job took precedence over the family at all times, evenings, nights, weekends, bank holidays, birthdays, anniversaries, Christmas and even holidays on occasions. Up to now I had usually been able to predict when I would get home, but not any more.

It used to be said that young doctors married nurses or barmaids because those were all that they met in their day to day life but I didn't run true to form, marrying in December 1946 while I was still a medical student. It had been our intention to wait till I was qualified before we married but Pat's parents had decided to emigrate to South Africa and mine were returning to Kenya. At that time it was not done for a young couple to set up home together outside the bonds of matrimony, so we married when I had started the clinical part of my training at St Mary's. My mother disapproved for a number of reasons including 'that it will be in Huddersfield - such a dreadful place' and that the marriage would be in 'a Methodist Church'. Pat was working at the Colonial Office in Whitehall at this time and we set up home in furnished accommodation in Teddington and later in Kingston on Thames, and we travelled daily into central London on the Southern Railway. Commuter travel is bad enough now but I think it must have been worse then: I wrote to my mother that the trains were like cattle trucks and that London businessmen carried umbrellas to prevent women, even if pregnant, from getting a seat. I also mentioned that I was glad to be seeing ill people at last, instead of dissecting corpses.

Money was tight and food rationing was still in force. Pat earned £350 a year and my father continued my allowance of £85 a quarter until I qualified. This was sent from the Standard Bank of South Africa in Kenya to their branch in Northumberland Avenue. Transfer was by air mail which meant that I spent many anxious days waiting for the next instalment to arrive. I estimated my annual expenses as £330.10s, made up as follows: food and travel £150, half share of rent £48, gas bill £20, pocket money £60, fees £52.10s. It soon became clear that this was below the mark but we managed. It wasn't possible to spend much on food because of rationing and meals out ('British Restaurants' excepted) were out of the question. The weekly rations per person at the time were: potatoes 3lb, tea 2oz, sugar 8oz, bacon 1oz, butter 1oz, margarine 6oz, milk 2½ pints, meat 1s worth. Other items such as tinned meat and jam were on 'points' and one had twenty-eight points a month. Fish was plentiful, un-rationed and cheap and my mother (before she had returned to Kenya) wrote to my father that she had bought four herring in Redruth at 1d each. My rail season ticket once expired a few days before my allowance was due and I went to see my Bank Manager at the Trafalgar Square branch of Barclays Bank DC&O (Dominion, Colonial & Overseas) as it then was, to ask for a £5 overdraft which was peremptorily refused. I was dreadfully hurt at the time but I have kept my account with Barclays to this day, enjoying considerable overdrafts with them in later years.

'British Restaurants' had been established by the Womens' Voluntary Service (it did not bear the prefix 'Royal' then) to provide cheap meals during the war and Pat and I had many a lunch or supper in these establishments. You could get a meal for 1s, a typical menu being beef stew with lumpy mashed potatoes with the eyes still in and over-boiled cabbage followed by spotted dick and a cup of tea. The premises were insalubrious with peeling paint and smelled of steam, sweat, cigarettes and stale cabbage; the tables were sometimes wiped with a damp cloth and hard chairs discouraged one from lingering any longer than was necessary to consume the needed calories. The food was slapped by staff onto greasy plates on greasy trays. Maybe there were some wholesome establishments but I did not have the good fortune to find one. They nevertheless were a necessary institution and a hungry young man could stoke away some much needed calories without infringing his budget or ration coupons.

Unaware of the dangers at the time we indulged in one luxury, cigarettes,sharing a packet of ten Woodbines a day. I suffered great anguish the day Pat took what she thought to be the last cigarette from the flimsy paper pack which she then threw into the fire with one remaining cigarette contained therein. I never let her forget it and used to chide her gently about this all her days. The Chancellor of the Exchequer did impoverished students an unwitting favour when he put the price of cigarettes up to 1s 8d for a packet of twenty which made exactly 1d a cigarette. This meant that I need no longer lay out the cost of a whole packet as I could buy a single cigarette at a time in the medical school canteen. I think that the Chancellor must have suffered a loss of revenue for it was but a short while till the price was raised to 1s10d which made us revert to buying whole packets.

My father had been demobilised and had returned to Kenya and my mother rejoined him there. Before she could travel she had to receive a Yellow Fever inoculation for which she had to visit a centre in Redruth and she told me that it was given by a Dr Rivers who was in his dressing gown in a bath chair, having suffered a stroke. Soon after this my parents-in-law emigrated to South Africa by air. We saw them off from Croydon aerodrome on a bleak winter's morn, watching them walk across the grass runway and clamber up a step ladder into a piston engined aeroplane, taking an elderly parent with them. Their journey took several days, stopping off at hotels *en route* each night. Very strict currency controls were in operation at the time (and for years to come) and there was consternation when the said elderly parent took a wad of £1000 worth of notes from his back pocket on reaching their destination. However he was beyond British jurisdiction by then and suffered no retribution.

Pat and I were the only married couple in our immediate circle of friends and used to invite them to come and eat with us in our furnished bed-sitting room with microscopic kitchen attached. We both worked five and a half or six days a week so our entertaining was often on a Sunday, for a late breakfast or lunch. Two or three persons would arrive, bringing with them something with which to supplement the meal and protect our rations; perhaps an egg, a sausage or a slice of bacon, a couple of potatoes, a slice or two of bread and some jam, some fruit, a little flour and sugar, all pre-arranged according to the plan for the day's menu. The meal would be simple, no alcohol (no money) but seemed like a feast because of good company and happy conversation. And in the winter each would bring a couple of lumps of coal to add to the fire. A year or two later after I had qualified I stole a suitcase full of coal from the hospital where I was working, to help with airing the nappies of our firstborn. I lugged it all the way from Edgware into central London and out again on the Southern Railway to Kingston on Thames, only to find that it would not burn on an open fire because it was anthracite.

We medical students were farmed out round the hospital departments, medicine, surgery, pathology, bacteriology, obstetrics, venereal disease and so forth, for several weeks at a time. We 'clerked' the patients, writing the examination notes, operation notes, test results and had to produce this record for signature and approval to one of the medical school lecturers. In order to become really familiar with all aspects of the examination of a patient we had to conduct a complete examination on every patient even if it was not relevant in a particular case. For example someone with heart disease was not exempted from a rectal examination and we would not have our record accepted if it was not complete in all respects. In this way we learned what was normal as well as what was not normal and we learned how to ask personal and intimate questions of people old enough to be our parents and grandparents and how to examine them without infringing their dignity. We attended lectures every day, observed operations and were expected to attend many post mortem examinations so as to become familiar with the internal appearance of disease. I recall Professor Newcombe showing us again and again how the lymph glands in the chest were swollen and blackened by the tar from cigarettes - and yet the students' common room was thick with smoke. It was not till another twenty years had elapsed that most doctors had learned the danger of cigarettes and had given up. The VD clinics were a powerful reminder of the dangers of indiscriminate sexual activity – and not only because of the diseases but also of the treatment thereof which was unpleasant prior to the discovery of antibiotics. The lecturer in venereal diseases told me to search for a body louse in one man and I plucked a pubic hair with louse attached. Much was my discomfort when, under the microscope, it turned out to be a knot in the hair.

Every few months there was an exam to be passed. Only two of us from St Mary's Medical School, Geoffrey Rose and myself, were taking the Oxford degree BM BCh; the rest were doing the London degree MB BS or the London Conjoint qualification MRCS LRCP. Because of the differing regulations Geoffrey (who had been my best man and whose best man I was to be) and I found ourselves doing finals (for which the entry fee was £20) three months ahead of our contemporaries and we returned to Oxford for this purpose, myself 'in an awful sweat' as I recorded at the time. The names of those who had passed the final examnations had been hand-written on a sheet of paper which a porter pinned to a notice board with a scrummage of about twenty five of us from various hospitals jostling to see if our names appeared on the list. Mine was by far the longest name and from the back of the scrum I could see it clearly. I hurried out of the building to tell Pat (now pregnant with our first) who was waiting anxiously outside and we hurried from there to the post office to send telegrams with the news to our parents in Kenya and in South Africa.

From first making the decision to study medicine while I was at school to achieving my ambition had taken eight years of toil, expense, struggle, the greater part of the second world war and at the end, triumph. We returned to London and celebrated with a cup of tea, a cigarette and an early night.

Now it was time for me to go out and get a job and I had to have a suit in which to be interviewed. I went to the "Fifty Shilling Tailors" (later Montagu Burtons) and bought a blue suit for £5, (a hundred shillings) which lasted me for many years.

Soon thereafter I received the treasured document, signed and bearing the seal of the University.

UNIVERSITY OF OXFORD

This is to certify that it appears by the Register of the Ancient House of Congregation of Doctors and Regent Masters of the University of Oxford that

Gareth deBohun Mitford-Barberton
St Edmund Hall

after having satisfied all the conditions prescribed in that respect by the Statutes of the University, was on the sixteenth *day of* July 1949 *admitted to the Degrees of*

BACHELOR OF MEDICINE and
BACHELOR OF SURGERY

as witness my hand this eighteenth *day of* July 1949.
C H Paterson Assistant Registrar

On 20th July 1949 I went to 44 Hallam Street to the General Medical Council and registered my qualification for a fee of £5 and was given Certificate number 79712 to prove it at an additional cost of 1/- and went to work as a doctor. This registration fee of £5.00 was supposed to be once and for all but an annual fee of £2 was introduced in 1970 and I was allocated a new registration number, 0549545. Annual charges were increased to £5 in 1972, £8 in 1976 and £30 in 1988. When I reached 65 years of age and retired I was exempted from further fees, my name remaining on the register till death, unless struck off.

With my brand new Certificate of Registration in my pocket I scanned the job pages in The Lancet and telephoned the Medical Superintendent at Edgware General hospital who needed a locum casualty house surgeon and was taken on at twelve guineas a week with two guineas deducted for board. This was a premium rate as it was a locum appointment. I was helping to set a broken arm in the afternoon on 23rd August 1949 when a phone call came through from Kingston hospital to say that our daughter Helen had been born and I was given the afternoon off to go and see mother and babe.

Next was a six month appointment as house surgeon in general surgery at Edgware and this was followed by six months as house physician in Redhill County hospital in Surrey. That appointment ended on a Saturday but my replacement did not start until the Monday morning. One girl of about twelve years was terribly ill with serious complications and could not possibly be left without resident medical cover so I did not get home till mid-day on the Monday. Nobody thought to offer to pay me for the two extra days work and I dared not ask.

The working conditions and pay of recently qualified

doctors are criticised now as unreasonable and it was just the same then. In many teaching hospitals young doctors often worked for nothing in their first job, receiving a grace and favour honorarium of perhaps £50 at the end of six months when he (there were few women) went on to another post. In 1949 the Spens Committee looked into the conditions of employment of young doctors who were compulsorily resident in their hospital appointments and recommended £350 a year for house surgeons with £100 deducted for compulsory board. I also had to maintain a flat for Pat and Helen out of this so we were not exactly flush with money. I was on duty day and night, apart from one half day a week and alternate weekends and loved every minute of it. An occasional indulgence came our way when I received a cremation fee, or 'ash cash' as we called it. In this manner I picked up £2 per cremation and we would spend this on a visit to the launderette (we had no washing machine) and a visit to the cinema (1/- each in the cheapest seats) followed by fried egg, chips, baked beans and a pot of tea in the cinema café. Another occasional source of cash was half a guinea (10s 6d) for giving evidence at an inquest. An elderly lady was found dead with her head on a cushion in the gas oven in a house near the hospital and, being the nearest doctor I was called to see her. I certified her dead, checked her temperature which enabled me to calculate how long she had been dead and was dismayed to receive only 10s after I had given evidence in court. I remonstrated with the Clerk to the Court who assured me that it was customary for him to retain the missing 6d. There was no money available for living it up but I continued with my interest in rowing for a couple of years. We saw Oxford win the first post-war boat race against Cambridge, I rowed for St Mary's hospital and at the first post-war Henley regatta for the 'Oxford Triads', a boat raised by three Oxford colleges which could not afford to send individual boats. We achieved no distinction.

It had always been my intention to return to work in East Africa where I had been born and bred and Pat embraced this idea with enthusiasm. So I applied for an interview at the Colonial Office with a view to joining the Colonial Medical Service and was accepted on the condition that I undertook a course of study leading to the Diploma in Tropical Medicine and Hygiene, which I did in London, on half my colonial service pay. As a house surgeon my monthly take home pay had been about £20 a month in my first post and £25 in my second. On half colonial service pay I had to go to the Crown Agents for the Colonies in Millbank to collect my money and was paid £36 a month in lovely crinkly fivers. The first time I received this princely sum, when I got home I passed it through the banisters to Pat who was half way up the stairs. She gave a whoop of delight when she unfolded it and saw what it was and it didn't take her long to think of a use for it.

My father had never met his daughter-in-law and granddaughter so he paid us a visit while I was studying for the DTM&H. He was a colonial born and bred and totally self sufficient and reliant in the wild territories of South and East Africa in which he had been brought up. With a map, the sun and the stars he could find his way across a barren landscape; with a gun, a sheath knife and a box of matches he could feed himself indefinitely. When he arrived Pat met him off a coach in Trafalgar Square and took him underground to the tube station, to the Bakerloo line to make for Waterloo station and was speechless (rare for her) when he took a compas from his pocket to check which line was southbound.

Chapter 6

1951 Kampala and Mengo District, Uganda

Uganda has been rightly described as the pearl of Africa and first caught public interest in England on the publication of Speke's Journal in 1863, being his account of the discovery of the source of the river Nile as it flowed from the mighty lake named after Queen Victoria. Uganda lies astride the equator, much of it three to four thousand feet above sea level, humid and sultry with abundant rainfall. Only a small part of it is mountainous and only the north-eastern district of Karamoja is in any way arid. On the whole it is intensely fertile. Winston Churchill saw the great potential of the country and remarked what fun it would be for the Nile to start its immemorial journey to the sea by plunging through a turbine. This event took place while I was in Uganda - the actual source of the Nile becoming submerged beneath the Owen Falls Dam which was built to harness the power of the outflow of water through turbines to generate electricity for Uganda and for export to Kenya.

Gaining the Diploma in Tropical Medicine & Hygiene was most necessary as medical students were taught almost nothing about tropical diseases when studying at the London medical schools. The DTM & H stood me in good stead for the next eleven years in Uganda until Prime Minister Harold

Macmillan's 'wind of change' speech resulted in my returning to England. This coincided with a career change to Obstetrics and Gynaecology, in which I became an NHS consultant after completing the necessary training which I had been able to start in Uganda. To the end of my professional career I displayed DTM & H among my other qualifications with pride, and I heard of no other UK Consultant Gynaecologist with a qualification in tropical medicine. We were a motley collection of mixed nationalities at the School of Tropical Medicine in 1950, many from India and the British Colonies in Africa. We all struggled with the unfamiliar names of tropical parasites and the insects which transmitted them. Many of the names were of Latin derivation which caused me fewer problems than the doctors of other nationalities as I had studied Latin for ten years at school.

While I completed the DTM & H, Pat took Helen by sea to visit her parents in South Africa; I had to borrow money from my father for their fares. On completion of my course I went by sea through the Suez canal to Mombasa on the coast of Kenya, arriving on 18 May 1951. Ocean liners of the Union Castle line used to sail regularly from England to the Cape of Good Hope round the east or the west coasts of Africa and provided the regular means of visiting relatives in the colonies and in England; no one went by air at that time. My fare was paid by the Uganda Government and I allowed myself £10 for spending on the journey - barely enough but that was all I had available. The Uganda Government Agent met the ship at Mombasa and advanced me a month's salary: the painful reckoning came when it was deducted in three instalments from my next three pay cheques. I went from Mombasa to Nairobi by overnight train where I met up with Pat and Helen again, spending a few days with my cousin Elaine and her husband until the next passenger train went to Kitale a few days later. I was then on familiar territory, having travelled that route to and from the Prince of Wales School thirteen years previously. We slept one night on the journey and in the morning I watched with mounting excitement for the first sight of the extinct volcanic shape of Mount Elgon where I had spent my childhood. My parents met us at Kitale railway station and I spent a week's holiday with them before reporting for work in Kampala.

On 5 June 1951 I started work in Kampala as Medical Officer in Mengo District of Buganda Province of Uganda Protectorate. Uganda was not and never had been a British colony - it was a Protectorate under the mandate of the League of Nations. There were three other Provinces, Northern, Eastern and Western and each Province was divided into three to five administrative Districts. I worked on Mengo district under supervision of Dr Ronald Ladkin for a few months until I was posted to Karamoja District in the Northern Province. Ronald Ladkin had a great influence on those around him and was destined for high office till cruelly slain by an overwhelming attack of poliomyelitis four years later.

"You must have a car" he said, so I asked a friend for a few tips on driving (having no licence and there being no driving schools) and took a test at the police station a few days later. I stalled the engine driving up the incline from the Police Station onto the main road but as I didn't slip backwards and had to have a licence anyway I passed. Impecunious Government officers could borrow the purchase price of a car from the government and repay it by monthly deductions from salary over three years. So I borrowed Shs 17,300 (£865, but the shilling was the unit of currency) which happened to be exactly the amount of my first year's salary, for a pale green Citroen light 15. It had polished chrome headlamps bolted onto the top of the mudguards and the spare wheel was bolted onto the boot at the back. I've had many cars since then but none could match that Citroen for beauty or the thrill of ownership and I would go out last thing at night with a torch to run my hands over its gleaming flanks. The monthly repayment deductions started straight away, together with the repayments for the advance of salary already taken and I was repaying Shs 2,700 borrowed from my father so my early months in Uganda were fraught with penury. It was many years before I saw any silver lining to the clouds. European cars built for European roads took a hammering on the dirt roads of Uganda and seldom lasted well. When my Citroen had done its useful service I sold it to a parish chief in Acholi district who ran it into the ground after a few more years. My last sight of it was as a rusting hulk without wheels, with weeds growing through the floor and chickens roosting on the remains of the upholstery.

To begin with I was accommodated in a government hostel in Kampala, which was known as Belsen because of the quality of the cuisine. Pat and Helen remained with my parents on the farm at Kitale in Kenya till a house became available. I went to fetch them after about a month, when I was provided with a furnished government house (the rent being ten percent of salary) in Elgon Drive on Kololo hill in Kampala. It was a new house with a stony patch for a garden and the first thing we did was to plant a lawn, after I had cleared the surface of stones, one the size of a coffin. I was advised to light a large fire over it and then to douse the fire with buckets of water, thus fragmenting the stone into manageable pieces. I obtained a sack of Paspalum grass seedlings from the Agricultural department which we planted at intervals of a few inches. I was posted to Karamoja before I saw the resultant lawn but did so later when the house was occupied by someone else and it was a resplendent green. I hired two servants, one for the house and one for the garden, the latter named Barnabas. The going rate for wages at the time was about Shs 50 a month, with accommodation and basic rations provided. While in Kampala there were some riots for a reason which I cannot now recall and Barnabas (whose day off was Thursday) asked if he might have Tuesday instead so that he could join in the riot. I said that I would really prefer it if he stuck to Thursday. He was disgruntled then but was even more so on Thursday by which time the riot had died down.

There were almost no General Medical Practitioners in Uganda at the time. The Uganda Medical Department ran a hospital, sometimes two or three in each district, with a British qualified doctor from the Colonial Medical Service in charge, usually assisted by one or two British qualified Nursing Sisters. Kampala had a large hospital named after Mulago hill, upon which it stood, staffed by British specialists and by Makerere University professors and lecturers. Mulago hospital served as the teaching hospital for the Medical School of Makerere University which stood on another hill nearby. Doctors trained in Uganda were excellent and their qualifications soon became recognised by the General Medical Council in the UK. In addition, there were a small number of hospitals run by the churches - the Church Missionary Society from England and the Verona Fathers from Italy - and these, together with Mulago Hospital, trained Ugandan nurses and midwives. These same Missions (and others) provided many of the schools throughout Uganda which were staffed by European missionary teachers and it was the children they educated who went on to train for work in the hospitals, schools, police and so forth. I soon found that I could discern the religion of a young Ugandan from their style of handwriting. Those educated at Roman Catholic schools run by the Italian Verona Fathers, wrote with a fine italic script, while those educated at Protestant schools run by English CMS teachers had a rounded upright hand. Once I had advertised for a clerk/typist - there was no such thing as a proper shorthand typist - and received an application copied verbatim from one of those books which tell you how to write a formal letter. He had copied exactly:

> 'I refer to your advertisement of *(insert date)* in the *(Times / Daily Telegraph / Daily Sketch)* newspaper for a shorthand typist and beg to apply for the same. My speed is *(insert number)* words per minute. Mr *(a well known person in this town)* has agreed to provide me with a reference ....'

He had good Roman Catholic handwriting, could spell well and type slowly but had no shorthand. He was the best applicant and got the job.

The distances between towns with a hospital were great so the Medical Department had set up small "dispensaries" in the intervening parishes. These were in the charge of Medical Assistants who had been trained to a point part way between a nurse and a doctor. They were skilled in the diagnosis and treatment of common tropical diseases, malaria, hookworm, tapeworm, bronchitis and simple injuries and would send more seriously ill people to the nearest hospital. Some dispensaries had a few beds but the majority treated out-patients only and they kept a stock of the commonly used medicines and dressings provided from the nearest hospital. The stock of medicine bottles at one dispensary were most beautifully labelled with delicate painted lettering instead of the scruffy, stained labels which had been applied at the hospital pharmacy. I asked who the calligrapher was and learned that it was the illiterate dispensary porter who had painstakingly copied the printing, which he was unable to read, from the disfigured label.

The only medical record kept at the dispensaries was in a hard backed foolscap book with a one line entry per attending patient which recorded a serial number, name, diagnosis and treatment. The patient was given an MF5 (Medical Form 5) recording the details and was asked to bring this on any subsequent visit. I was amazed at how carefully some of these were preserved, admittedly often damaged by termites, by people with the minimum of facilities for doing so. The Medical Assistant would produce a monthly return of the number of patients and conditions treated, these were collated into a District Return (by someone like myself) to the Provincial Medical Officer and by him to the Director of Medical Services in Entebbe. No doubt they eventually ended up in the statistics of the Secretary of State for the Colonies in Whitehall. The dispensaries were regularly visited by doctors like myself for special clinics but I would always call in unannounced when passing in case any help was needed with a particularly ill patient. On one occasion I found the person in charge had taken unauthorised leave and had written up the attendance register in advance for the days he expected to be away.

Venereal Disease was common and widespread and I used to do regular VD clinics at various dispensaries; I used to see seventy to a hundred new cases of syphilis and gonorrhoea a month - AIDS was not known then. At that time it was not known whether Penicillin would be effective against syphilis and treatment was with a rather toxic arsenical preparation named Neohalarsine, necessitating two injections a week for ten weeks. The syphilitic lesions on the genital organs would often disappear after four or five injections and it was uncommon for people to complete the course to achieve what we hoped would be a full cure. To begin with I made an attempt to trace contacts for treatment as I had been taught when a medical student but this proved to be a hopeless task - one man told me he had a different partner most days. Once as I was driving towards a dispensary for my regular VD clinic, I passed a couple of constables chasing a man running as fast as he could manage. Soon after I had started the clinic there was a commotion in the waiting room and when I popped my head round the door to investigate, there was the fugitive (who had by now been arrested) and the constables, the fugitive claiming in all innocence that all he wanted to do was to attend the clinic to which he had been hurrying. That being the case, said one of the constables they also wished to attend the clinic. So I ended up seeing all three together, a constable on either side of the fugitive, each dropping his trousers and each confirmed as having syphilis and one of them gonorrhoea into the bargain. Gonorrhoea was at that time highly sensitive to treatment with a single injection of penicillin and a quip then in vogue was that it took less time to cure than to catch.

Another of my duties was to visit the prisons in the district. There were two sorts of prisons, one under the jurisdiction of the central government for offences against the criminal law and the other under the control of the parish chiefs for civil offences such as adultery, failure to pay the bride price or non payment of poll tax which was, at the time Shs 5 a year. One such prison had four separate communal mud, wattle and thatch cells, one labelled 'Tax avoiders', another 'Adulterers', a third 'Women' and the fourth 'Lepers'. A visitor from England who was with me at the time thought that leprosy was being treated as a civil offence but I explained that this was so that prisoners with leprosy could be isolated. The Medical Assistant from the nearest dispensary used to visit daily for the sick parade; my visits were less frequent and were to see anyone who was more seriously ill, to check that the dietary and occupancy regulations were being observed and to hear appeals against fitness for hard labour. One prisoner (No: 51/51 Adaku son of Adabor) had chronic bronchitis and heart failure and had been passed fit for hard labour on the prison farm by the visiting Medical assistant. He clearly was not fit for hard labour so I countermanded the decision and he died not long after. I later identified an outbreak of Vitamin A deficiency in Luzira prison because the dietary requirements were not being observed; altogether I found 165 cases, one of whom actually lost his sight due to the condition. The outbreak gradually waned with the addition of red palm oil (rich in Vitamin A) to the prison diet. There was a small sick bay in the prison, used if possible rather than sending prisoners to hospital. The medical assistants were not very popular in the eyes of the prison authorities as they were always complaining about the prison diet, the sanitary arrangements, overcrowding in the cells and, particularly, as some had been found to be trafficking in illegal substances for the prisoners. The prison service in Uganda at the time left a great deal to be desired and an enquiry into the running of the main central government prison at Luzira revealed a disturbing state of affairs.

It was at this time that I first encountered a strike by hospital porters - later to become all too commonplace in the NHS in England. The function of a porter in a Uganda hospital was very different from that of a hospital porter in Britain: they gathered firewood for the kitchen stoves, kept the fires going for cooking and for hot water, emptied the latrine buckets, washed up the pots and pans, disposed of the refuse, filled and trimmed the wicks of the oil lamps and so forth. The railway line nearby was being extended and, to complete the project, wages somewhat higher than the going rate had to be paid to the railway workers, which meant that the hospital porters wanted the same remuneration. One thing was certain, the dispensaries and hospitals could not function without porters so we called in the Labour Commissioner from Kampala who recommended an increase of Shs 4 or 5 per month and this satisfied the strikers. There was no money available to increase the allocation for porters wages, so the increase had to be met by a reduction of the workforce.

Malaria was endemic throughout Uganda and was a major cause of ill health in the African population with a high mortality rate, especially in babies and children. The majority who recovered from repeated attacks of malaria gradually developed some resistance to the disease so that the attacks became milder with the passage of years. Government officers from England had no such resistance and became very ill if they contracted the disease; they were therefore required to take prophylactic tablets and to sleep under a mosquito net unless their house windows were adequately screened. Myself, Pat and each of our children took a drug called Paludrine for malarial prophylaxis every day from the time of our arrival in Uganda in 1951 till we left in 1962 and not one of us ever had a single attack of malaria. The babies had a quarter tablet a day from birth which we crushed into powder and put into a fold of paper. As they opened their mouths to clamp onto the nipple for a feed, the bitter powder was poured onto their tongues but the sweetish mother's milk soon dispersed the evil taste. Our middle child Philip seemed to develop a taste for it and used to chew his daily tablet while the rest of us shuddered. The prevalent variety of malaria was called Malignant Tertian, caused by a parasite named Plasmodium Falciparum, which was transmitted by the Anopheles mosquito: one of the first things I learned at the London School of Tropical Medicine and Hygiene was how to recognise this mosquito and identify the malarial parasite in a droplet of blood taken from a finger-prick. Locally trained African Laboratory Assistants were highly skilled at recognising the various malarial parasites. In the towns the Health Inspectors in the Medical Department used to take a pride in trying to eliminate all pools of stagnant water in which the Anopheles mosquito could breed so Kampala town was more or less free of malaria bearing mosquitoes most of the time.

The staple diet of the Africans in this part of Uganda was a variety of an unsweet banana called Matoke which was peeled like a potato and cooked by steaming or boiling and eaten with tasty sauces. It was delicious and provided sufficient calories but was deficient in protein. Meat was expensive and in short supply. The result of this was protein malnutrition starting in childhood, the condition being known as Kwashiorkor. The affected children developed brown hair and skin (not a healthy shiny black) and a distended abdomen; they failed to grow and many died young from a combination of this, hookworm and malaria. Groundnuts were a cheap source of vegetable protein which helped redress the balance and someone developed groundnut biscuits which were provided for schoolchildren for their lunch.

The Muganda people who lived in Buganda province of Uganda and who spoke Luganda, were the most advanced and civilised people in central Africa at that time. The men were friendly, cultured, of good stature and very few carried any excess weight. Their traditional style of dress comprised long white robes, now mostly replaced by shirts and trousers. The women were statuesque, exquisitely graceful, walking in measured pace and manner, often balancing some load - maybe only a single bottle - on their heads and often bearing a baby on their backs. Their clothing was more often traditional, long colourful cotton robes from neck to toe; on ceremonial occasions 'bark' cloth was used. Most of the trade lay in the hands of the Asian community and they helped greatly in the development of the country. But things had to change so that the local people became involved in the trading pattern of the country and the government set about trying to remedy this throughout Uganda. Two long term friends, Peter McLean and Harold Barker (I was godfather to one each of their offspring) were closely involved in this project but not sufficiently so to satisfy Field Marshall Idi Amin Dada, self-styled President for Life who eventually expelled the whole Asian population from Uganda.

My duties as a Medical Officer in Mengo district of Buganda province were not at all what I had been expecting - they were mainly organisational. Venereal Disease clinics apart, I treated no ill or injured people but was part of a team that provided the arrangements whereby the ill were treated at a few small hospitals in the charge of African doctors and at dispensaries managed by medical assistants. This meant a fair amount of travel by car, mainly day trips on dirt roads, sometimes with overnight stops in government rest camps. There were tarmac roads in the town of Kampala, from Kampala to the administrative capital Entebbe and from Kampala to Jinja, where the Owen Falls dam was being constructed. Because of the proximity of lake Victoria, some of the journeys were on causeways through papyrus swampland - I had to stop for a puncture in one swamp and was promptly bitten by a swarm of tiny flies aptly named Simulium damnosum. I made Pat close the car windows hurriedly, despite the sweltering heat, to protect her and Helen while I changed the wheel. This particular fly transmits a disease Onchocerciasis - river blindness - which was widespread in these swampy areas. Later on I was peripherally involved with the Government Entymologist in an attempt to eradicate this fly from another area: he threw a perforated hose across the Nile as it flowed into a swampy area and dribbled DDT into the river for several days, with immediate effect but to no lasting benefit.

The tarmac road from Kampala to Jinja was a miracle of engineering, having been cut for fifty miles through the tropical Mabira forest by an Italian company named Stirling Astaldi. Like the Roman roads in Britain it was almost dead straight and one could average sixty miles per hour through it. The Mabira forest was rich in tropical hardwood trees, notably mvuli, which was used for good quality furniture. Sadly too much of the valuable timber has now been felled. This forest later gained a sinister reputation as the place where Idi Amin's henchmen cast many of the bodies of their victims to be consumed by wild animals so that the evidence was destroyed - such was believed to be the fate of Mrs Dora Bloch who was killed at the time of the successful Israeli raid to rescue Idi Amin's hostages at Entebbe airport.

Jinja was close enough for us to visit at weekends where we had a friend who was working on the construction of the Owen Falls hydro-electric dam. We would go for lunch and would then go for a walk on the Jinja golf course alongside the river Nile after it had issued from the great Lake Victoria. The Nile was replete with hippo and these often wandered out of the river onto the banks, leaving large deep muddy footprints which served as pitfalls for the golfers. A local rule permitted a player to lift his ball from a hippo footprint and drop it onto flat ground over his shoulder without penalty. During convivial dark evenings at the golf club-house people would shine powerful torches to search for hippo which were identified by their reflective eyes. Emboldened by alcohol one member won a bet by sticking a postage stamp to the rump of a stationary hippo while it was dazzled by a powerful torch beam.

There was a small European hospital in Entebbe where most of the senior Colonial Service Officers worked; I was sent to do a short stint of duty there while the doctor in charge was ill and I was provided with a very superior house well above my station. Entebbe is on the lakeside with abundant rainfall, hot and humid with sparkling cool early mornings, the flowers profuse, colourful and heavily scented, the vegetation an intense tropical green, dripping with heavy morning dew and the bird chorus deafening - no need of an alarm clock there. One such bird was given its common name from its call - "quick-doctor-quick, quick-doctor-quick". I was soon reminded of the danger of malaria - a family returned from leave in England with their new born baby who was bitten by a mosquito on the first night in their hotel room; the baby was buried, with a favourite toy, a few days later.

There was a simple outdoor swimming pool in Entebbe which we often used for a day out with a picnic lunch. The two boys, Philip and Brian, were not yet born but we often used the pool on visits in later years. Brian, our youngest was laying down his views waving his sandwich in the air when a hawk swooped and snatched it from him. There was another more grandiose swimming pool at the Silver Springs hotel in Kampala, which had a high diving board and the two boys would jump off this with great nonchalance while adults, myself included, were too hesitant to do so. Another favourite outing was to Port Bell on lake Victoria where Bell beer was brewed and where the flying boats from England landed on their journey to South Africa. Passengers would stop overnight in an hotel, the whole journey from England to the Cape taking several days. We used to entertain each other in our homes and play the card game Canasta which was then in vogue. There was also the Kampala Club (then for Europeans only) but I couldn't afford to join that, nor could we afford other than the occasional bottle of beer - either Tusker or Bell.

There was a most colourful market in Kampala where we bought our vegetables and salad. To begin with Pat went with one of the servants till she learned enough of the language to get by on her own. Other household provisions were bought weekly at a store whose courteous Goan proprietor, Mr Pinto, had managed to corner much of the European trade. He would meet his customers at the doorway, escort them to a side room with a comfortable easy chair, offer coffee, gin and tonic or whatever took their fancy and would take their order in elegant handwriting with an indelible pencil in a duplicate book - there was no need of a shopping list before arrival for he thought of everything. The order was assembled by a young Goan relative and, when complete, was carried to your car by an African employee. No such vulgarity as payment was discussed - it was assumed that you wanted an account and this was submitted monthly together with the copies from the order book to verify the amount. Our early months were fraught with financial anxiety. When we went through the accounts at the end of the month we could not see how we would survive to the next, so we bought ourselves a bottle of Cointreau for consolation. Once a week we might have a tiny portion, other days we might remove the cork and inhale the aroma. Imagine then our total dismay when we found the bottle which we knew to be three-quarters full to be three-quarters empty. I thought Pat had drunk it, she thought I had drunk it and then we both realised that the servant had drunk it. After this experience my father told me how to mark the contents of a bottle. It was no good marking the level as it stood on the table, for the culprit would simply top up the depleted contents to the mark with water. The trick was to turn the bottle upside down and then mark the level which seemed to the culprit to bear no relevance to the contents.

While in Kampala we made a few trips to visit my parents in Kitale, it was the better part of a day's journey. On one such trip I ran over and killed an antelope - I did not want bloodstains in the car and my father was disappointed when I told him I had left it on the roadside. On another visit the rains had begun and the road was a quagmire in parts, quite impassable to a modern saloon car. We became hopelessly stuck and had to be shoved through the mud by a group of Africans who were making a useful addition to their usual remuneration. They wanted Shs 10 to push me through when one of them (whose syphilis I had treated) recognised me and persuaded them to do it for nothing for the 'Bwana Daktari'. There happened to be a sale on in Kitale before I returned and I bid for a second hand pair of car tire chains. When I came to pay I found that not only had I bought some chains but also a pile of gramophone records and a number of books in the same lot. So I had to buy a gramophone as well, a second hand wind-up HMV in a fine oak case. At that time and on those roads one was lucky to get more than ten thousand miles out of a set of tires and I couldn't afford a new set. A Danish neighbour of my father's named Wilhelm Heilbuth recognised my plight and called at dawn the next day leaving a set of used but not worn out tires for me. These did me for a few more thousand miles and I had retreads applied to my old ones.

I had learned to speak Swahili as a child and it rapidly came back to me after a few weeks in Kampala. There are numerous tribal languages in Uganda but Swahili was widely spoken and would get one round most of the Protectorate. Some years previously there had been some riots and the Governor realised that almost none of the British administrative officers could speak a word of any of the tribal languages, which was a great disadvantage when trying to understand the details which had led to the disturbance. As a consequence of this, a salary incremental barrier was applied beyond which one could not progress without having passed an examination in a local language at the required standard. So I started lessons in Luganda, the local language, whereupon I was posted (in February 1952) to Karamoja District in the Northern Province of Uganda where not a word of Luganda was spoken. I knew little or nothing about Karamoja (which was one of the most primitive parts of the world) until enlightened by my father who regarded the posting as the greatest good fortune a young man could hope for. I did not own a gun and for my birthday he gave me a .22 rifle which was successfully used to supplement our supply of meat. From the butcher it was beef and nothing but beef. We frequently had chicken but, with the rifle, I was able to vary our diet with guinea fowl and antelope.

Thomas Barber about 1810

Henry Mitford Barber 1899

Mary Layard Barber and son 1904

Raymond Barberton 1915

Wagon Transport - British East Africa 1917

Peggy Barberton 1928

Ivan Barberton and Spirit of the Wave 1955

Tarsectomy Patients - Gulu 1956

Chapter 7

1952 - Karamoja District, Uganda

The Karamoja District was either one of the most exciting places in the world in which to work or the worst if one had a different viewpoint. It was a 'closed district' which travellers were not permitted to enter without prior authorisation by the District Commissioner. Pat and I were thrilled to grasp the opportunity of living in this wild, barren, seemingly inhospitable, even hostile, land. Some found the going too much to cope with, too hot, too dry, too windy and too lonely and had to be posted elsewhere to preserve their sanity. The district was about a hundred miles from north to south and eighty miles from east to west, bordering on Kenya to the east and the Sudan to the north. It lay a little north of the equator, a hot, semi-desert area which turned green and burst into flower when the low annual rains came.

The 1948 census gave the population as 125,000 but as no reliable records of births or deaths were kept this figure can only have been approximate. The Karamojong people were polygamous semi-nomadic cattle owning people, the men tall and lean, often naked save for a short light cotton cloak worn across the shoulder, each and every one of them a fearless warrior, each carrying a long spear; to carry two was prohibited by law because it denoted men going to war. Each wore a finger knife - an iron ring worn on the middle finger with a curved blade on the dorsal surface which was sharpened for cutting meat and skinning animals. They shaved their scalps, saving the hair until sufficient had been collected to be pricked together like felt to fashion an elongated 'beehive' hair style, which was then decorated with coloured clays, brick red, azure and white, with different patterns for young men of differing age groups and this was worn on ceremonial occasions. The beehive was quite dense and ostrich feathers were pushed into it for decoration. Those who had killed a man dipped a feather in the victim's blood and wore it with distinction. These head-dresses took a long time to perfect and were tended carefully so the Karamojong carried a small wooden two legged stool to support the neck when sleeping in order to protect the hair-do; by day the stool served as a seat. Many wore a spent .303 brass cartridge case containing snuff suspended from a leather thong around their necks. The men and boys went off with the cattle to distant dry weather grazing grounds for several months of the year when the nearby grazing was exhausted.

The women wore skins and stayed at their homesteads with the little children, the chickens and goats and tilled, planted and harvested the limited crops of millet and vegetables. Some of the women were of surpassing beauty after the style of the Egyptian Queen Nefertiti and they anointed their skin with animal fat so that it glistened in the tropical sunlight. They wore animal skin clothing, their breasts exposed till marriage. The hems of their skirts were weighted with small pieces of lead so as make them swing seductively as they walked and I recall with delight the embarrassed laughter of a group of pubescent girls I came upon twitching their hips and swinging their skirts. Their homesteads, called manyattas, consisted of thorn enclosures (into which the cattle and goats were herded at night) containing several small round thatched huts for the adults and children. There was a single narrow entrance which was barricaded at night with more thorn branches, making a sound defensive enclosure against lions, leopards, hyenas and cattle rustling marauders.

Their diet consisted of the limited crops which could be grown, blood mixed with milk and meat derived from hunting or from the occasional ox which had been slaughtered for a ceremonial occasion. A man's wealth was measured by the number of his stock so they did not avoidably slaughter an animal. Blood and milk were particularly important to the men and youths when they went off to the dry weather grazing grounds away from their manyattas. An ox would be selected and its head held low by the horn and a thong would be placed round the neck, just tightly enough to make a large neck vein stand out. A young man would crouch about two feet away and take careful aim and shoot with a miniature bow and arrow, a small slip of wood being bound round both sides of the blade of the arrow so as to leave only a quarter of an inch exposed at the tip. This prevented the arrow from penetrating any deeper than the vein itself. The blood would flow out in a gentle arc into a hand-held gourd made from the skin of a dried marrow, perhaps two or three pints being collected. The thong would then be released and the young lad would walk the ox around for some minutes with the head held high by the horn until the small cut in the vein had sealed itself with a clot. Meanwhile another would swiftly rotate a 'swizzle stick' under the surface of the blood, to and fro between the palms of his hands so as to gather the fibrinous clot. When complete, the stick and fibrin would be thrown to a dog. The remaining blood would then be taken to a cow which would be milked into the gourd raising a bloody froth as it squirted in. This delicacy was then passed around those present, each drinking from the gourd and then wiping the bloody froth from the corners of the mouth with his arm after passing the gourd to the next.

The main rains fell in March and April each year and the main crop Mtama (millet) was planted at this time. There was a second short spell of rain in June and July with a secondary planting of crops and vegetables. These would last through to the end of the year but there were three months before the next crop, during which maize-meal had to be imported from Kenya. The heavy rain fell on parched earth - baked hard by the relentless sun of months - and the consequence was flash flooding as the rain poured across the surface of the earth into the river courses. I was camping by a dry river bed once when the rains began and I heard a rumbling rushing noise getting louder and nearer - the approach of fast flowing water. The first thing to appear was a couple of feet or so of dirty brown froth with sticks and so forth running down the watercourse at the speed of a fast walk. Then followed the water, soon to be three feet deep and flowing fast, often washing the road culverts away if the volume was too great. As the rivers were dry for three-quarters of the year there were very few bridges - you could drive across the river bed, even in up to two feet of water, in the hospital's Fordson truck. I got badly stuck once and it took forty men four and a half hours to manhandle the truck across sixty yards of wet sandy river bed, coupled with great anxiety on my part in case more rain came down again with a fresh flash flood. The rains used to fail from time to time and did so in 1952; Karamoja became completely dry with no grass, with most natural sources of water dried up, the cattle thin and in poor condition and the Karamojong in trouble all round their borders for infringing other tribal territories. The classical Karamojong diet of blood and milk had to be partaken of more frequently when other sources of food were in short supply. Double the usual number of cattle were sold so as to raise funds for the purchase of maize-meal, the price of which went up and up. In January 1953 the cost of two hundred pounds was Shs 43, in July Shs 59 and in November Shs 62 and the daily cost of feeding a patient in the hospital rose from fifty-four cents to eighty cents over the same period.

The capital of Karamoja was Moroto where the small new hospital under my charge had been built. There were a few small Indian dukas where you could buy the necessities of life. Indians had contributed greatly to the development of the whole of East Africa as traders who opened shops in the most remote parts of the hinterland. A typical Indian duka in Moroto had a wooden frame with corrugated iron walls and roof, a front shaded veranda, a single front room with a counter and shelves groaning with goods, a second room which was a store and maybe another couple of rooms which provided accommodation for the shopkeeper and his family. On the veranda there was usually an African tailor (always a man) with a rickety treadle Singer sewing machine running up khaki shorts and 'Americani' shirts for sale to the locals. Americani was a cheap cotton fabric which had been heavily dressed during manufacture to give the fabric weight and this imparted a characteristic sweetish smell. The new rolls of Americani often served as a mattress for the night-watchman. On sale within were local foodstuffs, posho (maize meal), dried beans and pulses, vegetables and fruit when available, tinned meat and fruit, condensed milk, bottled soft drinks and, of course, beer but no spirits unless the shopkeeper had a licence. There was no electricity so paraffin, hurricane lamps, Primus pressure stoves, torches and batteries were on sale. Also cheap clothing and fabrics, needles and thread, blankets, pots, pans and cheap proprietary medicines. One such was labelled *Hair and Brain Tonic* which was purple in colour and was sold in old gin bottles and smelled of methylated spirits and coconut oil. Also, hammers, screwdrivers, saws, nails and screws were usually to be found. When European Government officials and their families came on to the scene other necessities such as Tampax, Durex and Kodak film, razor blades (Gillette for the Europeans and Jumbo triple tested brand for the African market) were added to the stock. I had a monthly account and objected on one occasion when I discovered that an invoice had been raised for every single day of the month (including Sundays and a few days that I had been out of the area) for purchases I had not made.

The European population of Moroto, indeed of the whole district, consisted of nine British Colonial Service Officers: a District Commissioner, an assistant District Commissioner, a District Medical Officer (myself), a Veterinary Officer, a Police Officer, an Agricultural Officer, a Tsetse Control Officer, a Borehole Maintenance Officer and a Public Works Department Officer. I was the only married one, with two little children. Once there was a doctor in the district more wives and children appeared on the scene; prior to that Moroto had been a mainly bachelor station. There were no restaurants, no hotels, no pubs or bars and we made our own entertainment visiting and feeding each other. Pat was a good cook which meant that we frequently entertained visitors and our house was a refuge for lonely and hungry bachelors. One evening at about 6 pm a couple arrived and we opened a couple of bottles of beer, always keen to entertain visitors. After half an hour or so I had a return of memory – we had invited them to dinner and had forgotten about it. I took myself off into the kitchen, wrote Pat a note to that effect, came back to rejoin the visitors and told Pat that the cook wanted to see her. She was able to carry off the occasion without the truth emerging, but we did confess at a later date.

Some of the Indian dukas had licences to sell beer and spirits and we used to get through a case of sixteen bottles of Tusker beer a week. We hardly touched spirits and wine hadn't been heard of in Karamoja. The local water supply was not treated in any way and was therefore not safe for drinking so we used to boil three or four pints every day for the next day's consumption. We kept it in the refrigerator in the Gordon's gin bottles which fitted neatly into the door shelves. The refrigerators ran on kerosene because we had no electricity. There were no bar licences in the town but it was common knowledge that some of the bachelors would drive to the dukas after their evening meal where they would be plied with whisky in a back room.

All up-country stations in Uganda had a club for the government officers which were the scene of many convivial occasions whenever we could think of a reason - but not Moroto. So one evening, when the subject came up over a beer or two, we elected a chairman and treasurer and decided to build one ourselves. A whip around raised the necessary sum which had been 'guestimated' at about £100. The administration found a plot which was not allocated for any other purpose so we did not have to pay for the land on which it was built. The public works department found some damaged spare bricks which were going free and we bought some more, some cement, sand and timber. Somebody roughed out some plans on the back of a Clipper cigarette packet, we didn't need planning permission. The rest was up to ourselves: at the end of each day's work there were about two hours of daylight during which we would all gather at the site and do whatever was necessary under the guidance of our PWD officer. We demurred at putting on the corrugated iron roof ourselves and contracted with an Asian fundi to do so and in a couple of months the Moroto Club was up and running.

The only permanent stream in the district flowed through Moroto, all the other rivers dried up in the dry season and water only flowed in them briefly during the rainy season. Water could usually be reached by digging in the dry river beds and there were a few permanent, muddy and contaminated water-holes, so the supply of water for the local population and their cattle and goats was parlous. Accordingly, the government embarked on an aggressive programme of drilling bore-holes which gave a plentiful supply of clean but untreated water. The contract for this was awarded to Craelius, a Swedish Company, who employed a handful of bachelor Swedes throughout the district. It was hot, dirty and lonely work with no European contact but the pay was good. A hundred and forty four bore-holes had been drilled already and a further eight were drilled during my first year in the district There was a natural pool in the Moroto river which we enlarged to make a swimming pool, again untreated. Cattle drank from the river upstream and there were leeches in the pool, one of which once attached itself to my body. To pull a leach off was painful so the approved method was to touch its tail with a lighted cigarette whereupon it would release itself. I cannot remember anyone coming to any harm from swimming in what must have been pretty un-hygienic water. The path to the pool was fringed by dense bush on either side and we kept a sharp eye out for snakes as many poisonous varieties flourished in the district: the herpetologist from the Coryndon Museum in Nairobi came to stay and replenished his collection of deadly snakes. I once ran over a python so long that its head and tail were in the bush either side of the road and the wheels went bump-bump over its body. It was night time so I did not stop to kill it and collect the skin, which would have made a nice handbag.

Our house was a spacious bungalow with a corrugated iron roof which made a deafening noise when heavy rain fell. There was a wide veranda down one side to protect the rooms from the direct sun but it was hot, hot, hot nevertheless. In the dry season a hot dry dusty wind blew relentlessly, blowing the curtains out horizontally and slamming any open doors and loosening the plaster around the architraves. Precious rainwater was collected off the roof into a hundred gallon water tank but we also had a forty gallon petrol drum (filled from the bore-hole supply) mounted over a brick fireplace outside which would be lit for our daily baths. Water from this tank was piped into the bathroom and kitchen. We were allocated one cubic yard of firewood a day - delivered by prisoners - to heat the water and for the wood stove. We had a small vegetable patch which was irrigated with all the waste water from the kitchen and bathroom. I planted a grapefruit tree, sinking into the ground next to it an empty four gallon paraffin tin, with perforations in the base and the side adjacent to the roots and I filled this with water every day: none of this was lost by evaporation and the tree flourished. When the leaves went yellowish the agricultural officer told me to add nitrogen to the water by peeing into the tin daily. We had no water closet, the toilet consisted of a bucket under a wooden seat with a trap-door to the exterior. This was emptied daily by prisoners who would shout a warning before raising the trapdoor to remove and replace the bucket. I had always gone to work by the time this happened but Pat once suffered embarrassing consequences. A couple of years later we moved into a new house with the untold luxury of proper water borne sanitation. We took our faithful servant Yokana Koki to inspect the house before we moved in and he became quite dizzy descending the stairs, the first he had seen.

The mail came up from Kampala by bus once a week, a day of great excitement. My relations were only a hundred and thirty miles away in Kenya but the rest of the Europeans came from the UK and awaited the weekly letter from loved ones with bated breath. We all belonged by common agreement to different book clubs and most weeks one or another of us would receive the monthly book which would be read avidly and lent out to the others. Also came the voluminous official mail, directives, circulars, regulations and so forth. We would congregate at about 4.30pm and wait for the bus, crowding our way into the post office while the Postmaster sorted the mail into respective post boxes, grabbing personal mail and books as they were sorted. "But Dr Barberton it is not permitted to enter the post office while I am sorting the mail and you cannot take your letters before I have finished" remonstrated the Indian Postmaster. But he always got even by bringing his wife or sick child to see me just as I was on my way home at the end of the day - "but Dr Barberton I knew you were too busy to see me in the morning".

Karamoja, with its huge herds of cattle and goats, needed a Veterinary Officer to advise on cattle diseases - notably Rinderpest - and to organise the necessary inoculation programmes. The vet also used to inspect the meat killed for human consumption in Moroto and one of my reports recorded that forty eight percent of carcasses were infected with tapeworm cysticerci, so beef was never eaten rare, nor was any condemned because of tapeworm. The local butcher was a handsome lean Somali with eyelids and face wrinkled by tropical sunlight. His shop consisted of four stout poles with a flat sloping thatched roof without walls. There was no water and no counter, only a scale, a wooden box for the money and a block of wood (part of a tree trunk) for cutting up the meat. An ox was walked to the shop daily and ritually slaughtered by cutting its throat, it was skinned and dismembered, offal on the ground in one corner, the head in another and so forth, all under a cloud of flies. No matter which part of the beast, the price was one shilling per lb. Pat taught the butcher how to cut certain joints and how to save the fillet for her. It was tough and stringy unless carefully marinated, it couldn't be hung because of the hot climate. The butcher had been to see me with some malady and had a high opinion of my diagnostic skills. After that he always saved a whole fillet for us twice a week and fillet steak was a regular feature of my breakfasts at that time.

The hospital was brand new and I was appointed to commission it. The previous hospital comprised three dilapidated buildings of mud and wattle with thatched roofs. The new one had six small single storey buildings constructed of brick with corrugated iron roofs, and had proper windows, running water and proper water closets but no electricity or telephone. There was a ward for men and another for women, an office and a store block, an out-patient building, an operating theatre, a kitchen and a mortuary. It was a while before the boundary fence was completed and what a great boon when it was - goats had wandered around the compound and into the wards till then, chickens however remained a problem. The staff consisted of myself, Dr John Lubega who had been trained at the Medical School in Kampala, a male nursing orderly with one year's training, a trained laboratory assistant, a trained pharmacy assistant, a clerk and thirty five others who were untrained and unskilled - ward assistants, cooks, porters, sweepers and such like. The OC Police virtually closed the hospital down once when he conducted a waragi raid. Waragi was a spirit distilled illegally from pombe (beer) and he suspected correctly that this was taking place in the hospital staff quarters and arrested the key members on whom I depended.

The hospital compound, perhaps an acre, was totally bare. I laid out a road and planted about twenty ornamental trees - Persian Lilac and Tamarind, the seedlings of which were given to me by Rev Canon Bob Clarke from the Church Missionary Society mission at Lotome. I often wondered how many had survived and in 1980 had the good fortune to encounter someone who had recently visited the hospital. He told me that there were a number of good sizeable shade trees in the compound for people visiting their friends and relatives in the hospital.

Scattered through the district were six Dispensaries at Abim, Kaabong, Kangole, Karita, Kotido and Nabilatuk and these consisted of a single building staffed by a nursing orderly and a porter. They received a monthly visit from myself and a monthly supply of simple drugs and dressings for the treatment of common ailments and injuries. These units fulfilled a very useful function for those who lived nearby but seriously ill or injured people had to make their own way as best they could to the hospital in Moroto - there was no ambulance service at that time. The Catholic and Protestant missions also provided dispensaries at some of the sites where they had schools - at Kotido, Lotome, Abim and Nadunget and I would include these units on my tours round the district. The Roman Catholic Father in charge would observe my approach in the hospital Fordson van and would hurry away to don his cassock, calling to one of the nuns to prepare a tray with Cinzano and glasses.

I would arrange two working safaris per month, so that every dispensary would be visited once in each month. Each safari would last several days, perhaps four to six and I would sleep either under a tent or perhaps in a government 'rest camp'. Sometimes Pat and Helen would accompany me if the trip was not to be too arduous: I was much better fed when they were with me. When the departmental ambulance (in fact a Fordson truck) had arrived I would use that for the trip, or I sometimes borrowed a Land Rover from the District Commissioner. In addition to myself there would be a driver, a medical orderly, one servant, usually someone else needing a lift, sometimes Pat, Helen and the dog. On our return there would often be an additional passenger in the shape of a sick person needing to get to the hospital. The vehicle would be loaded with some spare petrol, supplies for the dispensaries, tents, camp-beds, bedding, clothing and my rifle and ammunition. We would carry lanterns, enough food, a crate of Tusker beer and clean drinking water to last out but had to shoot enough meat for our daily needs - usually a small antelope or a guinea fowl. At least one of the African staff accompanying me would be a Mohammedan so the game I shot for our evening meal had to be slaughtered according to their ritual to render it fit for his consumption: he would leap from the vehicle, sharpened knife in hand and run full tilt into the bush where the animal was in its death throes. He would raise its head by a horn so as to expose the neck and would then neatly cut the throat to fulfil the required ritual. On one fruitless trip we had found nothing for the evening meal and I was sitting disconsolately in the front passenger seat of the truck, rifle at the ready. I spied a hapless hawk gliding in a thermal current, loaded a cartridge and took a pot shot at it from the moving truck. To my shame and amazement the bird dropped mortally wounded onto the road behind the truck - it provided a meal that night for my passengers, I made do with a tin of bully beef. Another time it was Pat who bagged a duiker for the evening meal. She took careful aim and the dying antelope was despatched by our Mohammedan servant with a swift blade to its throat. She was mortified at this, but it didn't deter her from cooking its liver for the family meal.

Darkness fell by 6.30 so we had to have established our camp before that, either in a mud and wattle thatched rest camp or a tent. A good camp fire was made to keep us warm as the evening cooled, to heat water for washing and to deter nocturnal animals; cooking was done on the fire and on primus stoves. When Pat was with me she would, when our supply was exhausted, make bread in the embers of the fire. We would retire to bed on our camp beds with mosquito nets to protect us from malarial mosquito bites and my rifle and ammunition would lie ready to hand under my bed. We would rise at dawn, make maize meal porridge and coffee, break camp and make for the next dispensary to be visited. When I got there I would find a small crowd of patients waiting to see me. I would deliver the fresh medical supplies and inspect the register of patients seen since my last visit to try and assess whether the drugs used equated more or less with the patients treated. By now the heat of the day was blistering and we would set off for the next visit and the next camp.

Hospital admissions consisted almost entirely of emergencies. Malaria, acute dysentery, pneumonia, typhoid and injuries due to fights and wild animals were the commonest reasons for admission. There were periodic outbreaks of smallpox and infrequent cases of poliomyelitis. Most surgery was for injuries such as animal bites, fights, fractures and tusk and horn penetrations. A woman arrived at the hospital with her upper arm bitten through by a hyaena (she said), the humerus was fractured at mid-shaft with jagged ends protruding and the rest of the arm hanging gangrenous from skin, muscle and sinew. I told her it would have to be amputated which she refused, swinging her rotten arm as she went.

A man limped into the hospital with a leg wound saying he had run upon his own spear by mistake while hunting. The Karamojong spear has a wooden shaft perhaps six feet long with an iron blade about eighteen inches on one end and an iron spike of similar length at the other. This spike served to balance the spear when thrown so that it travelled true and was also used to stick the spear in the ground to hold it vertical when not being carried. He had been running full tilt after an antelope, had thrown his spear, which killed the animal and, as it fell dead, he was unable to stop in time to avoid running on to the spike end which entered his thigh just above the knee and snapped off where it joined the wooden shaft. He told me that the metal spike was in his thigh, which I found difficult to believe as there was very little to see apart from a wound about half an inch long on the inner aspect of his knee. Then I felt a small hard protrusion under the skin of his buttock. There was no X-ray to confirm his story but I found it to be true: under anaesthetic I put my small finger up the knee wound and could feel the tubular end of the spike into which the wooden shaft had fitted. I could not extract it through the knee wound so made a small incision over the protrusion in the buttock and was able to pull it through this. He recovered in a few days and walked home.

Another man was brought in more dead than alive with a huge wound from an elephant's tusk through his chest, in at the front and out at the back. Being blunt-ended the tusk had pushed the heart and lung aside without penetrating them and there was remarkably little bleeding. I cleaned out sticks, leaves and grass from his chest cavity, the heart beating strongly in my direct vision, washed it out thoroughly with plenty of saline, sewed him up fore and aft, inserted drains and gave him plenty of penicillin. Pat was with me on this occasion, it was night and she was holding an electric light running from my car battery through the theatre window. The man recovered fully in a few weeks.

A woman arrived with an axe wound to her shoulder straight through the clavicle and revealing (but not cutting) the great vessels from the heart to the arm, neck and head - she too recovered.

I received visits from specialist doctors at Mulago hospital in Kampala from time to time and one of these found a man by the roadside with a spear wound through the front of his chest and out at the back through the upper left chest, bleeding profusely. The doctor happened to be Group O rhesus negative, which blood group can be administered to people of any other group. So he gave him an arm to arm transfusion of his own blood, a shot of morphia and of penicillin. At this moment a Verona Father missionary happened to arrive on the scene, stopped and took him to hospital where he recovered. This was certainly the first blood transfusion in the district.

The Karamojong were an isolated polygamous community, reputedly free of venereal disease until it was introduced by a detachment of the King's African Rifles, who had been stationed in the North of the district in order to quell some earlier tribal disturbance. This resulted in a pocket of syphilis in that particular county which I confirmed by a disease survey. This was a long way from the hospital in Moroto and many of the people affected lived beyond the road-head which meant that it would be difficult to set up VD clinics. The only hope would be to carry out a mass treatment campaign of everyone at the same time with a large single dose of long-acting Penicillin which had by now been found to be highly effective against the disease instead of a long course of arsenical injections. I spoke of this to the Governor, Sir Andrew Cohen, on one of his visits to Karamoja and for good measure, buttonholed his wife on the subject with the consequence that I was supplied with sufficient long-acting Penicillin to administer a single dose of one million units to each infected person and his wife or wives and, if necessary, their children. I worked through the District Commissioner and the county and parish chiefs, arranging first to examine the population and identify those infected, returning on a second occasion to administer the Penicillin, with a third visit six weeks or so later to assess results, all this to be done during August and September after the crops had been planted and before the departure of the men and youths to the dry weather grazing grounds. The population assembled where there was good shade from a Tamarind tree while waiting their turn for examination. My team consisted of a couple of Nursing Orderlies to translate and carry out the preliminary examination, Pat, who undertook the clerical work and myself to take blood and other unmentionable samples for laboratory examination and make the final diagnosis and prescribe treatment. I intended to give an identification card to each person treated but the chiefs dissuaded me as they had no pockets or suitable place to keep such a card, so Pat had the idea of using some serially numbered aluminium infant welfare medallions I had found in some recess of the hospital stores. The number on the medallion and name were entered in the Syphilis Ledger, a medallion (with a length of string so as to wear it round the neck till our return) was issued to each person injected and we thought we were home and dry with a foolproof system. On my return the first few had not got their medallions - it was lost, the string had been needed for some other purpose, it had been exchanged for a chicken, were among the reasons given. Then we came upon one man who had a dozen medallions glinting round his neck and it became apparent that we had provided a means of decoration which failed to achieve the purpose intended. So I was never able to produce convincing figures about the effectiveness of the campaign to eradicate the disease from this small group of people. But certainly there were whole families affected, the man, his wives (one or two) and several children, who were all treated at the same time so I am sure that we did some good. Gonorrhoea was very uncommon in rural Karamoja but there was a pocket of it in Moroto, the capital of the district, fuelled by a small group of prostitutes. I was able to identify these and to arrange periodic examination and treatment.

Undertaking disease surveys gave me an unparalleled insight into understanding their form of polygamy and assessing the outcome of childbirth. The popular view of polygamy is of a man having his cake and eating it with a multiplicity of nubile women at his beck and call but this is far from the case. A wife was very expensive and had to be paid for with stock, the bride price at the time being sixty head of cattle. A man first married when he could afford the bride price, usually in his twenties and his bride would be a teenager, marrying perhaps soon after puberty. As the wife was responsible for building the huts and planting and harvesting the crops it was often the first wife, now with several children, who told her husband that it was time for him to take another to help her with the work. Judging by the age of the first wife's children when the second wife's children came along, I concluded that the commonest interval before acquiring a new wife was eight to ten years. Women who were widowed were automatically assimilated as an additional wife by another man in the extended family, maybe the brother of the deceased husband. As these women inherited the deceased husband's cattle they were readily taken on as an additional wife, as a plurality of wives, children, cattle and other livestock added to a man's wealth and influence. Many men had only one wife, relatively few had three and I only encountered one with five. Polygamy was their form of social security. There was of course no contraception but sexual intercourse was proscribed for a woman from the conception of a child until it was mobile and this resulted in an interval of about two years between births. Twins were bad news and were killed for the supposed reason that if she had conceived a second child she must have had coitus again within the proscribed time, and if not with her husband, then with whom? Lining the children up at the time of my surveys with the tallest on the right, shortest on the left it was easy to judge their ages and I found few women with more than six or seven children, not all of them surviving. When there was a larger gap in height than usual between two children this often indicated that the intervening one had died.

There were no maternity or paediatric services in the district and I knew nature to be profligate when it came to maternal and child mortality. I never obtained figures for maternal mortality but on my disease surveys I specifically questioned groups of parents about the number of children who had been born into the family and how many of them had died. There was no reliable system of registration of births and deaths, so the information was not obtainable from any other source. From one group of parents I learned that of 771 liveborn children 35 had died under the age of one month, 169 had died between one month and two years, and 81 had died between two years and puberty. Converting these figures to mortality rates per 1000 provides the following death rates: 45 per 1000 under one month, 264 per 1000 under two years and 369 per 1000 below puberty. You may wonder how I estimated the age of the children and I have to confess that it was intelligent guesswork based on experience; the height of the child, coupled with the birth or death being linked to some other event - the year the rains failed, the year the Governor visited, when so-and-so came to be District Commissioner, the year the sun went dark in the day (an eclipse) and so forth. In the case of a dead child I would date the year of its birth as half way between the living children born on either side.

Little surgery, apart from emergencies, was carried out as the Karamojong have a healthy suspicion of operations which are not absolutely essential. It was a tribal custom to mark the skin with decorative scars, to perforate the ears for ornamentation and to perforate the lower lip in the centre for a decorative lip stud perhaps half an inch in diameter. It was this lip stud which became a disadvantage when a man wanted to move out of his tribal environment into the army, the police or into office work. Just removing the stud was not sufficient for it left a hole through which saliva dribbled. I was asked to repair a number of stud holes - simple enough, but how they bled.

The Rev Canon Bob Clarke asked me if anything could be done for an eight year old boy with one leg paralysed by poliomyelitis some years previously and the other leg broken more recently. He had fallen out of a Tamarind tree he was climbing and had fractured the midshaft of the tibia of his good leg. He lay untreated on a blanket in a corner of a hut for weeks and the fracture united at an angle of 65° backwards, behind the knee. He was now only able to move around by crawling on his hands and good knee. He was terrified when he was brought to the hospital and put into a bed - at the first opportunity he climbed out and lay comfortably and securely on his blanket on the floor. He was desperately unhappy away from his home but cheered up when Bob Clarke brought a relative to see him now and again and gave him a bag of sugar. Weeks later, after I had refractured and reset the good leg we taught him to walk with crutches - how frightened and dizzy he was. I left Karamoja before he left hospital but heard later how he was walking well and confidently using a single wooden staff in preference to a pair of crutches.

A woman reported with a huge ovarian cyst more than the size of a full term pregnancy. She recovered after surgery and when she heard that I was to visit her home area she would stand at the roadside and raise her skin skirt above her waist to reveal her long scar as I passed in my car, thus identifying herself, a huge grin illuminating her features. I would draw up to pass the time of day with her and she would have a good laugh at my Karamojong accent. The Karamojong men were always game for a good laugh as I discovered when I stood on a chair to examine the eyes of an inordinately tall man - all the waiting patients were convulsed with laughter.

We had occasional outbreaks of smallpox, one of which affected thirty one persons that I knew about but I have no doubt there were more. The locals knew the disease was serious and would isolate an infected person in a hut by themselves till the scabs had all dropped off. I was sent calf lymph for a vaccination campaign, with the fringe benefit that I was issued with a refrigerator (which ran on paraffin) in which to keep it. I vaccinated everyone in the area and also everyone leaving the district on the bi-weekly bus. The locals were very suspicious of vaccination but readily agreed when Helen came forward as the first volunteer - goodness knows how many times she was vaccinated in all, but it did her no harm as she developed no reactions being already immune from previous vaccinations required for international travel. I trained a Karamojong schoolmaster from Lotome mission how to vaccinate and he did over a thousand.

Eye disease was very common because sick children (and adults) allowed flies to crawl on their faces and in the corner of their eyes. One particular disease, Trachoma, caused by a virus, often progressed to blindness. In cattle country where flies were abundant as many as four people in ten might suffer from the disease which results in the eyelashes turning inwards, scratching the transparent cornea every time the person blinked, so that they slowly become blind. A simple operation to correct this preserved any remaining sight and cost but ten cents, equivalent to 1¼d of pre-decimal currency.

Guinea worm was an interesting oddity transmitted by an insect called Cyclops (it appeared to have one central eye) which abounded in the ataparas (dams). When swallowed, the larva would develop into a worm which grew to eight or ten inches in length, migrating round the body and eventually reaching the skin. It would emerge from the skin to release its eggs, some of which would be shed into water to gain re-entry to the alternative host Cyclops. The treatment was to wait till the worm started to emerge through the skin, then wind the free portion onto a matchstick, taking it up day by day as a little more appeared, taking care not to break it off before the whole worm had been slowly extracted. On one occasion three guinea worms started emerging from the skin of a man undergoing an operation.

Each tribe in Uganda has its own language and most also speak Swahili which is used as a lingua franca - but not the Karamojong. I was therefore at a disadvantage and had to use an interpreter. I spoke English and Swahili and the interpreter spoke Swahili and Karamojong. My salary had reached an incremental barrier beyond which it could not progress without my passing an exam in another language in addition to Swahili. The problem was that no government officers knew Karamojong so there was no one who could examine me. I persuaded the powers that be that Canon Clarke (who had compiled a Karamojong dictionary and had translated the New Testament into the language) could both teach me and examine me and they agreed to this. My hospital clerk, Alakara, also helped me with an hour a day of conversation but, not knowing any grammar, he could not readily explain how the words changed to form a plural so I needed Bob Clarke to drill some of the complexities into my confused brain. For example, many plural nouns change both the prefix and the suffix - ekapolon (chief) becomes ngikapolok (chiefs). The possessive could be a prefix, an infix or a suffix in different parts of the district. For example, take the case of 'your name'. Kon (your) and ekiro (name) may be kon-ekiro, e-kon-kiro or ekiro-kon depending on which part of the district you were in. Anyway I struggled on and gained a working knowledge of the language, satisfied my examiner and gained my salary increment. Counting in Karamojong was done to the base five which translates into English thus: one, two, three, four, five; five and one, five and two, five and three, five and four; five twice and so on. Large numbers became quite complicated - for example ninety nine when translated back into English becomes five and four times five twice with five and four. This made for difficulties when rapid counting was needed, such as when counting a pulse rate. When I had achieved a reasonable fluency I was the only government officer who understood and spoke the language, which put me in a unique position and I was once able to intervene in a trial before the High Court. The Judge and prosecutor spoke English, the first interpreter English and Swahili, the second interpreter Swahili and Karamojong and the accused spoke Karamojong only. I was the only person present who spoke all three and I interrupted the proceedings (to the Judge's initial displeasure) when I heard a particularly inaccurate translation from English to Swahili, from Swahili to Karamojong and then all the way back to English

The Government Medical Officer in each district fulfilled many functions - physician, surgeon, obstetrician, pathologist, Medical Officer of Health, Police Surgeon - you name it, I did it. I had to do it. On 26th September 1952, as the sun was setting, I was having a beer with Sandy Field (the

District Commissioner) when he received a report that ten people had been killed and two wounded in Dodoth county in a raid by Turkana tribesmen from Kenya . He asked the OC Police and me to accompany him to the scene; we left by Land Rover before dawn the next day, accompanied by a few armed Police as far as the road-head at a place called Kalapata, where the local parish chief provided us with porters to carry our food, tents, bedding and so forth. From there we walked through arid countryside, about forty five miles in four days, until we reached the scene of the killing. On the way we encountered three wounded survivors, two with spear wounds in the legs and one with a bullet wound through the flesh of both thighs. The rest of the party went ahead while I tended the wounded and followed on later. My escorting Police askari was an excellent tracker and pointed out sandal prints in the dust - 'goojer' he seemed to say, which I did not understand until a bit later he pointed again and said 'dunlop'. I then realised he was recognising the tread marks of sandals made from old motor car tyres. He next showed me lion spoor overlying the footprints of the party which had gone ahead and they were not best entertained when I told them about it on catching them up - we knew we were in wild game territory and this sharpened our vigilance. We camped each night where we were able to find water - some foul and some crystal clear. One night we stopped by a slimy green pool which we filtered through cotton wool and then boiled - it made the coffee taste terrible, ruined the whisky but was quite palatable with Eno's fruit salts. Another night we found a hole in a split in a sloping rock surface which contained lovely clear water deep in the cleft, collected from the previous season's rains. We were told that it's name when translated was 'the place where God coughed'.

The scene of the killing, Dokomoru, turned out to be in the most northern point of Karamoja, about four miles South West of the trijunctional point of Kenya, Uganda and the Sudan at the source of the Kidepo valley. At Dokomoru I examined the remains of eight humans varying from an almost complete skeleton to only a portion of a skull. The vultures and hyenas had disposed of all but the skulls and the mostly fragmented bones. Later, when I had returned to Moroto with the remains, I referred to my textbook of Forensic Medicine and was able to determine the sex and approximate age of some of the victims. I could not determine the cause of death in any single case, nor were any bullets found in or near any of the bodies but several empty cartridge cases and two misfired rounds were found in and near the manyatta of the victims. About five miles from Dokomoru I found a complete human fibula with portions of other bones and a tuft of hair plaited in the manner common to Karamojong women. I was later able to estimate that the fibula had come from a person about five feet tall and a wounded young girl had in fact died here. From the assembled remnants I was able to estimate that the total casualty roll was nine dead and the three wounded previously treated. Some weeks later, nineteen Turkana tribesmen were arrested, charged and held on remand in Moroto prison, pending their trial before the High Court when it visited the district seven months later. When arrested they were found to have a motley collection of antiquated guns of unknown manufacture, with ill assorted ammunition, only some of which fitted the breech of some of the guns. One particular gun had such a wide bore that there was no bullet that fitted neatly into the breech and the owner showed how he bound a slender leather strip tightly round the cartridge case to make a tight fit in the breech.

The prison was a rectangular mud and wattle building with a thatched roof, accommodating perhaps thirty or forty prisoners and I used to visit it regularly wearing my Prison Medical Officer hat. The High Court met in an open half-walled mud, wattle and thatch building a hundred yards or so away and the prisoners waited patiently in the shade of a nearby tree for the proceedings to begin under the far from watchful eye of a single prison guard. One of the accused was given permission to go back to the latrine in the prison and was told to hurry back - that was the last that was seen of him. In the end all were released for lack of adequate ballistic evidence and because it was not possible to prove from the skeletal remnants how any of the victims had died.

The prison regime was hardly spartan and hard labour consisted of tending the prison shamba and cutting firewood for the kitchen stoves and hot water of Government Officers and the hospital. Half a dozen or so inmates would go out into the bush with a single prison guard, returning some hours later when their task was done. Pat, Helen (aged three) and I had driven to the Indian duka in the town for a supply of groceries late one afternoon when a wild eyed prisoner ran in saying that one of them had been shot. He recognised me from my prison visits. I told Pat to take Helen to friends and to return with the car. The prisoner and I ran off into the bush a mile or so, when we came upon the guard, the other prisoners from the wood-cutting party and one other prisoner who I confirmed to be dead. He had tried to escape and the guard had loosed off one .303 round which had felled him. Four prisoners carried him swinging by the arms and legs back to the duka, loaded him into the back of my car and Pat took him to the hospital mortuary. The OC Police had meanwhile arrived and I remained behind to relate my part of the affair. Pat returned half an hour later with her eyes starting out of her head for the body had seemed to groan as it was hauled from the car to put it in the mortuary. A nursing orderly was summoned hastily and confirmed that the dead man really was dead. The Pathologist - myself, wearing yet another of my hats, found that the single bullet had gone through the left renal artery causing the man to bleed rapidly to death.

That is not quite the end of the story. Some weeks earlier I had removed a tumour which I wished to send to the pathologist in Kampala for examination but at the end of the operation I found that it had been put in the incinerator. I threw a tantrum and warned all and sundry that if it happened again some member of staff would find themselves in the mortuary. The following week I had amputated a gangrenous leg which I did not want to send to the pathologist and Pat, to her consternation, had found this rotten limb lying in the mortuary when she took the dead prisoner there.

The Rev Canon Bob Clarke was greatly respected by the Karamojong. He had a cauliflower ear sustained when a slate tile had blown off a roof as he was walking by. His school taught not only the three Rs, but also important practical subjects, woodwork, farming, animal husbandry, brick making, building and so forth, and the boys (few girls attended) who were schooled by him really were able to improve their living conditions. In my time some even became sufficiently literate and numerate as to be able to go to Kampala for training as Nursing Orderlies. One day Bob told me that there was to be a great gathering of the tribal clans at Lotome, that an ox would be slaughtered and a feast and a dance would be held. A hundred or more

Karamojong men, women and children arrived the day before and well into the day of the festivity, which had been planned for the time of a full moon so that there should be plenty of light for the occasion. It was very dry and a pall of dust rose from the movement of so many people gathered together. The ox was slain with a single spear thrust and a number of young men set about skinning the beast and cutting it up into meal sized portions. The women had made a large fire nearby and cooked, or perhaps I should say barely singed the meat whereupon it was given out in generous portions to be eaten by hand. Later the dance began, the young men formed into a large circle watched by the women. They were tall and slender, bare footed, naked save for a light cotton cloak, chanting and jumping as high as they could from a standing position and landing heavily on their heels. The dust rose and the dance went on an on for what seemed to be hours, some leaving for refreshment and others joining, continuing well into the night after I had left for my bed. The day after a dance the hospital was unusually well attended with backaches due to the dance and headaches due to the refreshments.

I don't know whether people were already great characters before they went to Karamoja or whether Karamoja brought out the unusual in them. Certainly there were legendary personalities, none more so than an early District Commissioner named Preston who was there before my time, with his no less remarkable wife Bernice. Preston was dismissive of authority and was the scourge of the Treasurer's department in Entebbe who used to question some of his expense claims. His working journeys were mostly made on foot, in considerable difficulty and discomfort, with porters carrying all the paraphernalia of a camping safari lasting a week or more. He was asked to explain why it was necessary for him to employ twenty five porters for a certain safari, to which he made a one line reply - "because twenty-four would not have been sufficient". As already recounted, Karamoja was an arid semi-desert district but on one occasion Preston had to hire a canoe when he had to meet with his counterpart across the border at lake Rudolph in Kenya. Preston was asked by the Treasury to explain why it had been necessary to hire a canoe in this arid region to which he made another one line reply - "because, unlike the late J Christ Esq, I cannot walk upon the waters". It may have been on this visit to lake Rudolph that a crocodile attacked Preston and would surely have killed him but for the intervention of Bernice who was beside him under her umbrella because of the intense sun. She beat the crocodile about the head with her umbrella and poked it in the eye, with the consequence that Preston was released and survived. Back at Entebbe, the administrative capital, doubts were at one time entertained about Preston's mental stability and the Chief Secretary wrote about this in confidence to the OC Police, the only other officer in Karamoja at the time, being unaware that he and Preston used to open and deal with each others correspondence when the other was away on safari. Preston opened the letter and replied to the Chief Secretary that, to the best of his knowledge, Preston was sound in mind, signed J Preston (for OC Police).

Another character had been in Karamoja for a while before I arrived and was thought to be a confirmed bachelor. He was no stranger to alcohol, but was not afraid of hard work and did a good job. Out of loneliness, I suspect, he would often drive his truck down to the dukas after dark and be offered a scotch or two or more in a back room with the Indian proprietor who did not, of course drink alcohol himself. He would drive home to his bed and go off to work the next day seemingly none the worse for the events of the previous evening. One morning he awoke to find that his truck was not at his house and hurried on foot to the police station to report the theft. Such a thing had never been heard of before in Karamoja where you could leave your house unlocked for weeks with full confidence that nothing would be stolen. The Indian with whom he had spent the evening before, hearing of the reported theft, hurried to the police station to explain that he had driven his visitor home the night before as he had flaked out and was quite incapable of driving his truck.

After the statutory three years work his long leave of three months in UK fell due. To our amazement this confirmed bachelor returned with a wife who had never been away from her home territory before. She found it difficult to adapt to the great changes she encountered, a small mainly male community in one of the most primitive semi-desert areas of the world and a husband of established habits which he did not change after her arrival. He continued to patronise the dukas of an evening, returning home in a state to which she had not been accustomed. Not long after her arrival I chanced to meet her, clearly unhappy and asked if there was anything I could do, at which she burst into tears and told me what was upsetting her. He had, she said, returned late the evening before and fallen into the marital bed and into a deep sleep. In the morning he had opened a bloodshot eye, focused it on her face and asked "who the hell are you?"

The authorities were, on occasion, most insensitive when posting people to Karamoja. A young bachelor, whom I shall call Robinson, the only son of a widowed mother and not long out of school, applied to to join the

Colonial Police. He was in due course sent to Uganda and, after a very brief spell in the capital Kampala, was posted to Karamoja where he was placed under the supervision of a more experienced police officer. Cattle rustling and murder were commonplace and often involved him in making journeys of several days duration. He lived on his own in a small house, employed a barely trained servant to look after the house, prepare his food and accompany him on his working safaris - he was lonely and insecure. He had to spend perhaps ten to fifteen days a month on safari, visiting outposts, investigating cattle raids and killings and so forth. He would travel by Land Rover on some of the worst roads in the world carrying a tent, camp bed, table and chair, provisions, primus stove, paraffin lamps, some water and the all important crate of Tusker beer. Water was only available at considerable intervals and was often unfit to drink so the crate of beer was essential if one was to try and avoid dysentery. Once he was at Amudat, a most isolated small township of about three substandard stores, a full day's journey from Moroto, when he heard of a cattle raid and killings way out in the bush off the road. He set off on foot with a police askari, walked half the day in the burning sun to the place of the crime carrying a little food and enough fluid, made his investigations and a few arrests and arrived back at Amudat as it was about to get dark. He was tired, footsore, dirty, lonely, dishevelled and depressed but had been sustained by the knowledge that a single bottle of Tusker beer remained at his camp to refresh him. He washed in a basin of cold water, put on clean clothes, sat at his folding camp table and his servant brought the bottle of warm beer and poured it into the silver tankard given to him by his mother when he left England, placed the tankard on the rickety camp table which collapsed, spilling the beer on the dusty earth. At this Robinson cracked, unable to cope with the conditions any more and unable to carry out his duties. He spent a miserable fearful night in his tent with lions nearby roaring (I heard them myself when camping there) and returned to Moroto in acute depression the next morning. He returned first to Kampala and then to England.

Some time later the Veterinary Officer was on a walking safari with a young Assistant District Commissioner who had not heard of Robinson's misfortune, when the porter carrying the case of Tusker beer stumbled, with the result that every bottle but one was broken. The young ADC said that he would carry the remaining bottle safely to the end of the day so that they could then share it, but the vet said "not bloody likely, remember Robinson", removed the cap and poured it into two glasses and they drank it there and then. A consequence of this sad tale was that, whenever there was only one of anything left, it became the custom to say "remember Robinson" and finish it off lest some disaster befall.

Another great character was Wreford Smith who came to Kenya at the same time as my father and farmed nearby. In addition to running his farm he made a monthly safari, lasting about a fortnight, to buy cattle in Karamoja for Liebig's corned beef factory in Nairobi. At one time Liebig had sought to advertise how good their corned beef was for growing children by putting the smiling face of a small African child on the label but this backfired when the locals boycotted the product thinking it to be tinned baby – they couldn't read and, after all, tinned pineaple did have a picture of pineaples on the can! Wreford would travel on a lorry with all his provisions for his Karamoja safaris and a safe chained to it containing enough shilling coins to pay for the cattle. The Karamojong had no trust in paper money and would bring a narrow necked gourd into which the coins were counted one by one. Wreford had established regular camp sites where he stayed for a few nights and, when he was near Moroto, we would always be invited to join him for a lamp-lit meal by his camp fire under the stars. He had a huge, long handled, blackened saucepan permanently on the fire and a servant would carry this two handed to those seated round the table. We would dip in with a large spoon to see what came out. "What's in it Wreford?" Pat would ask: he kept it replenished with whatever had been shot the day before. Helen was three and Wreford, knowing she loved biltong (salted and dried eland) and Cadbury's milk chocolate, always brought some for her. She would retire to sleep in the car while Wreford plied us with Tusker beer and Mellowood South African brandy under the brilliant African starlit night. He had a resident cat (and kittens) at each camp and I saw one of the kittens playing in the dark with I knew not what. I rose from my camp. chair to investigate and found it to be the biggest scorpion I had ever seen, striking at the kitten with its poisoned tail, the kitten cuffing it playfully with its forepaw. I crammed the scorpion into a two pound jam jar and sent it to the Cornydon museum who informed me that it was the largest specimen so far recorded. Wreford always carried a police whistle in case he needed to attract attention: I left his camp by car late one night after his usual generous hospitality and turned northwards into the darkness when I heard his whistle blowing urgently: I had turned the wrong way.

Sandy Field, the District Commissioner, was another great character. He had a private income and an independent frame of mind which made him fearless of authority, big game and warring Karamojong tribesmen. He was a dapper figure who would go off big game hunting for days in spartan conditions of great hardship which he would surmount without any hesitation. He had a fine collection of elephant tusks and he once took me into his spare bedroom to show me his collection of gleaming ivory, perhaps a dozen fine tusks. He once faced down with great courage a Karamojong war party which was advancing to kill him and his small armed escort. He ordered his escort to stand easy, remained seated himself and looked the spear wielding warriors fearlessly in the eye and, at the last moment, they lost courage and abandoned their intent. Later Sandy became a game conservationist as Chief Park Warden at Serengetti National Park and then Chief Warden of the National Parks in Tanzania. He was a skilful pilot and flew his own plane for years over distances great and small and was eventually presumed dead some where in the bush at the age of seventy eight when he and his plane failed to return from a flight. It was many weeks before his body and the wreckage of his plane were found.

Violence was a way of life among the Karamojong and I was often asked to carry out post mortem examinations. One particularly sad occasion was when two young Suk lads from a neighbouring tribe who were herding the family goats were speared by Karamojong as they fled from their attackers. The motive was believed to be for the purpose of spear blooding so that the killers could sport an ostrich feather dipped in human blood in their head-dresses but, more likely, it was a dispute over grazing grounds. Shortly after this a party of thirty Suk warriors retaliated by killing the Government Agent Lorika and his companion Ekapolon Nangiro, spearing them to death, together with another unidentified man, at Nakumoathing. I got to the scene the next morning and found the bodies partly eviscerated by vultures, one actually crouched within the thorax of Lorika, picking away at the last morsel of lung and struggling to get out and away as I arrived. Filled with misplaced anger with the vulture (mainly because I knew the dead man) I could have shot it there and then but forbore to do so for they are a protected species. I had attended a meeting with Lorika the morning before and could identify him only by his clothing, the same green and yellow stockings and brightly coloured check shirt that he had worn at the meeting, his features having been stripped away by the vultures. Nangiro was similarly identified by someone else. The suspected killer was arrested but escaped from custody. Eighty Karamojong, armed with spears, pursued the Suk and were challenged by Uganda Police who shot and killed two and I carried out post mortem examinations on those as well. Continued skirmishes took place between the two tribes, odd bodies being found here and there. There was long term hostility between them because Suk tribesmen from the eroded Karasuk area had been infiltrating the Karamojong dry weather grazing grounds for years. Later some Suk tribesmen were tried before the High Court and acquitted to the consternation of the local chiefs who said that only a public hanging at the site of the crime would prevent disturbances the next time. The Karamojong involved were collectively punished by communal fines of cattle. Some months later there was the inevitable sequel with further civil disturbances, some Karamojong absconding with eight hundred Suk cattle. I treated many wounded, one with his face largely severed by a spear thrust from the side so that his upper lip and nose remained attached to his face only by the skin of the opposite cheek. He had tied it back more or less in position with a piece of rag round his head. I made a better job of it with sutures and persuaded him to come back to the hospital with me, where I could treat the infection (which was sure to develop) but he lost his courage and absconded. The final death roll of this fresh episode of disturbances was reported by the chiefs to be about forty.

Suicide by hanging was quite common among the Karamojong and, among the men, by leaning upon or running upon their spears. I carried out a a sad post mortem examination on a girl of about thirteen who hanged herself a couple of days after undergoing infibulation, the so-called ritual circumcision of girls approaching puberty. This barbarous procedure involved the excision of the clitoris and labia while the fully conscious girl was held down by older women, the resultant wound being crudely approximated, sometimes by stitching or by binding the thighs together. It had been prohibited by law for years but continued nevertheless, its purpose being to preserve virginity till marriage. A further consequence was dreadful trauma during subsequent childbirth.

I was a member of the Moroto Township Authority and with the District Commissioner helped draw up a Town Plan. We thought we did pretty well but the Town Planner from Entebbe thought little of our efforts and threw out our ideas. The Township Authority had to arrange for refuse disposal and this was undertaken by prisoners with wheelbarrows. We had tried an ox cart but this was not successful because of the scarcity of trained oxen. Cattle there were a-plenty but they were the mark of a man's wealth and none were trained as draught oxen. One of the things we got right was the cemetery with different areas for Protestants, Catholics, Muslims and heathens - they segregated themselves to the best of their ability in life and certainly did not want to lie next to each other in death. The only heathens to be buried in the cemetery were those Karamojong who died in hospital. If they died at home the relatives put the body out in the bush to be cleared away by hyenas, jackals and vultures. If they died in the hospital the prisoners would be commissioned to dig a grave, often little more than three or four feet deep because of the very hard stony earth. It was but a simple task for the hyenas to dig up the corpse at night and the scanty remnants were to be found lying round the cemetery the next morning. One night the hospital staff were too fearful to take the body of a man who had died to the mortuary some distance away in the dark so they put it under a nearby tree overnight and forgot all about it when they went off duty in the morning. Pat and Helen had the car for shopping and came to collect me for lunch and it was Helen, alerted by the smell of decay, who found the corpse. On another occasion a bloodstained hospital mattress was put under the same tree to be cleaned up at daylight but the hyenas smelt the blood and consumed most of the mattress. It was a brand new expensive 'Mattress, Dunlopillow, African for the use of' (to use the store-ledger jargon) and my explanation that it had been eaten by a hyena was received with some scepticism by the auditors who happened along a week later. The auditors were giving me a hard time about this and other matters but my day was made when they lost the stores ledger, never to be found again and had to make a new one from scratch.

I also sat on the Coronation Committee. King George VI had died and we had heard the BBC news bulletins on an old style short wave wireless which ran on wet batteries with terrible reception. When the time came for the Coronation of his young daughter Elizabeth we were provided with bunting and flags; there was a ceremonial parade by the police with the District Commissioner in full ceremonial uniform and the rest of us perspiring in our English suits brought out of mothballs for the occasion. There was also a firework display that night.

I was a member of the Local Education Committee and attended interminable meetings at which my usual input was to encourage the provision of latrines and washing facilities at all schools. After one such fruitless meeting I asked Yakobo Lowok (the Chairman of the District Council) how he felt about the proceedings: "Pepo, pepo zaidi" he replied; "too much hot air" will suffice as a colloquial translation but a better understanding of what he meant is obtained if you know that pepo means not just air, but also flatus. Most of the bush schools were primary only, first, second and occasionally third year. I used to call in and inspect these bush schools when I was passing; they were of mud, wattle and thatch construction, no whitewash, no latrine and no facilities for washing. The equipment consisted of slates, blackboard and chalk and they learned reading, writing and elementary arithmetic. There was but a single secondary school at Lotome operated by Bob Clarke. He turned out such reliable school leavers that they were in demand by people like myself for employment. We were asked not to offer work to any of them before the end of their second year in secondary school lest they were tempted to leave prematurely.

Cotton was an important crop in Uganda but not in Karamoja District. In the 1940s the price of cotton on the world market happened to be higher than usual and the Uganda Government decided to retain a small portion of the value received in what was named the Cotton Price Assistance Fund so as to be able to subsidise the price should it fall in later years. When Sir Andrew Cohen was appointed as Governor he found a large amount of money languishing in the fund with the price of cotton as high as ever so he decided that this should be spent on Community Development projects and Karamoja benefited from this. Ideas were put up by the local people who were expected to make a contribution to the project by supplying free labour. We received Shs 16,000 (£800) for an ambulance and Shs 23,000 (£1,150) for a leper settlement. Other funds were supplied for the cleaning of ataparas and for the fitting of hand-pumps, needed because this source of water was readily fouled by animals. Another project was the fencing of the dry weather grazing grounds in the forlorn hope of keeping out the Suk and their cattle. A total amount of Shs 260,000 (£13,000) was allocated but the whole idea was not a great success because Karamoja had difficulty in spending its allocation of Community Development finance due to lack of artisans, lack of a community anxious to develop itself, lack of transport and lack of officers to supervise the work.

Helen was so excited when she knew that another baby was expected. Government officers' wives were supposed to go to Kampala for their confinements but Pat came into labour early with Philip and later with Brian. Philip was born in Moroto and was designated the only white Karamojong at that time. Pat did a bit better with Brian, who was born at Mbale on our way to Kampala three weeks before she was due. Helen had been left for the occasion to stay with Ruth and David Sharpe (he was an ADC) and they took her shopping at the local store. She had been told not to ask for sweets and did her very best not to do so but, as they returned to the car, she hit on a stratagem which proved successful: "My Daddy sometimes gives me chocolate if I don't ask". With two young brothers her cup of happiness was full and she helped to bring them up with love and enthusiasm, teaching them how to brush their teeth, wash themselves, wipe their bottoms, dress themselves, tie their shoe laces and anything else you can think of. When Brian died aged forty she and Philip were totally desolate and part of them died with him.

In 1954 we went on leave with the three children to visit Pat's parents in Harrismith in the Orange Free State. We flew by Dakota (a relic from the 1939-45 war) from Kampala to Nairobi and then joined an international flight from London to Johannesburg. While we were there, Pat's brother David arrived home one night - at six o'clock in the morning - disturbing his mother in the process and was sitting on his bed having removed one shoe when she opened his door to investigate. With great presence of mind he said "I have to go to work early today mother", replaced his shoe and left the house.

We returned by sea from Durban to Mombasa where we were to be met by Arthur Brown, a bachelor friend from Karamoja. He had bought a farm near Arusha and we were to stay with him for a week or so but his ancient truck had broken down. We stayed in the Manor Hotel for a day or two before I located Arthur, who had meanwhile found other means of transport for us. He had seen a couple of new Land Rovers destined for Arusha 200 miles away being unloaded at Mombasa and offered to deliver them for a small consideration, thereby providing us with the required transport. His home was made from two wooden houses which he had bought for a song at the closing down sale of the disastrous Kongwa Groundnut Scheme, introduced by the post war socialist government in the UK. Pat took over the cooking while there and Arthur enjoyed unaccustomed *haute cuisine.* Late one evening (when nobody, but nobody, used to call) there was a knocking at the door and Arthur admitted a furtive looking man dripping with rain known as Jimmy the Greek, who asked did Arthur want some meat, free, twenty pounds weight or thereabouts? Smelling a rat Arthur asked for more information and learned that it was giraffe (a protected animal) which Jimmy the Greek had shot; now he was going round his friends trying to get it eaten so as to conceal the evidence. Arthur tried to pass it off as beef, knowing that Pat would throw a tantrum if she found out that it was giraffe - which she did. She refused to touch a mouthful but the rest of us, farm labour included, enjoyed it greatly - very like beef. Jimmy the Greek salvaged his battered reputation with Pat when he took us at dawn in his ancient short wheel-base Land Rover to the railway station at Arusha, five of us, our baggage, two sacks of maize-meal and three large milk churns.

When I got back to Kampala, the railhead in Uganda, I found that having learned the language and done much to open up the medical services in Karamoja I was to be posted to Gulu, the main town in Acholi, the next district to the west. No matter that I spoke not a word of Acholi, nor they a word of Karamojong: I had passed my two language exams and my future salary increments were secure. However it was not long before I had a working knowledge of that language as well, in addition to English, Latin, French, Swahili, Karamojong and now Acholi. Not knowing who was knocking at my office door I would call out "Come in, Jangu, Karibu, Bin bin" etc and would await events.

Chapter 8

1955 - Acholi District, Uganda

I was appointed District Medical Officer of Acholi District in the Northern Province of Uganda in October 1954. The Acholi word for a witch-doctor was *ajwaka* and I was known as *ajwaka madit*, the head witch-doctor. Acholi district was a more prosperous area than Karamoja and Acholi men made disciplined soldiers, many of them joining the King's African Rifles and the Police force. One such soldier, a sergeant in my day, was called Idi Amin. The district was about the size of Wales, with a population of 215,000 and was fertile with good food crops - millet, maize, vegetables and good cash crops - cotton and tobacco. The river Aswa (a tributary of the Nile) flowed through it. I had charge of two hospitals at Gulu and Kitgum, eleven dispensaries at Attanga, Anaka, Attiak, Awac, Awere, Patongo, Naam Okora, Palabek, Pajule, Paimol and Madi Opei and one leper settlement at Alelelele. There were also two Roman Catholic Mission maternity units at Kitgum and Kalongo which provided excellent services. During my tenure the government provided funding to establish the first Midwifery Training School in Uganda outside Kampala and this became a great source of local pride. The district was served by a single ambulance which also served to deliver supplies to the eleven dispensaries and Kitgum hospital over dirt roads, with frequent breakdowns. The Acholi District Council provided two more so called ambulances which had been on the road for a total of only ten days in the previous year. The British-American Tobacco Company gave me half a dozen bicycle trailer 'ambulances' (one for each county of the district) made to my design. I provided the simple metal single bed frames from the hospital and the BAT Co fitted bicycle wheels, one on either side and a tow bar, so that it could be drawn by a cyclist. The Divisional chief (Jago) had charge of the bicycle ambulance and would loan it out free to relatives when someone needed taking to the hospital and it would be returned at the first opportunity. If relatives were unavailable or too old or frail to tow the sick person, then the Jago would volunteer some able bodied man to do so. There was no payment for this - the tradition of community work, called 'ber lobo' was strong and the Acholi could be relied upon to turn out and give a hand when any project benefiting the community needed labour.

Acholi District had the usual administrative structure of a District Commissioner, Charles Fulford-Williams, with three or four ADCs. One of these, Rex Hunt, was based at Kitgum. He was later knighted for the distinguished part he played at the time of the Argentine invasion when Governor of the Falkland Islands. The European population of 264 comprised mainly Government service officers and their families, plus a few Missionaries. The chief town was Gulu and the Provincial Commissioner for the Northern Province, Chris Powell-Cotton, had his office in the town, as did Nick Twohig the Provincial Medical Officer. There were about twenty Indian dukas and the Asian population was 628. The British appointed the chiefs, mainly from the same clans who had held authority before British rule. The Lawirwodi was in charge; under him were six County Chiefs and below them were twenty four Divisional Chiefs. They enforced the laws, collected taxes, made bye-laws and were supposed to keep registers of births and deaths. The annual death rate, according to notifications, was 1 per 1000 whereas it cannot realistically have been below 20 per 1000. Similarly the birth rate was said to be 2.5 per 1000 against a probable figure of 25 per 1000. To try and encourage better records I instigated the issue of informal birth certificates at Gulu maternity unit and the Roman Catholic Mission maternity units and the mothers were instructed to take these to the Jago to register the birth. They had other opportunities of updating their records at the periodic sleeping sickness inspections, of which more later.

I was allocated a house with mains water, mosquito proof windows and flushing toilets and we felt we were in the lap of luxury but there was no electricity. Later I was to install my own generator - a small petrol engine which charged car batteries which supplied electric light to our living quarters. Pat and I and the children lived there happily with four servants for the next five years. We employed a cook, a gardener, a house servant and also an Ayah to help look after Brian who was a baby at that time. The cook, gardener and house servants were always men who came and went with the passage of several months but the Ayah, Sevarosa Kabanya, stayed for a long time and became a faithful family retainer. I sought to encourage one male servant who was particularly good to remain in my employment for a long time by setting up a scheme whereby he would receive a lump sum gratuity when he eventually left. I increased his wages above the norm conditional upon him putting the excess into the gratuity fund and said I would pay a similar amount each month into the same fund, to be drawn when he left. The end result was just the same - he went after a few months. I then realised that the reason many of them worked at all was to accumulate the necessary finance for a particular project - most usually for the 'bride price' or perhaps a new roof for the family house. Having achieved this there was no continuing need for work so off he went till he next needed some cash. Sevarosa was the archetypal buxom nanny, full of kindness and love. Helen was by now at school and each morning Sevarosa would take Brian and Philip, with a flask of fruit juice and a few biscuits, on to the golf course where she would meet up with half a dozen other ayahs under a large shady tree. The children would play happily together for a couple of hours and brush up their social skills, picking up a lot of the local language from the ayahs as they chatted amongst themselves. "Briany" she would call in peremptory tones when his mischief got the better of him. He loved her and would run for solace to her comfortable bosom when hurt or upset. The children sampled her diet when given the chance and told us how lovely fried flying ants tasted after they had pulled the legs and wings off. Sevarosa stayed in Acholi district when we moved to Kampala but always remembered us. When we eventually left for England she sent the three children a pillowcase each, hand made with hand sewn seams and embroidery. Some years later we heard that she had retired to her homeland where she died from a snakebite.

The drive to the house had a small roundabout with a sweet-smelling frangipani tree in it's centre and I erected a notice reading 'SLOW CHILDREN' as a warning to visiting motorists, and this caused some merriment. Apart from children there were other hazards for motorists, as the children often left a rusty scooter round the bend in the drive where it couldn't be seen till the last moment. I remonstrated with them to no avail and jumped out of the car in a fury when there it was once again. My anger abated as quickly as it had risen when the scooter turned out to be an Egyptian cobra which first raised its hooded head and then slithered away as I approached.

Our neighbour was Kate Gray, Provincial Education Officer for the Northern Province, a Lancashire woman of great wit, charm and humour who was loved by all, especially Philip and Brian. They would rise early (about half past six) run through a gap in the hedge to Kate's house and into her bedroom where she was enjoying her early morning cup of tea. After a brief conversation she would send them on their way with a sweet. We knew nothing of this until we found one of them still eating a sweet when he got back to our house where we knew we had none. We then learned that this had been a regular occurrence for some time - "Kate gives us a thweet every day" said Brian. Pat remonstrated with Kate about this and told the boys that they were not to ask for sweets, so on the next visit she did not offer any. The conversation grew desultory for lack of the usual subject so they rose to return home. Brian managed to restrain himself till he reached the door, then turned big reproachful eyes on Kate and asked "No thweeties"? I only learned this last detail from Kate when she was eighty five and Brian had died. Later it fell to me to deliver Kate's funeral oration.

Central Government promulgated the usual plethora of Public Health Ordinances which applied to the whole of Uganda Protectorate. In addition the local councils of the various Districts in each Province were empowered (and expected) to pass relevant bye-laws appropriate to the state of development of their populations. Protection of Health,

Leprosy and Sleeping Sickness bye-laws had been passed by the Acholi District Council, couched in plain simple English, very unlike the legal terminology used in the United Kingdom. As an example I quote their bye-law relating to housing, verbatim:

THE HOUSE:
(a) Size: If the house is of round design the width across shall not be less than four yards, but if it is intended that more than two people shall sleep in the house, the width across shall not be less than five yards. If the house is rectangular with one room, the size of the room shall not be less than four yards by three yards in length and if it is intended that more than two people shall sleep in the house one side of the room shall be not less than five yards in length. If there is more than one room the sides of each room shall not be less than three yards in length. This rule does not apply to stores.
(b) Roof: When grass is used to thatch the roof the slope of the roof shall be sufficiently steep to ensure that rain falls off the roof and does not come through.
(c) Floor: The floor of the house shall be at least six inches above the height of the ground outside the house. The floor shall be rammed earth and smeared with cow dung or swamp sand.
(d) Walls: The walls shall be plastered sufficiently smoothly to prevent cracks which harbour insects, and they shall be not less than seven feet high.
(e) Windows: Each room, except for stores, shall have at least one window.

LATRINES: The owner of each compound shall ensure that a pit latrine is dug for each compound, but if there are more than six houses in the compound two latrines shall be dug. The latrine shall be not less than ten feet deep and shall have walls of not less than six feet high, with a roof sufficiently steep to prevent rain coming through. The floor shall be not less than six inches higher than the surrounding ground. The latrine shall be built not less than ten yards from the nearest building.

RUBBISH: All refuse from the house or compound shall be burnt or buried. It shall be an offence to leave any refuse in or near the compound.

ANIMALS: Cattle, goats, sheeps *(sic)* or fowls shall have separate houses built for them; it shall be an offence to allow these animals to occupy a house at night in which persons sleep.

PENALTIES: Any person disobeying these provisions shall be guilty of an offence and shall, on a first conviction, be liable to a fine not exceeding Shs 10 or to imprisonment not exceeding two weeks, or to both such fine and imprisonment and shall, on any subsequent conviction, be liable to a fine not exceeding Shs 20 or to imprisonment for a period not exceeding one month or to both such fine and imprisonment.

A Leprosy bye-law allowed for the establishment of leper settlements by the County Chiefs not less than two hundred yards from a village for the admission of men only in the first instance and, when large enough, women and children. Wives and children were not permitted to visit without written permission from the Jago *'who will give such permission only in very special cases'*. In no circumstances were visitors allowed to sleep in the same room as a leper who was considered to be infectious. The settlement was to be self supporting, all crops were to be owned in common - no private cultivation was allowed. Each leper might receive an allowance of Shs 2 per month from the local government chief for personal expenditure.

Central government established a leper settlement under my charge at Alelelele and when this became operational the local government settlements fell into disuse. On completion of treatment, certificates of cure were issued, with copies to their divisional chiefs who would thereby know that it was in order for the individuals concerned to return to their homes. I had a visit from the Specialist Leprologist from Kampala who carried out a survey and told me that the incidence of leprosy was 16.9 per 1000, in which case there were about four thousand cases in the district, only one quarter of whom were being treated, so we then had a blitz. The day the Specialist was due to return to Kampala I had done a post mortem examination on a man whom I suspected to have died of bubonic plague. I asked him to take a bottle of pus from one of the glands to the central laboratory in Kampala but he refused, as he was too fearful in case he should have an accident and the bottle be broken.

Another bye law concerned trypanosomiasis (sleeping sickness) which was transmitted by the Tsetse fly, which had itself acquired the parasite by biting another infected person. Divisional Chiefs were required to keep river crossings and the approaches to watering places clear of grass and vegetation to protect people from being bitten by the fly. The size of the sleeping sickness clearing was to be fifty yards by fifty yards with one porter to maintain each clearing. Sleeping sickness inspectors were required to help the

District Medical Officer and Chiefs, with periodic mass inspections for the ascertainment of cases of the disease, to make house visits for the same purpose and to assist with mass examinations for other conditions, such as leprosy, if not engaged on sleeping sickness work. Their regular work consisted of making counts of tsetse flies in an area. Two men in white shirts would walk along pathways in the bush and the one behind would count the number of tsetse flies landing on the back of the shirt of the one in front in an hour. If the number was high the area would be cleared of game by shooting, a low or nil count was good news. They had to bring flies back for identification, this being confirmed by the presence of a hatchet shaped cell in the wings – a skill I had learned at the London School of Hygiene and Tropical Medicine.

Sleeping sickness led to drowsiness and then coma, followed by death. It was therefore of paramount importance to identify, isolate and treat infected persons so that they could not pass the parasite to the tsetse fly for onward transmission to other people. This was achieved by mass examinations of the population - for example 70,024 persons (of which three were infected) were examined in 1958. The number of cases picked up was not large - 44 cases from 1950 to 1958 inclusive. Notice of the date and place of a sleeping sickness inspection would be sent to the Divisional Chief and the local population, perhaps a thousand, would gather at some convenient shaded spot for what turned out to be an informal public holiday. I would have arrived the night before with three or four other members of staff so as to be able to start early the next morning. The Jago would be present with his hand-written register in a hard-backed book, ticking those attending, updating his records of births and deaths and noting absentees. I would stand under a shady tree, a clerk at one table, a laboratory assistant with microscope at another, a medical assistant at a third table with syringes, needles and microscope slides. There was also a pan of boiling water on a primus stove for sterilising the glass syringes and needles. I would examine each person in turn, checking for enlarged lymph glands in the neck and under the armpits. If there were any enlarged glands I would take a blood sample, inject a tiny amount of saline into the gland, rub it vigorously and then aspirate the saline and pass them to the laboratory assistant for examination of both specimens under the microscope to see if the trypanosome parasite was present. If any were found I would check the result myself and would often show the parasite to the infected person. At the end of the day I was hot, tired and thirsty with distinctly grubby hands from a thousand necks and two thousand sweaty armpits. Then back to my camp where my servant had prepared four gallons of hot water over a wood fire for my bath and a chicken stew for my meal, which I washed down with a couple of bottles of beer. Trypanosomiasis was such a serious disease that those found to be infected were sent to Mulago hospital in Kampala for confirmation of the diagnosis, isolation and treatment which was prolonged and rather toxic.

There were few sinecures attached to my job but one of them was my responsibility for Public Health in Murchison Falls National Park. This was a large reserve in which the game was protected and through which the Nile plunged ferociously through a narrow gorge, perhaps twenty feet wide, to the broad river below. The game park was prohibited for human habitation apart from staff employed there - game rangers and the staff at the Paraa Game Lodge for tourists. Big game abounded - elephant, lion, leopard, buffalo, rhino and countless antelope of every description.

The river contained hippo and crocodiles galore. There was abundant and varied bird life, some of which would feed on ticks from the backs of large animals and on leeches from the open jaws of crocodiles. Tourists, perhaps eight to ten at a time, would stay in huts at the Lodge and be taken game spotting. They would also make a launch trip up the river for two or three miles to the base of the Murchison Falls.

I used to take my duties as MOH to the Murchison Falls Park very seriously, visiting at least once a month and seizing the opportunity to take Pat and the children along as well. We would stay overnight and the next morning would check around our sleeping hut for spoor, finding lion on one occasion and leopard on another. I would check the food, the kitchens, the water supply and the staff in case anyone was ill. In 1959 we were to receive a visit from Queen Elizabeth, the Queen Mother so imagine my consternation when I detected two cases of sleeping sickness close to the park shortly before her arrival. For once my visit was not a sinecure and my inspection of the staff was rigorous but, fortunately, there was no sign of the disease in the park so her visit went off smoothly. She travelled with her physician for the occasion, Dr Alec Alderdyce, who was medical superintendent of Mulago hospital. On her trip to Murchison Falls his flight was delayed for a couple of hours during which I stood in for him obtaining in the process the best view of big game that I had ever seen. That night a *Bwola*, a ceremonial tribal dance, was held in her honour in the open air by lamplight from pressure paraffin lamps. Chanting Acholi tribesmen with bells around their ankles and wearing ceremonial skins and head-dresses, bearing a spear and shield, formed a large circle and danced to drum beats stamping to a tribal rhythm, raising a cloud of dust. At a signal the circle opened at one point to admit the Provincial Commissioner and the Queen Mother into the cloud of dust, she in a dazzling white gown with a diamond tiara glinting in the lamplight. Acholi women, dressed in colourful skirts and head-dresses and wearing bright green brassieres for the occasion, were gathered to one side and added to the excitement with their shrill ululation and clapping, encouraging the men in the splendour and vigour of their dancing. Charles Fulford-Williams, the DC, later told me that the Jago had included in his expense claim for the Queen Mother's Bwola 'twenty four pairs of breast suspenders'. The Acholi word for a brassiere is '*kilega*', meaning a garment for praying in: this was because early missionaries had always insisted that women should cover their breasts whilst in church. The next morning the Queen Mother took off from the Murchison Falls dirt airstrip in a Heron of the Queen's flight, seen off, amongst others, by myself in an unaccustomed suit smelling of moth balls. A Land Rover made a preliminary transit to and fro to scare big and small game from the take-off path.

Gulu Hospital was a much grander unit than Moroto with no fewer than five doctors: myself, Dr Deogratias Byaruhanga from Uganda, Dr David Rosanelli from Austria, his wife Dr Irmtraud Rosanelli and Dr May Wreford-Smith from Kenya who was in charge of the Midwifery Training School and maternity unit. Dick Woollard from Devon was the District Health Inspector and probably did more than the rest of us put together when it came to improving the health of the population. He helped train African Health Inspectors and was also an examiner in their final examinations: he told me that one candidate answering a question on fly borne diseases wrote "diseases carried by flies is so many that not even one fly can carry them all".

There were three British Nursing Sisters: Barbara Martin,

Betty Mitchell who was a Health Visitor and Jessie Abrahams the Midwifery Tutor. Dr May Wreford Smith was the daughter of Herbert Wreford Smith the cattle buyer mentioned in the Karamoja chapter; she and I had been born within a year and a few miles of each other. In an earlier era our proximity would probably have led to our being married but she went to Cape Town and I to Oxford to gain our respective medical qualifications and our paths diverged. May's mother, Dos, was a great character, deaf with a penetrating voice and when she was introduced to Pat in Kitale main street when we first arrived she said "So you are the one who has married Gareth. We always hoped he would marry our May, you know". Pat loved and respected her greatly. Paula Hirsch (of whom more later) told of being present on the Wreford-Smith farm at the time of their golden wedding anniversary. A young reporter came to interview Dos and had the temerity to ask whether she had ever, in her fifty years of marriage, considered divorce. She pulled herself ram-rod straight and said "Young man, divorce - NEVER, but MURDER often".

I looked after the health of the European Officers and their families and used to reserve the first hour of the day for the Europeans so that they could then get on with their days work and I with mine. To get to my consulting room they had to pass Sister Barbara Martin's office and she was very hot on Europeans coming at the prescribed time and not later. A young Police Officer (his limping dog in tow) turned up at 10am one day and Barbara Martin intercepted him: "It's no good you coming at this time you know, the Doctor can't see you now" to which he replied "I'm all right but my dog has been hurt". "That's different" she said "he'll see you right away". She was a pushover when it came to an animal in trouble and, as the government vet had no facilities for pets, she ushered in the Police Officer and dog. The dog had a broken leg so I set and plastered the limb and unleashed a hornet's nest about my head from the Mohammedan community. How could one of them needing an operation possibly go to the same hospital and the same doctor who was operating on dogs, they complained to the DC, the PC, the Governor, the Director of Medical Services, the United Nations and Uncle Tom Cobley and all. I was suitably reprimanded.

The Colonial Civil Servants from Britain all underwent a stringent medical examination before being appointed and were pretty healthy; they did not make a significant inroad to my day to day work. I suppose that most of my consultations were for the wives and children - minor ailments, injuries and childhood infectious diseases. The latter often involved home visits, one of which was memorable because I saw a small crocodile walking hastily along the roadside. I couldn't believe my eyes but there it was, miles from it's normal habitat in the river Nile. Crocodiles have only one emotion and that is hostility and they are invariably dangerous. So I got out of my car and went to the boot where I kept an American army trenching tool, with which I despatched the crocodile with a single blow across its neck. Only later did I learn that it was the pet of a teenage girl in the town.

Because of the international travel of Government officers and families from Uganda to UK and back, everyone had to be repeatedly inoculated or vaccinated against the major infectious diseases - small pox, yellow fever, typhoid and cholera in particular. Greatly feared was poliomyelitis, commonly known as infantile paralysis, of which epidemics occurred in the African population from time to time. I would see someone with poliomyelitis in the hospital and would then go home to Pat and the children, fearful of transmitting infection to them, so I was doubly scrupulous about hospital hygiene. When a healthy young doctor in Kampala caught the disease and died in the space of forty eight hours we all shuddered - there but for the grace of God went any of us. I knew a vaccine against poliomyelitis to be under development in the USA and when it was released for use there was a rush of applicants. Only a small supply was available and every dose had to be accounted for and paid for - a sum of about two or three shillings each. The vaccine came in vials containing ten doses, each to be injected and, at the end, I was one dose short, for which I could not account. I painstakingly scrutinised the list of people who had been injected and discovered that Maria Rosanelli, a doctor's daughter aged about seven years, had received her injection and then went to the back of the other queue and received a second. She came to no harm.

I was Medical Officer of Health for the town and district and much of this aspect of the work was undertaken by Dick Woollard the Health Inspector who kept an eye on food premises in the town, promoted housing improvements, clean water supplies, urban and rural sanitation. He set up a housing improvement competition with prizes for those who best observed the housing bye-law with Dr Nick Twohig the Provincial Medical Officer as judge. Nick was never slow to criticise shortcomings in the departmental staff for any perceived failings and I recall an incident in the housing competition on a hot day when we were all tired and spirits were flagging:

The scene: a substandard Acholi homestead. The characters: Nick Twohig (PMO) myself, Dick Woollard and an African Assistant Health Inspector (AHI).

PMO to AHI: "Tell me what you have done at this homestead".

AHI: (already under some strain and in halting English): "I have told the man to put a window and he has put it. I have told him to put the floor up and he has done it. I have told him to build a chicken house, but he will not do it".

PMO: (plainly exasperated) "And WHY will he not build a chicken house"?

AHI: "Sir, he has no chickens".

As MOH I was taken by surprise one day while having a beer in the club when I was offered some potato crisps, said to have been made in Gulu, which I did not know about. The next day the premises were inspected and were spotless, with good washing facilities, clean white coats for the staff, covered waste bins for the potato peel - everything seemed to be in order. The man packing the crisps had suffered from leprosy and parts of his fingers were missing because of the disease - there was no harm in that for his leprosy was burned out and was no longer infectious. But having stumps for fingers made it awkward for him to open the packets to insert the crisps, so he held the packet up to his mouth and blew hard to inflate it and was then able to fill it. Then came the culmination of the process, he held the packet up, licked the end like an envelope and sealed it down! Needless to say, this was promptly corrected.

The club was the social centre of the district, for Europeans only - at that time we did not think this to be at all unusual. Pat and I once took a visiting Ugandan doctor into the club for a drink and received a few dark looks but no one dared complain. It was our equivalent to an English pub and we would go there with the children for a beer after a swim. There was an annual fireworks party to celebrate Guy Fawkes day and an annual fancy dress competition and Pat and/or I often won a prize. Her best was when she went as a bat (flying, not cricket) and my best was in a suit of armour which I made from empty kerosene tins.

Most government officers were married - there were a few bachelors but very few spinsters - so weddings were a rarity. When one did occur it was a great social event and out of mothballs came all the finery. One of the few weddings was between Paula Hirsch, a Hungarian anthropologist and Philip Foster, a schoolmaster at the Sir Samuel Baker school. During World II Joachim von Ribbentrop, Hitler's Foreign Secretary, had been made responsible for eliminating the Jewish population in Hungary and Paula, her parents and younger sister had been sent to Auschwitz concentration camp. They joined an interminable queue, moving slowly towards a bunch of prison guards. Her parents and younger sister were directed to a group on one side and Paula to a group on the other. In this arbitrary manner were her parents and sister sent to the gas chambers and Paula to work in a salt mine. She was eventually liberated by the American army. A GI, coming upon her skeletal frame, gave her a jar of peanut butter from his knapsack which she devoured ravenously and was violently ill. After many vicissitudes she emerged tough and determined, with her charm and gaiety unimpaired. As her parents had not survived the Holocaust, Pat and I organised the wedding. Pat made the bridal dress and all the ladies of Gulu helped in our kitchen preparing the wedding feast. Pat and Paula struck sparks from each other and enlivened any gathering.

Malaria was and still is the scourge of central Africa and thousands upon thousands of local people were affected every year. European expatriates were expected not to get malaria by careful attention to prophylaxis with a daily Paludrine tablet and by sleeping under a mosquito net. In the town any standing water provided breeding places for the mosquito so these were drained where possible and we did this to a swampy area within the town boundary. This anti-malarial drain yielded such a lot of water that the European population subscribed the funds to collect it into a swimming pool, which would be emptied once a fortnight to flush the drain lower down. Monthly mosquito catches were carried out to assess the success or otherwise of our measures. I used to supply large quantities of anti-malarial drugs to the dispensaries as this was the commonest disease encountered. Imagine my dismay when I checked and found that only two of the medical assistants actually knew the correct treatment for this condition.

I used to write a monthly and annual report to the Director of Medical Services which passed "u.f.s" (under favour of signature) through the Provincial Medical Officer who added his comments if appropriate. These reports were a good discipline as it made me keep an eye on all aspects of medical work throughout the district. Mostly they comprised statistics, the number of cases of typhoid and so forth and were pretty dull so I tried to liven them up by including bits of entertaining information. Once I attached a burned out valve from the ambulance engine in case any one questioned the mechanic's account. Other times I let off steam when I felt let down by staff. Once I expostulated:

> "The number of persons giving cause for suspicion as to their honesty continues to rise and the ethical standards of the well educated, well trained and now well paid Acholi can only be described as deplorable. The ill assorted

> combination of arrogance and alcoholism, idleness and desire for self aggrandisement, casual indifference and intense selfishness appear so frequently that it is difficult to appreciate how the Acholi myth ever arose. The Kitgum area seems to bring out the worst in medical and nursing staff and the incidence of pregnancy, drunkenness, insubordination and assault is prodigious. Fortunately the magistrate is lenient when it comes to a prison sentence, otherwise half the hospital staff would be there."

Dictaphones, photocopiers and word processors hadn't been invented. The hospital clerk had no shorthand so I used to write the monthly report in longhand and pass it to him for typing on an ancient machine. The original was for the Director of Medical Services, the first carbon copy was for the Provincial Medical Officer and the second copy for the office file. I always had a further carbon copy made, pretty faint by now, for me to keep. It is from these that I have reminded myself of much of the information on this stage of my life. My annual reports were a source of pleasure and pride and I livened them up by including black and white photographs. The Provincial Medical Officer, his adrenaline rising, wanted to know under what head of expenditure I had charged them and was taken aback (unusual for him) when I told him I had paid for them from my own pocket.

The hospital had no electricity so no X-ray. Broken arms and legs were set and plastered by feel and the results were surprisingly good but with no X-ray before and after to confirm that the bony alignment was satisfactory. Broken limbs have to be watched most carefully in the first twenty four hours in case they became swollen within the plaster of Paris, so cutting off the blood supply and becoming gangrenous. The nurses had to check the limb frequently, especially through the night to be sure that the toes remained warm with a good circulation - if they became cold the plaster would be split if necessary but one night this was not done. The next morning I was sickened to find the leg stone cold and dead and had to amputate it. Daylight operations were not a problem but at night I ran a lead with an inspection lamp through the operating theatre window from my car battery parked just outside. To save the battery, pressure paraffin lamps were used for all the preparation but these could not be used during the operation as the ether used for the anaesthetic was highly inflammable and explosive. Once two nurses, one carrying a bottle of ether and the other a paraffin lamp, collided in mid theatre and the bottle fell on the cement floor and broke. I bellowed at everyone to run like mad, which they did, including the nurse with the lantern. We were fortunate that no explosion or fire resulted.

We had no telephone at that time so if I was needed at night a porter would walk or cycle to my house about half a mile away with a lantern and would waken me by knocking on the bedroom window. Later he obtained a torch with a powerful beam and would shine this through the bedroom window to waken me. One night I climbed out of bed naked and took refuge from his probing torch in a curtained wardrobe and fumbled in the dark for a pair of trousers; it was only when I got to the hospital that I found I was wearing my dinner suit trousers.

Tulio Lam had been trained as a theatre orderly while in the King's African Rifles and now worked for me in charge of the operating theatre in Gulu. He looked after the surgical instruments, kept them in perfect condition and made sure that the correct ones were put out for each operation. He spoke several African languages and was very useful as a translator when explaining matters to patients and their relatives, who would often wait on the grass outside the theatre for a report at the end of the operation. He was a much respected figure, more than was his due, for I later discovered that he often told the relatives how difficult he had found the operation and how he had needed my assistance. Poor Tulio came to a sticky end for he had learned how to copy a key while in the army. Items were going missing from the store to which I held the sole key. I was unable to explain this until one night there was an almighty explosion. It turned out that Tulio had entered the store with a hurricane lamp which he had placed on a leaky forty gallon drum of industrial spirit which exploded, killing him and blowing the roof off the store. The copy of the store key was found on his body. After his death I was told that he used to charge relatives for the operations he claimed to have performed.

Artificial limbs were not available in Uganda - the only source of supply was Nairobi in Kenya where the Salvation Army had a hostel where people being fitted could stay. The limbs were expensive and it took two days travel by train to get there, so very few people could afford an artificial leg. The only exceptions were men from the King's African Rifles who had lost a leg while in the army and they were fitted free with a wooden leg, admittedly not a high quality article, but serviceable nevertheless. The great majority of men who lost a leg never received an artificial limb and struggled about with a single staff, which they seemed to prefer to a pair of crutches. From time to time I would come across an ex-soldier with his artificial limb and would wonder how I could find someone with the skill to make these for me. Then I thought I had struck lucky - I found a man in a local government prison who had not only been fitted with an articulated leg but who had made his own replacement from wood when the original wore out, somewhat primitive to be sure, but it worked. "What are you in for?" I asked and he replied "for adultery", this usually being a euphemism for failure to come up with the bride price. Would he come and make limbs for me at the hospital if I could secure his release I asked, to which he readily agreed. So I spoke to the Jago who said his prison sentence could be cancelled if he paid compensation, or the full bride price to the girl's father, provided the District Commissioner agreed. So I went to the DC to discuss the matter, the amount of compensation was agreed and paid and the man was released. I sent him a travel warrant to come to Gulu on the weekly bus - and he was never seen again.

Dr David Rosanelli was one of our team of doctors and when I discovered his wife also was a doctor it was as if I had won the football pools; in no time I found enough money to employ her on a part time basis. He had served in Field Marshal Rommel's Afrika Korps as a doctor and we were all surprised to find him serving in the British Colonial Medical Service after the war but his charm and skill (and hers) soon disarmed any thoughts of prejudice. When the German army was being driven out of North Africa he found himself squeezed into a pocket of territory between the British and American forces. He told how he thought that the Americans would be a softer option for a prisoner of war so got himself captured by them rather than by the British and spent the rest of the war in the USA organising a prison camp orchestra and improving his skills on the viola. We had a number of ex Desert Rats who had served with General Montgomery in North Africa. They used to organise an annual El Alamein reunion dinner in Kampala and David was very touched and honoured to be invited to attend. David was what I have always called a proper doctor - a physician rather than a surgeon such as myself and the Acholi benefited greatly from his skills. He was a wily bridge player and passed on some of his skills to me.

Blindness due to trachoma was common but now we had the staff to do much more about it. Dr Irmtraud Rosanelli took a special interest in trachoma and became very skilled at the operation of tarsectomy, which preserved and improved that sight which remained. In the year 1955 she did 536 such operations, all under local anaesthetic. She operated once a week doing perhaps a dozen in a morning. Well in advance she would get in touch with a Jago from a certain area and he would send along an agreed number of patients on an agreed date, usually people who knew each other and who would give each other moral support whilst at the hospital. They would arrive the day before, together with a relative to care for them and prepare their food for the four days that their eyes were bandaged. We provided no beds, no food and minimal nursing: there was a thatched shelter in the hospital compound where they all slept. Before doing the tarsectomy on the first patient Irmtraud would have injected the local anaesthetic in the next so that she could move on without delay. At the end of each operation the patient would sit on the grass, eyes bandaged till the last was done. Then, hand on the shoulder of the one in front, they would be led in crocodile to the shelter. After four days the cotton sutures would be removed from the upper eyelid and home they would go on foot, sometimes many miles. The pain of inward turned lashes scratching the cornea had gone, the inflamed cornea had started to heal already with the four days of bandaging; not only was the remaining sight saved but there was some real improvement in vision as well.

The doctors and sisters would meet for morning tea and I would bring the most recent issue of the British Medical Journal or The Lancet if there was anything interesting to discuss. On one occasion David Rosanelli told the incredulous group of a report that some tablets containing a combination of sex hormones had been tested on women in Puerto Rico and had been found to exert a contraceptive effect - I opined that I doubted that it would catch on. On another occasion we spoke of the nuisance of stray dogs wandering in the hospital compound, scavenging from the dustbins. I had just seen one enter a ward while I was doing a round, put its front paws on the bedside locker and steal the food that was there. So I decided to do something about it, Sister Barbara Martin, who was the local RSPCA representative, insisting that we must be kind about it. The first thing I tried was giving an overdose injection of time expired human insulin - the dog went into coma in a shady place and recovered a day later, by now ravenously hungry. So I discussed the problem with John Oakley, the Township Officer who said he would come along with a van and half a dozen men and nets to catch the dogs. They would be put in a pound and shot after an interval if unclaimed. I thought it prudent to arrange a date when I knew Barbara Martin would be away from the town doing a clinic elsewhere but I had not bargained for Irmtraud Rosanelli's reaction. We were gathered as usual for morning tea when we heard a commotion outside, men shouting, dogs barking and howling as they were netted and clubbed. Irmtraud threw a mega-tantrum, far worse than I would have expected from Barbara Martin and she didn't speak to me for days. We were dog free for a week or so and then a new lot took the place of the dead ones.

Sometimes when I was in town I would call in for cinnamon tea with JB Patel who had a motor spares shop with a hand operated pump atop a forty gallon drum of petrol. He made strong cinnamon flavoured tea by mixing equal measures of cold water and milk in a saucepan on a primus stove, adding two tablespoons of tea leaves, two or three more of sugar and a few sticks of cinnamon and boiling for ten minutes. The resultant brew was coppery in colour with a fiery flavour which brought one out in a profuse refreshing sweat on a hot day. One day an Asian competitor turned up uninvited and unannounced and sat himself down. "Are you com-for-table" asked JB with ill concealed sarcasm. "No, I am come for tea" was the reply.

Preventative measures undoubtedly did more for the health of the public than curative measures could ever do. Uganda was a very poor country in terms of government revenue and my budget for medical services was equivalent to a few old pence per head of population per year. I have already mentioned the housing improvement competition and these became a regular feature. Various government departments - education, agricultural, veterinary and medical, clubbed together to put on county shows from time to time. The medical exhibits included a model house and we provided latrine stances and wooden window shutters for sale. We had a microscope and laboratory specimens so that people could learn how parasites were transmitted and how they could be avoided. We sold an illustrated vernacular booklet entitled 'Gwok Gangi' explaining the Protection of Health bye-laws and we had a good food and cookery demonstration with free samples to taste. We sold a calendar with a different photo for each month illustrating some aspect of public health - I featured in October 1956 examining a person with leprosy at Alelelele leper settlement. The Nursing sisters devised a five foot square snakes and ladders game featuring aspects of healthy and unhealthy living. They organised a baby show which was a complete failure as we did not realise that it was considered bad luck to parade a baby's charms in public. There were talks with question and answer sessions, lots of good humoured banter from the Acholi but I wonder how much of my propaganda was ever put into practise. There was a tribal dancing competition, several teams performing the Bwola fuelled by draughts of pombe, millet beer. As darkness fell the youths and maidens would perform an impromptu dance called the 'Dingi-Dingi', with much tut-tutting and shaking of heads by the adults at the erotic movements of the young girls. The end of the Aswa county show in 1955 was marred by disaster; a lorry taking participants home overturned with two killed, eleven serious and twenty five minor injuries.

The Acholi diet consisted mainly of grain with relatively small amounts of meat. On the whole the diet was reasonable as they were a robust people of good stature with very few of them too thin or too fat. There was an important dietary taboo for women past the age of puberty - chicken and eggs were forbidden for some reason thus withdrawing a valuable and cheap source of protein from the childbearing population. Cattle could not be kept in large numbers because of the tsetse fly and were killed on ceremonial occasions only, similarly goats and chickens. The planting season was from March to July when more goats than usual were killed by farmers in exchange for help with tilling and planting the land. The main source of meat was obtained from hunting, every division being permitted two hunts per year. Three to four thousand men would take part forming a large circle, driving the game closer and closer into the centre when it would be set upon by men with spears and a few guns. This would result in a huge amount of meat having to be consumed in a short time, not particularly valuable from a nutritional point of view - there being no refrigeration facilities for meat storage. Another method of hunting, which was outlawed because of its cruelty, was to ring the game with fire. Fish was available for those living close enough to the Nile. One of the Nile ferrymen at Pakwach, on whose wife I had operated, used to send me a Nile perch from time to time.

I used to receive official visitors from Kampala and Entebbe, some of them welcome, such as surgeons, physicians, tuberculosis specialists, eye specialists, nutritionists and so forth. Some were unwelcome - such as the auditors who turned the hospital upside down once a year looking for fraud. Some visitors from England seemed to be on a swan - for instance, what on earth was the Chairman of the London University Appointments Committee doing visiting me in July 1955? I also received a visit from a bunch of Members of Parliament from Westminster. When government officers went to areas where I knew venomous snakes to abound I used to issue them with syringes and ampoules of anti-snakebite serum, and I did likewise to this visitation of Parliamentary personages. One lady MP asked if the Acholi population received the same issue, to which I replied in the negative - I couldn't afford it from my budget. Back in the UK a Parliamentary question to the Secretary of State for the Colonies resulted: "Why was anti-snakebite serum only issued to Europeans and not the African population of Acholi district, how many Africans had been treated for snakebite during the year and how many deaths due to snakebite had taken place"? This question winged itself back to the Governor of Uganda who passed it on to the Director of Medical Services, who sent it on to the Provincial Medical Officer and in due course it landed on my desk. So far as the hospital figures were concerned I knew the answer - no snakebites and no deaths. So I was told to search the death registers kept by each Jago. These were known to be incomplete but were interesting nevertheless because of their simplicity and probable reliability. Causes of death were not medically certified but were as reported by the relative who made the notification - deaths were recorded as having been due to 'fever', 'coughing', 'fell off a lorry', 'diarrhoea', 'witchcraft', 'drowning' and so forth as the case may have been, but not one was said to have been due to snakebite. I have no doubt that my reply went back by the reverse route and I heard nothing more.

Unexpected deaths were often ascribed by relatives to witchcraft or to poisoning and one of my most distasteful duties in such cases was to undertake on-site post-mortem examinations on exhumed corpses. The District Commissioner and the Magistrate would have issued the necessary order for the exhumation which I would attend, together with a posse of police and my own assistant, often watched by the relatives of the dead person. The stench of decay was overwhelming and permeated my clothing, hair and lungs in spite of a face mask, rubber aprons, gloves and boots. After removing samples and establishing the cause of death the body was re-buried and I would return home to a bucket of Jeyes fluid on the back step into which I put my clothes. I would then walk naked to a hot bath, don fresh clothes and go for a long, long walk to discharge the smell from my lungs. I suppose I did about half a dozen exhumation post-mortems and in each case the cause of death was innocent.

Physicians and Surgeons from Mulago hospital used to

visit from time to time and we would line up cases relevant to their speciality, at the same time observing their surgical techniques. These visits were always welcome and worthwhile. One of the most beneficial skills we learned was the skin-grafting of tropical ulcers on the front of the shin bone. These started with a simple enough injury which then spread to the bone and became chronic, never healing and sometimes progressing to crippling due to loss of the limb. Modern antibiotics, plus good surgical technique cutting and chiselling away infected tissue and bone, then grafting with skin from the thigh, plus a fortnight or three weeks in hospital, produced a dramatic cure.

Less welcome were the auditors - it was beyond their comprehension that a ledger discrepancy could have an innocent explanation. They would spend days at a time going through the books and disrupting my life. I always had difficulty with sugar and tea, the weight of which seldom tallied accurately with the amount on the ledger because of the effect of the weather: a sack of sugar weighed nominally 200 lb but when it was damp in the wet season or dry in the dry season this could vary from 210 lb to 190 lb and I would have to argue the toss with the auditors about this. Once I blew my top when the auditor insisted that I add the excess weight of tea in the store to the ledger. I refused, telling him that it was because the tea was damp and that I would prove it. The next dry day a sack of damp tea was weighed and then spread out on a tarpaulin in the sun, raked, re-bagged and re-weighed and I was right - it now weighed less than was on the ledger. I asked him to explain what he had done with the missing weight and received a jaundiced look; he redoubled his efforts to find other evidence of skulduggery, failed to do so and left discomfited in due course.

The British Medical Association had an active branch in Uganda and while I was in Karamoja I had presented, on one of my visits to Kampala, a paper on the pattern of disease in that district. I had been nervous as a kitten but warmed to my subject as I got into the talk and was totally amazed and surprised when everyone burst into applause at the end. It didn't go to my head but set a pattern for the future and I was never again frightened to speak before an audience. While I was in Acholi district I was asked to organise a BMA meeting in Gulu and leapt at the opportunity. Nineteen doctors from all over the protectorate attended, I spoke myself and arranged for a programme of other speakers and we finished with a party in my house arranged by Pat. In later years when I was living in England I came to disagree with some of the political activities of the BMA and resigned. Later I rejoined, only to resign once again when my subscription was, in my view, improperly applied to some political posturing and I never rejoined.

The Maternity unit with its associated Midwifery Training School was the jewel in the crown of the medical services in the whole of the Northern Province of Uganda. It consisted of four single story buildings costing a total of Shs 214,000 (£10,700) and was opened in December 1955 by Mrs Trim, the wife of the Director of Medical Services. Dr May Wreford Smith had been appointed six months before to commission and run the unit together with Jessie Abrahams, Midwifery Tutor. As the great day of the opening approached it became plain that the Public Works Department would not be able to complete everything in time so Dr Wreford Smith and Sister Abrahams set to with brooms to sweep up and brushes to apply the final coat of paint. Local worthies were invited to the ceremony which was timed for ten o'clock in the morning. I was worried about the Jago for Gulu who was always inebriated by then and was advised that he would probably not notice if he did not receive an invitation. Every seat was filled except for four reserved for May Wreford Smith, Jessie Abrahams, myself and Mrs Trim who was expected at any moment, when the Jago for Gulu arrived unsteadily and cast a rheumy eye on the scene, staggered to the empty seats and said "You did not ask me so I came". We hastily found a chair for him and the proceedings went off without further hitch.

We admitted eleven midwifery trainees all of them with primary education only. They knew very little English and had to receive lessons from Pat in order to understand their midwifery lectures. The training period was twenty seven months, at the conclusion of which the first five qualified as midwives, a real triumph for May Wreford Smith and Jessie Abrahams. Early in the first training period a toilet became blocked when a pupil tried to flush a placenta away and they were told to take the placentas to the manhole cover over the septic tanks for disposal. One morning soon after, three artery forceps used for clamping the cords were missing and Jessie Abrahams correctly surmised that they had been dropped by the night staff into the septic tank together with the placentas. They were summoned from their beds, told to remove their uniforms and to wear their own clothes in order to retrieve the valuable surgical instruments.

To obtain new surgical instruments was a long, laborious and expensive matter. First one had to accumulate the necessary finance from one's annual allocation of funds. Then one had to satisfy the PMO and DMS of the necessity of the purchase and, if approved, the DMS would place an order with the Crown Agents for the Colonies in Millbank. And then, about a year later the instrument would arrive. We needed a vaginal speculum badly and its arrival was eagerly awaited. A vaginal speculum has a screw operated ratchet which holds the two curved blades apart while one removes a polyp or suchlike, and the ratchet has to be reversed to close the blades and remove the speculum. Soon after we had received the speculum a patient on whom it was being used gave a shriek, leapt from the couch and legged it down the road with the speculum in situ and that was the last we saw of it.

The new maternity unit rapidly gained a reputation for excellence and many mothers and babies lived who would not otherwise have done so. When we first started work in the new unit the mortality rate for mothers was 2 percent and in the first year we reduced this to 0.7 percent - appalling figures compared with the United Kingdom where the figure was a thousand times less in 1990, but what an improvement on leaving childbirth to the forces of nature which is so profligate of the lives of mothers and babies. I remember with horror a seventeen year old girl in her first pregnancy who was brought into hospital in profound pain and shock after having been in obstructed labour for three days. When I operated I found her baby to be dead and her uterus to be gangrenous. I removed her uterus but she died nevertheless. There were so many other sad occasions but no human can have suffered more than this young girl.

Many maternal deaths (and others) were due to haemorrhage and we were able to start a rudimentary blood transfusion service while I was in Acholi district. I had lectured about the idea to prisoners and to secondary schools but this was altogether too advanced for the people to accept at that time. Then in May 1957 I had a stroke of luck when a small child who had lost a lot of blood from an injury was brought to hospital by its mother. She realised that the child was in danger of dying and she and other near relatives agreed to give some blood for the child. When I had checked the blood groups of two or three relatives I found the mother's blood to be suitable so I used this to transfuse the child, who recovered before their eyes and the news spread round the town and then the district like wildfire. I carried out another blood transfusion soon after, using my own blood: a woman had a serious haemorrhage in labour and needed a Caesarean section. She was the same blood group as myself so I gave a pint of my blood, transfused her with it and carried out the operation while the blood was running in. After this, blood transfusion became accepted gradually. It was all rather time consuming; we did not have a refrigerated blood bank but I was soon able to set up a register of volunteer donors whose groups were known who would turn out when needed. I found a particularly valuable source of donors among the prison population who earned a month's remission of sentence per pint given. The sixth form boys at Sir Samuel Baker secondary school also provided a panel of donors. The result of this was that the blood transfusions administered mushroomed from one in 1957 to a hundred during 1958. The development which really got our service going was the new Maternity unit and Midwifery training school - you cannot run a maternity service without blood. Other benefits also accrued and we were able to introduce closed circuit anaesthesia with muscle relaxants and endo-tracheal intubation. In the UK this would have been undertaken by doctors only, but we didn't have enough of them for this so we trained Medical Assistants in the technique.

Acholi district was a haven of peace compared with Karamoja so far as tribal disturbances were concerned but we received many refugees from troubles in the Belgian Congo (as it was then called) and from the Sudan. We had plenty of fights and murders but these were domestic or alcohol related. I would be called upon to do the post-mortem examinations and to give evidence to the High Court when it visited Gulu twice yearly. Full ceremonial was always observed with a guard of honour parading for the Chief Justice but this once had to be postponed for a day when his long trousers went astray on his journey to the district.

The entry wound of a rifle bullet is always smaller than the exit wound and this will reveal whether a man was killed by a shot from behind as he fled or in front as he approached and this may well have a bearing when it comes to the verdict: it is difficult to prove self defence if the man was shot from behind. So I was not popular when I once gave conflicting evidence before the Magistrate's Court and later to the High Court. When I was speaking at the Magistrate's enquiry I did so correctly from notes in my hand, but at the High Court I got muddled and got the entry and exit wounds mixed and was properly admonished by the Judge. On another occasion a man had died from a shotgun blast having half a dozen pellets in the side of his knee and a similar number in the side of his neck, one of which had perforated the carotid artery from which he bled to death. I couldn't understand the strange distribution of the pellets unless there had been two shots but only one had been heard. Then I realised that the man could have been squatting with his knee near his neck bringing the pellet wounds close together. Then someone gave evidence that the man had been found dead with his trousers round his ankles and it became clear that he had probably been squatting behind a bush in order to defecate when he was shot. With shotgun pellet wounds the spread in inches approximates to the range in yards so I was able to estimate that his attacker had fired at about fifteen yards distance.

Some entertaining episodes took place. I was dining in Kitgum with Mavis and Rex Hunt when there was a hammering at the door. Rex's servant went to investigate and returned with the bizarre information that it was a prisoner who had been locked out. He had been out foraging for firewood for the prison and had returned late but the gate-man had refused him entry, telling him to return in the morning as he was not permitted to open the prison gates after dark. The prisoner, who was not a local man, was hungry and frightened of the wild animals he might encounter so went to the ADC's house and Rex sent him back with a note authorising the opening of the gate.

While I was in Gulu there were serious civil disturbances in the Belgian Congo when the Belgians left, orchestrated by one Patrice Lumumba who was regarded as a hero or a villain according to one's viewpoint. Those who live by the sword also die by it, which was his eventual fate, but not before streets, avenues and squares had been renamed after him by left wing zealots in other countries. While Lumumba held sway thousands upon thousands of unspeakable atrocities were reported. Many Belgians, teachers, missionaries, traders and their children fled, quite a number through Acholi district. Their belongings were stolen and they arrived with virtually nothing. Those who resisted were shot or bludgeoned to death. The women, nuns included, were raped, not once but again and again - "I stopped counting" said one to me. The contraceptive pill was by now available and it is ironic that among the first Roman Catholics to take it were some nuns who knew they faced the probability of rape as they fled. One of Lumumba's military commanders had occasion to meet with a member of the Uganda administration on the border and did so resplendent in his uniform with gold epaulettes, many watches up both forearms and his pockets lined with fountain pens, also looted. When it came to signing the agreed document he selected a gold Parker 51 pen, removed its cap, smeared ink on his thumb and applied his print to the paper. Katanga province of the Congo was rich with copper deposits and for a while sanity prevailed there under the leadership of the much respected figure of Tshombe, but he too fell prey in due course to the forces of revolution.

The southern province of the Sudan revolted against their northern rulers while I was visiting Kitgum in northern Acholi. Rex Hunt the ADC at the time heard that there had been an ambush on our side of the border and asked me to accompany him to the area in case there were any casualties. We travelled by Land-Rover and were held up at machine gun point by one of the northern soldiers, a sergeant. We thought it prudent to stop and he was relieved to know that we were friendly, and we to find that he was. He told us that two army trucks full of rebel soldiers, their wives and children had just been ambushed, the drivers killed and the passengers in the back sprayed with machine gun fire. I climbed over the tail board of first one truck and then the other into about an inch depth of warm blood in the process of clotting. There were several corpses in each truck and two more were groaning, seriously wounded. I took the wounded to Kitgum hospital where bullets were extracted and wounds repaired and they eventually recovered. Red tape reared its head at this point: the Sudanese sergeant wanted to take the wounded to Juba hospital many miles away in the Sudan. I knew they would not survive the journey and we reached an agreement that I would sign a receipt for the two wounded if he signed a receipt for the dead, so we parted amicably. A few days later a hundred and forty rebel Sudan Defence Force refugees arrived in Acholi district complete with their medical orderly and first aid box - albeit empty. They later paraded and marched very smartly with buglers and drummers at our annual Remembrance Day ceremony. They were used as labour for Township projects and at the hospital as well until they eventually returned home to an uncertain fate.

In the absence of the telephone it may be imagined that communications were somewhat primitive but it was amazing how well and quickly they worked. An alert Jago in northern Acholi saw a man who had crossed from the Sudan who he thought to have smallpox. He arrested the man, isolated him in a hut and put a guard on him with instructions to shoot if he tried to escape. He sealed the border so that no other Sudanese could cross, cycled several miles to the Police station at Kitgum and sent a police radio message to Gulu police and they walked fifty yards down the road to me with the message. I telegraphed the Director of Medical Services asking for fifty thousand doses of calf lymph for smallpox vaccinations to be sent by air the same day, motored to Kitgum, cycled with the Jago to the ill man, confirmed the diagnosis as smallpox and got back to Gulu the same evening to find that the calf lymph had arrived. At dawn the next day I set off with a team, formed two other teams from staff in Kitgum and we vaccinated fifty thousand people in the area in three days. No other cases occurred on our side of the border.

Later we were supplied with a telephone service in Gulu - my number was Gulu 6. It was a manual exchange operated from the Post Office. The exchange closed down at night but they plugged my house in to the hospital before going off. The pitfalls of night nurses with limited English and myself with limited Acholi were many and I would often have to get out of bed and go to the hospital to find out what they were trying to tell me. Once on the phone I asked in exasperation "is he breathing?" to which I received the reply "not much, sir". I went down to find a man tusked through the thigh by an elephant. He eventually recovered, the nurse had thought I had said "is he bleeding". The misunderstanding would never have happened when a porter brought a note by bicycle.

Before the telephone arrived I would communicate urgent messages to the Director of Medical Services by telegram from the local Post Office; being a small town where everybody knew everybody else one could be sure that anything interesting rapidly did the rounds. We used a simple code for confidential matters which was based on a single code-word issued by the DMS, which was changed from time to time. In my time in Acholi district the code word was AUREOMYCIN. These letters were written out in a line followed by the remaining letters of the alphabet in order in two rows of thirteen, one below the other. One then substituted the upper letter for the lower or vice-versa and set out the resultant jumble in five letter blocks and took it to the mystified postal clerk for transmission. To ensure that we had understood how to use the code we had to send a message in code back to the DMS. Dr George Nelson (in the next district to mine) replied in code to the effect that he had no idea what they were talking about and would they please explain more clearly.

While in Gulu an event took place which was to change the course of my life: the Royal College of Obstetricians and Gynaecologists in London recognised the training provided by the Makerere Medical School at Mulago hospital for its higher qualification, the MRCOG. At the same time it had become plain that independence for Uganda would take place over a much shorter time scale than we had previously thought and it had become government policy that Uganda nationals should be promoted preferentially to available vacancies so as to prepare for independence. At this time Professor Rendle-Short advertised for a registrar post in Obstetrics and Gynaecology at Mulago hospital and I applied for and obtained this appointment in order to retrain myself for re-entry to the practise of medicine in the United Kingdom. Thus I came to leave Acholi district in 1959 after five very happy and busy years. I concluded in my annual report for 1958 as follows:

> "I came to this district in 1954 and I shall be leaving it in 1959. These years have been a period of intensive development and interest. Expatriate staff has more than trebled. In Central Government hospitals about £25,000 worth of building has been done and another £10,000 is approaching completion. About £10,000 worth of building has been completed in Local Government institutions. The Northern Province Training School for Midwives has been opened and I count myself privileged to have been concerned in some way in its conception, its birth pangs and its emergence as a vigorous and thriving unit. It is my earnest hope that the emblazon 'Gulu School of Midwifery' will become a prized possession, a mark of efficiency, compassion and humanity.
>
> We have come a long way since the 15th August 1926 when the Acting Governor wrote in our Visitors Book: 'Paid a surprise visit to the Native Hospital today at 5.30pm. Only a native caretaker in charge, and a few patients scattered about the compound. I could not inspect the building as it was closed. The female wards are of a very poor type. A medical Officer should be posted

> to Gulu as soon as one is available'.
>
> On this note I pay tribute to the past Medical Staff of this District for their work and vision, I thank the present staff for their unstinting efforts on all occasions, and I look to the future staff to carry the art of Medicine beyond the confines of our present knowledge and conditions".

When it came to my departure a party was arranged and unbeknownst to myself a collection was made and a presentation chiming clock bought. I only heard of it just before the party when someone discovered that Colonial Service regulations prohibited presentations except on retirement. I learned later that Chris Powell Cotton the Provincial Commissioner had been consulted; he checked the regulation and saw a way out: "Don't present it" he said "just leave it around for him to take away", which I did. That night, having drunk too much, I was sick as a dog. It wasn't till daylight (no electric light - I had sold my generator) that I saw that I was vomiting and passing blood and was ill as well as being drunk. However I survived both the illness and the night, with the clock chiming every quarter and striking every hour, which it still does half a century later. As I drove away from the hospital to take up my new post Aldo the head porter, in a freshly pressed uniform and smart red fez, stopped me, saluted and presented me with a fine pair of Acholi spears which have since been wall mounted in eight successive homes. They and the clock are a daily reminder to me of times past and of friends of all races and creeds, some of them later wantonly and cruelly slaughtered under the yoke of self-styled President for Life, Conqueror of the British Empire, King of Scotland, Field Marshall Idi Amin Dada.

Chapter 9

1957 - South African Safari

While in Gulu my periodic 'long leave' fell due. The great majority of Colonial Civil Servants came from Britain and their long leaves enabled them to return to their homes and renew contact with their relations. This often included some of their children who were at secondary school in England because of inadequate facilities in Uganda or Kenya. The duration of the leave was six months after three years service or pro rata; travel with fares paid had always been by passenger liner but now,1957, many people travelled by air. The Comet airliner, the first commercial jet, was the pride of British aviation and provided a service from London to Nairobi. My situation was different. My close relatives were in Kenya and Pat's parents lived in South Africa so we determined to go there by car, camping all the way. I had a fairly new Vauxhall Cresta saloon which I thought would stand up to the journey. This threw the Uganda administration into confusion as there was no precedent for this and they had no idea what amount of money I would be entitled to for the journey. I made the suggestion that they pay me the going government mileage rate plus a bit extra as I was saving them five fares - two adults and three children. They eventually agreed to this but had serious misgivings in case I actually made a profit out of it all - such were the thought processes in the Treasury department.

There wasn't much to decide so far as the route was concerned as there was only one main road from Uganda to South Africa but I had to calculate very carefully how much we could carry in one saloon car. The distances between petrol pumps, mostly hand operated on a forty gallon drum, were often a hundred miles or so and in one case, in Northern Rhodesia (now Zambia), over two hundred miles so I felt that I had to carry a spare couple of gallons at all times. The same consideration applied to water; with three children we could never risk being unable to find water fit to drink across tropical Africa so I carried a couple of gallons. Tents, inflatable matresses (no camp beds), bedding, clothing, emergency medical supplies, towels, toiletries, primus stoves, lantern, torches, some paraffin and food for a day at a time soon filled the car. I had fitted a roof rack and bought a waterproof tarpaulin. The journey had been planned for the dry season so we did not encounter any rain till we were well on the return journey. Passports, inoculation and vaccination certificates, international driving permits, travellers cheques, some of the currency of each country through which we would travel were all sorted. But one item was no trouble whatever - visas - for we were travelling through British Protectorates, Colonies and Dominions all the way. Sure enough we had to show our passports but there was no let or hindrance to our passage. Being a doctor I carried more than a first aid kit - I carried my emergency bag in case of accidents and it came in useful on the very first day when I came upon an accident on the road through Kenya. At every border I declared the contents of the bag which contained a few injections of morphine as I did not want to be accused of smuggling drugs and had no trouble until the Tanganyika - Kenya border on my return. It wasn't the morphine that bothered the customs man: "Of course if it was sulphonamides we should have to confiscate them" he said, waving me through. I had several bottles of several types of sulphonamides (used for serious infections) and it transpired that these were in demand by the Mau Mau rebels for treating their wounds. Several people advised me to carry a gun but I did not want to do this as it would only create problems when crossing borders. Besides, Africa was at that time a very safe place, excepting perhaps Mau-Mau territory in Kenya which was one of the two places where the car broke down. The only item I carried which might have been regarded as a weapon was a panga, a machete which was commonly used as a farm implement, carried for the purpose of splitting firewood at our nightly camp sites. Never did I feel the need to use it as a weapon but it would have severed an arm or sliced a jugular very effectively if required. It travelled under the driver's seat by day and I slept with it beside my inflatable mattress.

The route took us through countries that have now become fully independent, some of them changing their names in the process. At that time we went from Uganda to Kenya, Tanganyika (now Tanzania), Northern Rhodesia (now Zambia), Southern Rhodesia (now Zimbabwe) and into the Dominion of South Africa (now the Republic of South Africa) to Cape Town and the Cape of Good Hope. The names of some of the towns through which we passed will mean nothing to most people but I record them here as they are music to my ears: Gulu, Kitale, Nakuru, Nairobi, Kajiado, Namanga (Tanganyika border), Longido, Arusha, Makuyuni, Mbugwe, Babati, Beroko, Kolo, Kondoa Irangi, Dodoma, Iringa, Sao Hill, Makumbako, Igawa, Chimala, Mbeya, Tunduma (Tanganyika - N Rhodesia border),

Isoka, Mpika, Chitambo (Livingstone died here), Kanona, Serenje, Kapiri Mposhi, Broken Hill (now Kabwe), Lusaka, Kafue, Mazabuka, Monze, Chume, Kalomo, Livingstone (NR-SR border), Wankie, Gwai, Bulawayo, Gwanda, Beit Bridge (SR-SA border), to Johannesburg, across the Karoo desert to Cape Town and Hout Bay. From Gulu to the Cape, including many diversions and return, we covered 12,500 miles all told.

We left Gulu for Kitale where we stayed with my parents for a few days while we made final arrangements for our departure. In the Colonial Medical Service one often returned from leave to find that one had been posted elsewhere but on this occasion I knew that I would be returning to Gulu so packing up our house was not too traumatic. The car was serviced, new tyres fitted, the tank filled plus a couple of spare gallons in a can, our bedding, clothes and provisions were packed, my medical bag was stocked for contingencies, the water can was filled and off we went. We left at mid morning so as to be well past Mau Mau territory by dark, the only danger zone on the whole route - the Mau Mau rebellion was in full swing at the time. As we approached Nakuru in the afternoon, more or less on the equator, I heard the unwelcome sound of a leaf spring breaking and the car developed a list to the near side. I stopped to confirm my diagnosis and then drove on at a crawl for a hundred yards or so to a place where I could safely draw off the road. I decided to stay with the car with Philip and Brian (aged five and three) overnight while Pat and Helen (eight) thumbed a lift to Nakuru to collect a new pair of main springs, reinforced with an additional leaf in each. The spring had broken because the car was overloaded so I immediately reduced the load by not carrying spare petrol and water, apart from a couple of pints of drinking water in a canvas bag hung on the outside of the car to keep cool.

I knew Pat and Helen had arrived safely in Nakuru when a couple of African policemen arrived at dusk to mount guard over us through the night. They wanted me to abandon the car and to go with them to Nakuru for safety but I demurred as I knew that the car would be stripped of its contents, wheels and battery by morning. So I jacked up the car on the side of the broken spring so as to level it, built a fire, cooked the two boys a meal on the primus stove, put them to sleep together on the back seat and I slept fitfully on the front bench seat. It was a bitterly cold night and I woke from time to time and joined the policemen around the fire, drinking strong sweet tea, smoking and chatting. We woke early, had a good breakfast and I unloaded the car in preparation for removing the broken spring in anticipation of Pat's return. I was worried about working under the car with only a simple jack to support it when a lorry drew up to see if I needed help. It was a Post and Telegraph lorry laden with telegraph poles with a European officer on board. He was laying a new telephone line to Nakuru and lent me his lorry jack. He was working nearby and said that he would stop from time to time when passing to see how I was doing and invited me to spend the next night at his camp site a few miles further on. By mid morning I had removed the mainspring when Pat and Helen returned with two new springs, each reinforced with an additional leaf. The Asian shopkeeper who had given them the lift the day before had dropped them at the Nakuru hotel where they happened to meet Mitford Bowker who was a kinsman of mine. The garages were by then closed so next morning Mit took them to the Vauxhall agent where they collected the two reinforced springs and he brought them back to where I was waiting. I fitted the new spring and reloaded the car (now tilting the other way) and we made our way to the campsite of my Posts and Telegraph friend. I unloaded again, removed and refitted the other (reinforced) mainspring and returned the borrowed jack. It was now about sunset and I was tired and dirty. Pat had prepared a hot meal for us and invited our new found friend to join us to repay some of his kindness to me. He reciprocated with a few bottles of beer and we feasted like kings off simple fare by a camp fire under brilliant tropical starlight. I slept the sleep of the just and we set off on our adventure with a light heart the next morning. We motored south through Nairobi, across the Athi plain and its abundant wild game and into Tanganyika at Namanga. Here we set up our first camp of many on the journey.

Each afternoon we would stop at about 4 pm, often by a river, to set up camp before tropical darkness engulfed us soon after 6 pm, each of us falling without delay to our appointed tasks. Philip would at once set about his task collecting dry firewood for the campfire, twigs and small sticks in one pile with which to start the fire and larger pieces with which to keep it going. He soon learned to recognise a good place for the fire on a bare bit of ground, close enough for us to keep warm but far enough away so as not to be a danger and situated so that we should not be troubled by smoke. Brian, the youngest, had custody of the bag containing tent pegs and mallet and travelled with them at his feet in the back of the car. He would jump from the car with his bag of pegs and help me erect the two small tents in which Helen, Pat and I slept, Brian and Philip sleeping on the car seats. When we had erected the tents he and Philip would help me blow up the inflatable mattresses and put out our sleeping bags. In the meanwhile

Pat and Helen had set about preparing the evening meal and setting up the folding camp table and chairs.

As soon as the fire was going I would set a four gallon tin of water on it, collected at our last stop or from a nearby river, to heat for our baths. Pat would put the vegetables to cook on the fire, the meat or whatever cooking on the primus stove. By now it was dark and I had lit the hurricane lantern and the Optimus pressure lamp which gave us a bright light. For bathing we carried a mortar pan known locally as a korai into which I put about a gallon of warm water. Each of the boys would in turn strip and stand in the korai and be soaped and washed from top to toe and would step out onto a wooden duckboard to be dried and don their pyjamas, by now ravenous for their meal. Helen, more modest would bathe herself in the same manner in fresh water, keeping a maidenly eye open for passers by of which there were remarkably few. Having finished she would step onto the duckboard and pick up the korai of bath-water and pour it over herself from shoulder level before drying and donning pyjamas whereafter we would set about our meal with gusto. None had to be sent to their beds, they were dog-tired and couldn't wait. So a quick brush of their teeth, hop behind a bush to spend a penny and fall into bed and to sleep with barely time to say goodnight.

Pat and I would wash up and put everything away in the car boot to protect the food from insects and rodents. We would sit awhile with a cigarette and a glass of beer or maybe a tot of South African Mellowood brandy. We would bathe as had Helen, make up the fire and retire to our sleeping bags, each with a torch and a box of matches, myself with the panga as well. The tropical nights were cold and far from silent, cicadas chirping, bullfrogs croaking, jackals barking, hyenas whooping, children calling "I'm cold" or "I want a wee-wee". It often fell to me to attend to the childrens' calls as it was my task to make up the fire from time to time during the night.

Come daylight we would be awakened by the dawn chorus of birdsong, the children would struggle from their sleeping bags shivering in the cold misty early morning air. As the dazzling sun rose above the horizon, they would be revived with steaming enamel mugs of sweetened tea. We would dress hastily, don jerseys only to remove them, sweating, a short hour later. The boys and I would break camp as Pat and Helen prepared breakfast on the revived fire; the tents would be dismantled and folded, Brian collecting the pegs and placing them on the floor of the car where he sat. Our bedding was rolled and the boys held open the canvas army kitbag at my waist level while I packed it. As we nearly reached the top the three of us would pack it more tightly by raising the bag in the air and dropping it firmly to the ground so as to compact the contents - "up down, up down" several times in chorus went the ritual. Then breakfast and how welcome it was, always cooked - bacon, egg, tomato, fried bread, coffee and toast made on the dying embers of the fire. I would then find a suitable place behind some bushes and dig five small holes to which we would repair as the mood took us, armed with some toilet paper. Philip would rake over the ashes of the fire and cover them with loose sand so as to be sure that nothing could catch alight when we had gone. By 8 am we were on our way again and would stop mid morning for a drink of orange juice or water.

At intervals of fifty to a hundred miles we would come upon a small town and would stop for petrol, fresh water and provisions. Little boys have little bladders and frequent stops were needed for a roadside pee. Traffic was very light and hardly ever did another car pass while we were stationary, but one did. Philip continued his pee unabashed but Brian admonished him "you should turn it off like I do", gripping his penis to arrest the flow and waving to the passing occupants with his other hand.

Our tent was but small with a central pole which took up a disproportionate amount of the available room. At one camp there were two trees not far apart and I slung a rope clothes line between them and hung the apex of the tent from this line which enabled me to dispense with the pole. This proved much more satisfactory and I did this whenever possible for the rest of the trip. Sometimes I would throw the rope over a high branch and hang the tent from that, once this was under a Baobab tree, but never again. Baobabs have a huge spongy trunk to store sufficient water through the long arid season and this applies also to the branches and leaves. Through the night I was intermittently wakened by the sound of heavy drops falling onto the tent. In the morning I found numerous sticky messes adherent to the surface of the tent and spent an hour or more trying to clean them off before folding it away for our next day's journey. The tent was indelibly stained and was regarded with disdain by the person to whom I tried to sell it a year or two later.

We were driven from a campsite by bees one morning in central Tanganyika. We had come upon a roadside rest camp at Kondoa Irangi, where people on the long distance bus could alight and rest for a day or two till the next train fell due at Dodoma, on the east-west railway line from Dar-es-Salaam on the coast to Kigoma on Lake Tanganyika. True, there was no actual railway line at the rest camp but there was a connecting bus and we were glad to take advantage of the chance to sleep under thatch rather than canvas.

The buildings were simple wattle and thatch with no other facilities but provided adequate shelter. We enjoyed a leisurely evening meal without having to set up camp and slept soundly, waking to a glorious cloudless dawn. Pat and Helen had bacon in the frying pan when we were set upon by a swarm of angry bees. I shut the children in the car, we threw away the bacon and coffee, dumped loose bedding and cooking utensils in the boot and fled un-stung, hungry, thirsty and in disorder towards Dodoma a few miles distant on our route. Dodoma was a small town serving the farming community and I knew there to be a hotel which had been built by the Germans before the first world war when Tanganyika was a German colony. Our adrenaline levels soon subsided and everyone cheered up when I promised them a big breakfast as soon as we got there. A mile or so before we got to Dodoma Brian piped "I want a wee". I told him it was only a short way and asked if he could wait till we reached the hotel, which he assured me he could. The hotel was built in a pre-war German style with thick walls and as we mounted the steps to the entrance Brian (not knowing exactly what a hotel was) asked if this was it. On learning that it was he hoisted the leg of his shorts and peed there and then on the steps. After a moment of surprise and confusion we realised that no one had witnessed the episode so we entered in all innocence and were served a full English breakfast with fine starched linen and marmalade from a silver dish. We re-packed the car which was a shambles and took the opportunity of a good wash in the cloakrooms before resuming our dusty journey.

A most welcome chance of a clean up came at the border between Tanganyika and Northern Rhodesia (now Zambia) at Tunduma. All the roads on which we had travelled had dirt surfaces and, as it was the dry season, we travelled in a cloud of dust which permeated our hair, ears, noses, clothes, bedding and the car. So we were none too clean after a few days travel despite our nightly bathing routine. At Tunduma we found a Government rest camp with sleeping and cooking accommodation and, *mirabile dictu*, a bathroom with running water. The African superintendent made us welcome for some nominal charge and we stayed two nights. Pat took the opportunity to wash every item of clothing and bedding so we were able to resume our journey as clean as we had started. The children enjoyed a day off from travel and a day in the open air - it was somewhat cooler by now as we were well south of the equator. We were on schedule to get to Pat's parents in Harrismith in the Orange Free State on our appointed date; we were well pleased with our progress despite the loss of a day's travel with the broken spring and set off into Northern Rhodesia on a good but unmetalled road.

Near Mpika I saw a European man thumbing a lift, a most unusual occurrence in central Africa, so I stopped. He climbed into the back of the car with the three children telling them entertaining stories. He was a Protestant missionary and had missed the long distance bus which had gone through Mpika several hours early. Apparently this bus had a six day route, three days outwards to the north, then three days homeward to the south; the drivers (two of them, taking turn and turn about) had a day off before resuming the next scheduled journey. If they could make good time they would get home after five and a half days on the road and have a day and a half with their families, so I was told. Most people knew the bus would arrive early on the return journey and turned up at the bus stop in good time. Our missionary passenger was travelling to Chitambo, a mission station five miles off the road where Livingstone had died, which we reached late that afternoon. He said he would bicycle from there but I left the main road and took him right to his destination, recognising on the last mile an ominous sound. It was a burned out rear wheel bearing. Having experienced this some months before in Uganda, I had had the foresight to buy a spare which I carried in the glove compartment. That is, until Dr Deogratias Byaruhanga in Gulu asked my opinion on a strange noise emanating from the rear wheel of his Vauxhall. He was impressed with my expert mechanical knowledge and was most grateful that I could supply the necessary part as well, but I never got around to replacing my spare bearing.

I then experienced an unlikely succession of coincidences. The missionary to whom I had given the lift took me to meet a Dr Blaikie, who turned out to be the brother of Dr Ken Blaikie whom I knew and who was in charge of the next district to mine in Uganda. He offered help at once, Pat and the children could stay at the mission station while I went to Broken Hill some hundred and fifty miles away to get a new wheel bearing. There was a further problem - I had to have a special 'puller' to pull the half shaft from the differential, not a tool that one is likely to find except in a well equipped service station. Dr Blaikie had himself experienced the same problem some months earlier and had, as a consequence, ordered a puller which had arrived that very week. I removed the rear wheel and brake drum and pulled out the half shaft complete with the faulty bearing, had some supper and went to bed early so that I could rise in good time to be at the bus stop by 2am for the 5am bus.

True to form it arrived early, at about 3 am and I set off with the half shaft and bearing, a razor, pair of pyjamas and some cash. The bus was ramshackle and full of African passengers and the driver drove like Jehu along the dusty road reaching Broken Hill around mid-day. I located the Vauxhall agent a short way from the town centre, handed over my half shaft which they took into a workshop, pressed off the old bearing and pressed on the new all in about five minutes and for a surprisingly small charge. I hadn't eaten since the evening before so found a snack bar and assuaged my hunger, setting off northward on foot, much refreshed, having learned that there was no bus till the next day. "Oi, you" I heard someone call and knowing that it couldn't be for me as I knew no one in the town, I walked on. "Oi, don't you want this" he called, so I looked round and saw the proprietor of the snack bar hurrying after me with the half shaft and new bearing which I had left under my chair. I walked on northward out of town into open country - it was now my turn to provide the unusual spectacle of a European on foot seeking a lift.

A woman in a small car stopped but she was only going a short way down the road. After another mile or so a Cadillac two blocks long glided to a halt, an African driver in front and a solitary middle aged European with a clipped South African accent on the back seat. He was going to Elizabethville (now Lubumbashi) in the Congo (later Zaire, now Congo again) and could take me as far as Kapiri Mposhi where the road forked, left for Elizabethville and right for Nairobi and Cairo, my route. We conversed about this and that and every now and again he would lean forward to examine the speedometer, admonishing the driver - "Ali, you are going too fast, slow down". Did I play bowls, he asked and I replied that I had done so when I was a medical student as it was very cheap, about sixpence (pre-decimal pence) for two or three hours. "Ali, stop" he commanded and took me round to the rear of the Cadillac and opened the boot. There was a well polished leather case which he opened to display his set of bowls, the best that could be obtained in the whole of South Africa he claimed - he was a top player in South Africa and was on his way to compete in the pan-African bowls championship in Elizabethville. We continued on our way talking about bowls, interspersed with periodic commands to Ali to slow down, till we reached the fork in the road where he went left and I was to go right.

I alighted with many thanks to my kind host taking care not to leave my half shaft with new bearing. It was mid afternoon with hot sun blazing down and I looked around for shade in which to await another lift. There was no shade from the vegetation which was low scrub but in the fork of the road was a notice-board proclaiming that this section of the great north road from Cape Town to Cairo had been constructed with money provided by the British taxpayer. It cast a shadow in which I sheltered, lighting a cigarette as I made myself comfortable squatting on my haunches.

I felt very small and lonely but before I had finished the cigarette I heard a small engined car approaching and up drew a Morris Traveller with a wooden estate type body. A European was driving with an African in the passenger seat and the rear was full of baggage and camping gear, almost to the roof. I didn't think there was room for me, but "hop in" he said and his African servant clambered into the rear on top of all the baggage, looking most uncomfortable. I felt bad about this, but not bad enough to chance waiting for another lift with darkness due to fall in a couple of hours. We introduced ourselves and it turned out that he was Curator of the Coryndon Museum in Nairobi on a trip collecting specimens. He knew my father and had visited the caves on his farm near Kitale to examine old fossils. The back of the car was full of specimens and he was now on his way back to Nairobi and could take me right to Chitambo. As we were driving along there was a muffled explosion from the glove compartment just in front of me, followed immediately by a strong smell of fermentation. The driver sensed my anxiety and explained with a laugh that it was due to his forgotten butterfly trap: he used to put a tot of whisky and an over-ripe banana into a Tate & Lyle Golden Syrup tin still containing a little syrup and the resultant fermentation was, he said, highly attractive to butterflies. He would stop and leave the opened tin under a shady tree while he wandered around for a quarter of an hour and when he returned there would be hundreds of butterflies of which he would take his pick for the museum with his butterfly net. We reached Chitambo well after dark; he camped there overnight and went on his way next morning. The mission station, Pat included, had not expected me till the next day and had battened down the hatches for the night so it took me a few minutes to gain admission, tired, dirty and hungry. It didn't take me long to remedy this and I fell into the deep, deep sleep of satisfied achievement.

In the morning, now being an old hand at this, I rapidly replaced the half shaft with the new bearing. I took the opportunity to change the engine oil and lubricate the grease nipples; we then re-packed and set off in the afternoon. We were now another day behind schedule so we decided to drive through the night and the next day to catch up, one sleeping fitfully while the other drove. In the small hours of the night, while Pat was driving, I woke and wondered how far we had gone; I glanced at the compass which I had fitted to the windscreen near the rear view mirror and saw that we were going south-east to Salisbury (now Harare) instead of south-west to Livingstone. Pat had taken the left fork at Kafue instead of the right, so back we tracked to get on the correct route. We crossed into Southern Rhodesia over the Zambezi bridge south of Livingstone and onto roads which were part metalled: they had two strips of tarmac in the centre of the road, the width of car wheels, on which one travelled until one met another vehicle when each slowed and moved over with the offside wheel on the near-side strip till they had passed. We now made rapid progress, stopping twice to meet relatives. My uncle Alban Barberton had married a young widow Mary Matthews (whose husband Bernard had fallen victim to that dire complication of malaria, blackwater fever) with two young daughters Ann and Jill. Jill had married Jack Wylie, they lived near Bulawayo and we visited them, camping on their ground, bull frogs the size of dinner plates honking away on marshy ground through the night. We also met up with my cousin Louis Braithwaite in the toy department of a department store (name forgotten) in Bulawayo. The store assistants were very patient with my children who had never seen such a display of toys in their lives. Louis met us in the store restaurant in his lunch hour; I had last seen him when I was a child of four or five years old and have never seen him since.

We crossed into South Africa at Beit Bridge on 21st September 1957 and onto real tarmac roads, now impatient to get to Brian and Gladys Thorpe, my parents-in-law. We arrived there full of euphoria and the children ran wildly free in their spacious garden after days of confinement in the car. Their house was but modest, the children slept in the spare bedroom and Pat and I slept in what was intended to be a servants room attached to the garage. Apartheid was the way of life at the time and park bench seats, beach areas, public toilets, hotels, shops, restaurants - in fact everything - were segregated with the choice areas and zones reserved for the white skinned races. Negroes, half castes, Asians and Chinese were regarded as non-white, but Japanese (good trading partners) were officially designated as white so the system was bound to break down with the passage of time: the question was whether it would do so with or without bloody revolution and when. In the event, it took another thirty five years and was more peaceful than many had dared to hope.

We were shown round a model deep alluvial gold mine and I remembered that it was my grandfather, Hal Barber, who had started the gold rush in the foothills of the Drakensberg mountains in 1884, the resultant camp becoming the town of Barberton. I had visited Barberton on a previous occasion, being received by the Mayor and Corporation because I was the grandson of the founder. The jobs in the mines in Johannesburg were segregated by race with the best paid reserved for the whites. The African labour force was housed and fed on the mine compound - no wives were allowed. Because the quality of accommodation and feeding was quite good the white people thought that the natives (or 'Kaffirs' as they were called) were being well looked after and this was self evident because there was a heavy demand for jobs in the mines. At the end of our visit we were shown gold ingots the size of a brick and were told that we could have one if we could carry it away, which we couldn't - the sides sloped inwards towards the top and it was far too heavy to pick up.

After an interval we went on our way to the Cape of Good Hope, camping across the Karoo desert. The Karoo was not sand like the Sahara but a desolate area with low scrub vegetation crossed by a dead straight tarmac road with but scanty traffic, which took a day and a bit to traverse. The accompanying telegraph poles mesmerised one with the sound "whit, whit, whit, whit" as they sped past the whole day long with the consequence that many drivers fell asleep at the wheel on what seemed to be the safest road in the country. We entered the coastal area and camped at Beaufort West which I remember for two reasons, the hardness of the ground and the puncture which my inflatable matress sustained. The ground was so hard that I could barely drive in the tent pegs. Our inflatable matresses were placed on a groundsheet on the bare earth and mine developed a slow puncture. Pat complained that her night was intermittently disturbed by the sound of me blowing it up. I awoke un-rested and believing myself to be black and blue.

We motored on to stay with my uncle Ivan Barberton at Hout Bay - he and his wife Pam offered us the use of their guest rooms where we stayed in luxury. I learned many years later that Ivan had commemorated our visit in stone in his garden. He was a renowned sculptor at Cape Town university where we saw many of his works. One, an eight foot bronze outside the South African Mutual Life Assurance Society offices in Pinelands, Cape Town commemorates Wolraad Woltemade (on horseback) who was a national hero. He was a coast farmer who made repeated journeys on horseback into the raging sea to a shipwreck on the coast rescuing about six people on each trip. On his last sortie he was drowned.

Ivory was Ivan's favourite medium and we saw his Spirit of the Wave, a nude female figure atop a bronze wave on his mantelpiece - the family cat had knocked it to the ground and snapped the hands clean off. A Barberton cat, maybe the same one, is depicted in haughty pose in African stinkwood; a bronze leopard stands guard on a rock overlooking the southern oceans at Hout Bay. A bronze group, man woman and child, commemorating the 1820 settlers stands prominent in Grahamstown. He made statues of many dignitaries and African tribal figures and several public buildings are adorned by and contain his work. He carved the arms of the Republic in oak and these grace the Senate house in Cape Town. I like to feel that our ancestor the artist Thomas Barber's talent has cascaded down the generations to Ivan and now beyond to his sculptor sons Michael and Nicholas Barberton. I am the present custodian of two bronze busts created by Ivan and six bronze medallions of members of the family which will pass down the generations together with Thomas Barber's paintings and drawings.

We returned to Johannesburg, at first by the coastal route. Our first camp was by a cemetery in a small place called Riversonderend. As we breakfasted the next morning in brilliant sun we heard the sound of an African man whistling cheerfully as he dug a grave with pick and shovel. The children ran to see what he was up to and returned to say that he was sweating with the effort so we sent them back with some toast and marmalade and a mug of steaming tea. The next night we camped by the sea at Plettenberg Bay and swam before breakfast. Philip became lost ten yards away on the other side of a sand dune and let out a piercing yell of fear when he could not see any sign of us. Great was his embarrassment when we stepped over the dune and his young brother asked "what wath you thcweaming about"?

We returned to Harrismith for a week or two to prepare for our return journey to Uganda. We had decided to send Philip and Brian back by air with Pat's mother, while her father returned by car with Pat, Helen and myself. It was now near the end of the dry season and we hurried back with the rains pursuing us, sometimes catching us up as we journeyed northwards. We camped at different places on our return and were able to make rapid progress without the two little boys and because we were now familiar with the route. We camped near the Victoria Falls at Livingstone and walked along the riverbank becoming saturated by the spray. At our camp site we were pestered by monkeys crawling over the car and trying to steal our food. Approaching Broken Hill the rain overtook us and was so heavy that we could not stop to strike camp so we drove on into the night. We became so hungry that Pat prepared vegetables for some soup as we drove. I stopped to light the primus stove in the rain and we cooked the soup in a pressure cooker in the middle of the road lit by our headlights, confident that there would be no traffic. We saw the steam spurting from the valve and after a few minutes restored our spirits, drinking the soup from mugs in the car as the rain teemed down. The rain eased as we got to Broken Hill and I asked at a petrol station for a hotel. There wasn't one so we went to the railway station where we slept, Helen on the front seat of the car, Brian Thorpe on the back seat and Pat and myself under the table in the ladies waiting room - all the seats and benches were already occupied. Next day we hurried onwards, storm clouds heavy with rain on our heels all the way through Tanganyika where, at our last camp, half a dozen giraffe ambled past us with no more than a languid look.

We crossed into Kenya and on to Kitale to my parents where we enjoyed the luxury of hot baths, clean clothes and linen sheets on real beds. Gladys Thorpe, Philip and Brian had arrived before us and we made a quick trip to the Murchison Falls Park before the Thorpes returned to South Africa. And then back to work, stony broke having spent all that we had and more on a journey of twelve thousand five hundred miles, through countries that became for the next third of a century unsafe to undertake such an adventure.

Chapter 10

1959 - Kampala and Mulago Hospital, Uganda

In 1959 we packed our precious belongings on to a lorry for the journey from Gulu to Kampala, to take up my new post as Registrar in Obstetrics and Gynaecology to Professor Coralie Rendle Short at Mulago hospital. We followed the lorry along the road as I did not trust the driver not to 'lose' a case on the way. We nearly lost the lot on the Nile ferry because the river level was lower than usual so that the lorry had to climb a steep bank as it left the ferry. The driver lost momentum and ended with spinning wheels unable to make the ascent until he had unloaded our belongings. The ferry was a simple wooden platform floating on empty forty gallon petrol drums with room for one lorry or a couple of cars; it was propelled across the river by a motor launch attached alongside. I was waiting for it to return to collect my car for the crossing and was a helpless witness of the drama unfolding before my eyes across the river, but all was well. There were other very simple hand propelled ferries in Uganda across short stretches of swamp. These consisted of a smaller floating wooden platform with room for one vehicle only, propelled by a couple of ferrymen with long poles. Traffic was light, perhaps only four or five cars a day, so there was no schedule. One would often arrive to find the ferrymen on the far side enjoying a smoke or a siesta but, at the sound of the horn, they would pole their craft like a punt across to collect the waiting car. A tropical swamp is a silent place and the crossing was soundless apart from the occasional grunt of effort from the ferrymen, the dripping of water from the poles, desultory snatches of conversation in the heat of the day and the occasional chatter of birds as they hopped from one floating water lily leaf to another.

Kampala is built on several hills, one of which is Mulago hill where the hospital stands. The city of Kampala - a city it is for it boasts not one but two cathedrals - was at that time but a medium sized town and had changed since I was there eight years earlier when I first arrived in Uganda. The traffic had doubled and redoubled and there was now a rush hour twice a day - but no traffic lights yet. There was an air of expectancy as independence and self rule approached at an accelerating rate. The new Parliament building was complete even if the vote had not yet been extended to the populace. There were two good restaurants with excellent cuisine and you could even order a bottle of wine, mostly South African. Hawkers would come in during the meal and offer flowers or wooden carvings of african animals. There was a night club, the Black Cat, which we used to frequent. It was little more than an upmarket bar with a tiny dance floor which kept the rif-raf away by dint of the admission charge and the price of the drinks. Some young magenta skinned girls were usually present and soon found themselves partners for the occasion from among the attendant bachelors. There was also the Kampala Club (for Europeans only at that time) of which I was not a member - I couldn't afford it. We made our own entertainment with friends - swimming, tennis, bridge, picnics and so forth.

I was allocated a house on Mulago hill just outside the hospital compound, close enough to walk to work, except when it was too hot, the rain too heavy or when there was an emergency. It was a typical spacious colonial style bungalow with overhanging eaves and a wide veranda to prevent the heat of the tropical sun entering the rooms. Heavy rain and hail were deafening on the corrugated iron roof and we were often disturbed by the Mulago hill monkeys running across it. They were cheek personified and would climb on to the top of the open front door, peering inside to see if there was any food to be pinched, which there often was. We would have tea and biscuits on the veranda table and there was often a bunch of ripe bananas hanging from the rafters; a monkey would dash in and steal anything if no one was in sight. Heloise, our Siamese cat, would sit on the lawn sunning herself in the late afternoon and a monkey would creep up silently behind her, grab her tail and give it a yank and dash away. There were mature fruit trees, mango, avocado, grenadilla, tree tomato, orange and lemon. The lawn sloped down from the front of the house to a large fig tree, ideal for children to climb.

Mulago hospital hadn't changed since I last saw it but was to do so over the next fifteen years when it was completely rebuilt, courtesy of the British taxpayer, to be handed over when Uganda achieved self-government. The old hospital consisted of separate brick built wards, bungalow style with corrugated iron roofs, interconnected by concrete pathways. We had two maternity wards at the upper end of the hill, two gynae wards lower down and an operating theatre lower still. Patients going to the operating theatre would be wheeled down the path in the open air, a waterproof groundsheet thrown over them when it was raining. There were many other wards for other specialities and, although the premises were pretty basic, the medical standards were high. There must have been a dozen or more British trained nurses and midwives in charge of the maternity and gynae wards and operating theatre. The medical staff of the Obstetric and Gynae Departmen comprised Professor Coralie Rendle-Short, her first assistant Dr Richard Trussell (later Professor at St George's, Tooting), her second assistant Dr Daphne Kayton (later an NHS consultant), two Colonial service specialists Dr Hugh Mansfield and Dr Derek Scotland (both later NHS consultants), three registrars, Dr Frederick Bulwa (later Professor at Mulago), Dr Nergesh Tejani (such a graceful woman, later a specialist in New York) and myself (later an NHS consultant). Lastly there were about half a dozen young recently qualified house surgeons doing their hospital posts before going to work in the districts of Uganda. The volume and pace of work were tremendous. Dr Bulwa, Dr Tejani and I did successive nights on call and it was far from unusual to do a normal day's work, continue through the night and through the next day so our sleep was very important when off duty. On one occasion, after a hard night's work with emergencies, I was surprised to see Dr Bulwa arrive worn out after his night off. His brother, a farmer, had called him to see a cow in obstructed labour and he had performed a caesarean section.

The labour wards were bedlam. There was no system of referral by general practitioners as in the UK. Many pregnant women had no ante-natal care whatsoever - they just turned up unannounced in labour and had to be accommodated whether there was a bed or not. Others had attended the ante-natal clinic a few times and later attended for the birth. Many never came near the hospital, just having their babies at home with the help of an older woman - there was no such thing as a trained midwife for home deliveries. When things went wrong, such as severe haemorrhage or obstructed labour, some would die undelivered at home, others would make it to hospital near unto death. It wasn't unusual for two urgent caesarean sections to be needed at the same time, trying to work out which should have priority. There was quite a good supply of blood available for transfusions but no laboratory technicians to do the cross matching - that was yet another task we had to undertake before we could get on with the operation.

My first port of call in the morning would be the labour wards to see those women who had delivered during the previous twenty four hours. Every bed would be occupied and some who had delivered in the night would be lying on thin mattresses on the floor between the beds, with their new-born babies. I lived in fear that I would mistakenly tread on one of these babies. Like it or not the labour ward had to be cleared to make room for the anticipated influx of the new day. Unless they were ill or had undergone anaesthesia and forceps delivery, or Caesarean section, the women didn't want to stay in hospital anyway so getting them to go home was no problem. I never ceased to be amazed at their fortitude for they had to travel perhaps many miles, maybe on foot or balanced on the cross bar or carrier of a bicycle, sometimes by bus with their new-born baby, many of them with stitches in a delicate and painful part of their anatomy. A fortunate few would go by car or taxi.

Obstructed labour was common, but for the women who had booked into the hospital for the birth, this was recognised by the midwives and doctors on duty at the time and appropriate action was taken, with either a forceps delivery or a Caesarean section. These mothers and babies did well and they went home hale and hearty when they had recovered. Women who developed obstructed labour at home underwent a terrible ordeal, labouring into the second and third day with no medication for pain relief. Some would make it into hospital in time for a Caesarean section to save themselves and the baby. Others would arrive exhausted and shocked, with infection having set in and the baby already dead. We would try to deliver these with forceps in the hope of avoiding a fruitless Caesarean and the mother would make a slow and stormy recovery with the aid of antibiotics and intravenous fluids. The infection which had set in might well have the consequence that she was unable to conceive again.

Others would continue to labour with a crescendo of pain until the uterus ruptured and the baby was expelled from the cavity of the uterus to lie free in the mother's abdomen, followed by major internal bleeding from the torn uterus. All these babies and many of the mothers died without ever reaching the hospital. Those who did arrive underwent immediate blood transfusion and surgery to remove the dead baby and the ruptured uterus; sometimes it was possible to repair the uterus with the possibility of a future pregnancy. I was once faced with two women with ruptured uteri, knowing that which ever I chose to operate on first was likely to live and the second to die because of the delay.

Professor Coralie Rendle-Short was at that time the world authority on rupture of the uterus in women undergoing neglected childbirth. She and her staff published papers in the medical journals which had a major influence on the management of this dread condition. Doing a Caesarean in obstructed labour saved the mother and her baby at that time but had a long term consequence in that the uterus was weakened by the Caesarean scar, which meant that these mothers had to be persuaded of the necessity of booking in for all future births in case another Caesarean were to be found necessary. Failure to attend the hospital for the next confinement usually had dire consequences and later I published a paper (with Dr Elsie Sibthorpe - an NHS consultant and a previous first assistant to Professor Rendle-Short) on the outcome of labour following a previous Caesarean section in 801 women attending Mulago hospital from 1953 to 1959. All young doctors aspiring to eventual Consultant status knew that two or three publications would be regarded as a sign of industry and would provide useful discussion points when being examined for higher qualifications or being interviewed for more senior positions.

Vesico-vaginal fistula (a hole from the bladder through to the vagina) was another dread complication of obstructed labour which went on and on in the woman's home for two or three days without surgical intervention. The head of the baby (dead by now) was pressed by the forces of labour on the internal tissues against the pubic bone, cutting off the circulation to the wall of the bladder at that point with the result that some of the bladder tissue died and decayed. This had the consequence that urine now leaked from the bladder into the vagina and dribbled down the woman's legs, saturating her clothes, cushions and bedding. She now became a social outcast, smelling of urine, without child and unable to conceive again and useless to her husband. This complication was sadly common and the repair of these fistulas was the only condition in the gynaecological unit for which there was a waiting list. The woman would bring herself along to the out-patient department and we would record her address by county and parish (gombolola) - there were no street names or house numbers. When, after a few months, her turn for an operation drew near, the gombolola chief would be alerted and he would get the woman to attend on the required date. Repairing these fistulas was technically very difficult and they had to wear a catheter for ten to fourteen days after the operation to keep the bladder empty while the fistula healed: disaster struck if the catheter became blocked for any reason or if it became kinked as the woman turned over in her sleep. The repair would break down if the healing process was not sufficiently advanced and one would have to start all over again in a few months time. During waking hours the woman could be relied upon to watch her own catheter but we found that we could not always rely on the nurses to do so through the night.

A woman whose fistula had healed after an operation underwent a total transformation. She no longer smelt of urine and was welcome wherever she went, including the marital bed. If she conceived it was essential that she was delivered by Caesarean section to protect the healed fistula and this was impressed upon them even before the operation was carried out.

Ectopic pregnancies in the Fallopian tube were common because of the frequency of infection in the pelvis. These were emergencies (the tube having ruptured with resultant serious internal bleeding) necessitating urgent surgery to remove the tube and transfusion to replace the blood lost but many women died in their homes because they could not get to the hospital in time. In very rare cases the tube would stretch without bursting as the baby grew but the baby would almost always die at some stage and become calcified within the mother's abdomen. One such woman arrived at the out-patient department saying that she was passing small bones from her vagina from time to time, which I found difficult to credit. I couldn't find anything wrong and couldn't have an X-ray as the apparatus was broken down awaiting a spare part from England, so I asked her to bring the bone along if it happened again. She returned a month or two later with a tiny scapula the size of my small finger nail, wrapped in a slip of paper. The X-ray machine was now working and revealed the bony remnants of a tiny collapsed foetus. She declined an operation as she was not ill or in pain. Another young woman arrived saying she had been pregnant for over a year now and wasn't it time the baby came? She had an advanced tubal pregnancy with, miraculous to say, the baby still alive. I operated on her and she went home very happy with a live baby. Later I encountered two more such cases, one of them with a living baby. I then searched through the hospital records from 1955 to 1961 and found another six cases and I published a report about these in one of the medical journals. This proved a useful talking point when I was later being interviewed for jobs.

Great care was needed to ensure that the correct patient was presented for an operation. In the UK the system is almost foolproof, with patients being identified by full names and date of birth, both orally and by identification labels attached to the wrist. In Uganda many people had the same or very similar names, often with a variety of spellings and most did not know their date of birth. One brought to my operating list for a hysterectomy for fibroids was clearly in advanced pregnancy. I later learned that the theatre porter had gone to the ward and called out "Nsuburga", a common enough name in Kampala. A woman of this name who was expecting a Caesarean section in a few days responded, but said that she was not due for operation today. "Hurry up, the doctor is waiting for you" said the porter. Uganda women always deferred to the menfolk so up she climbed onto the theatre trolley, only to be returned when I checked her identity.

Cancer was reputed to be less common in Africans than in Europeans but the British teaching staff at Mulago hospital showed this was a fallacy. Certainly there was plenty of gynaecological cancer and Richard Trussell, first assistant to the Professor, developed a technique of intra-arterial chemotherapy with Methotrexate for the treatment of cancer of the cervix. The standard treatment of this condition in Britain was either major surgery, radiotherapy or a combination of both but there was no radium or radiotherapy available in Uganda. I assisted Dr Trussell with this work and he published the results in The Lancet in 1961 (with myself as co-author) showing a substantial reduction of the size of the tumour in most cases. The treatment was rather toxic but the results were sometimes remarkably effective. This served as a landmark on the development of chemotherapy for some other cancers.

I was being trained as a specialist by Professor Coralie Rendle-Short and this necessitated a great deal of private study in addition to the heavy clinical work load. She would gather the registrars for a weekly tutorial in her office and would, with her gentle manner and disarming smile, reveal our lack of knowledge, sending us away with a load of reading to do before the next tutorial. She would give us a subject to read up and present at a seminar to the senior medical members of the staff who would expose any deficiencies. We were farmed out to give lectures to the pupil midwives, to help in the Pathology laboratory so that we learned how to describe, cut and stain sections from tissues we had removed during operations; on ward rounds we were expected to present problem patients with our diagnosis, suggested treatment and complications which might be anticipated.

Before being allowed to sit the MRCOG exam one had to submit a book containing detailed treatment of forty patients and a couple of short theses and I took great pains and pride in mine which, when completed, contained 448 typed pages. It was bound, with gold lettering on the front and went by expensive airmail post to the Royal College of Obstetricians and Gynaecologists in London. I then waited anxiously to learn whether it had been approved, which it was. It was returned to me at the conclusion of the examination for the MRCOG seven months later. This masterpiece, now obsolete and useless, remains a treasured possession.

I had a desk in an alcove in the house where I kept all the papers for my book while it was in preparation and I worked on it day after day in short snatches between eating, sleeping, working and enjoying myself. I often had to stop in mid sentence and no one, but no one, was allowed to touch anything on the desk - not Pat, nor the servants, nor the children. Brian, aged about six, needed to borrow my bottle of ink and the inevitable happened, he spilt it on my papers. In a rage I grabbed him by the hair and shook him like a rat and bellowed imprecations at him. I released him, white and shaking to find a handful of his hair remaining in my grip. Mortified at what I had done I made my peace with him - he was less upset than I was. I carefully gathered the hair together and stuck it with a drawing pin at eye level above my desk as a permanent reminder of what I had done and it remained there till we left that house.

Pat took a job as a teacher while we were in Kampala, first at the school at the Kabaka's palace (the Lubiri) and later at the Aga Khan's school. At the Lubiri the children were all Africans, at the Aga Khan's school they were all Asians. She also produced the school plays and found it somewhat incongruous how they enjoyed Shakespearean productions. One of her pupils at the Lubiri school was a lad named Erasmus Kagwa who was about twelve years old at the time. His mother was a widow, trying to bring up her family of several children and Erasmus was going to leave school and go out to work as she could no longer manage the school fees. Pat was horrified that his education should be cut short for this reason so we offered to accommodate him and pay his school fees, which was accepted by his grateful mother. Our house was already full with our own family but we had a disused kitchen which we converted to a study-bedroom for Erasmus. When the house was built there had been no electricity so the kitchen, containing a wood stove, had been built a few yards apart from the house, in case of fire and to avoid the nuisance of smoke in the living quarters. We now had an electric stove in the house so the old kitchen was spare. Erasmus stayed with us as a member of the family and became a good friend but we lost touch with him when we left Uganda. He would go home for the weekends and his mother would sometimes send him back on Monday morning with a present of a few eggs in a banana leaf cleverly fashioned into a shallow basket shape. He hoped to become a meteorologist and many years later I wrote to the Director of Meteorological Services in Kampala to try and regain contact but received no reply.

Our neighbours were the Huttons and the Mansfields and their families. Philip Hutton was a physician and Hugh Mansfield a gynaecologist working at the hospital. There were four Hutton children, one Mansfield, plus our three who formed a happy and carefree gang who could wander around the hill in complete safety. Nearby lived a Ugandan doctor, Dr Kibuka Musoke. He had three children who were terrified of our dogs. One sunny day 'the gang' arrived back at the house, red in the face and hot and sweaty with the dogs panting on their leads. Where had they been, Pat asked. "Hunting" was the reply. Hunting what, she asked. "The Kibuka Musokes" we were dismayed to hear.

Chewing gum was banned but one day I caught Helen chewing away at the forbidden substance. Where had she obtained it I demanded. From the hospital shop she replied. What with? - her pocket money for the week had all been spent. The gang of eight had set up a roadside stall and sold off old toys and books, along with flowers from their mothers' gardens, thus gaining the necessary funds. We had a huge tree with dense foliage in the front garden and we would hear a variety of invisible children chattering away in the branches. No one ever fell or hurt themselves.

The Drs Rosanelli, David and Irmtraud, who had worked with me in Gulu had been posted to Jinja hospital some sixty miles away so we were able to continue our close friendship with weekend visits to each other once or twice a month. Their daughters Veronika and Maria slotted neatly into the ages of my three children and these happy days were marked by the conversation and laughter of children, able to wander the area with unrestricted freedom. The neighbourhood was completely safe and we had no fears that they would be molested or harmed in any way. The visiting family would depart on Sunday after an evening meal. One Monday morning, as I was shaving, the phone rang and I learned that Irmtraud had died in a road accident on their way home from our house the evening before. She had died instantly and Maria, asleep on the back seat, was unharmed, her sister Veronika was away at boarding school with Helen at Eldoret in Kenya. A widower with two young children could not manage to do his work as a doctor without help so I told the Director of Medical Services that Pat and I would help him look after his children if he could be posted to Kampala. So he was posted to Mulago hospital and was allocated a house close to ours and Pat found herself helping to care for two families of children. She had been told years before by a fortune teller that she would have two families and this was the closest she came to it.

We had tremendous storms from time to time with frightening flashes of lightening striking the ground and trees nearby, coupled with violent wind. We were wakened by one such in the small hours of the night with rain hammering on the corrugated iron roof and screams of terror coming from Philip and Brian who shared a bedroom. I had to put my shoulder to the door to open it against the wind and found that a tree had blown down against a window which was smashed in with heavy rain pouring through. The wind snatched the door from my hand and slammed it shut, I gathered the boys to my side, dragged the door open, which promptly slammed again the moment we had escaped through it, our pyjamas saturated. They stayed in our bed for the rest of the night, paying uneasy attention to the story I told to try and divert their minds from the storm. The next morning the sun shone as though nothing had happened and the boys, dressed for school, ran to me with delight saying they would not be able to go because another tree had blown down across the road. "Hard luck" said I, "walk round the tree and ask David (Rosanelli) if he will take you." On another such occasion it happened to be my turn to collect the children from school, huge warm drops of rain beginning to fall as they hurried into the car. On the journey home the heavens opened and monstrous flashes of lightning and bolts of thunder clapped about our ears - we were all terrified of the awesome power of the storm. I hurried as fast as I dared for shelter in case we were struck, driving with relief into our garage, where we sat in the car singing songs at the top of our voices trying to drown the sound of the thunder. The storm passed as quickly as it had come; out came the sun, steam rising from the sodden earth, the birds singing, no doubt sunning themselves after their unscheduled bath. Nearby was Lake Victoria which would be whipped into dangerous conditions by these violent storms.

Dick and Betty Woollard had been posted from Gulu to Mbale in the Eastern Province so we would visit each other now and again. One of their visits to us in Kampala was memorable because of a drunken fight which took place late one night in the servants' quarters attached to my house. I went to see what was going on and discretion led me to the opinion that there were too many people involved for me to sort it out, so I telephoned for the police. An hour later there was no sign of the police and the rumpus was getting really noisy so I went again to the servants quarters. There was a bright moon and perhaps a dozen Ugandan men in heated altercation, half within and half without a small room containing a single bed with a straw mattress and lit by a spluttering home made oil lamp. This consisted of a tin containing paraffin, with a small hole through it's metal lid from which protruded a wick made from a length of rag. I elbowed my way to the doorway and stood with my hand on the door frame, shouted for attention which I did not receive, when a bottle came flying towards me. I dodged the bottle which hit my hand on the door frame, striking my signet ring which absorbed the force so that I was uncut and unbruised. Fearing that the makeshift oil lamp would be upset and set the grass mattress alight I dashed into the room, grabbed the lamp and made my escape. This had the unintended consequence that those involved in the fracas in the room were plunged into sudden darkness which impaired the progress of the fight and they stumbled through the doorway into the moonlight looking sheepishly at me and each other. Their ardour was now dampened sufficiently for them to agree with me that enough was enough and that it was time for bed. One by one they went their ways and I to my bed, only to be awakened by the arrival of a pick-up truck full of police an hour later. "Where is the fight" asked the Sergeant. "What fight?" I replied.

A spell of long leave fell due in 1960 while I was at Mulago hospital. We had saved Pat's earnings as a teacher and used them to buy a Fiat Cinquecento. We went to the Fiat agent in Kampala and arranged to pick up the car in Rome, drive around Europe and ship it back to Uganda. While we did this the three children went to South Africa by air to stay with Pat's parents. We flew first to London and stayed for a week with David Buxton and his wife. We had known David well at Oxford, he was godfather to Helen and remained a close friend for life. But for the war taking him off into the Navy he would probably have married Pat but I intervened. David booked us into a hotel in the Via Veneto in Rome to which we flew on the fabled and ill-starred Comet. I was staggered at it's speed: I bought an Evening Standard at the airport before we left, opened it to read when we had taken off, was interrupted by the arrival of a meal, reopened it at the end of the meal and was unable to finish it before we landed. We were devastated when this marvel of British technology had to be grounded after one of them fell out of the sky into the Mediterranean because of metal fatigue, with the loss of all lives.

We picked up the Fiat in Rome and arranged to deliver it back to the docks in Genoa some weeks later, for shipping to Uganda. We motored north through Italy and into France stopping overnight in small hotels. At one, I ordered mussels, the sight and smell of which Pat could not abide so she took herself off to eat at the next table, intending to return when I had finished the mussels. The waiter, sensing a marital rift, spoke to the head waiter who came over and tried to pour oil on troubled waters - at least that is what I think he was doing for we could not understand what he was saying. Meanwhile I had finished the mussels and Pat returned, the head waiter attributing this to his timely intervention. He was so pleased at the outcome that he brought us a complimentary bottle of Orvietto Abocato to cement our reconciliation.

Another stop was at Carrara - a Uganda bridge friend, John Bernacca, had given us the name of his cousin Mario who lived there and he entertained us royally for a couple of nights. As we entered Carrara I spotted a traffic policeman on a powerful motor cycle and asked for directions. I showed him a slip of paper bearing the name and address - "Oh, Mario" said he, "follow me", which I did with difficulty as he sped through the town with myself in desperate pursuit. Mario was a local worthy. We accompanied him and his wife on the evening promenade through the town; it was like a royal procession, people greeting them with varying degrees of deference according to their station, ourselves basking in reflected glory. Mario took us to see the marble quarries where the finest stone is obtained, which had been used by Michaelangelo. We drove north through southern France and across the Rhine into southern Germany - Pat was admitted without any let or hindrance because she was travelling on a British Passport but I was denied entry because of my Uganda Passport - I was supposed to have a visa. The German at the border control went off to make enquiries, returning to say that I would be allowed to enter on payment of DM 30. I suspected that this was probably a bribe but didn't quibble; my evil thoughts were confounded when I was issued with an official receipt, so we went on our way into Austria and to Graz where we met and stayed with David Rosanelli's old mother. We re-entered northern Italy, spent a day in Venice and made our way across to Genoa where we went to the docks to hand the car over for shipment to Uganda. The dock gates were closed, sealed with a heavy chain and a big padlock with not a soul to be seen within. This posed a problem as we did not have the luxury of any time to spare for we had to catch the Paris-Rome express at 9.15 the next morning and the plane to Uganda the same evening.

"Chiuso, chiuso" said the policeman, without looking up from his hand of cards. We had located a police station to find out how we could gain entry to the docks and found four policemen playing cards around a small table. Not knowing what he was saying I thumbed through my phrase book and learned that chiuso meant closed. So we booked into a hotel whose receptionist spoke good English and she explained that it was Ascension day, a public holiday. She found me the telephone number of the British Consul who was away, so was the Vice Consul. Eventually I obtained the number of the shipping clerk at the consulate who met me at the docks with a huge bunch of keys, opened the gates to allow me entry with the car, saying he would sort it out in the morning. I went back to the hotel and checked my money, discovering that I hadn't enough cash to pay the hotel and the train fare. I couldn't get any more till the banks re-opened the next day - no credit cards at that time.

The next morning I was waiting at the bank with my travellers' cheques at 9 am sharp, obtained some money, tore back to the hotel, paid the bill and we rushed with our bags to the station catching the train with but a minute to spare. Two nuns in our compartment crossed themselves every time we went over a bridge, a mournful looking man selling ice cream walked up and down the train intoning "Gelati Motta, gelati Motta" and an Italian mother with three children produced a packed lunch from her basket, reeking of garlic. She had more than they needed and offered us what was left, for which we were very grateful. We arrived in Rome, caught a taxi to the airport, caught our plane and were back in Uganda the next day.

After a week or two I enquired of the Fiat agent if he had any knowledge of the arrival of the car. "Not yet" was the reply, time after time, so that I began to wonder whether the shipping clerk in Rome had made off with it. The car was supposed to arrive at Mombasa on the coast of Kenya and then be put on one of the two trains a week to Kampala; the Fiat agent would send one of his drivers to the station to meet each train, all to no avail. Then one day I spotted it being driven in Kampala still with its Italian number plate, so I dashed along to the Fiat agent and asked innocently whether it had arrived yet. "Not yet sir" was the reply whereupon I lost my cool. It transpired that the driver sent to collect it had sensed an opportunity to run a car free gratis and for nothing for a week or two.

I was now on the last lap before going to London to sit the examination for Membership of the Royal College of

Obstetricians & Gynaecologists (MRCOG) and redoubled my studies. Political events in Uganda were now gathering pace under the Governorship of Sir Andrew Cohen and it became plain that independence from British rule as a Protectorate could not be long delayed; soon we learned that this would take effect in 1962 when I would actually be in London. The policy of Africanisation of all possible posts in Government employment was already taking place, so I knew that I would not be appointed a specialist in Obstetrics & Gynaecology when I obtained the MRCOG as there would be Ugandan doctors with the same qualification at the same time. I had therefore to make up my mind whether to stay on indefinitely in a subordinate position in Uganda or whether to emigrate to Britain, Australia, South Africa or Canada. Pat and I discussed this endlessly. I knew what the answer had to be but could not bring myself to make the break with East Africa, where my parents lived and I had been born, so I made no decision till I was actually in England. Political change was taking place in Kenya also and independence there was imminent - what I did not know at the time was that my father had decided that it was time for him to retire, sell the farm and move to Spain.

I was by now very well read in medical terms, very well taught, very experienced in my specialist subject and began to feel confident that I would make the grade when it came to the MRCOG exam - indeed it was vital that I did so if I were to burn my boats in Uganda. Senior examiners from the UK would visit Uganda for the annual final medical examinations of Uganda trained doctors. One of my tasks was to see that the necessary patients were in the right place at the right time for the medical student being examined, so I had the opportunity of meeting some of the senior members of the College who were later to examine me. I realised from conversations with these examiners how very different they found the type of medical practice in Uganda from that in Britain; for instance my skill at repairing vesico-vaginal fistulas would not cut much ice in London where the problem barely existed. They advised me not to rely on capitalising my unusual experience but also to familiarise myself with the UK scene by attending a course aimed at the MRCOG exam at the Institute of Obstetrics & Gynaecology at Queen Charlotte's hospital. I booked myself into a four month course starting in February 1962 and was later to learn that my fellow registrar at Mulago, Dr Nergesh Tejani was booked into the same course. Pat and the three children would remain in Uganda while I did the course and the exam, either to await my return if I did so, or to join me in England if I decided to leave Uganda.

I flew from Entebbe airport on my thirty seventh birthday, very much aware of how I was dicing with our future. I had a secure job in Uganda, albeit with uncertain prospects because of political change and was contemplating abandoning this for a new career in Britain. I hadn't even sat the exam and if I passed I would have to re-enter the UK ladder with junior hospital posts, taking a considerable drop in salary at the same time. The timetable for Ugandan independence had now been published and it turned out that I would have to communicate my decision to the authorities before knowing the outcome of my examination. I arrived in thin tropical clothing to an English February, bought an overcoat and checked in to my spartan accommodation. My colleagues on the course were a mixed bunch, English, Indians, Pakistanis, a Persian, an Israeli, a Chinese and a few others I can no longer recall. We attended lectures, teaching ward rounds, demonstrations, seminars, discussions, libraries at the Institute itself, and at Queen Charlotte's, Hammersmith and Chelsea hospitals. Our knowledge was mercilessly probed by our lecturers who assured us that this was but a gentle introduction to the actual examination. At the end of each long day we would re-discuss the days events and challenge each-other's understanding of what we had absorbed. I found Nergesh Tejani's clear, lucid mind and manner of speech a great help and I give credit to her part in my satisfying the examiners at the end of the course. Having now made a firm decision to stay in Britain I bought a Ford Anglia estate car and took her around and about, to the ballet at Covent garden wearing her most resplendent golden sari, to the south coast, to communion at Christchurch College in Oxford. Crossing a deserted Blackfriars bridge late one night I stopped the car. "No woman should cross Blackfriars bridge on a night like this without viewing the Thames by moonlight" I said.

I wrote on 23 June 1962, just in time to beat the deadline, to the Director of Medical Services in Uganda saying that I had decided to leave the Colonial Medical Service under the terms of Compensation which had been offered. I was informed that I would receive a pension gratuity of £2332.17.5d, a pension of £452.17.7d a year and, in addition, I would receive Compensation payments in five annual instalments of £2002.19s, £2142.8s, £2053.3s, £1962.18s and £1874.12s. This seemed to be a lot of money at the time and just lasted long enough for me to put a deposit on a house and to subsidise my salary until I obtained a Consultant post. My Certificate of Entitlement to Compensation which bears serial number 119 is an imposing document on top quality paper and stated at the end 'This certificate is given without alteration or erasure, and no copies or duplicates will be issued'. It was promptly altered by the application of a rubber stamp of Assignment to Barclays Bank and the word ASSIGNMENT had been crossed out and replaced by LETTER OF AUTHORITY, in manuscript! I wrote to Pat to sell up and pack up.

I completed the examination and Pat arrived with the children before the results were published. I had to vacate my accommodation at the Institute and had rented a small cottage at Margaretting Tye, Ingatestone in Essex as a stop-gap until I had lined up a job. I met them at Gatwick airport and took them through London and out on Eastern Avenue towards Chelmsford. Philip, aged nine, had never seen such a density of houses and asked "How do you know which is yours?" Pat explained about houses being numbered, odd ones one side, even the other and, light dawning, he observed "Oh I see, you have to count them." We settled in at Margaretting Tye and I set about applying for jobs. We planned a camping holiday across Europe to Austria while awaiting anxiously the result of my examination. The cottage was for sale and as I had received my pension gratuity and first instalment of compensation I was in a position to consider a purchase but I was horrified when I learned that the asking price was £2000 - there was no way that I was going to pay that, which explains why I am not now the owner of a valuable country property within twenty miles of central London. We arranged to drive to the RCOG in Regent's Park on the day that the results were to be posted on the College notice board but I received the result that I had passed by the first post before we had set off . The whole family cried with joy to see this culmination of years of study and hard work. A few days later I attended an interview at Chelmsford with David Brown, Consultant in Obstetrics & Gynaecology and was appointed as his Registrar. So, in a few days I learned that

I had passed the exam, obtained a job and set off on our camping holiday and my cup of joy was full to overflowing. On return from the holiday we moved from Margaretting Tye into a spacious but cold hospital house with five WCs, two of which used to freeze in the depths of winter. I attended the ceremony at the Royal College and received my Certificate which was signed by the President, Arthur C H Bell, Ian Jackson, Chairman of the Examination Committee and T L T Lewis, Honorary Secretary of the College, on 28 September 1962.

Our baggage arrived from Uganda in a huge sealed crate and a man from the customs came to witness it being unpacked in case I was smuggling anything. He nearly fainted when the first item to emerge was a huge Uganda cockroach.

Chapter 11

1962 - Chelmsford and Cambridge

As I had been well educated at Stamford School I thought it appropriate for Philip and Brian to go there as well; I had written to the Headmaster about this some years earlier and now renewed my application, also seeking a place for Helen at the Stamford High School for girls. I anticipated two or three moves before I obtained a Consultant post so it seemed sensible for them all to board in order that their schooling would not be interrupted every time I moved. The boys were interviewed and admitted to Southfield house in the junior school. I was so pleased to find that two of the masters, H E Packer and "Squibbs" Bowman, who had taught me would be teaching my sons. Helen, already thirteen, was accepted into the Stamford High School for her secondary education. Boarding fees for three children were way beyond my salary as a comparatively junior hospital doctor so I used the Uganda compensation to make up the shortfall, hoping that I would obtain a Consultant post before the money ran out. If it didn't pan out, I would try for Australia, New Zealand or Canada. At that time these countries were not able to train enough doctors for the needs of their populations and were partly dependant upon attracting British doctors, which ceased to be the case before many years had passed. Working at Chelmsford hospital was very convenient as it was only a short journey to and from Stamford for several visits per term. The boys and girls schools shared the same governors and the same dates for the beginning and end of terms and for *exeats* so we could visit everybody at the same time.

My sister Hazel and her husband Richard with their two children had left their Kenya farm in 1962 at the same time as we were settling in England from Uganda. I met them on their arrival and not long after, they took up a smallholding in Grantham so we were able to see a lot of them on our journeys to and from Stamford. Grantham was a penance for them, so cold with a relentless winter wind from the direction of Siberia and back-breaking work with chickens, pigs and horticulture from dawn to dark seven days a week. After a few years they decided to move to Western Australia. Our parents had left Kenya as well by now and lived in Spain; they too upped sticks for Western Australia, so it was a fair number of years before I was able to see them again.

The maternity unit was on the main hospital site in Chelmsford with the gynaecological unit the other side of the town at Broomfield hospital. The house allocated to me had originally been built for the Medical Superintendent of Broomfield hospital in pre-NHS days and was inordinately grand compared with the squalid accommodation commonly provided for young hospital doctors all over the country. Living on the hospital site was compulsory, the pay at that time was derisory and the working hours were punishing: five and a half long days a week, plus alternate nights on call, plus alternate weekends on call day and night. The very least the administration could have done would have been to provide half decent accommodation for young doctors who were required to be resident - I was the sole exception.

David Brown was a single-handed Consultant Obstetrician and Gynaecologist and was supported by myself, another registrar and three young, recently qualified, house surgeons. David had established an Australian connection and received a succession of applications from Australian doctors who came to England to sharpen their surgical skills and to sit the MRCOG examination. The population of Australia was much smaller than that of the UK, so these young doctors could be sure to get a lot more operating experience in the UK. They were all men of quality who took their duties very seriously but who possessed an air of irreverence which brought a breath of fresh air into the somewhat stuffy NHS atmosphere. Later I was able to establish an Australian connection myself when I became a consultant in Kettering and they served the department most loyally, filling our lives with laughter as well. Sadly for us the Australian specialist Colleges developed their own excellent post-graduate training schemes so that fewer of their doctors now need to come to the UK to augment their training. David also established a scheme for UK General Practitioners who wanted to up-date their obstetric skills and knowledge. At that time there was no formal programme of continuing medical education for doctors who had qualified some years previously and it was all too easy for a doctor's knowledge to become locked into a time-warp of his years at medical school. All this has changed - not only is continuing medical education now available everywhere in Britain, but it is also obligatory. David Brown's initiative in this respect displayed a yawning gap in the NHS which learned from his example.

Pat's parents had been living in South Africa since 1947

and twenty-five years later her father was due for retirement. Their hopes of relative prosperity in South Africa had not been realised and it was plain to Pat and myself that they would live in straightened circumstances in old age unless they received some help. I anticipated that when I became a Consultant I would have the resources to do this for them so we took them into our home, with the plan that I would build an extension for them as soon as I could afford to do so. They came by sea to Rotterdam and crossed on a Channel steamer to Harwich where we met them on a cold winter's dawn and, from 1962 to 1965, we lived a cramped existence all in one house. Brian Thorpe was one of nature's gentlemen who had been born and bred a Yorkshireman with a fierce loyalty to that county and to the Huddersfield Choral Society (of which he had been a member) and to Malcolm Sargeant its renowned conductor. Apart from earning it, he was hopeless with money. Gladys was attractive, vivacious, funny, demanding and enjoyed admiration and having her own way. Pat's loyalty to and care for both her parents knew no limits and it was a great relief to her when I was appointed a Consultant in Northamptonshire and was able to extend our house to provide a separate wing for her parents. Sixteen years later, when we again moved house, I bought another property for them which they occupied for the rest of their days.

Our first Christmas in England in 1962 was spent in Broomfield, Chelmsford; Pat's parents were with us. We had become accustomed to the fact that we were worse off in England than we had been in Uganda. There we had two cars and the children all had bicycles but these had been sold in preparation for the move so we now had only one car which I usually needed for my work. The family had accepted without complaint the reduction in their fortunes for the long term benefits which all were confident would accrue. When odds and ends of residual finance started to arrive from Uganda I concluded that I would be able to afford a modest second car for Pat and that I could replace the childrens' bicycles. Early in December I enquired the cost of three different bicycles and when the proprietor realised that I wanted all three he readily agreed to my suggestion of a fleet discount and we closed the deal. He kept the bicycles for me till Christmas eve and, for good measure, he threw in three bicycle locks. I smuggled the bicycles into the garage and wrapped and hung the three locks on the Christmas tree. Ever since my first hospital Christmas when I first qualified we had continued to celebrate on Christmas eve and, after dinner, we distributed the presents, starting with the three bicycle locks which mystified the children. I offered no help in solving the puzzle and it was Brian, the youngest, who first saw the light. "Where are the bicycles then?" he cried and they all dashed out to ride them in the dark, a hard frost on the ground. That night heavy snow fell and lasted for weeks and weeks, the bicycles lying untouched in the garage.

Pat's car presented more of a problem as she was always preoccupied on Christmas eve with the preparation of the feast to which she had accustomed us. I told her that I wanted her for one hour between four and five pm, her mother was there and would help and that I would brook no refusal. She grumbled mightily and grudgingly agreed. Not only did Broomfield have a bicycle shop but also a motorcycle shop which sold three wheeled bubble-cars. I had bought, taxed and insured a German Trojan three wheeler, two at the front and one at the back with a front opening door. I dragged her protesting from her kitchen to walk to the shops with me and the family, steering her towards the motor cycle shop. "What are we going here for" she demanded and was, unusually for her, dumfounded when she realised why. The night frost had already started to form on the road and she skated uncertainly home on the icy road in her unfamiliar vehicle. That too became snow-bound with the bicycles, but we garaged it in the oversized container which had brought our goods and chattels from Uganda. It was just wide enough to reverse the car into it and, having a forward opening door, the driver could open up and emerge. I used it many a time to go to work when Pat needed the proper car. I found it unstable and dangerous, the body being made of glass and tin affording no protection in the event of an accident. I was relieved when we were able to replace it with four wheels.

I was soon locked into the British style of work, finding conditions which were common here and rare in Uganda, such as utero-vaginal prolapse, rhesus antibodies, mild pre-eclampsia and undesired pregnancy. Others were common in Uganda and rare here, such as maternal deaths, still-births, vesico-vaginal fistulae, eclampsia, ruptured uterus, severe pelvic infection and neglected pregnancy - and in Uganda every child was wanted. Some of my surgical skills honed in Uganda lay infrequently used here and I had to learn new ones which were taught to me by David Brown to whom I pay my tribute: he was so delicate and neat a surgeon. There were some unexpected surprises. I had, in Uganda, encountered one set of locked twins and never expected to see another in my life - till Chelmsford and later Cambridge where I encountered two more sets. In each case the first twin was being delivered as a breech birth to be followed by the second coming head first, but locked chin to chin. I was conducting the confinement and was immediately able to displace the head of the second back into the uterus which allowed the head of the first to descend and be delivered, followed quickly by the second, both being healthy. And the same applied to the Chelmsford and the Cambridge sets of locked twins. I have earlier complained about the crippling work load which I and thousands of other young doctors had to undertake but here is the other side of the coin - it is under these circumstances that one gains the greatest experience of rare conditions and how to deal with them.

I found myself doing plenty of teaching in Chelmsford, lecturing to nurses and midwives, to general practitioners on refresher courses and to medical students who came from the London medical schools to do their midwifery training.

The next step in my career was to obtain a senior registrar or university lecturer post so I started scanning the advertisements in the medical journals. I wondered about an academic career in a teaching hospital when I found how much I enjoyed this aspect of my work at Chelmsford so I applied for a lecturer post in Bristol which I did not get. In truth I never had a hope as I had not carried out any basic research and did not have the type of brain required for this highly cerebral style of work. My dedication and application to clinical work could not be questioned, but research - no. I was probably short-listed on the strength of the research done by Richard Trussell in Uganda on treatment of cancer of the cervix with Methotrexate, with which I had helped in a small way; but it was to no avail. Nevertheless I really enjoyed the grilling I received at the hands of the interviewing panel of academics at Bristol. It was at about five o'clock one summer's day in an upstairs oak panelled board room, myself seated alone on one side of a long polished oak table, the sun dazzling me through leaded lights with my five inquisitors ranged opposite me. Each probed my knowledge and ideas searchingly and minutely, questioning me in detail on the papers I had published and intended to publish and on what research I proposed to embark. I had anticipated many of the questions I was asked and had my answers prepared but they weren't good enough - the right person got the job and it was not I. But I came away feeling happy that I had been properly and thoroughly assessed, that I had given a good account of myself and that they had made the best choice.

So I applied for a non-academic NHS post in Cambridge on David Brown's suggestion. A senior registrar post was coming up and he advised me to go for it, "God knows why" he said "for I don't want you to leave". Senior registrars were on the last lap before achieving Consultant status. They were still so called 'junior' doctors but frequently acted up for Consultants and down for registrars in their absence. I applied and was appointed, to my great delight, not just because of the post but also because of its location. Looking back on my medical career I had trained in Oxford and then London, followed by eleven years in the tropics, then London again and now Cambridge. What more could anyone ask for than to have worked in the two greatest and oldest Universities in the world and the greatest city, coupled with a wealth of experience obtained in Uganda.

In Cambridge at that time there were two consultant Obstetricians & Gynaecologists, Oswald Lloyd (universally called Ossie) and Janet Bottomley and I was responsible to both of them. There were also a couple of registrars, one senior house officer and four house surgeons. David Brown warned me that I would need to enter all the great sporting occasions in my diary - Ossie Lloyd would be sure to be there leaving me to look after his patients in his absence and this proved to be the case. One of his out-patients commiserated with him because he seemed to be wearing a hearing aid but the truth of the matter was that he was listening to a Test match commentary from a small radio in his pocket with a lead to a small ear piece

Up to now all my hospital posts had come with housing provided because residence on the campus was obligatory. With a house surgeon, a senior house officer and a registrar on call before being called myself, it was no longer essential to be on the hospital campus so we set about house hunting. We settled on a new property in Little Shelford, with a nine hundred and ninety-nine year lease, one of a group next to the village cricket field, each with its own garden, with communal courtyards and gardens. It backed on to a wood with a stream running through it; ours was Number 13 Courtyards and we were very happy there for the short time till I moved to Northamptonshire. Senior registrars were not well paid and were not supposed to be able to afford property of this quality. The only reason I could was that an instalment of my Uganda compensation had come through which I used as the deposit. Ossie Lloyd commented that I must have private means to purchase such a property and I did not disillusion him because I knew that if I was thought to be independent financially, people would be less inclined to try and push me around. Our neighbours included two university lecturers, one of whom planted a circular lawn so as to be able to mow it without following his motor mower around. He mounted a post in the centre of the lawn to which the mower was attached with a rope the length of the radius of the lawn. He would start the mower on its tethered journey, the rope shortening with every circuit of the lawn so that it eventually reached the centre. He had meanwhile retired to his study to prepare his next lecture, keeping an eye on the proceedings through the window.

Living next to a cricket field, a wood and a river was paradise for Philip and Brian - except that they lacked a canoe. We saw a two man (or boy) canoe in one of the shops and I told them they could have it if they contributed a third of the cost, which they did. They slaved away at any jobs which would attract payment and before long the money was there, the canoe was bought and on the river; I had no fears for their safety for they were good swimmers.

Cambridge was a wonderful place to live with the colleges, the backs, punting on the river, first class cricket at Fenner's, afternoon tea in the orchard at Grantchester, theatre, music, debate and many other attractions. I was surrounded by first rate people and brains and once again I saw the attractions of an academic lifestyle but knew it was not really for me. I now discovered what a lot of backbiting went on in academic circles - the like of which I had not seen in the NHS - and I fell foul of a senior lecturer in Pathology who had issued a test report which proved to be incorrect. This was pasted into the patient's notes and, in case anyone were later to attach significance to it, I had crossed it through with a double line and signed the erasure. He threatened to blight my career unless he obtained a written apology so, anything for a quiet life, I ate humble pie.

Left to Ossie Lloyd he would have monopolised my services whereas I regarded myself as Senior Registrar to the whole department of Obstetrics & Gynaecology. I had to make sure that I gave half my time to Janet Bottomley from whom I learned many surgical skills. She kept the departmental statistics and I helped with these when she was away for any reason. This stood me in good stead when I later had my own department to run. I enjoyed assisting at her operating lists - except when she rapped my knuckles with a compression clamp. "Sorry" said she "I forgot you weren't the house surgeon".

Ossie Lloyd worked me mercilessly and I enjoyed and profited from it. He had a large private practice which he ran from consulting rooms in his house in Lensfield Road and, while I was there, he had to have a new front door fitted - "worn out by private patients" I quipped, to his feigned indignation. I used to claim that I had been 6ft 6inches tall when I went to Cambridge but that Ossie had ground me down to 6 ft. I used to assist with his private operations, for which he paid me a fee. I would leave these to accumulate and claim them three times a year to help with the school fees. "What do you do with all the money"? he asked in mock alarm at the amount and I told him it was enough to pay for Brian's school fees for the term. "My God" said he "I've educated two families of my own and now I'm bloody well paying for yours as well".

My predominant memories and impressions of Cambridge were of much happiness, great job satisfaction and unremitting hard work. The registrars and house surgeons undertook night calls in their respective rotations; being the only Senior Registrar I was at the permanent beck and call of everyone all the time. I would act up for a consultant, down for a registrar and even for both at the same time on one occasion, as well as carrying out my own workload. The telephone service was still nationalised so pagers hadn't been invented and I would be pursued by phone calls day after day and night after night, everywhere I went.

Radiotherapy was a new field for me at Cambridge for none of the hospitals in which I had previously worked had this facility. Professor Mitchell was in charge of the University Department of Radiotherapy - his title, in keeping with an ancient school of learning, was *Regius Professor of Physick* and I attended his weekly radium insertion sessions for patients with cancer of the uterus. He was meticulous and painstaking, writing up all his findings in detail in his own hand on each and every occasion: he never left it to an assistant. Patients with cancer of the cervix would be brought back to theatre at intervals, twice, perhaps thrice for re-examination to assess their response and to decide whether further treatment was needed. I would also attend another follow-up out patient clinic at which the long term results of treatment were observed. I learned a great deal from this great and modest man.

Rhesus sensitisation was a condition which was rare in Uganda and about which I had little experience in Chelmsford. In Cambridge I was able to remedy this deficiency in my training. All rhesus negative women were checked for antibodies at intervals during their pregnancies and it was my responsibility to receive and analyse all reports showing the presence of rhesus antibodies. This I did in a weekly meeting with Professor Gairdner, the renowned Paediatrician with an unrivalled experience of the management of rhesus affected babies. From him I learned the tricky art of judging the best time for intervention: many babies had to be delivered early to protect them from dangerous degrees of rhesus disease, which then exposed them to another danger, that of prematurity. When Professor Gairdner and I had reached our view of what should be done I then had to take the information to Ossie Lloyd or Janet Bottomley for their sanction. When babies were severely affected they had to undergo exchange blood transfusion, a major and laborious undertaking involving several medical and nursing staff for two or three hours, during which they could not be interrupted by other emergencies. Since then major advances in the prevention of rhesus disease have taken place so that exchange transfusion is now less commonly needed.

I started the study of cervical smears for the early pre-malignant diagnosis of cancer of the cervix in Cambridge in 1964. Cervical cytology was already well established in the USA and on the European continent before it was put into practise in Britain and I had attended some training sessions under Professor Navratil in Graz, Austria while there in 1960. Janet Bottomley and Ossie Lloyd delegated me to get the smear service under way and I set up a weekly clinic run by the registrars and myself, at which women could attend on a walk-in basis. Before long the clinic was flooded out with more than we could cope - but with women least in need of cervical smears. Women who had the lowest incidence of cancer of the cervix attended in droves, while those with the highest risk hardly attended at all. General Practitioners of that era had not been trained to take smears and it was to be twenty years before a new generation of doctors would be able to get to grips with the matter and carry out regular smears on nearly all women.

Cambridge was one of the centres at which the MRCOG examination, lasting three or four days, was conducted. Janet Bottomley and Ossie Lloyd (who were among the examiners) would look out suitable patients from those attending their clinics and would give me the list; it was my job to get the right patient in the right place at the right time, before the right candidate and the right pair of examiners. Half of the patients were pregnant but not all could be relied upon to remain so for the full duration of the examination. To test the candidates' knowledge we looked for patients with some medical problem but occasionally, to make up the numbers, I had to slip in a completely normal pregnant woman, much to the puzzlement of the candidate and the examiners.

At the end there was a celebration dinner for the examiners and those who had helped with the arrangements and, after the wining and dining, came the speeches and reminiscences. One hilarious tale concerned Fothergill, a renowned Gynaecologist from a previous era, who had given his name to a particular operation for the repair of prolapse of the uterus. His name was still in daily use and was spoken of with reverence. The tale was told of Fothergill's last house surgeon before he retired, by when the great man was becoming somewhat forgetful. After being interviewed and appointed, the house surgeon had broken his leg but was well enough to take up his post at the appointed time with his leg in plaster. "What's your name, my boy" asked Fothergill. "Bevis, Sir". "Tell me, where do you come from?" asked Fothergill, receiving the reply "Bingley, Sir". "It's nice to meet you, Bingley" continued Fothergill, shaking him by the hand. After a few weeks the leg had healed and the plaster was removed and Fothergill, puzzled by the change asked "What's your name, my boy?", again receiving the reply "Bevis, Sir". "Nice to meet you Bevis, what ever happened to that bugger with his leg in plaster?"

Huntingdon, Doddington, Newmarket and Royston hospitals were satellites of Addenbrooke's in Cambridge at which some gynaecological clinics and operating sessions were undertaken. I used to operate at Huntingdon once a week for Janet Bottomley while she did the gynaecological clinic and at Doddington once a fortnight for Ossie Lloyd while he did the gynaecological clinic there. These sessions were a valuable part of my surgical training as I was separated from the full supporting services of Addenbrooke's hospital and was thrown wholly onto my own resources.

There were resident medical staff at both hospitals who would look after the patients' post-operative recovery and only once was I recalled to Huntingdon to see someone on whom I had operated. It was on a winter's night with dense fenland fog obscuring the A604 as it then was. I asked if the Police could escort me and was told to follow the rear light of the police car and stay there at all costs, which I did. The road was straight and I learned that the police would go as fast as they could if they were able to see a red rear light in the distance ahead, which they then overtook with myself glued to their tail. They would then proceed at a slower pace till the next red light came into view when they would speed up again. I was in fear of my life throughout this journey but arrived safe and sound. "You are on your own, chum" was the reply when I asked for an escort for the return journey. The patient needed a second operation and did well - I got home in time to stay up and go straight to work at Addenbrooke's.

In 1965 I started applying for consultant posts which culminated in my appointment to Northampton and Kettering hospitals in the Oxford Region. The first post for which I applied and was unsuccessful was at Bury St Edmunds. The interview was in Cambridge and the short listed applicants waited in a cold tiled room (like a public lavatory) on hard rickety chairs. Hospitality consisted of a cup of stewed tea. Next I applied for Chelmsford, a post I would really have liked as I knew the hospital and local doctors well, but it was not to be. Then I applied for Romford. I went to see the senior consultant who made it plain that whoever was appointed could not expect any share of the available private practice so I withdrew in case I got the job. Finally I applied for Northampton and Kettering and went to see Tony Alment who was the senior consultant and later became President of our Royal College. He received me with courtesy, charm and civility. The interview was in Oxford where the candidates waited in a warm, carpeted, comfortable room. We had been entertained with a sherry (only one) and salad lunch with the interviewing panel beforehand, each member of which had sought out and conversed with each candidate. The omens looked good and proved so to be. I dashed out to 'phone Pat and drove very carefully home.

Chapter 12

1965 - Irthlingborough and Kettering

I started as a Consultant in Obstetrics and Gynaecology in Kettering and Northampton on 1st July 1965. I had ascertained my timetable and learned that my very first work session would be a morning operating list in Northampton. A locum Consultant had been in post pending my arrival and had prepared a list for me, so I arrived to find theatre staff, anaesthetist, house surgeon and registrar waiting to start operating. The locum had left a message apologising for landing me with one of the more formidable operations for cancer of the cervix on my first day but he had no option: he had, some weeks before, set in train all the necessary investigations and preliminary radiotherapy before realising that the operation would by chance fall due on my first day. This particular operation taxes even seasoned surgeons so I was more than anxious that it should go favourably, which it did. I came through my baptism of fire exhausted but successful, with the respect of medical and nursing staff established. The patient was a woman in her thirties and she came to see me for check-ups every three months for five years when I was finally able to discharge her as completely cured. I related the circumstances to her and told her that she was the first patient I could claim to have cured from her cancer following my appointment as a Consultant.

My first out-patient session at Kettering hospital the following day was memorable for a different reason. Being a brand new Consultant I had not received any new referrals but there were a few old patients to see, mainly cancer follow ups who had been operated on by my predecessor Robert Watson whose retirement vacancy I had filled. I was soon to learn that Robert Watson was regarded as tantamount to God in the eyes of his old patients and the Northamptonshire General Practitioners. The very first patient I saw sat bolt upright on the couch as I entered the examination room. "Where's Mr Watson?" she demanded. I explained that he had retired and that I had taken his place. "In that case I'm off" she said, sliding off the couch and replacing her clothes without ceremony. I left the room and the attendant nurse was shocked and in a twitter when the patient stomped off. I was reminded of this twenty years later, when a comparable event took place. I was now the senior Consultant with a holiday due. A young Australian doctor named Greg Hicks was working for me at the time and I arranged which patients he was to operate on while I was away, which he did very competently. A few weeks later one of them returned for her check up. As I entered the examination room she sat bolt upright - "Where's Dr Hicks?" she demanded.

I bought a house in Irthlingborough more or less half way between Kettering and Northampton. A condition of my appointment as a Consultant was that I live within ten miles of the hospitals to which I was appointed, which did not leave me an awful lot of scope: I drew a circle on the map centred on Kettering and another centred on Northampton each with a ten mile radius and went to the estate agents asking them to find me something within the intersection of the two arcs. No 15 Wellingborough Road, Irthlingborough was a fine red brick Victorian house in good condition within half an acre of walled garden with a stable block and orchard. It had five bedrooms, two bathrooms, three loos, a dining room and two reception rooms, one of which would serve me as a private consulting room. There was room to accommodate my own family and Pat's parents. There was also a good brick garden shed close to the house and I worked out that I could connect this to the house to provide completely separate accommodation for the Thorpes. On the down side there was no central heating, the mouthpiece of the telephone was caked with dried food droplets and the hand set was grimy. Pat agreed to the purchase of the house provided central heating be installed, a dishwasher (a rare luxury then) and a new washing machine purchased, a cleaning lady employed, the extension for her parents built and a new telephone obtained. And so it came to be - except that I put in two telephone lines, Irthlingborough 283 and 736 with eight extensions. My Cambridge house was not yet sold and Barclays Bank agreed to lend me the purchase price of £8000 against the security of the Cambridge house and the remainder of my Uganda Medical Service Compensation payments yet to come. When the Bank became restless about my loan repayments I negotiated a mortgage with the Abbey National Building Society and I wrote to my father "I am taking out a £3,500 mortgage over fifteen years. The penultimate instalment of compensation comes through on 1st March and will clear my overdraft and loan on the previous house. Then I'll have no money which is quite a lot more than I have got at present". I sold the house sixteen years later for £74,000 (the effect of inflation), it was resold for £125,000 a few years later to become a residential home for elderly people (known as Barberton House) and a few years later again for £250,000 to become an up-market Nursing Home.

For a month or so (until the house was ready) I commuted to and from Cambridge except when on emergency call when I slept at the George Hotel in Kettering. They were quite taken aback when I asked for a room with telephone - they had none. The night porter would answer the phone at the reception desk then come and waken me to take calls from the hospital. When the Irthlingborough purchase had gone through Pat and I (and my father who was on a visit to UK) camped there, cleaning, painting, fitting cupboards, carpets and curtains while the children remained in Cambridge with the Thorpe grandparents. Then came the day when the whole family moved from Cambridge with the cat, the dog and our remaining goods and chattels. We lived there happily for the next sixteen years, through three family weddings, two births, a divorce, a death and other memorable events.

Amongst our earliest visitors were the Woollards from Uganda who gave us a Visitors Book in which they were the first signatories. This evolved into a Special Occasion Book over the years when all those present signed their names, adding a witty comment, a drawing or whatever. It records parties, birthdays, weddings, christenings, funerals, Christmases, the assassinations of Indira Gandhi, her son Rajiv and also of Yitsak Rabin, the weights and heights of grandchildren, their signatures from when they could first fashion the initial letter of their names till their writing became well formed, the funerals of my parents-in-law, Pat and our son Brian. It records my second marriage and we took it to Australia to gather the signatures of my sister and brother-in-law, my niece and nephew and great nieces and great nephews. I have become a bore producing the book over the years but how they all enjoy turning back the pages to recall past occasions. The book became dilapidated and the cover fell off so I took it to Woolnough Bookbinders in Irthlingborough to be rebound and titled 'THE BARBERTON BOOK' in gold lettering.

Slightly more than half my working time was allocated to Kettering, the rest to Northampton. A strange fiction had passed into NHS folklore about the working pattern of Consultants, namely that they did nine half-day sessions per week for the NHS, leaving two sessions for private practice. Nine working sessions equates to a four and a half day week, whereas I actually had to be available all the time and work nights as well. For this privilege one's salary (and ultimate pension) were reduced to nine elevenths. So I had five sessions in Kettering and four in Northampton; two colleagues in Northampton, Tony Alment and Arthur Bates and one, Sadie Lehane, in Kettering. They all made me very welcome and showed me the ropes. We shared the nights on call - they recognised that I could not possibly do one in three in Northampton and one in two at Kettering so I only did one in two in Kettering, which proved to be a substantial enough burden. Kettering only had one registrar grade doctor in Obstetrics at the time which meant that the Consultants had to do a great deal of night emergency work in addition to a full day's work the day before and the day after. No Trades Unionist would have stood for it but everyone expected it of doctors. I never worked in the same place in the afternoon as in the morning and would spend my lunch hour driving from one part of the county to another, usually late and often hungry. This experience stood me in good stead for I later turned the necessity into a virtue, by starting the day with a good cooked breakfast and then working through my lunch hour. This then enabled me to get home by about 7pm, an hour earlier than would otherwise have been possible.

I now saw more of my parents (now in Spain) and sister (in Grantham) than I had done for years. Hazel and Richard struggled to make a living on their smallholding, rearing pigs and chickens, growing chrysanthemums and so forth in bleak conditions and soon realised that the rewards would never be commensurate with the grinding input of their labour. Before I had settled on Irthlingborough I looked at a large property with several acres of land and suggested that I buy this with a view to their farming the land and occupying part of the house but there just was not enough land to make an adequate living. So they looked at pastures new and emigrated to Australia in November 1965. It was a well chosen move. My parents followed on to Bunbury in Western Australia about a year later. The precipitating reason was the devaluation of sterling by Harold Wilson, Prime Minister of the day, whose profligate socialist government had brought the United Kingdom to the verge of bankruptcy. "The pound in your pocket" he lied to the nation on Television, would be unaffected. The resultant collapse of stock market values hit my father hard so they upped sticks with the remains of their savings and lived happily in Australia for the rest of their lives.

My father gave me the family portraits before they departed. They had been painted by my great-great-grandfather, Thomas Barber, in Derby and Nottingham from about 1790 onwards. I have his self-portrait which had been restored after being damaged in a fire, a portrait of his first wife Mary Atherstone, one of his sons, Tom, who died young, himself a promising portrait painter. I also have one of an unidentified 'boy with a pitcher', a portrait of two young grand-daughters Mary and Emily and a rather severe portrait of a Mrs Gill, the mother-in-law of one of his sons. She hung over the fireplace in my consulting room for many years, keeping a stern watch over the proceedings. My father had offered to sell the portrait of Mrs Gill to one of her descendants but this had been declined as she was remembered as somewhat of a termagant. It is remarkable that these portraits have survived upwards of two hundred years to the present day, considering the journeys they have undertaken, starting in 1839 with Frederick William Barber to the Cape of Good Hope on a sailing ship named the Robert Small. They then moved from homestead to homestead by ox-wagon over the next seventy years or so. In about 1912 the portraits were taken by steamship to British East Africa by my grandfather Henry Barberton. Again they moved round the colony by ox-wagon to various homes, passing in due time to my father. They hung in his house on the farm near Kitale where I remember them from my earliest childhood. The portraits left Kenya by rail and then steamship for Spain in about 1963 and returned to England in the boot of a motor car in 1966 when they passed into my possession. They were now only about seventy miles from where they were painted, having travelled many thousands of miles in the two hundred year interim.

I set up one private consulting room in my house in Irthlingborough for patients in the north of the county and another at 21 The Drive, Northampton for patients from the south. I rented this for three guineas a week from St Matthew's, the only private hospital in the county. 21 The Drive was a large Victorian house which had been converted into several private consulting rooms. My fees at that time were three guineas for the first consultation and one guinea for subsequent visits. The fee for a minor operation was ten guineas, twenty five for an intermediate and fifty for a major operation or a confinement. By the time I came to retirement, inflation had increased these fees about ten-fold. It was not long before I had built up a private practice which brought in more than my NHS salary. I needed the extra sorely in order to pay for the childrens' school fees.

My private in-patients were on three different sites. The only private obstetric beds were in Northampton General Hospital. The private gynaecological beds were in Northampton Hospital, at St Matthew's and at Wellingborough Cottage Hospital. My NHS work was at three different hospitals, Kettering, Wellingborough and Northampton and, in addition, I had out-patient sessions at Corby and Rushden. I seemed to spend my days (and nights) traversing the county, pursued by telephone messages, often recalling me to the place I had just left. The 'bleeps' of the time were little help as their range did not cover more than the individual hospital compound and there were no mobile 'phones. A recent innovation which was useful was the 'Ansafone' and I installed one in my house, a large machine about the size of a personal computer containing a six inch diameter tape to record telephone messages. I signed a five year rental agreement at five shillings a day.

An increase in the establishment of Obstetric and Gynaecological consultants took place in 1967 and enabled me to drop my NHS sessions in Northampton and transfer them to Kettering. Sadie Lehane, an Irish consultant of the greatest integrity, decided to leave Kettering for a post in Eire. When she left, the Oxford Regional Hospital Board decided to replace her with two consultants, making three in Northampton and two in Kettering. I was the one most affected as I would have to decide in which centre I wanted to work. I knew I would make more money in Northampton than Kettering but Kettering had the additional lure that a spanking new Obstetric Unit was planned for the not too distant future. Kettering had one added attraction in that the relationships between the hospital consultants and the general practitioners were outstandingly good without the back-biting and power struggles so often seen in larger hospitals. So Kettering it was and John Ritchie was appointed to join me there. The new appointment in Northampton went to Bob Van Amerongen who joined Tony Alment and Arthur Bates. The five of us maintained a loose informal professional association for years which was mutually beneficial to both hospitals.

The 1967 Abortion Act was a watershed in gynaecological practice. Prior to then procurement of an abortion was illegal and was punishable by imprisonment and erasure of one's name from the Medical Register, except for the most grave and life-threatening circumstances. However, it was plain that some pregnancies, where the mother's health or sanity were threatened, ought not to continue and a great debate took place on how to determine which could and which could not be terminated. One of my Obstetric teachers at St Mary's Hospital Medical School had been Alec Bourne, a colossus in the world of obstetrics and gynaecology at the time and he was the first to grasp this nettle some time in the 1930s. A schoolgirl had fallen pregnant as the result of being raped by several guardsmen and he announced that he proposed to terminate the pregnancy and openly took her into the gynaecological unit of St Mary's Hospital in Paddington for the purpose. He was tried at the Old Bailey and was acquitted, it being held that he had acted lawfully in order to protect the mental health of the girl. Thus, by case law, it became established for the first time that the mental health of a person could be taken into consideration.

Slowly over the years more terminations were undertaken by doctors who always took the precaution of obtaining other medical opinions to protect themselves from the possibility of imprisonment and erasure from the Register. During my training in Cambridge I had learned that a consultant who was sure that his opinion was correct and who was supported by the woman's general practitioner and another consultant had nothing to fear from the law and I followed this course when I myself became a consultant. When the new Act came into force in 1967 the population at large leapt to the conclusion that abortion was now freely available more or less on request. Some doctors shared this view, others (myself included) did not and it took several years for society, medical and lay to reach some degree of equilibrium on the matter.

There were some serious problems to be ironed out. The first was one of hospital resources to undertake a large and sudden increase in workload for which no provision had been made. The second problem was that gynaecologists really had little or no experience of the procedure, which is not particularly difficult with an early pregnancy but, when complications did occur, they could be serious with even a rare death taking place. The third problem was that the necessary surgical hardware had not been developed and refined because there had not been any need to do so.

The first problem resulted in abortions taking priority over almost all other gynaecological procedures; they could not be placed on waiting lists because the pregnancy would progress beyond the stage of safe termination and the natural consequence of this was lengthening waiting lists for other procedures. Because the NHS could not cope with the demand a thriving trade in private abortion hospitals grew up but the Northamptonshire consultant gynaecologists agreed informally among themselves that they would not go down this pathway.

One of the requirements of the Abortion Act was that all abortions and complications be notified to the Chief Medical Officer and this led to an early recognition of the second problem: gynaecologists who were widely experienced in all other aspects of the speciality lacked expertise in this new procedure. Soon the Royal College of Obstetricians and Gynaecologists set up a research study on the incidence of and the circumstances under which the various complications occurred. The results of this study led to an understanding of how these complications could be minimised, the single most important factor being the termination of pregnancies prior to the twelfth week if possible.

The third problem, that of the most suitable surgical instrumentation, took a couple of years of trial and error before the safest hardware had been developed. It was not long before an enquiry into the working of the Abortion Act was set up by the Oxford Regional Hospital Board and I was a member of that. Another enquiry was set up under Justice Lane, the so called Lane Committee, to which I gave evidence.

The Abortion Act contained a conscience clause which permitted gynaecologists, anaesthetists and nurses to opt out of this work - no doctor could be made to do an abortion. The Chief Medical Officer at the Department of Health appeared to try and circumvent this when he wrote to Regional Medical Officers saying that they might state that, when appointing a consultant "it may be stated that the post includes duty to advise on, undertake or participate in termination of pregnancy". He added, darkly in my view, "No reference to such duties should be included in the advertisement of such a post" perhaps in the hope that applicants would not rumble what was actually going on. There was an uproar in the press and from the profession, myself included. I was by then Chairman of the Oxford Region Obstetric and Gynaecological Committee and used my position to expostulate with the Regional Medical Officer, the President of the Royal College of Obstetricians and Gynaecologists, the Secretary of the British Medical Association, the Medical Defence Union and my Member of Parliament. I even reported the Chief Medical Officer at the DHSS to the General Medical Council for what I believed to be unprofessional conduct. On the evidence of the replies I received it was all to no avail, my views being rejected on all sides.

I will never know whether my protestations had any hidden effect but, up to the time of my retirement, I never heard of a consultant appointment being conditional upon willingness to undertake terminations of pregnancy. Mrs Barbara Castle (known in the profession as the Red Queen) was Secretary of State for Social Services at the time and had not endeared herself to the medical profession and I cannot believe that she had no part in the matter. My final word on this subject is to dispel the illusion that I was anti abortion - I was not. I was the first person to undertake abortions in the Kettering area, even before the 1967 Act and continued to do so all my working life; I was just not going to be party to any attempt to circumvent the provisions enacted by Parliament.

Pat had always had an acute interest in politics which she had not really been able to indulge. In Uganda, Colonial Service staff and their families did not have the vote and were not allowed to take any part in any political activities - that was reserved for the indigenous population. When we arrived in England I was on the move from post to post so there was not time for her to get to grips with the local political scene but that changed when I settled into a post which was likely to be permanent. Northamptonshire County Council elections fell due in 1967 and she stood as a Conservative candidate in Irthlingborough, a Labour community through and through. The children and I all buckled down to helping her with the canvassing and, to our amazement and delight she was elected. District council elections took place a month later and again she was elected as a district councillor for Irthlingborough. She was never short of an apposite comment in debate and many a socialist opponent learned to fear her interventions. However, their fear turned to respect when they realised that she was not in politics to satisfy any personal ambition but because she had a genuine interest in securing the best deals for the town and county in which she and they lived. Labour councillors had always had an easy ride when it came to elections in Irthlingborough and it took her shock election for them to get their act together with the result that she lost her seat at the next election.

About that time she turned her eyes towards the House of Commons and tried unsuccessfully to get herself adopted as Parliamentary candidate for Kettering. She knew Peter Fry, MP for Wellingborough, very well and had worked tirelessly for his election campaigns and they had many a stimulating political joust together. Ten years or so later we moved to Kettering and coincidence served us well when the Fry house came on the market. Pat had by then become resigned to not playing an active part in local politics but that changed when she was persuaded to re-enter the fray. So she found herself on the Kettering Borough Council till she lost that seat four years later.

The Irthlingborough house was full of fun and laughter through these years, with the children growing up and leaving school to embark on their adult lives. I resuscitated the unused grass tennis court and the children filled it with their friends and even the Thorpe in-laws played till late in their lives. It was covered with daisies (not much of an exaggeration) and for a couple of years I went on a daily foot patrol with an old daisy grubber the previous owner had left behind and it wasn't long before the court played true and straight - not much advantage for me, for I was the worst tennis player in the family. Bad at tennis I may have been but I excelled in one respect: no one could touch me when it came to a barbecue where my tropical experience from an early age gave me the advantage. I built a brick stove and we filled the garden on fine summer evenings with people, young and old. The house and stable loft were capacious and we were able to sleep any number of friends, in sleeping bags if necessary. Breakfast the next morning would be served in the kitchen in relays as they surfaced, the latecomers wakened by the aroma of coffee, bacon, eggs and sausages. We erected a marquee and hired a band for Helen's eighteenth birthday and filled the house and garden with friends; Pat excelled herself with the cuisine and all were well wined and dined. And one guest's proposal of marriage was made and accepted among the rhododendrons.

The River Nene flowed nearby and the boys went camping on their own on a number of occasions, returning home after a couple of nights or so when they had run out of food. One golden summer day I answered the front door to a policemen who asked if he might have a word with me and my sons. My fears that they had been up to mischief were rapidly dispelled when he asked if they would be able to help search with their canoe for a young lad who had gone missing - he lived near the river and they wondered if he might have been drowned. The boys did not need to be asked twice, they could think of nothing better than an excuse to spend a couple of days on the river so we set them off with thermos flasks and sandwiches. They returned at dusk, tired and disappointed and set off again the following morning. On this occasion they found the lad floating out in the country a couple of miles from any habitation. They decided that Brian would stay in the canoe near the body and that Philip would go for help. He ran as fast as he could manage with his heart bursting till he found a farmhouse and asked to use their telephone, waited there till the police arrived and guided them back to the river bank to retrieve the body. They returned home pale, shaken and subdued. A few days later they received a letter of thanks from the Chief Constable.

I learned a few days later that the boy had been born in the Maternity Unit where I worked and this knowledge led me to add one item to the advice that I gave to women when they came to see me for their post-natal check-up. After we had covered all the medical considerations consequent upon their confinement I would call out to them as they made for the door: "By the way, teach him/her how to swim. There's no point in having ante-natal care if they are going to drown in the brook". I never knew if anyone took any notice of this till several years later when I went into the anaesthetic room to speak to a woman on whom I was about to operate. I had known her because of her medical problems for a number of years and had seen her through her only successful pregnancy ten years earlier. "Can you remember what you said to me at my post-natal"? she asked. Inspiration came to me in a flash and I replied "Did you teach her how to swim"? "Yes" she replied "and she passed her life-saving test yesterday". Many years later this sad drowning came to mind again. In my last year of work I saw a patient, with her husband and, when we had concluded the consultation and they were about to leave, the husband turned to me and said "The paths of your family and mine have crossed before; it was your sons who found the body of our son in the river Nene many years ago".

The Nene was the scene of several river holidays. I would hire a boat from Barnwell marina, cram the family and the dog on board and we would set off for a week which was either a success or a disaster depending on the weather. A good week was a delight with the sunshine, the grassy meadows, the bird life, the smells of home cooking, the lazy progress on the slow flowing river, frequent stops to go through locks, visits to village shops and country pubs, the evening mists and deep, sound restful sleep. Another week was a disaster with heavy continuous rain, the river fast flowing in spate, the boat trapped for days between locks which had been declared closed by the River Authority. Everything was damp, food was running short, we had read all the books and done all the crosswords, we were fed up with Scrabble and Monopoly and the dog was smelly and bored out of his mind. Then glory be, the rain stopped and the locks were declared open and we set off downstream in good spirits. We approached a three arched bridge as slowly as I could but the boat was impelled by the speed of the current. I made for the centre arch which clipped the windshield of the boat, Helen was thrown into the water with a nasty cut on her shoulder. Brian dived in and helped us get Helen back on board. While Pat and I tended Helen's wound, Brian went ashore to find a public telephone in a nearby village and he called our friend, Don Rawlins, from Irthlingborough who came to our rescue. He took Pat and

Helen to Kettering hospital where Tony Grabham, surgical consultant who had been appointed about the same time as myself, removed various fragments of glass and repaired the wound.

I decided to abandon the holiday so Brian and I turned the boat around and headed as fast as we could upstream through a number of locks, bustling at top speed as we had a long way to go before we reached Barnwell where I had left the car. We arrived home tired and hungry to find Pat with a big bowl of steaming stew, with the news that Helen was not badly hurt and would be home in the morning. Her main worry was that her beauty would be marred by a large scar but in a few weeks this turned to disappointment that there was so little to show for it. Philip, on holiday in Austria had missed all the drama.

Dr. David Rosanelli, our Uganda friend was now practising as a physician in Graz, Austria. He had remarried following the death of his first wife and his second wife was looking after his daughters Veronika and Maria. Then he wrote telling us that he had developed lung cancer and was to undergo surgery and radiotherapy. Our hearts were filled with foreboding for the children who were now in their teenage years but he seemed to make a good recovery and returned to work. Then I heard he was ill again and was not going to recover. A letter came in due course to say that he had died 'in great sickness', a literal translation of an Austrian phrase. The daughters continued under the care of their step-mother until they were old enough to leave home.

The years 1972 to 1974 were best forgotten when it came to trades union power and medico-political matters. The most powerful union in the land was the National Union of Miners who set an example which was later followed by many other unions, including the public sector unions working in the hospitals. In 1972 the NUM went on strike and threatened to cripple industry and throw private households into darkness. We conserved what coal we had in the cellar, bought paraffin, oil heaters and lamps. We had a few 'camping gaz' stoves for our camping holidays and laid in a stock of gas cylinders. The strike was settled at the price demanded and our precautionary supplies remained in store unused. A couple of years later the electricity workers went on strike. We switched off our central heating, lit an oil stove to heat my private consulting room, placed candles and matches in strategic places in case the lights went out. That same year, the oil exporting near-east states doubled the price of oil with the consequence that a national speed limit of 50 mph was imposed to save petrol. Coupons were printed and issued in case rationing became necessary, which it did not. I remember that my needs were accorded pretty low priority. I did have a bicycle and was determined to use it if necessary.

In 1974 there was another miners strike, putting industry onto a three day week. Edward Heath called an election on the basis of who governed the country - the unions or the elected government - and lost out to Harold Wilson. Barbara Castle became Minister for Social Services and tried to outlaw the private practise of medicine; Dennis Healey became Chancellor of the Exchequer and promised to tax the rich till they squealed. He was true to his word and introduced penal taxation rates which put me into the 80% tax bracket. Barbara Castle was less successful but not for lack of effort. She was unable to outlaw private practise for one particular reason among others, too many socialists (including Members of Parliament, herself included it was rumoured) used private medical facilities. I wrote to my parents about these troubled times, strikes present and planned, by lorry drivers, train drivers, hospital cooks and cleaners, sewage workers, water supply workers, all smarting under imaginary grievances and consumed with greed and envy. In truth working conditions had never been so good.

The medical profession felt that it suffered from implacable hostility from Barbara Castle to the extent that I, who had loved my job, came to dread the contempt in which I felt she held us. Her attitude rubbed off on some public sector trades unionists who were working in the hospital service, who now felt that they could take it out on private patients in particular (her pet aversion), knowing that they would not be rebuked or disciplined. I must make it clear that the great majority of ancillary hospital workers were loyal to all patients but a few were not and others were coerced for fear of victimisation. One particular embargo which was placed upon private patients was the refusal to take them to or from the operating theatre - never once did the hospital administrators take any action about this refusal to carry out this small part of their normal duties. For my part I took matters into my own hands and wheeled my private patients to and from theatre myself, receiving black looks or muted admiration according to the view of the observer. I had always used St Matthew's private hospital in Northampton but from this time did so for preference whenever possible as I did not feel that I could rely implicitly on all the ancillary staff in NHS hospitals.

In 1974 I was Chairman of Kettering Hospital Medical Advisory Committee and it fell to my lot to accompany Barbara Castle round the hospital when she came to visit for some reason or other. During our tour I told her of the misgivings of the consultant staff and was rewarded with a haughty glare and a stony silence. I wrote to the Prime

Minister Harold Wilson about the unsettling effect she was having on the profession. I had no reply for a couple of months and then received a long socialist treatise which I filed carefully in the waste paper basket.

Notwithstanding the trials and tribulations of the Medico-Political scene, work was fun and the whole staff put their backs into providing the best service we could. Plans for the new Obstetric unit were in the pipeline, medical and surgical advances were taking place and were being introduced. The days of the old isolated, antiquated Maternity Unit at St Mary's Hospital were numbered and we looked forward to the future with anticipation.

We did have some laughs in amongst the traumas. An Irish Gipsy woman, travelling the country with her husband and other children, finished up in Kettering at the end of her pregnancy. She was clearly far from well but I could not put my finger on a diagnosis. She went into labour and delivered uneventfully and only then was I able to feel a swelling in her abdomen which had been hidden by her pregnant uterus. I arranged for her transfer to the Surgical Ward across the town when her husband said he wanted her to be admitted to the private ward. I explained that this was not really necessary and that it was, in any case, somewhat expensive, whereupon he went out to his battered old van, returning with a suitcase. He opened this to reveal densely packed five pound notes stacked like filing cards in their thousands. "How many rooms are there?" he asked as he wanted to bring his wife's relatives over from Ireland to be with her, thinking that we could accommodate them hotel fashion. She, more pragmatic, said she wanted to go into the surgical ward for the company.

Chapter 13

1970 - Kettering

Helen completed her training as a teacher in 1970 and became engaged the same year. Six years and two children later she and her family emigrated to New Zealand and Pat, myself, Philip and Brian motored to Heathrow airport to see them off, my heart desolate at the thought of her going so far away. My ancestors had gone to the Cape of Good Hope, many of them never to see their loved ones again. I suppose I felt as they did, forgetting how the telephone, air mail and air travel had transformed our ability to maintain contact.

We kept in touch with frequent letters and would telephone from time to time but that was before satellite linkage of telephone calls and getting through was often problematic with reception indistinct. We had agreed to think of each other when we were able to see the constellation Orion at night. I knew that she had remembered this when she wrote that Orion was upside down in the southern hemisphere. Three further years down the line I decided to raid my income tax reserve and hang the consequences so that Pat and I could go out and visit her; we returned home with an uneasy feeling that she too was desolate at the loss of close family contact. The last straw was the fire which destroyed their wooden house and most of their possessions and they returned to England not long afterwards.

1971 was the year in which the British currency was metricated, preceded by many announcements to explain the new money. The 100 new pence to the £1 (twenty shillings) would replace the 240 old pence to the £1. A local reporter on the Kettering Evening Telegraph interviewed people for their reactions in the market and received the comment from one elderly man "It'll never catch on in Kettering you know". I happened to be in Gozo when they metricated weights, having for many years used the imperial system of lbs and ozs running parallel with an old Arabic measure used for farm produce called the ratilo, which was approximately equal to 2lb. I bought some potatoes and asked how the shopkeeper was coping with kilograms. "Oh its easy" she replied, "a kilo is a ratilo and a quarter of a lb".

Metrication of the UK currency provided an easy route to inflation as the conversion was always rounded upwards to the benefit of the trader. We were now in inflationary times in any case due both to government policies and to wage demands. My old letters remind me that in 1974 inflation forced postage up by 1p to 3p for second class mail and 3.5p for first class mail. And, a year later, the inflation rate for the twelve month period had risen to twenty six percent, playing havoc with prices, pensions, investments, house values and wages and perpetrating a gigantic fraud on thrift, to use Margaret Thatcher's memorable phrase. Another sad consequence of metrication has been the loss of the old English usage: tuppence and threepence sadly became two-p and three-p; and we lost the 'tanner' for 6d, and a 'bob' for a shilling.

I made a resolution that I would publish one medical article a year but only managed one as a consultant and that was as co-author with Professor Alan Stephenson at the Department of Medical Genetics at Oxford. The result was a paper in the December 1971 issue of the Journal of Medical Genetics entitled 'A patient with 45, X/46, XXq/46, XXq-DIC karyotype'. Few of my colleagues could understand it and I must admit that I also found it pretty heavy going. Another of my resolutions came to nought because it priced itself out of my range. I determined that I would give each house surgeon who passed through my hands a medical text book of their choice at the conclusion of their six month appointments. To begin with there were four house surgeons per year and text books cost in the region of £10 - £15. Later there were eight house surgeons a year and the price of books had doubled and trebled so that resolution did not survive.

In the Obstetric unit we were able to employ a succession of Australian registrars who were of great value to the NHS. They were, without exception, doctors of the highest quality who entered into the work of the unit with zest coupled with plenty of irreverent humour. The NHS was in some turmoil (when was it not?) due to political machinations and I often wondered whether the grass was any greener in Australia or New Zealand. I had visited my parents in Western Australia and Helen in New Zealand and I loved the wide open spaces, which reminded me of my childhood in Kenya. I took my courage in my hands and applied for some posts out there but was not appointed to any of them. So I buckled down to the job I had and enjoyed it immensely for the rest of my working life.

My private practice was pretty well organised but confinements interfered with everything - sleep, the day's work, birthdays, speech days, dinner parties, Christmas - you name it, they messed it up. Even holidays could be disturbed unless I was very careful and I soon learned to book the next holiday as soon as I returned from the last. Now and again I struck lucky and in a letter to my father I wrote "I had a confinement today and told the lady in jest not to have it before 4.30 as I was too busy and she obliged me at 4.45 which made my day".

My private gynaecological operating was mostly done in St Matthew's hospital in Northampton and later on in the Woodland hospital, Kettering. I suppose I must have travelled to St Matthew's perhaps three hundred times a year for twenty five years, which gave me plenty of thinking time so I would carry my dictaphone on the car seat beside me to make mental jottings while in transit. On one such journey I was much perturbed by the impending fate of Zulfikar Ali Bhutto, previous Prime Minister of Pakistan, who was languishing in jail under sentence of death. I stopped at a Post Office en route and sent a telegram to General Zia ul-Haq (the then Prime Minister) at Islamabad saying (to the best of my memory) "Your name and that of Pakistan will be sullied if you execute Zulfikar Ali Bhutto and I urge you to spare him", but he was hanged nevertheless. Those who live by the sword die by it so it was not surprising when Zia ul-Haq was himself later killed by a bomb in the aircraft in which he was a passenger.

Philip and Brian both left school to make their way in the world and from modest beginnings did brilliantly. Philip started at the very bottom of Sartoris Ltd in Irthlingborough, manufacturer of steel educational and storage equipment for schools, sports centres and industry and, after twenty four years, became the sole owner and managing director of this prospering concern. Under his successful management the firm outgrew its premises and he had to move to a new and larger site in Wellingborough. He licked me into the last decade of the twentieth century when he gave me his old fax machine. "What do I want with a fax"? I asked but within a short while I found it very useful; this was before e-mail became so useful.

Brian started as a trainee journalist with the Wellingborough Evening Telegraph but soon transferred to market management. He started at the bottom of Neilson Clearing House and later returned as Managing Director. He was joint Managing Director of his own concern, MRM promotions, when his life was cut short at the age of forty by a cerebral aneurism.

When Brian married Theresa her father was unable to attend the ceremony as he was in hospital, so she and Brian left the reception in their wedding finery to visit him. To enable them to get away on their honeymoon without returning to the reception I had given them the key to my office in the obstetric unit so that they could change and then leave. They were running late and ran from visiting Theresa's father to the Obstetric unit, Theresa's veil flying behind her. A waiting husband whose wife was in labour laughed at them and called out "Just in time"?

My grandchildren, Matthew and Benedict, Sarah, Simon and Francesca, Thomas and Ruth all show promise and have become enthusiastic and worthy members of the Barberton clan. They all seem to be good physical specimens, in good shape to transmit the family genes down the future generations.

About the time that the first of them, Matthew, was born I gave up smoking with great benefit to my health and with the probable consequence that I am still alive to pay my tribute to them and their future. I had started stealing the occasional cigarette when I was about eight years old and, at thirteen years of age, I discovered the thrill of nicotine inhalation when goaded into doing so by Ebbie

Smith at the Prince of Wales School in Nairobi. By the time I was eighteen I was addicted to cigarettes and later to cigars and pipe tobacco. Later I developed a smoker's cough which caused me years of pain when I damaged a disc in my spine through a violent coughing fit. I am now convinced that cigarettes are more addictable than heroin and it was the acceptance of the fact that I was a tobacco junkie that eventually gave me the determination and stamina to kick the habit. Before I gave up I never felt that I had the right to badger my patients into doing so but, for the last twenty years of my working life, felt able to discourage them. I never hassled them repeatedly and told them that I would only mention it once, as I did not want to make them fearful of coming to me again. To the best of my knowledge I only managed to persuade three people to give up, one of them being myself. One was a pretty girl in her early twenties who came to see me for a minor problem which necessitated a minor operation. She had a cough so I advised her to give up smoking and I would admit her a month later when her chest had improved. As she left the consulting room I called after her "and besides it makes your breath and clothes smell". She had her little operation and, on returning for her check up, she told me she had given up because she couldn't bear to think that she smelt. The third was a fourteen year old who came to see me seeking a termination of her early pregnancy. She was terribly nervous and as I was explaining the arrangements for her to come into hospital her handbag fell onto the floor spilling the contents, among them a packet of cigarettes. As she gathered everything together I said sharply "Put them in the bin". She flashed a look at her mother who said "Do as the doctor says". She gave me a hostile look, did as she was told and made to replace the lighter in her bag. "And the lighter" I continued. When she returned for her post-operative check up six weeks later I had forgotten all about this . "I want to thank you Doctor" she said. Thinking she was referring to the termination I told her to make certain that she was never again in the same predicament. "Oh it's not that Doctor, for stopping me smoking".

Building of the new one hundred and four bed Maternity Unit in Kettering commenced in 1972 at an estimated cost of £1 million, though I have no doubt it over-ran its budget. When finished in 1976 it lay empty for the better part of a year due to lack of funds to open it. The gynaecology beds in Wellingborough were due to be moved into an upgraded ward in Kettering Hospital and we eventually reached the compromise of amalgamating the maternity and gynaecological wards in the new Maternity Unit, which proved to be of great benefit in the long run. It now became possible to supervise everything much more closely. Another hidden benefit was that it made us much more conscious of efficient bed usage with the result that we were able to admit more patients than previously.

So, in 1977 the new unit was opened and, at the same time, we appointed a third consultant obstetrician and gynaecologist, Robert Smith. This reduced my 'on call' commitment from one night in two to one in three and I cannot adequately describe the sense of relief from this nocturnal drudgery. I had been on call one night in two for twenty years. Even now few people realise that a consultant who has been called out of bed for two or three hours in the night still has to be at work the next day as if nothing had happened the night before. As a young doctor I found emergency calls to be challenging and fun because of the job satisfaction involved. In my middle years the demand lay within my physical capacity but, in some cases, stress begins to tell and is most often manifested by narrowing of the arteries, resulting in coronary artery disease. In the last ten to fifteen years of my professional life the stress of night calls were an unmitigated burden. I was heavily committed with other demands on my knowledge and experience, with committee work, lectures, marking of examination papers, departmental management, plus my normal day to day work with patients. My family were last in the queue.

Private consulting rooms in my house and in Northampton and private in-patients in the three towns in the county made for a lot of travel and long, long hours. In 1965 my accountants told me that my gross NHS earnings had been £2,794 and my gross private earnings £992 (with a bad debt of £4 written off). A year later my NHS earnings had been overtaken by my private earnings of £3,829. In my last year prior to retirement my gross NHS salary was about £40,000 and my gross private income £37,932 with bad debts of £375 written off. These figures are not in any way comparable with those of my early years because of rampant inflation which had taken place in the interim.

Private practice was no sinecure and the income earned was not easy money. Confinements for instance were an open ended commitment. Some were straightforward, others were complicated with a great deal to be fitted in with my other work and social programme. One advantage was that I came to know the women concerned quite well, as obstetrics and gynaecology create a long lasting association between patient and consultant. Fitting in holidays between confinements was problematic and I soon found that I would never have any holidays if I accepted all the confinements available. A few women who knew me well would telephone to ask when I was taking my holiday the next year so that they could plan their next pregnancy while I was available.

There were many entertaining episodes. A woman turned up for her appointment one day with a large crumpled brown paper bag. At the end of the consultation she opened it and brought forth a femur she had found on an excavation site. She asked my opinion as to the cause of death and of course I hadn't a clue. Her opinion was that the head of the femur showed evidence of tuberculous infection. She may well have been right for she was a very knowledgeable person.

When I conducted an uncomplicated confinement I would hold the baby upside down by its feet, facing the mother so that she was the first person to identify its sex before I handed it to her to cuddle. One of these babies, a boy, rewarded me for my pains by choosing this moment to pee all over my spectacles and face. The father later made amends by bringing me a case of wine.

Over the years I employed a succession of part-time nurses, receptionists and secretaries to help with the private patients and they served me faithfully and reliably. Pat was a whole time underpaid standby and she and the part-timers had a good working relationship till her untimely death a year before I retired. I want to pay special tribute to the two who were in post at that time, midwife nurse receptionist Jane Jackson and secretary Sarah Taylor who loyally helped me to get on with and enjoy my professional life when I first became a widower. Jane Jackson's predecessor had been another stalwart, Ann Hensman, whom I had known professionally for many years - her predecessor had been another Jane and to begin with I was for ever calling Ann, Jane. I was sad when she moved to another county a couple of years later and I composed a bit of doggerel to go with her farewell gift:

Dear Jane, I mean Ann
I'm sad that I can
Neither scan,
Nor what's worse
Write verse.
Suffice it to say
That I'll miss you today
And do the best that I can
Not to call Jane, Ann.

This account would be incomplete without mention and tribute being paid to Andrea Austen, gynaecological theatre sister who worked with me for about twenty five years at Wellingborough and then at Kettering, with thousands of NHS and private operations. She was expert beyond comparison, ran a good operating theatre, was totally reliable and full of fun and laughter to boot. She knew my operating technique down to the finest detail and knew which instrument I would need next without ever being asked. She had acute powers of observation: during one operation she noticed the faintest change in colour in a patient's toes on the operating table and raised the alarm. The patient had just suffered a cardiac arrest and owes her complete recovery without any impairment whatever to Andrea's timely observation. One night I received a phone call in the small hours from a consultant friend in another hospital at which I did not work, asking if I would come to operate on their teenage daughter who had been admitted as an emergency with a ruptured ovarian cyst. I was filled with apprehension about operating in a strange theatre with strange staff, so I phoned Andrea who agreed without a moment's hesitation that she would come: her husband brought her to a convenient point on the route where I met them and she helped me through a difficult operation on a deeply shocked young woman who made a good recovery.

In 1973 I was elected chairman of the Obstetric and Gynaecological sub-committee of the Oxford Region Hospital Board, as it then was. I had no inkling whatever that I was held in sufficient esteem for this when the out-going chairman asked me if I would stand. I agreed and drove home heart a-flutter to tell Pat the news. The election took place and I found myself in the chair, unprepared controversies to come. The position carried with it membership of the Regional Medical Advisory Committee and, after a suitable interval, I was proposed for chairmanship of that but lacked the necessary support and finished up as vice-chairman. I had by then become fearless of the administrative hierarchy and what I said was not always welcome. A year later I was elected chairman of the Kettering hospital Medical Advisory Committee (MAC) and served in this capacity for two terms. I was on holiday in Tenerife when the election took place and had arranged with the hospital administrator (whom I had known in Uganda years before) to telephone me with the result, which Pat and I duly celebrated with Spanish champagne.

It turned out that there wasn't much to celebrate - all three of these committees were only advisory, without any executive or management function. They were turbulent years with much dissent between the clinicians who did the real work night and day, bank holidays and weekends and the administrators in the Department of Health and the Regional Hospital Board and their political masters. At the end of my terms of office I cynically went through all the minutes of all the meetings to try and assess whether I had actually achieved anything, finding but two items. The first was the abolition of extra beds in the middle of hospital wards. Hospital consultants (notably the general surgeons) had for long insisted that they could not manage with the number of beds provided and demanded that more be placed in the centre of the ward. This placed an impossible burden on the nursing staff and the Medical Advisory Committee had a long and difficult meeting at which the decision was taken to abolish these extra beds forthwith. This had the consequence that we all had to limit our admissions for 'cold' surgery to the number of beds available, having made due allowance for some emergency admissions. Within a month the new system had settled down; with disciplined management the need for extra beds had been found to be flawed. The second item was an administrative one - the sharing out of the annual allocation of funds to each department for the purchase of new equipment. This had always been done by the whole MAC at a long and acrimonious meeting: I managed to divert this task to a sub-committee of departmental heads which did a more efficient and better tempered job than had previously been the case.

Irthlingborough was a town with a soul and a lot of ancient inhabitants. Pat saw the need for a day centre where old and frail people could find company, food and warmth. There was already an established Old Peoples' Welfare Association which was operated by some of the stalwarts of the town, Town Councillors Midge Bailey and Reggie Bland, Town Clerk Cecil Palmer and a local teacher Janice Childs, who was Midge Bailey's daughter. Pat was on the town council at the time as a true blue Tory but she hit it off famously with Midge Bailey and Reggie Bland who were Labour councillors and the three of them together were unstoppable. Irthlingborough was a settled community, most of whom had been there for generations and the three councillors reckoned that they could raise the money to build a day centre without going to the Government or the County Council with cap in hand. So they nominated me to be Chairman, persuaded the Town Council to sell us a town centre site at a peppercorn price and detailed Pete Childs (a builder and Janice's husband) to build it for us. The architects Cook, Culling and Illingworth gave their services free. The scheme got off the ground in 1974 and was in operation in 1978 by which time we had raised £26,000 to pay for it in full. We raised money from all over the place, none of it from central or local government, the largest single contribution being £5,000 from Help the Aged. For that we had to thank Peter Fry, MP for Wellingborough, who somehow shamed them into this sizeable donation.

My particular contribution to fund raising was to hold four annual auction sales, aiming at the Christmas market. I wrote to patients (mainly private ones) asking for a donation of £1 - we had £1 notes at that time which could easily be sent by post. I told them that I expected to turn it into £2 at the sale and most were so relieved that I was not asking for more that they coughed up happily. I went to wholesale outlets and bought items that I thought would sell well for Christmas. The sales were held in the Civic Centre in Irthlingborough, rent free for a good cause; Pat and a cohort of helpers prepared a lavish buffet and a local publican operated a bar at generous prices. When all were well lubricated Don Rawlins and I would conduct the auction. At the first sale we raised £400 and at the last £1160, by when we were home and dry.

The management committee which was overseeing the project would meet in my house, perhaps once a month, to conduct the necessary business. I would place a few bottles of lager, some wine and a bottle of whisky in clear view at one end of the oval dining table round which we sat. Those present knew that these would not be opened until all matters had been discussed, so our meetings never lasted any longer than strictly necessary. The management committee consisted of the individuals already mentioned, plus Rev John King. We also had a social worker who became too busy to attend but as he was useless anyway we didn't miss him or replace him when he left. The centre was named the College Street Day Centre when it opened in 1978 and it proved to be a winner from the start. The Old Peoples' Welfare Association took over the management, providing voluntary staff who worked without any remuneration whatever, which meant that the hot lunches could be provided very cheaply at cost price. Regulars also paid a small monthly subscription and the centre was let for evening functions, wedding receptions and so forth. These activities brought in sufficient income to keep it going. When I moved away from the town in 1981 I was presented with some fine porcelain bird figures and was made an honorary life member of the centre. When Pat died in 1989 a bronze memorial plaque was erected naming her as its founder, which indeed she was.

I had been an examiner for the Central Midwives Board since 1966 but gave this up in 1973 when I became too busy and moved on to become an examiner for the Royal College of Obstetricians and Gynaecologists. In the fullness of time one may be elected to Fellowship of the Royal College (FRCOG) and may be asked to assess the MRCOG book which candidates had to produce before being allowed to take the examination. Both of these events happened to me in 1975 and in 1976 I attended the College for the admission ceremony for new Fellows with Pat and Helen. I hired the academic gown trimmed with kingfisher blue for the occasion. I took us out to a slap-up celebration lunch at the Dorchester Hotel which cost £9 a head.

The MRCOG book is an account of work undertaken. Many months are spent in its preparation and candidates have their eyes on a particular date for their examination so assessors have only limited time to review the book. This means burning the midnight oil and spending hours in the medical library checking references in addition to all the normal days (and nights) work. Most candidates have put enough effort into their book for it to be accepted, pity the ones whose books are rejected who have to start again. Later on I became an examiner for the Diploma of the Royal College (DRCOG) which is taken by doctors who are already qualified, after they have undergone a further period of training in Obstetrics and Gynaecology, usually prior to their entry into General Practice. The examination would be sat in various centres and the papers would then be sent by special courier to the examiners who would have but a few days to mark and return them. A few days later the examiners would congregate in various centres for the oral and practical sections, concluding with a meeting to collate the marks and allocate passes or fails. A modest fee was payable for this but the College usually managed to persuade the examiners that it was their duty to protect the College finances by forgoing any payment.

Non emergency surgery was not undertaken in the ten days up to Christmas so we could usually close the gynaecology ward, apart from emergency admissions such as miscarriages. The maternity wards were emptied as far as possible but there were always some mothers who were too ill to go home and there were usually a few Christmas babies. The consultant on call would come into the maternity unit on Christmas day to carve the turkey - until 1975 whereafter hospital kitchens produced air-line type meals which were much more impersonal. The first Christmas turkey I carved was nearly a disaster as I was presented with a blunt hospital carving knife. Pat and the children were with me so she dashed home to bring my own carving knife and sharpening steel. We would have nuts, crisps and a glass of wine with the midwives on duty and would then go on a tour of the other wards. As I grew older and my family left home, new, younger consultants with young families were appointed. Mindful of my own experience when I was their age I made it my business to place myself on call on Christmas day so that they could spend it with their children, hence my family always celebrated on Christmas eve.

Consultant pay in my day was augmented by a system of Merit Awards. I received one in 1976, which was worth £1600 per annum. This brought my income into a higher tax bracket (from 75% to 80%) which reduced the additional amount I actually received to £350 per annum - the Labour government Chancellor of the Exchequer was being true to his word and was taxing me till I squealed. Nine years later I received the next award.

Alec Turnbull, Professor of Obstetrics and Gynaecology at Oxford, submitted my name for the Confidential Enquiry into Maternal Deaths on which I served between 1985 and 1990. The Royal College and the Department of Health had for thirty five years been publishing triennial reports into the causes of maternal death in association with childbirth and these had been studied throughout the world. These reports had a major beneficial consequence in the widespread recognition of dangerous obstetric situations, with a progressive reduction of maternal deaths over the years in the United Kingdom and in other countries who took on board our experience. Alec Turnbull was himself a major contributor in this field, undiminished to the premature end of his life.

My parents were living in Bunbury, Western Australia and in 1973 I paid them the first of several visits. I then went out every three or four years until they had both died at a ripe old age. To begin with they lived modestly in their own house but it became apparent that they were following the family trait of living a long time and becoming frail. So they negotiated their admission into Elanora Villas, a church based sheltered housing association. Here they remained happily till the end of their lives, my father continuing with his life long interest in heraldry and family history - not just our own, for he earned some useful additional finance researching Australian families back to their English roots. In 1977 he was so pleased to be the recipient of one of the ancient Orders of Chivalry when he was admitted Knight of Grace of the Military and Hospitaler Order of St Lazarus of Jerusalem, the admission ceremony taking place at St Boniface Cathedral in Bunbury. I maintained a correspondence with my parents, too seldom to begin with but much more frequently as time went by as I realised how important it was for them. When he died I found that all my letters from childhood right up to date had been preserved, to which I have been able to refer in composing this record. My parents had always been good correspondents with a wide circle of relatives and friends who gradually died off so that they received fewer and fewer letters. I realised how they missed these on one of my visits, noticing my father walking (limping now) to and fro' the letterbox at the gateway to their drive every quarter of an hour to see if the postman had been, only to conclude disconsolately that there was no mail on that particular day and on many others. I therefore made up my mind that I would always write once a week. Later, when I had a word-processing programme on my first computer I would keep a letter on the go all the time, adding to it almost daily and posting perhaps twice a week.

Chapter 14

1976 - Gozitan interlude

In about 1970 I had the good fortune to meet Diana and Michael Chudley. Diana had written a hugely entertaining book about her large family entitled 'The More the Merrier' including an account of a family holiday in a bus (known as the Chudbus) across the United States of America. She was a financial genius and built up a highly successful Conference Centre in Creaton. Diana had been a foundling, wrapped in newspaper and left in a telephone box: "It must have been the Financial Times" she claimed.

Dr Brownie Dalgleish used to give anaesthetics for one of my Northampton operating lists and I grew to know her and her husband Peter very well - he was the doyen of the Northamptonshire general practitioners. They had bought an old rectory in Kislingbury and invited us to come and see it and there we met the Chudleys again and so began a close friendship between their family and mine which has endured to this day. After inspecting the property in the chill autumn air and hearing about the planned restoration, Michael Chudley disappeared to his car for a couple of minutes, returning with a bottle of Bollinger and cut glass champagne flutes. We lit a brazier with scraps of timber in the sitting room to warm ourselves and drank a toast to the house which was to become a family home again filled with love, laughter and friends. As we left, Diana asked us to a meal and a couple of days before we were due to visit she telephoned to say that she was confined to bed for a few days but that we were to come nevertheless. We found a table prepared in her large bedroom, Diana reclining on pillows with a couple of telephones making and receiving calls, running her conference centre from her sickbed. Tall, wide bay windows faced south with luxurious ceiling to floor brocade curtains which, she explained, she had paid for by selling the Rolls. She had an office but that was occupied by her staff, not herself, she worked on her feet and on the phone. There were telephones everywhere, including her cars, her memory and organisation were faultless, as I came to realise. Many years later I went to visit Diana for the last time as she lay on her deathbed. She had arranged for me to have lunch at a table in her room and lay propped on pillows with two phones, making and receiving calls, issuing directions for the planting of the gardens the next year.

The Chudleys had bought and renovated a village property in Gozo, an old mill house which had previously been the village bakery. Pat and I used to take our main holiday in the Canary islands and resisted Diana's blandishments to visit Gozo for too long, for we later came to love the place and bought a holiday home there ourselves in 1979, three years after our first visit to the Chudley property in Ghasri village. Diana would fly to Luqa airport in Malta and take a taxi from Billy's garage to the Gozo ferry at Cirkewwa. If she was too late for the ferry she would telephone for Father Hili in Gozo to fetch her in his boat. When she got to Mgarr harbour in Gozo she would pick up a pre-arranged hire-car from Mayjo in Victoria. On our first visit in 1976 the ferries from Malta to Gozo were infrequent and our flight was late so we missed the last ferry of the day. We stayed overnight in the Ramla Bay hotel in Malta and caught the first ferry next morning. Back home at the end of the holiday Diana gently chided me - "I told you I would send the priest's boat if you missed the ferry" she said. I learned then to listen closely to what she said: what might have been construed as a throw-away remark wasn't, her word was her bond.

We went to see John Debrincat the estate agent at Mgarr harbour about buying a Gozo property. The 'phone rang as we entered and he motioned us to sit down - he was talking to a client in England. Sensing a sale, he picked up his other 'phone and dialled a lawyer in Gozo, conducting a three way conversation with a 'phone to each ear and clinched the deal. He took us downstairs for a coffee at a pavement cafe beside the harbour. "I do not have a mill house on my books at the moment" he said "but I can show you a good apartment overlooking the harbour" pointing up the hill. This was not what I was after but we agreed to look. We mounted two flights of stairs in a sandstone apartment block, entered an unfinished flat, clambered over builders rubble to the balcony which had no rail and looked out over the harbour, crowded with fishing boats, to the island of Comino with its blue lagoon and beyond that the island of Malta. I could imagine the scene by moonlight and, without consulting Pat (she was standing beside me), said "I'll have it".

So home we went to work out how to pay for it. We borrowed some from the bank, some from Pat's cousin Barbara Tinker, raided my income-tax reserve and gave up buying wine altogether: I made my own wine for a couple of years but could not recommend it. When the time for completion came in April 1979 I was visiting my parents in Western Australia so Pat completed the formalities. Josephine Grech had my Power of Attorney, her son-in-law Michael Refalo drew up the contract and thus we came to own 6 Belvedere Court, Hamri Street, Ghajnsielem, Gozo. Joe Zammit, a retired headmaster friend of ours oversaw the completion of the work remaining to be done.

That August Pat and daughter-in-law Theresa, followed later by son Brian and myself, went out to furnish and equip the place. The following Easter and every Easter thereafter the apartment was blessed by Father Joseph from Ghajnsielem church, it being the custom for him to visit every household in the town to collect the annual contribution to church funds. It became the happiest of holiday homes for ourselves, our families and many friends and I eventually sold it in 1994 to friends Frank and Susan Baker who had themselves enjoyed many holidays there. Two people who died, one of them Pat, spent their last happy holidays there. It was the scene of three honeymoons, one my own when Judy and I were married two years after Pat had died. It was there that Sylvia Cauchi (who lived on the ground floor) ran up the stairs calling "They kill the Queen uncle, they kill the Queen uncle" and we knew at once that Lord Louis Mountbatten had been slain by the IRA.

The Queen visited Gozo and friends who were there at the time recorded in the GOZOBOOK "Imagine our surprise when the Queen and Prince Philip popped over from Malta in Britannia to see us". Pope John Paul visited the island and I stood on the pavement when he passed by in his pope-mobile. All the roads on which he was to travel were resurfaced and, for some time after, any roadworks were met with an enquiry whether the locals were expecting a visit from the Pope. All these events and many others were recorded in the GOZOBOOK which had started as a record of visitors to the apartment. It was Brian who first enlivened it with a Maltese recipe, others followed with entertaining comments, doggerel, water colour sketches and it became a source of much amusement.

I would spend hours looking round the boats in the various harbours around Gozo and made the acquaintance of John Azzopardi who said sure, he would look after a boat for me during my absence if I bought one. He had served for twenty years in the British navy and was now a ferryman for the Comino hotel plying between Comino, Malta and Gozo. He had a weather beaten face, eyes creased against the Mediterranean sun and sea spray, a quizzical smile and an inexhaustible fund of anecdotes. He knew I was a complete novice and would not let me buy anything that I could not manage safely. So, on his advice, I came to own a 13' 6" fibreglass fregatina with a 9.5hp diesel inboard Ducati engine which I used around the coves and beaches of Gozo and Comino. I named it 'Barberton Daisy' after the Transvaal daisy (Gerbera Jamasonii) first described by my grandmother Mary Layard Barberton in about 1890. This name I transferred to my next boat, a 17' 6" fibreglass Fletcher Scorpion speedboat with two 60 hp outboard Johnson engines which took me further afield, round Gozo and to Malta. A stranger, noticing the name, enquired about the connection. He was South African and knew about the town of Barberton.

To insure the boat I was advised to see a man who worked at the Mid-Med bank in Xaghra. When I reached the head of the queue he closed his bank books and reached for his insurance papers below the counter and conducted his other occupation as an insurance clerk on the bank's premises in the bank's time with no let or hindrance and with no complaint from those in the queue behind me.

Moorings in Mgarr harbour were a free for all but John Azzopardi looked after my interests to prevent mine being appropriated by someone else while I was away. My bow mooring rope was attached to a heavy chain which was, in turn, attached to a concrete sinker and, one day, the rope became cut by some underwater wire. I tried to connect a new rope myself but could not hold my breath for long enough under water so I turned to Father Hili for help - in addition to his duties as a parish priest he ran three boats which he used for tourist trips and he also worked as a diver. He came along with his aqualung and did the job for me in a trice and I offered a contribution of ten Malta pounds for his church funds. "Oh no, no, doctor" he exclaimed, "it is much too much too much", as he reached for and pocketed the proffered note.

After my experience with the boat insurance I was not surprised when I was advised to go to the Milk Marketing Union for a new part for the boat engine, I was to ask for 'Il Bogi' who was the Gozo agent for the engine. Hesitant about using a nickname I was told that his real name was Joe Vella, for whom I asked. A somewhat mystified Joe Vella was summoned to see this strange Englishman and was even more mystified when I spoke to him about a spare part for a boat engine. Then light dawned, "Oh, it is Il Bogi you want" he said. In this manner I learned the importance of nicknames in a country where so many people have the same Christian and surnames, for it is by the nickname that the Joe Vella you want is distinguished from the Joe Vella you don't. I was speaking of this to Michael Refalo who told me that nicknames were often used for that very reason in legal documents. My local nickname was II Professore.

I was obsessive about filling the boat tanks with petrol as soon as we returned from an outing and Pat would become exasperated, wanting to hurry back to the apartment to prepare the evening meal. However, I always insisted because we could never be sure that we might not need to go out of our way to rescue someone or such-like. I also insisted because I knew how much more fuel the boat consumed if the weather should chance to blow up rough on our next trip. It so happened that I was twice called upon to go well out of my way to tow other boats, which had suffered engine failure, back into harbour. One lovely day Pat, her cousin Barbara and I went round to the other side of the island to Marsalforn for lunch at the Republic Restaurant. I had full tanks, knowing that the round trip would use about half the petrol. A south-west gale blew up as we set off on our return journey. We made very slow progress, driving into the force of the waves and wind arriving back to my mooring in Mgarr harbour safely enough. I dropped Pat and Barbara off while I went to re-fill the tanks and found to my alarm and dismay how right I had been - I was down to about a pint of petrol in each tank

Ta Pinu is a magnificent religious shrine near the village of Ghasri, which had been built on the site of a vision of the Virgin Mary by a young Gozitan woman named Karmni Grima. It is a very large ornate church of sandstone and marble with stained glass and mosaic portraits of various saintly figures. It was a popular spot for tourists arriving on foot, by car and by coach, from all over the world. Large marble statues had been imported from Italy which depicted the various stations of the cross and these had been erected at intervals up to the top of Ghammar hill, where there was a huge concrete cross visible from miles away across the island: at Eastertide there was always a large procession led by the Bishop along the route.

On one of my visits to the shrine I heard a plaintive English voice "Does anybody here speak English?" which I identified as coming from a woman in a wheelchair. She was one of a party of disabled people on a visit to Gozo and needed to go to the toilet so I wheeled her along and we came to a couple of steps, a narrow iron gate and a narrow passage through which her wheel chair could not possibly go. Her legs were paralysed but her arms were strong so I bent down facing away from her and she grasped me around my neck, clambered onto my back and clung to me piggyback fashion. I reversed her into the toilet, eased her down onto the seat, closed the door and waited outside. "You won't go away, will you?" she called and, after a minute or so, I heard the urine begin to flow and it went on and on and on. "Are you still there, I won't be long" she called, urine still flowing. I then realised that disabled people had to develop huge bladders because of the infrequent opportunities they had to get to the toilet. Eventually she called "I've finished now" so I reversed into the toilet, she clung around my neck, I walked her back to her wheel-chair, reversed her into it and wheeled her back to the rest of her party. She took my name and address and that Christmas I had a card from her.

There were multi-lingual forms at the entrance to Ta Pinu on which one could tick an appropriate prayer request. I remember in particular 'Happy Death', 'Success in Business', 'Girl-friend (Catholic)' and there were others. There was also a room devoted to miraculous events which were believed to have been due to divine intervention. There was a painting of a child in mid air falling from a roof who had survived; another of a violent storm at sea when the boat and crew had been rescued, a set of car seat belts, a crash helmet and so forth. Beside each was a framed record of the disaster and its happy outcome, believed to be a consequence of divine intervention. High up on the wall, perhaps ten feet from the floor was a rusty pair of dressmaking scissors with a framed and faded photograph of a little girl with a hand written legend of the event, but it was too far away for me to decipher. A few years later a young Maltese woman came to see me in Kettering. She needed a minor operation as a day case and, as I checked her blood pressure, heart and lungs, I noticed an ugly jagged scar over her heart. I asked how this had happened and she told me that, when she was a little girl, she had been jumping up and down on the bed while her mother was sewing and that she had fallen on the scissors which had penetrated her heart. She had nearly died but had been saved by the surgeon who repaired the injury and gave her a blood transfusion from her father. It was inappropriate in a busy clinic that I spend time asking about the scissors at Ta Pinu so I determined that I would take my camera, telephoto lens and tripod on my next visit. I carefully focused on the display, took a couple of photographs from different angles and posted the film to Colab in Coventry for expert processing and enlargement. When I got home to England the photos had arrived and I opened the package with mounting excitement, only to find that it was not my patient.

Crime was almost non-existent in Gozo so imagine my surprise when I heard of an attempted bank robbery at a small village branch of the Bank of Valetta, open one morning a week. At each branch an armed security man was in attendance throughout opening hours and one such was seated by the entrance; an English tourist and a young Maltese man waiting their turn at the counter. The security guard yawned, scratched, stretched and went outside for a cigarette. The young Maltese (he was assumed to be Maltese as a Gozitan would never have behaved so) seized the opportunity to draw a weapon and demand money from the cashier. The waiting Englishman picked up the chair vacated by the guard and felled the would-be bank robber. The security guard, hearing the commotion dashed in and arrested the Englishman whom he had caught red-handed wielding the broken chair. The cashier resolved the confusion, the Englishman was released and the would-be robber, now recovering was arrested. The security guard was later rewarded with some civic honour.

Pat and I kept on trying to arrange a Gozo holiday with the six grandchildren who were old enough - Francesca was too young to be included - but events kept conspiring to make this difficult. Matthew and Benedict proved the ultimate stumbling block because Helen thought they could not be spared from some school commitment or other, so in 1987 we settled for the remaining four children and I booked the tickets. Helen was quite indignant when I told her what I had done, "What about Matthew and Ben" she remonstrated. So out I went and bought another two tickets. Pat went out a week in advance, filled the freezer with ready cooked meals and hired a mini-bus. I followed on a night flight with six young children, an experience not to be lightly repeated. There followed a holiday to be remembered and savoured for the rest of time. The next year Pat was taken ill and died a year later. So, by good fortune, the aim was achieved at the first and last possible opportunity.

Shortly before we left Uganda in 1962 Peter and Margaret McLean had a daughter, Catriona, to whom I became a godfather and who I proceeded to neglect for the next eighteen years. Peter wrote to tell me that she had been accepted as a medical student at St Bartholomew's hospital. From that moment I have watched her progress and now bask in her reflected glory. To begin with I gave her a skeleton and a textbook of anatomy with which to start her studies and, as I came to know her, I realised what I had missed over the years. I helped her obtain a student surgical attachment in Kettering and, before her finals, she came to stay and we would sit late into the night going through old examination papers. She passed at the first attempt of course, and thereafter made her way to the top of her field. Now I can speak with pride of my god-daughter who is a Consultant Oncologist in Edinburgh. Then came my crowning moment: she asked me to propose their health and happiness at her marriage to Cliff Cully at Dundas Castle in 1996. Amongst other tributes I told of the only skeleton I knew to be in her cupboard, the one I had given her in 1980.

The McLeans and Catriona (before her marriage) came to spend a holiday in Gozo with Judy and myself and I showed them the church at Xewkija which I claimed to have helped to build. Xewkija had been a small village with a church to match but grew considerably in size with the arrival of several factories, so that the church became too small for the community. The local community decided to build a large circular new church around the old one, which was then dismantled and carried out through the new doors. Much of the money for this came from Australia where many Gozitans had emigrated and prospered after the 1939-1945 war. Some had returned to Gozo and Malta to retire and had built large houses, one named 'God Bless Australia', another 'Sydney House' and Ghajnsielem sported the 'New Sydney Haven' Night Club. On successive Gozo holidays I would call in to see the progress at

Xewkija church and some of the stone masons came to recognise me - I would photograph them at their work as they cut and shaped a stone to size from measurements called down by a man at the top of the scaffolding. This would then be hoisted with a block and tackle and eased into place, fitting exactly. By good fortune I happened to be there when they were finishing one of the several side altars: "It is the very last stone" one said "then the church is finished". Seizing the moment I asked if I could hoist it and was handed the rope to do this. I pulled the stone perhaps twenty feet up to the pulley where the workman at the top took it and slipped it into position, tapped it with his mallet and checked its alignment with his spirit level. Thus I have been able to claim that the church building was not completed until my fortuitous intervention.

Chapter 15

1985 - Kettering

I continued with my visits to Australia every three years or so to see my now very elderly parents and, on one visit, found my father to be dreadfully lame with severe osteo-arthritis of one of his hip joints. He believed that he was too old to consider a hip joint replacement but I urged him to consult an orthopaedic surgeon and I went along with him. His hip joint was so unstable that he had taken to retaining the head of the femur more or less in position in the remains of its socket with a leather belt applied tightly around his hips. The X ray showed the joint to be totally destroyed. The head of the femur, instead of being a neat rounded shape, was blunt and jagged; the socket was likewise with its upper aspect worn completely away allowing the head of the femur to slip out of the socket when he walked. No wonder he was in pain and had to resort to the leather belt. I wasn't really surprised as he had learned to make do and improvise as a Kenya farmer in the 1920s but the surgeon was quite taken aback. So it was arranged that he would undergo a hip replacement operation after I had returned to England and this liberated him from the confines of his house for several years. I visited them again in 1983 when he was still relatively mobile. He was by then becoming increasingly deaf and frail and I was desolate when he died in 1985 at the age of eighty eight. He had researched his antecedents for many generations and had found no ancestor or relative who had reached that age. Alban, the youngest of the four brothers had described him years earlier as "a very special man of God, the best of the Barbertons". I paid my mother a visit later the same year and she died in 1986, both of them having had wonderful fruitful and interesting lives.

The Rev Philip Jepps of St Andrews Church in Kettering had a special interest in the care of the elderly and disabled and he found a willing ally in Pat. She had pursued with vigour her promotion of the interests of the old and infirm and had become Chairman of the Northamptonshire branch of Age Concern and a member of the governing body of Age Concern, England. She had also been Chairman of the Kettering Community Health Council and had been shocked at the conditions in which demented old people were kept in National Health Service units at that time. She and Philip Jepps joined forces to see if they could make some additional provision for frail old people in Kettering.

At the same time Dr John Smith, who was the senior partner in his practice, was in the process of moving into a new custom built surgery which meant that the old surgery at 31 London Road, Kettering would come on to the market. The building was a solid red brick Victorian edifice which had been a Veterinary surgery before it became a doctors surgery. It was large enough to accommodate about twenty residents, so we entered into negotiations and agreed a price - but had no money. So Philip Jepps set about raising it with the aid of the Kettering Council of Churches and, over a period of about a year, sufficient money came in to allow us to proceed. The building was purchased with a mortgage and the money raised was used to make the necessary conversion and adaptation. I was persuaded to be Chairman of the Management Committee but the driving force behind its completion and success was Pat, who wisely decided not to sit on any committees - she just got on with commissioning the building within the limits of our finance and it was opened to the first residents in 1987.

We named the project St Francis House, a nursing home for the frail elderly under the auspices of the Kettering Council of Churches - it was not a hospice although many of our clients stayed with us till they died. I prepared the draft documentation for its registration as a charity and Philip Jepps saw this through the cumbersome bureaucracy of the Charity Commissioners. I drafted our constitution and George Ellam, a solicitor on the Management Committee, licked this into shape. One item I incorporated into the constitution was to place a time limit of five years on the chairmanship, my own included. I had seen too many Chairmen outstay their usefulness in the past, with no mechanism in place for their painless removal. Our first Matron was a fairly senior import from the NHS and didn't last long: she resigned because she could not accept the necessary financial restraints - she had never had to work to a budget in the NHS. St Francis House served the needs of the community well for about ten years but eventually had to close in 1997 because it could not compete with the rising numbers of custom built nursing homes with single rooms and en-suite facilities.

One of my special interests in my gynaecological work was the treatment of sub-fertility. Quite remarkable advances took place in this field in my working lifetime. Sometimes there was nothing wrong at all - it was just a matter of timing. A healthy young woman came to see me and I noted clear signs that she was ovulating. I told her to go home and do what was necessary without delay. "But we don't do it on Wednesdays" she said, "only Saturdays". She explained that they both had full-time jobs, that they were tired out during the week, that they did the shopping on Saturday mornings, drew the curtains and watched wrestling on the TV on Saturday afternoons, one thing leading to another - but not to pregnancy. However, she took my advice and it was not long before she was attending the ante-natal clinic.

Fertility drugs were needed for many women who were failing to ovulate and I had countless single births after such treatment, a number of twin pregnancies - and one set of quintuplets. That mother had already had a single baby using a particular dose and combination of drugs and returned to see me for a second pregnancy. She had the same dose with the same hormone level tests as the first time round but the scan showed three babies. She moved away to another town during the pregnancy and imagine her surprise when she had five babies. All were born hastily and normally, all survived and all did well in infancy and childhood. She used to bring the whole family to see me now and again. They would crowd into my congested office and I would wonder however she managed at home. Marian Pinnell (of whom more later) invited them (and others) to come along to my farewell clinic when I retired. Seventeen years after they were born I was filing old letters in my archives when I came across the letter I had received from their mother at the time of their birth. I was thus able to re-establish contact and to send them eighteenth birthday wishes. Their mother told me that they had all achieved entry to university.

I asked women who were using fertility drugs to keep a daily early morning temperature chart, a rise in temperature often indicating that ovulation had taken place. My phone rang one morning about 8am - "Mr Barberton, my temperature has risen and my husband is in Edinburgh at a conference, what shall I do"? "Phone him up and hire a plane from Sywell" I replied, knowing she was able to afford this. The husband left his conference and met her in his hotel room at lunch time, not best pleased - "Mr Barberton says you have to" she had told him. Their efforts were happily rewarded nine months later.

Another woman laughingly asked as I was tidying up after conducting her delivery, "Did I ever tell you how this baby was conceived"? I already knew some of the tale for I had chanced to see her on the day that she ovulated, telling her that she must have intercourse that day without fail. "My husband is away on a contract but I'll get him to come home" she had said. It transpired that her husband was on duty that day and night and couldn't come, "Mr Barberton says you must" she insisted. He managed to get a stand in for a few hours, drove fifty miles home, came through the front door grumbling that he was in a dreadful hurry and that she really had made difficulties for him. "So we made love downstairs on the carpet straight away and he got back into the car and returned to work" she said.

There were others who did not get pregnant and I would refer them on to Mike Newman a consultant colleague with greater expertise than myself in this field. After I had retired and was doing my own shopping I recognised an ex-patient in the supermarket queue, plainly pregnant. She was chattering happily to the check-out operator whom she knew: "Mr Barberton tried ever so hard to get me pregnant but couldn't manage, so he sent me to Mr Newman".

I put the collar of my coat up, pulled my hat lower over my face and turned away in case she should recognise me. Later, in the same supermarket carpark I came upon a couple and teenage boy admiring my new car. We struck up a conversation on its merits and the woman paused in mid sentence and said "Are you Mr Barberton"? I said "yes" and she coloured up and said "Ooh, you've seen all me bits".

I had discovered a talent for fund-raising when we built the College Street Centre in Irthlingborough and decided to put this to further use when I became frustrated by the lack of some equipment in my NHS work. Funds for new equipment in the hospital were provided every year by the Regional Health Authority but were never sufficient to meet everyone's needs: bids were placed in priority order by the Chairmen of the various departments and this meant that one would often have to wait a year or two before a particular item reached the top of the list. The bit of equipment I wanted at that time was a Colposcope - a special microscope for the examination and treatment of women with positive cervical smears - the cost being about £4000.

Marian Pinnell was the Sister in charge at the Rushden Memorial Clinic and had run my weekly clinic there with style, authority, efficiency and good humour for years; she offered to help. She had in her youth been a Rushden Carnival Queen and had then joined the Carnival Guild which consisted of ex-Carnival Queens who would undertake fund raising for various projects. Marian and other members of the Guild were to do a sponsored walk around Battersea Park and she offered to fix it for me to join them; she was sure that some of them would walk for my Colposcope fund. So I became an honorary member of the Carnival Guild for the occasion (and on another occasion a few years later). We had several months in which to set up the necessary publicity and the local Evening Telegraph, with which I did not usually have friendly relations, turned up trumps and I collected loads of sponsors. I was pretty fit but unaccustomed to walking long distances so I set about some serious training with some long walks at weekends with my dog Toby. I was soon doing about fifteen miles without difficulty - I knew I could do more but didn't have the time to spend finding out.

I planned to go on holiday to Gozo immediately after the walk - Pat would go a few days beforehand to open up the apartment. On the appointed day a bus load of young and not so young members of the Carnival Guild descended on Battersea Park and we walked and walked, circuit after circuit. The NHS was in turmoil at the time with demonstrators appearing on our television screens and I was not best pleased to see some banners being waved as I completed another circuit. As I drew close enough I was able to read "SHAKE A LEG GRANDAD" and "KEEP IT UP GRANDAD". Helen and her two young sons Matthew and Benedict had come to encourage me. I managed twenty one miles, many of the girls did twenty four and Marian, dear Marian, did twenty eight. Helen took me to Heathrow airport where I had booked a hotel room for the evening before catching a night flight for Malta and Gozo. I had a long soak in a hot bath, sank a couple of whiskies and stood them all a good dinner. I had prepared adhesive address labels for my ninety nine sponsors and after a couple of days, sent off postcards to each telling them how far I had walked and asking them to cough up - which they did and so did the girls and so did Marian. I only needed £4000 but the final tally was £9456-20, which was a serious embarrassment. According to the law as it was explained to me, I was supposed to return the excess but how could this be done? So I formed a charity - The Maternity and Gynaecology Charity Fund - and deposited the excess funds into that account. The Consultants in the department were the sole Trustees so that the Hospital Administration should not be able to have any influence on how the money was spent. We continued to top up the funds with donations and fund-raising events: needing a portable baby scanner for the Obstetric unit, John Ritchie did a sponsored walk on the Waendel Walk from Wellingborough; Mike Newman and I did another Battersea walk with Marian Pinnell and guild members for battery driven syringe pumps.

The Irthlingborough house had become too large for our needs with the departure of the children but I still hesitated to grasp the nettle and move because of the enormity of the task. Then, Peter Fry's house in Barton Seagrave came on the market - it was a house I knew and would suit Pat and myself very well, having a room suitable for me to use as a consulting room for my private patients. So, in 1981 I sold the Irthlingborough house, bought another at 87 High Street, Irthlingborough for my in-laws, Gladys and Brian Thorpe and bought 27 Poplars Farm Road, Barton Seagrave, Kettering. Smaller than the previous house, it was still large enough to accommodate family and visitors and was the scene of many, many parties and gatherings for large numbers of people. In 1982 I installed a heated swimming pool in which all the younger grandchildren learned to swim.

After I had left Irthlingborough I maintained my connection with the town. I was still President of the Cricket Club which did not own the field on which they played. In the 1960s they had been offered the ground for about £250 but had not been able to raise the money. The old wooden pavilion was damaged by fire in 1983 and it was not going to be worth rebuilding this without the security of owning the cricket field. By now the club's finances were in better shape and with some fund-raising by the members, some donations and a bank loan, it was possible to buy the ground and rebuild the pavilion. My last act as President was to write to all the seventy five vice-presidents asking for donations to pay off the last of the bank loan and this was achieved.

My next, and last, fund-raising effort for Irthlingborough was for the church roof which was found to be dangerously infested with death watch beetle. The townspeople had become accustomed to my annual sales for the College Street Centre and had supported me most loyally at that time so I repeated that format with very satisfactory results.

Being older than Pat and being in a high stress, high profile job with long hours and much night work, I was sure that I would pre-decease her, leaving her a widow with many years ahead of her. My financial planning over the years had been directed with this in mind and also because NHS widows' pensions were known to be parsimonious. In 1989 Pat complained of increasing abdominal discomfort but resisted going to see her doctor, John Smith, who was also our friend and neighbour. She awoke one morning in August with indigestion and I said to her that if she didn't ring her doctor I would and together we went to see him. She had X-rays and went to Oxford where she had a gastroscopy. Dr Jewell called me into his consulting room and said "I think your wife has an adenocarcinoma at the junction between oesophagus and stomach and I have taken a biopsy". "Have you told her?" I asked, to which he replied that he could not till he had the report from the pathologist. We drove home, Pat alert as always but intermittently drowsy from her medication for the gastroscopy. "It's got to be cancer" she said. A few days later on a Friday in the lunch hour John Smith phoned that he had the result and that he was coming to see her. "You know what I have come to tell you" he said. In September she had an oesophago-gastrectomy in Oxford by Michael Kettlewell and made a remarkable recovery. Diana Chudley provided me with a chauffeur driven car so that I could continue at work and visit Pat every day: I would finish my clinics and operating and take my notes and reports to work on during the journeys to and fro Oxford. Helen came from Somerset while her mother was still in the Intensive Care Unit and recorded the occasion in rhyme:

Ode to the Mighty Atom (or a first experience of the ICU)

I stood before the bolted door, my legs like melting butter;
My mouth was dry, I felt I'd die, my heart began to flutter;
And when the nurse tried to converse, my words were all a-stutter:
"I think I've come to see my Mum" at last I seemed to utter!

I found a means (between machines!) to pick a careful route
Through bleeps & clicks & whines & ticks which somehow all compute!
I should have known where Mum lay prone (had I been more astute),
But the mask and hose and tube up her nose put identity in dispute!

Then I saw feet beneath the sheet just half way down the bed -
Unless she'd grown (as yet unknown!) they must be hers! She said:-
"I want to move where I'll improve so put me upstairs instead!"
I thrilled to hear her voice so clear, & her still being one step ahead!

My attitude is now renewed: I know she'll be all right,
For one thing Mum has always done, is put up a damn good fight.
For all her sins - she always wins & puts her foes to flight!
To strength she'll grow, for this I know - the Atom moves with Might!

In March 1989 we had a holiday in Gozo which she loved dearly and it was plain that she was not doing well. In April Michael Kettlewell operated again and found that the cancer had returned and was widespread. John Smith drove me to see her and I told her the outcome of the operation; "So I'm going to die?" she asked, looking me straight in the eye, to which I had to reply "Yes". After a few days she came home and saw all her family and friends with remarkable good humour and gave them strength to face the coming sadness. Philip Jepps came to administer the Sacrament to us. On Sunday 14th May the whole family congregated for a lunch-time barbecue and she came downstairs for a short while to add gaiety to the day. The next night it was plain that she was dying. John Smith gave her a sedative and his wife, Ann (a nurse) helped to make her comfortable. I sat up through the night with her and recited the Lord's Prayer, to which she assented with a loud and clear "Amen" and that was her last word; I continued reading passages from the Old and New Testament to her into the night until it was plain that she was sleeping or in coma. About 4 am I phoned Philip and asked if he would come and share my vigil while I rested for an hour or two and he stayed with me till the end. During the afternoon Pat died. I made to look at my watch to check the time but did not need to do so for my Uganda chiming clock struck four. It was Tuesday 16th May 1989 in the forty third year of our marriage.

The days up to her funeral (and after) passed in a blur. The local press paid tribute to her many achievements. Hundreds of people attended her funeral, which was conducted by Rev Philip Jepps and Rev John Phillips who had been the Rector in Irthlingborough and she was laid to rest in Irthlingborough cemetery. Many people came back to my house afterwards and the Barberton Book bears witness to the occasion with their signatures.

Mrs Shirley Toon who worked at the house three mornings a week volunteered at once to come five mornings a week; in addition to keeping the place spick and span she took over the washing, ironing, the dishwasher and would do shopping if I needed her to do so. Mr Stallwood, the gardener, also increased his hours and maintained Pat's high standards. Sarah Taylor my private secretary and Jane Jackson my private receptionist, midwife and nurse, helped me keep my private practise going uninterrupted and filled my house with chatter and laughter on Mondays and Thursdays. My colleagues at the hospital looked after my interests while I was unable to do so and offered me as much time off as I wanted but I needed to get back to work which I did without delay. My friends and neighbours in Poplars Farm Road, John and Ann Smith, John and Janet Keeble, kept an eye on me, called frequently and often asked me for a drink or meals and made me feel that there was more to life than death.

The two dogs transferred their affections to me and I would rise early so as to be able to take them for a walk at 6.30 in the morning and again in the evening. I was clearing a space on Pat's dressing table for something or other and placed her photograph in its frame on the floor. Toby, the Cavalier King Charles spaniel, wandered up to it, recognised her and waved his tail disconsolately. I had a serious discussion with Toto, the fifteen year old dachshund. He had belonged to my father-in-law who had died, then to my mother-in-law who had died, then to my wife who had died; I explained that I was not keen that this pattern should continue and he took me at my word, predeceasing me when he was nineteen years old. Mary Bland and Val

Stock had spent an hour or more with Pat the day before she died and later they asked if they might arrange a fund raising occasion for St Francis House in her memory. This was a great success and played a real part in my recovery from grief. At this function I re-encountered someone I had first met fifteen years previously when I operated on her.

I had never learned to cook but had seen Pat working at the kitchen table so many times that some of it must have penetrated the innermost recesses of my memory and, to my surprise, I found that I could get by quite well for one so ignorant. I even started to enjoy cooking but my main problem was time at the end of a long working day and an emergency call out while something was on the stove or in the oven did little for its flavour.

One late afternoon the doorbell rang and there was the driver and car which Diana Chudley had provided while I was visiting Pat in Oxford. He opened the boot and brought out a case of Moet et Chandon and a large insulated box full of frozen meals from her conference centre which I packed into the freezer. Pat had always kept the freezer well stocked and in this manner she and Diana continued to feed me for months. And my friends and members of the family plied me with invitations and I responded in kind, gaining in culinary experience all the time: Pat would have been amazed. But I had been married for so long and had so often been out late at work or meetings that I had always felt the need to hurry home to Pat as quickly as possible - and so it continued. When invited out I could not relax and stay out till the natural end of the evening; I still felt I had to get home.

I should have retired from the NHS in February 1990 on my sixty fifth birthday but worked for another five months. I had been born during a lunar eclipse and chance had it that there was another on the night of my sixty fifth birthday. I took the family, camera, tripod and telephoto lens out to dinner and broke off during the meal to capture the moon in partial eclipse. About a year before retirement was due I had warned my younger colleagues (and had kept reminding them) that they should prepare the job description of my successor but they had failed to complete this in time. I think that they, like myself may have been distracted by Pat's illness and I am now very grateful that I had the extra months of work to bring me back to the real world before being thrust into a solitary retirement. So I worked on and took my leave of patients, colleagues and staff at leisure and was able to meet and get to know my successor Paul Wood and to hand over to him in good order those patients who needed his continuing care. I had resolved to continue with private gynaecology for another year at the Woodland private hospital and so I came gradually to terms with my widowerhood and retirement. I still had the Gozo apartment and enjoyed a couple of holidays out there with family and friends. During this time Mary Bland also kept an eye on me, asking me to dinner with friends. One of the guests, who was seated next to me was the same woman I had operated on fifteen years earlier, Judy Constable. Again I felt I had to get home without delay, made an excuse that I had to pay a late visit to someone I had operated on that morning and was the first to leave.

Diana and Michael Chudley plied me with many invitations that helped me through the process of grief. Diana was herself now ill but continued to run her conference centre and entertain her large family and large circle of friends. We had been a foursome for so long and to begin with when we were a threesome conversation and laughter did not come to me so easily or fluently as before. But the Chudleys persisted and saw me emerge from my state of sadness to one where, eighteen months later, I could laugh and joke, exchange banter and stay out late. They had a holiday home in Brancaster and used to pass near my house on their way to and fro. Sometimes they called in for an hour or two while I tested my elementary cuisine on them in response to the times without number that I had enjoyed their hospitality. Out of the blue in mid conversation one evening Diana smiled and looking me in the eye said "What's her name, then"? I was momentarily nonplussed for there wasn't a name that I could at that moment divulge. I had years previously learned to respect Diana's intuition, perhaps she knew something I didn't. I promised that if there ever was a name she would be the first to know - and so it was.

Not long after, I made up a foursome to a concert in Northampton with Mary and Dick Bland - and Judy Constable. Judy and I were married on Trafalgar day, 21st October 1991. Imagine my embarrassment - brand new suit but empty pockets. I had to borrow the "Bride Price" for the Registrar's fee from one of the assembled guests. Michael and Diana had been invited but she was by then too ill so we called on her on our way to our honeymoon hotel in Burford, taking her one of our wedding flower arrangements. We were married by the Superintendent Registrar, Mrs Josie Pearce, who was well known to both of us and to Pat with whom she had sat on Kettering Borough Council. Josie was married to the legendary Rev Frank Pearce who bestowed his blessing on us - they had between them buttoned up most of the matrimonial business in the town. Judy, as Pat had been, was a Northamptonshire County Councillor and I have often joked in conversation that all my wives have been County Councillors, Conservatives to boot. Our wedding photos were taken by a young woman professional photographer whose serious cancer I had cured when she was but eighteen years of age. Marrying at the age we were, enabled us to be photographed with our grandchildren.

When we married, Judy was working as Agent to Roger Freeman who was the Conservative Member of Parliament for Kettering and she saw this job through to the general election in 1992 when her efforts played no small part in his re-election. He lost his seat (along with many other Conservatives) in the 1997 election. He had finished his House of Commons career in the Cabinet as Chancellor of the Duchy of Lancaster. A few months later we were privileged to attend his ennoblement in the House of Lords as Lord Freeman of Dingley.

To begin with we lived in my house in Poplars Farm Road, which was too big for our needs, with a larger garden than I would want if I became old and frail. So we looked about for a property which we could manage in old age, within walking distance of the shops, the bank and a few restaurants. We found a bungalow, 39 St Mary's Road, Kettering and in April 1993 we moved in. We bought the bungalow in the autumn of 1992 but went to Australia for a six week holiday while workmen started on modifications. I had not yet been able to sell the Poplars Farm Road house so we continued to live there until most of the work on the new one had been completed. Although the bungalow was smaller, we found it large enough to entertain the whole of our combined families and I was able to have the smallest bedroom as a study for my computer and numerous family papers dating back to 1819.

My youngest offspring Brian lived nearby in Stoke Albany with Theresa and their children Tom and Ruth. Brian had developed into a most successful marketing manager and, in the process, was a creator of opportunity and wealth not only for himself but for his employees. He died on 20th March 1994 aged just forty, great promise lay before him. He had telephoned me a couple of months earlier to say that a brain scan had revealed a swelling behind his left eye whose nature was unknown at that time. A huge sigh of relief went up when an arteriogram showed that this was an aneurysm and not a cancer - although extremely serious and needing hazardous surgery; we all had high hopes that he would make a full recovery. He wrote in characteristic vein and good humour to the managers under him:

> I have an "aneurysm" behind my left eye, or "a sac formed by abnormal dilatation of the weakened wall of a blood vessel". This means an operation within the next few days in Nottingham so, for the time being, you'll be delighted to hear I'm going to be off work. Peter will be taking over all my responsibilities but I'll be back soon, with a clear head!

His operation was in the neuro-surgical unit at the Queens Medical Centre in Nottingham and he spent the next five days in the Intensive Care unit without regaining consciousness. Repeated tests showed there to be no remaining cerebral activity so the life support system was switched off and he died at 5.30 pm on Sunday 20th March 1994, leaving despair and an overwhelming aching void in hundreds of hearts.

I had been to early communion in Kettering on the Sunday Brian died and the priest, knowing he was mortally ill, gave me two wafers, one for Brian. Theresa and their children are Roman Catholics and one of their priests came to Nottingham a few hours before Brian died to anoint him. The funeral service, according to the rites of the Roman Catholic church took place on Friday 25 March 1994 at Our Lady of Walsingham Church in Corby which was packed with about four hundred mourners. Brian's coffin had lain there overnight and I had arranged for an envelope to be placed in it containing a card from his sister and a lock of my hair to take with him to his grave. The family wreath was in the form of the Barberton coat-of-arms. His son Tom read from the Book of Wisdom, his daughter Ruth said a bidding prayer, his niece Sarah composed a poem but was unable to get the words out but her brother Simon managed to do so. I read the Desiderata, having done so from the same spot in the same church at Brian's marriage to Theresa sixteen years previously. His brother Philip and his nephews Matthew and Benedict were among the pallbearers. At the cemetery it was a bitter cold day with driving wind and rain, people huddled together against the cold, umbrellas blowing inside out. There followed a gathering of family and friends, there were a few speeches and Helen read out a valedictory letter to her brother written on the evening of his death, then dazzling sun shone through the clouds.

We met again at the cemetery the next day in cold sunshine and then went on to Brian's place of work, previously known as Premier House but already renamed Barberton House. Theresa had planted a memorial willow tree in the grounds which was already marked with a marble plaque.

My first wife and now my son had died before their time. I have urged my remaining offspring Helen and Philip and my second wife that they should await their due turns.

Diana Chudley too died not long after Judy and I were married and we joined his family in helping Michael through his period of grief. It had been Diana and Michael who had first introduced me to Gozo; they had sold their property there some years previously and we were now able to invite him to stay with us in our apartment in Ghajnsielem. The conference centre in Creaton which Diana had created continued under the management of one of her sons and who should attend an obstetric conference there but Glen Groocock, who I had known for many years - first as a young midwife at the old maternity unit at St Mary's hospital in Kettering, and finally when she was in charge of all the midwifery staff in Kettering hospital and the Kettering health district. Unusually Michael was in the conference dining room during the lunch hour and struck up a conversation with Glen. Each of them found that I had known the other for more than twenty years and I was able to fill each of them in about the other. Then Judy and I sat back and observed developments. In this manner I came to be Michael's best man at their wedding and they spent their honeymoon in my Gozo home.

Judy and I spent another couple of holidays in Ghajnsielem. I thumbed through my passport, counted thirty seven visits to date and decided to sell. So we made one final visit - this time by car as there were some fragile items I wanted to bring home, notably Pat's paintings and my family photographs which hung on the walls. So we put the car on the Dover/Calais ferry, drove across France, through Italy to Villa San Giovanni, took the ferry to Messina in Sicily, motored to Syracusa, took the ferry to Valetta in Malta, drove to Cirkewwa and caught the midnight Gozo ferry to Mgarr harbour six days after we set off. We slept in small hotels all the way there, had a good holiday while we were in Gozo and returned in five days, (five weeks later) triumphant but tired.

The Poplars Farm Road property took a long time to

sell because of the slump in the housing market. I had paid £48,000 for it in 1981, currency inflation and house price inflation took the supposed value to £180,000 in 1992 but it eventually sold in 1995 for £140,000. We were at last down to one property, having at one stage been the unwilling owners of four - Judy's flat in Petherton Court, my house in Poplars Farm Road, my Gozo apartment and our bungalow in St Mary's Road. Then we bought another - 15 Park Rise, Dawlish in Devon in 1995. We had already decided that when the Poplars Farm Road and Gozo properties sold we would have a holiday home in Devon which we could reach easily and quickly at frequent intervals, with the dogs. The Dawlish house was a great joy to us and has a DAWLISHBOOK after the style of the GOZOBOOK and the BARBERTONBOOK. But after five years of visits, maybe five or six times a year, we tired of the motorway travel and sold up in September 2000.

While on one of our many holidays in Dawlish we had a surreptitious phone call from my son-in-law Howard, he told us that Helen was to be 'surprise surprised' by Cilla Black on TV in Taunton and we went along to witness the occasion. Helen was completely bamboozled and reacted in a manner as to make for good television, particularly when she discovered that her sons Matthew and Benedict were part of the surprise: Matthew had been given the day off from his law firm and Ben had been flown home from his Australian safari for the occasion.

2001 saw the death of my sister Hazel in Western Australia. She had suffered a succession of small strokes and lost most of her cerebral function. Judy and I made a further visit to Australia to see her that year by when she was comatose and I don't think she recognosed me at all.

Not long before we sold the Dawlish house, we had a

visit from Peter and Margaret McLean. Whilst in Teignmouth one lovely sunny day, we were walking along Powderham Terrace, a fine Victorian terrace when Judy struck up a conversation with a man cleaning his garden bench in Dolphin Court. We asked whether properties came on the open market from time to time and learned that they seldom did, because they sold very quickly by word of mouth. We exchanged names and addresses and he promised to let us know if something became available. A few months later we heard from him that his circumstances had changed and he had to sell, so we bought his flat, 1 Dolphin Court, in April 2001 and sold 39 St Mary's Road. And here we have lived since and plan to do so for ever.

The medical changes which have taken place in my lifetime have been breathtaking, starting with the metrication of the weights and measures which were used for drugs and medicines. When I was a medical student my pharmacology lecturers used the apothecaries measures - who now has any idea of what a grain, a drachm or a scruple mean as units of measurement? And believe it or not we were taught how to wrap a bottle of cough mixture neatly in a sheet of white paper and to seal it with a dab of red sealing wax. At that time many medicines had little real pharmacological effect, unlike today's products which do - but which may also have serious side effects.

The first of the modern wonder drugs to be developed even before I was a medical student were the sulphonamide anti-bacterial drugs, the first being sulphanilamide which was serially numbered M&B 693 by the world famous British firm May & Baker, whose name disappeared from our annals in the 1980s when they were taken over by Rhône-Poulenc. Other new and potent sulphonamides continued to be developed and Guy's hospital gave its name to a cream known as Guy's Paste for the treatment of burns which contained a mixture of three different sulphonamides which was at the time a great advance in the treatment of burns.

The next weapon to be developed against infections was Penicillin, the first of the antibiotics from which stemmed so many new derivatives with differing actions. Now that our fear of overwhelming infections has disappeared into history it is being replaced by the fear of bacteria developing such drug resistance as to render our present antibiotics useless and by the fear of 'superbugs' which are sensitive to nothing we can throw at them - witness drug resistant Staphylococcus Aureus and Acquired Immuno-Deficiency Syndrome in humans and Bovine Spongiform Encephalopathy in cattle and its human variant.

The development of the contraceptive pill and of cortisone, conferred great benefit on humanity on one hand but with serious, even lethal side effects on the other. Two great infective scourges of mankind have been brought under control, indeed one of them (smallpox) has been eradicated from the face of the earth. The other, poliomyelitis (known earlier as infantile paralysis) has been largely eliminated in the developed world. Childbirth left to nature was (and still is in parts of the world) a traumatic and wasteful matter - how the fortunes of mothers and babies have been transformed by advances in their care.

The era of transplant surgery burst upon the world when the first heart transplant was carried out by Professor Christian Barnard in South Africa. And now we almost take it for granted - hearts with and without lungs, kidneys, livers, bone marrow and what next? One field in which transplant surgery has not so far been found useful is my own speciality, obstetrics and gynaecology, but who knows? The thought has crossed my mind, should we freeze-preserve our umbilical cords from the time of our birth in case the vessels were to come in useful in later years? At least there would be no problem with tissue matching but think of the storage problems which would far outweigh the 1996 controversy which arose from the storage for five years of frozen embryos whose parents could not be traced.

Chemotherapy for various cancers has transformed the outlook in many previously lethal conditions, travelling hand in hand with transplants at cellular level, notably bone marrow. And does gene therapy and stem cell therapy hold anything in store for future generations?

Gynaecology and Obstetrics led the field in two major developments, laparoscopy and ultrasound scanning and both these techniques have since been widely adopted in other specialities. Laparoscopy initially had its main place in the investigation and management of sub-fertility in women; this later became an essential tool in the development of In Vitro Fertilisation and is now used for complex 'key-hole' surgery in several specialities. One of its great advantages is that patients seldom need to stay in hospital for more than a day or two compared with seven to ten days if the abdomen has to be conventionally opened. When laparoscopy was in its infancy surgeons and anaesthetists had little experience or knowledge of the incidence and types of complications which might ensue and the Royal College of Obstetricians & Gynaecologists in London set up the first national study of these; the lessons learned were published world-wide with resultant benefit to countless patients.

Ultrasound scanning of the foetus within the mother's uterus was developed and pioneered in Glasgow by Professor Sir Ian Donald and has since swept the world and been adopted for use in many other specialities, including Veterinary medicine. It has helped us to find lost intra-uterine contraceptive devices, to count and harvest ova for IVF, to check foetal viability or otherwise with suspected miscarriages, to look for foetal abnormalities, to date the age of the foetus exactly, to count the number of babies, to locate the placenta in early pregnancy for biopsies and in late pregnancy when bleeding has taken place, to check the position of the baby when this is in doubt and to check the foetal growth rate when placental insufficiency was suspected. Most particularly it has helped to take samples of liquor, blood and tissue for testing for foetal abnormality. For the first half of my consultant career ultrasound scanning did not exist. In the second half we could not imagine how we had ever managed without it - and likewise foetal monitoring in labour. Before the apparatus had been developed the foetal heart rate would be checked every quarter of an hour or so; now we expect to have a continuous record of the foetal heart throughout all high risk labours.

Identification of chromosomal abnormalities (notably Down's syndrome) and of spina bifida (and other associated neural tube defects) became established and commonplace during my working lifetime as a consultant. Both depended on taking samples of amniotic fluid with a needle in about the sixteenth week of pregnancy, for which an accurate knowledge of the placental position (obtained by ultrasound) was essential. It should be noted that an essential precursor of these new procedures was the change in the law, which took place in the 1967 Abortion Act, which allowed doctors finding an abnormality to lawfully terminate pregnancies when the foetus was likely to be seriously adversely affected, if the mother so wished. I guess that I found an abnormality necessitating termination of pregnancy in perhaps one in a hundred and fifty tests and sometimes a normal foetus was lost by miscarriage as a consequence of such a test. So the need for a less invasive method is apparent and no doubt research will come up with new tests in the future.

Looking back on my life I have led a charmed existence. My early life was spent on a farm in Kenya when the country was first being opened up, no tractors, no electricity, no piped water supply, no WCs, no telephones, few doctors and fewer dentists. I had to attend boarding school (there were no day facilities) which was a long way from home. Wild dangerous animals roamed the countryside, you could expect to lose your crops to locusts perhaps one year in four. There were no luxuries but it was enormous fun. I travelled to and fro South Africa and England on passenger liners before air travel was possible. I went to Stamford school in England at the age of fourteen through the 1939-45 war and was spared the dangers of participating in that conflict; Stamford was one of the loveliest market towns with a goodly proportion of fine medieval buildings. From there I went to Oxford, the oldest and greatest university in the world. My college, St Edmund Hall, claimed to be the oldest in the university - that claim may be apocryphal but it is so old that no other college can convincingly gainsay it. Then from Oxford to medical school at St Mary's, Paddington in the greatest capital in the world where I was taught by pre-eminent men (no women I am sad to say) in the world of medicine. Through these formative years, and for more than forty years thereafter, I was supported and encouraged by my loving and loyal first wife.

Then out to Uganda where life was hard for the African population, none more so than the Karamojong among whom I spent three rewarding years which served to hone my character and skills. Then followed three years in the

Medical School in Kampala where I started my training as an obstetrician and gynaecologist under Professor Rendle-Short. She was a great taskmaster who taught me that there was nothing I could not achieve with hard work and diligent study.

Then came my leap into the unknown, back to England. Could I regain a foothold on the ladder which I had left when I went out to Uganda? I could and did, first at the Institute of Obstetrics at Queen Charlotte's hospital, then at Chelmsford where David Brown licked me back into shape for the UK, then to Cambridge, the second greatest university in the world. Here Ossie Lloyd and Janet Bottomley worked me mercilessly to turn me into suitable material for a consultant post in middle England.

Then followed twenty five working years in Northamptonshire which could not have been happier, with fine colleagues, job satisfaction in abundance, sincere friends and a family and descendants of whom I am proud. In the lottery of life who could have asked for anything more than all this, plus a loving and kind second wife, and to have been born an Englishman and a Barberton to boot?

EPILOGUE

While on holiday in Gozo in June 2004 I saw in 'The Times' that a firm called 'Oxford Ancestors' had been set up by the Professor of Human Genetics and that it would undertake DNA analysis on persons interested in ascertaining their origins. In July 2004 I received their report to the effect that my Y Chromosome signature indicated that I am of the Clan Oisin originating from West Eurasia some 40,000 years ago, and that I am probably of Celtic origin some 4000 years ago. Accompanying information supplied by Oxford Ancestors include the following excepts:

> The vast majority of native Europeans are members of six clans: Oisin, Wodan, Re, Gilgamesh, Eshu and Nentsi. The Oisin clan originated approximately 40,000 years ago in the Middle East and correlates with culture that colonised Eurasia as the glaciers retreated. The clan can be divided into two subgroups that correspond to the scientific clades Ria and Rib. The distribution of Rib is more significant in western Europe with particularly high concentrations running from Italy to the north and west to Spain, the British Isles and Iceland.
>
> We are pleased to tell you that, having checked your results against our database, we have identified your Y-

chromosome as being of probable Celtic origin. This means it is likely that your ancestor belonged to one of the groups of people that first colonised the land that was to become these islands. These original colonisers gave rise to the ancient Celtic tribes that lived in Britain and Ireland many thousands of years before any organised invaders (Romans, Anglo-Saxons, Vikings, Normans, etc.) arrived.

When the Romans left Britain around 400 AD to defend Rome, they left the islands to the mercy of Anglo-Saxon invaders from Germany and the Danish Vikings from Denmark. These invaders changed completely the language and culture of southern and eastern Britain, but their influence never extended into Ireland, Wales or northern Scotland, where the original Celtic languages are still spoken and your Y-chromosome haplogroup is most commonly found.

On balance, your Y-chromosome results indicate that your paternal ancestor was one of the original Celtic people who lived in the British Isles at the time that the Romans invaded. If you trace your paternal ancestry to Wales, Scotland or Ireland, then this is almost certainly the case. However, if your origins are in southern or eastern England, then there is a small possibility that your ancestry is, in fact, Anglo-Saxon. Unfortunately, some Y-chromosomes from these parts of Britain are impossible to assign with precision.

The origins of the Celtic tribes first encountered by Julius Caesar are shrouded in mystery. From what we can tell from archaeological discoveries, Britain was first settled after the last Ice Age, about 9,000 years ago, by hunter-gatherers moving up from southern Europe. Three thousand years later, the first signs of farming appeared. However, that does not mean that the original hunter-gatherers were necessarily replaced by the farmers; it is more likely that they learned and adapted to a new agricultural way of life.

About 3,000 years ago, during the late Bronze Age and Iron Age, material artefacts from the thriving Celtic cultures, like weapons and jewellery, began to appear in Britain. However, like the spread of farming, this vivid cultural change may actually have involved relatively few people.

Our analysis shows that it is most likely that you have inherited your Y-chromosome from one of the early inhabitants of the British Isles, perhaps even from one of the first settlers who arrived 9,000 years ago. There are intriguing genetic connections between Y-chromosomes such as yours and those found in the Iberian Peninsula, especially among the Basques. This hints at the existence of vigorous connections between Ireland, western Britain and the Atlantic seaboard of France and Spain, which archaeologists have long suspected. This connection began with the pre-farming hunters and fishermen and continued with the peoples who built the large stone monuments, the megaliths, which also connect these western sites from Spain to Scotland.

GLOSSARY

ADC - Assistant District Commisioner

Arap - 'son of', used in conjunction with the father's name

Americani - cheap cotton material used for clothing

Atapara - a dam in Karamoja, constructed to collect water

Askari - an African soldier or policeman

Auger - carpenter's manual boring bit

Ayah - a woman servant employed to look after the children

Banda - a temporary building of grass and poles

Barberton - town in South Africa named after Hal Barber who found gold there

Barberton Daisy - a large South African daisy alternatively known as the Transvaal daisy; Gerbora Jamesonii. A common Barberton nick-name was 'Daisy'

BEA - British East Africa, later Kenya

Biltong - dried salted meat, usually eland

Boma - an enclosure of thorn branches for livestock. Also the early administrative centre of a district

Bugishu - a Kenya tribe, the area from which they came

Bushvelt, bushveld - countryside, especially un-cultivated, in South Africa

Bwana - the master or employer of labour

DC - District Commissioner of an administrative area of a Colony

Dassie - a hyrax or rock rabbit

Dietz lamp - hurricane oil lamp

Disselboom - draught pole of a wagon or cart to which oxen were yoked

Drift - a river crossing where there is no bridge

Duka - a small shop, usually owned by an Asian

East Coast Fever - a severe viral cattle disease

Ekapolon - a Karamojong chief

Fundi - a skilled artisan, carpenter, brick-layer and so forth

Garri, gharri - a simple cart

GEA - German East Africa, subsequently Tanganyika, now Tanzania

Ghee - butter clarified by heating

Gunnybag - a hessian sack for maize, wheat and so forth, 200 lb capacity

Guano - fine, dusty bat droppings, used as a fertiliser for coffee trees

Highveld - highlands

Inspan - yoke the draught oxen, break camp

Jago - a divisional chief in northern Uganda

KAR - Kings African Rifles

Kaross - a cured hide with its fur, commonly leopard, used for warmth and ceremonial, worn by a tribal chief

Kavirondo - a Kenya tribe, the area from which they came

Kerai - a mortar pan, alternatively a small cooking pan of similar shape

Kikuyu - a Kenya tribe, the area from which they came

Kiswahili - the lingua franca of East Africa, see also Swahili

Kitosh - a Kenya tribe, the area from which they came

Koss, kos - food, provisions

Kraal - an African village enclosure, also an enclosure for farm animals

Kuke - abbreviation for Kikuyu

Lucerne - a rich variety of grass grown for cattle fodder

MLC - Member of Legislative Council

Manyatta - a thorn enclosure for a family and their stock in northern Kenya and Uganda

Masai - a Kenya tribe, the area from which they came, also called Wanderobo

Mealie - maize cob or maize meal, posho

Mooi - pretty, attractive [Afrikaans]

Mtama - millet

Mutungi, mtungi - a large clay pot for food or water storage

Naartjie - tangerine [Afrikaans]

Nandi - a Kenya tribe

Neopara - a headman in charge of farm labourers

Ngombe - a bullock

Outspan - un-yoke the draught oxen, strike camp

Panga - a machete, mainly fror agricultural use

Pombe - beer, usually fermented from millet

Pomelo - a citrus tree with a large fruit resembling a grapefruit

Posho - maize meal, mealie meal

Rinderpest - a very infectious disease of cattle

Rondavel - a round building of mud and wattle with a thatched roof

Rupee - a unit of currency worth about two shillings or somewhat less at the time - 1918-1919

Shamba - a farm field

Shauri - a meeting, discussion, often about a contentious matter

'Sixty Four' - a trading post on a farm of that number, later the town of Eldoret

SHO - senior house officer, a junior hospital doctor grade

Spider - a light passenger cart, horse or mule drawn

Squatter - an African who lived rent free on a farm in return for occasional paid labour

Stoep - veranda

Swahili - a Kenya coastal tribe, also the lingua franca of East Africa

Taak haar - [Afrikaans] - low class

Tembo - beer [Swahili]

Tilapia - a tasty tropical fresh water fish

Trans Nzoia - an administrative district of Kenya across the Nzoia river

Trek - travel, especially by ox wagon

Uasin Gishu - an administrative district of Kenya, a treeless plateau

Veld, velt - field, countryside, especially un-cultivated

Veldschoen - robust waterproof shoes, boots, made by the early settlers.

Vlei - a swamp

Wakiti - a Kenya tribe, the area from which they came

Wanderobo - a Kenya tribe, the area from which they came, also called Masai

Waragi - an alcoholic spirit illegally distilled from pombe

Watu - workmen (Mtu - workman)

Wimbi - millet (Swahili)

'Wire' - send a telegram, by morse code along a telegraph wire

SIX GENERATION FAMILY TREE SHOWING THE CONNECTION BETWEEN THE BARBER AND BOWKER FAMILIES

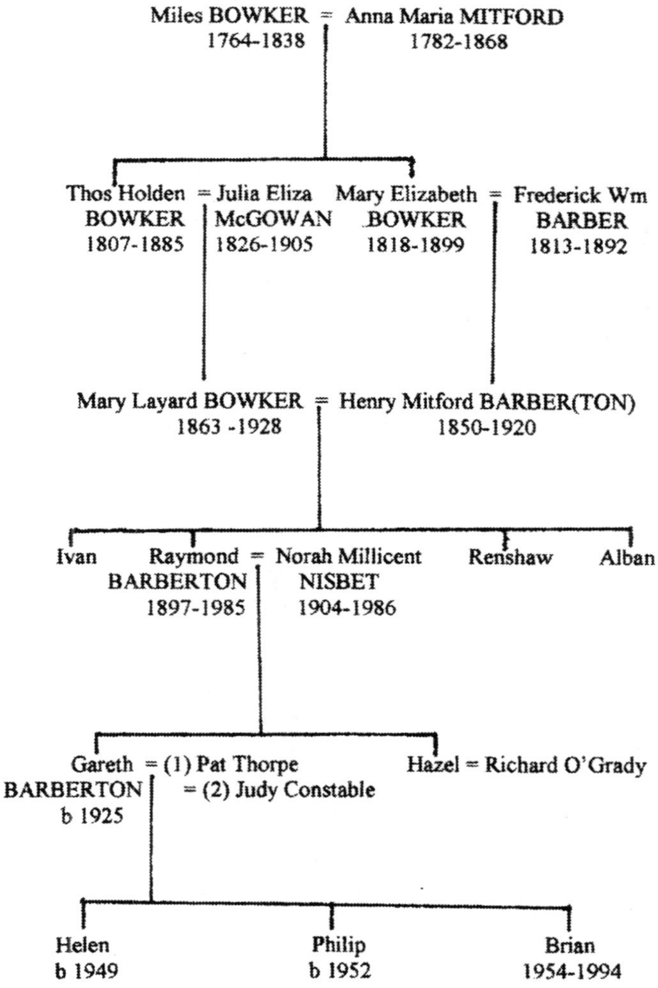

ISBN 141208546-2

9 781412 085465